Shaping Prose

SHEENA GILLESPIE
LINDA STANLEY
ROBERT SINGLETON

Queensborough Community College
City University of New York

Little, Brown and Company
Boston   Toronto

Library of Congress Cataloging in Publication Data

Main entry under title:

Shaping prose.

   1. College readers. I. Gillespie, Sheena,
date. II. Stanley, Linda, date.
III. Singleton, Robert.
PE1417.S385   808′.0427   81-15931
ISBN 0-316-31344-0   AACR2

ISBN 0-316-313440

9 8 7 6 5 4 3 2 1

ALP

Published simultaneously in Canada
by Little, Brown & Company (Canada) Limited

Printed in the United States of America

Design by Edith Allard/Designworks

To Julius, for his strength and sensitivity
To Ruth, sine qua non

Contents

"But if each one would employ a certain portion of each day in looking back upon the time which has passed, and in writing down his thoughts and feelings . . . not only would his daily experience be greatly increased . . . but he would be ready to turn over a new leaf."

"And yet my life does not go well *without* writing. It is my flywheel."

"One day I awakened from my amnesia. No longer a dancer. Miralles turned ashen and grey, was snuffed out. He became again an old, weary dancing teacher."

"It's an odd idea for someone like me to keep a diary. . . . Still, what does that matter? I want to write, but more than that, I want to bring out all kinds of things that lie buried deep in my heart."

"I put down my sweeping opinions, prejudices, limitations, and just here the book fails me for it makes no comment. It is even my wailing wall, and when I play that grim, comforting game of noting how wrong everyone else is, my book is silent, and I listen to the stillness, and I learn."

"To accept the world and to accept pleasure—but only when I am stripped bare of everything. I should not be worthy to love the bare and empty beaches if I could not remain naked in the presence of myself."

Contents

FIVE   Definition   155

NINE   Cause and Effect   291

TEN   Argumentation   335

Contents Grouped Thematically

Humor

Work

Education

Sports

Politics

Relations Between the Sexes

Language and Writing

History

Preface

Great writers are usually great readers. "Reading maketh a full man," says Lord Bacon, ". . . and writing an exact man." Students of writing need to read experienced writers for both content and form—for ideas, information, and technique. The selections in *Shaping Prose* were chosen for their high quality and their ability to stimulate student writing. Approximately one-fourth have never been anthologized before. Nearly all are complete essays; only a few are excerpts. They are grouped according to the traditional four types—narration, description, exposition, and argumentation—although they have been placed in their chapters, not because they use one single mode or type of development—such purity is not often found—but because of the mode or type that predominates in each essay. Instructors may not want their students to imitate any specific author or essay, but they will probably want to discuss the techniques of each mode; and they will ask their students to write an essay following a specific type or mode. They will certainly want assigned readings to "prime the pump."

Writers, both professional and amateur, know that exactness does not come without practice. For this reason, *Shaping Prose* begins with a selection of journal entries. It is the rare professional writer who does not confess to a heavy dependence on his or her journal or notebook for a place to ruminate and practice writing in private. Sheer quantity of writing, especially in journals, plays a part in the transition from incompetence to competence. Students whose long years of schooling have included very little practice in writing, students for whom committing thoughts to paper is agony, will especially benefit from the journal, or prewriting, stage.

After this introductory chapter on the journal, *Shaping Prose* arranges the four types in the order of increasing difficulty: narration, or storytelling; description, or word painting; exposition, or explaining, which is divided into six modes; and argumentation, or persuasion. Since the modes are not treated as totally discrete, later chapters tend to build on the lessons of earlier chapters. The thematic table of contents allows instructors to group essays differently if they wish to pursue one subject rather than one type or mode. The Glossary explains terminology.

Introductions to each chapter are addressed to the prospective writer. They analyze the techniques of the four types and six modes from the viewpoint of one whose reading will lead to writing; these techniques are summarized at the end of each introduction. The techniques are reinforced in a special section of Questions on Method following each essay and form the basis for the writing topics.

Each essay is preceded by a biography of the author and is followed by a group of Writing Topics and by three kinds of questions. Questions on Meaning provide a test of comprehension and a basis for classroom discussion. Questions on Method draw attention to writing techniques used in particular essays. Questions on Vocabulary and Diction focus on particular words. A second set of writing topics, some drawing on the chapter selections and others independent of them, appears at the end of each chapter.

We wish to acknowledge David Shimkin for his thorough work on the *Instructor's Manual* accompanying *Shaping Prose,* Hana and Kurt Wehle for their meticulous footnotes on the Arendt and Bettelheim selections, and Margaret Cavanaugh and Evelyn Pomann for their typing of the manuscript. Special thanks go to Paul O'Connell, former Chairman, Winthrop Publishers, Inc., whose support and encouragement have sustained us through this last decade.

Shaping Prose

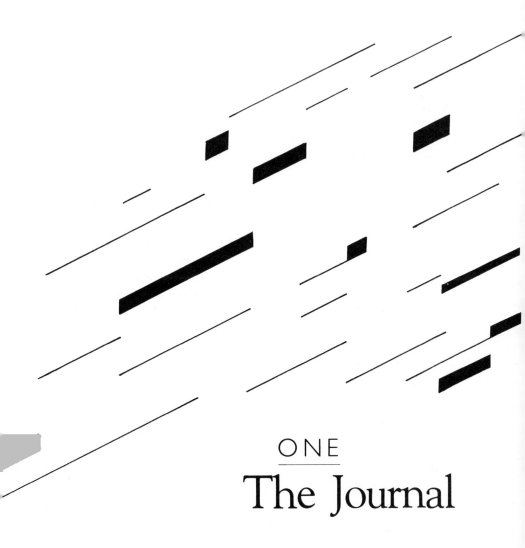

ONE
The Journal

People have been recording their daily thoughts and activities in diaries, journals, and notebooks since writing was invented. David wrote his psalms centuries before Christ, and St. Augustine his *Confessions* in the fourth century A.D., to cite two famous examples. And in the twentieth century certainly one of the best-loved books is *The Diary of a Young Girl* by Anne Frank, a Jewish teenager living in the Netherlands during the German occupation.

Why do people write in journals? According to the writers in this chapter, the reasons for keeping a journal are many: to have a

1

friend, to help oneself mature, to clarify one's identity, to avoid repeating mistakes, to store ideas for future writing, and to record thoughts for posterity.

What does a journal (or diary or notebook) consist of? Thoughts, feelings, experiences, and reactions to study and reading are the subject matter as Henry David Thoreau analyzes it in his journal entry here. The format is as varied as the content: short notes, short stories, whole essays, and anything in between. What is written and how it is written are the journal keeper's private concerns.

Of course, all the journals from which we have excerpted entries here have been published. Some journal keepers, then, obviously write with an audience in mind. Anaïs Nin published several volumes of her diaries during her lifetime, and one has been published posthumously. Other journal keepers, certainly the majority, write intensely personal matter for their eyes alone. Anne Frank could have had no idea at all of the millions of people who, in many languages, would read her "Kitty."

How do you begin a journal? Simply by obtaining a notebook and writing in it. The easiest way to start is to record an experience you had during the day and examine your feelings and thoughts about it, as many of the writers here do, or to react to something you read or overheard or saw on television or in a film.

Even though you may not be interested in keeping a journal, you might find through experimenting with writing in one that journal writing does fulfill one or more of the purposes listed above: communication, self-understanding, source for formal writing, and a record of your thoughts.

The writers of the journal entries that follow are very different from one another—one is very young (13), one is very old (over 90); two are men, four are women; five are professional writers, one is not; some write very personally, others very formally. Perhaps one writer's method of keeping a journal will serve as your model, or perhaps you will develop, as you proceed, a style of your own.

Writing a Journal

1 Purchase a notebook or diary, or set aside a section of a notebook for your journal.
2 Write for at least fifteen minutes every day.

3   Write about anything that comes into your mind—the events of your day, your emotional response to a person or incident, or your thoughts about something you read or saw.

4   Write freely, without stopping, to encourage a flow of ideas and discourage writer's block.

5   Do not rewrite or correct unlesss you want to.

HENRY DAVID THOREAU (1817–62) was an American essayist
and poet who was part of the American Romantic literary
movement. In 1845 he built a cabin at Walden Pond in
Massachusetts, where he lived for the next two years. He is
recognized today not only for his prose style but for his
individualism, which challenged the social status quo of his
contemporaries and ours today as well. The following excerpt,
taken from his *Early Essays and Miscellanies, The Writings of
Henry David Thoreau*, discusses the personal benefits of keeping
a journal.

From the

Journals

Henry David Thoreau

January 17, 1835

Of keeping a private journal or record of our thoughts, feelings,
studies, and daily experience,—containing abstracts of books,
and the opinions we formed of them on first reading them.

As those pieces which the painter sketches for his own amusement 1
in his leisure hours, are often superior to his most elaborate productions, so it is that ideas often suggest themselves to us spontaneously,
as it were, far surpassing in beauty those which arise in the mind
upon applying ourselves to any particular subject. Hence, could a
machine be invented which would instantaneously arrange on paper
each idea as it occurs to us, without any exertion on our part, how
extremely useful would it be considered! The relation between this
and the practice of keeping a journal is obvious. But yet, the preser-

vation of our scattered thoughts is to be considered an object but of minor importance.

Every one can think, but comparatively few can write, can 2 express their thoughts. Indeed, how often do we hear one complain of his inability to express what he feels! How many have occasion to make the following remark, "I am sensible that I understand this perfectly, but am not able to find words to convey my idea to others."

But if each one would employ a certain portion of each day in 3 looking back upon the time which has passed, and in writing down his thoughts and feelings, in reckoning up his daily gains, that he may be able to detect whatever false coins have crept into his coffers, and, as it were, in settling accounts with his mind, not only would his daily experience be greatly increased, since his feelings and ideas would thus be more clearly defined, but he would be ready to turn over a new leaf, having carefully perused the preceding one, and would not continue to glance carelessly over the same page, without being able to distinguish it from a new one.

Most of us are apt to neglect the study of our own characters, 4 thoughts, and feelings, and for the purpose of forming our own minds, look to others, who should merely be considered as different editions of the same great work. To be sure, it would be well for us to examine the various copies, that we might detect any errors, but yet, it would be foolish for one to borrow a work which he possessed himself, but had not perused.

In fine, if we endeavoured more to improve ourselves by reflec- 5 tion, by making a business of thinking, and giving our thoughts form and expression, we should be led to "read not to contradict and confute, nor to believe and take for granted, nor to find talk and discourse, but to weigh and consider".[1]

Questions on Meaning

1 What would you add to or delete from Thoreau's list of subjects to be included in a journal?
2 Do you agree with Thoreau that our best ideas occur to us spontaneously rather than when we are trying to think? What examples can you give for or against his argument?

1. Thoreau is quoting here from Francis Bacon's essay "Of Studies." (Editors' note)

3   Do you agree that it is generally difficult to express ideas on paper? If so, why is this true?

4   For what reason does Thoreau think everyone should keep a journal? To what extent can this objective be fulfilled without keeping a journal?

Questions on Method

1   Thoreau says that the ideas recorded in a journal are like the pictures a painter sketches for his own amusement: both are better than those forced by work or study. What other direct or indirect comparisons—in other words, similes or metaphors (see the Glossary, pp. 403–4)—does Thoreau use in discussing the value of a journal?

2   To what extent does this journal entry fulfill the purpose of keeping a journal for which it argues?

3   We usually think of journals as private diaries that no one else will read. Thoreau's journal, however, was published. Even though he described it as private, do you think he intended others to read it? How can one be spontaneous in a journal, knowing it will be read? How different would your journal be if you knew you were writing for an audience than if you knew you were writing for yourself alone? Is it possible to write for yourself and others as well?

Vocabulary and Diction

1   Because this journal entry was written a century and a half ago, Thoreau uses some words and phrases in contexts that may be unfamiliar. What do "sensible" (2) and "reckoning up" (3) mean as Thoreau uses them?

2   Thoreau's phrasing seems elaborately formal. Rewrite his journal entry as someone today might write it. For example, his first sentence might be written: "Just as those pieces that the painter sketches for his own amusement in his leisure time are often superior to his most elaborate productions, our spontaneous ideas are more beautiful than those we have when applying ourselves to a particular subject."

Writing Topics

1   Write a journal entry in which you discuss your ideas about the value of keeping a journal.

2 Write a journal entry in which you react to one or more of the following
   ideas Thoreau expresses:

   "Ideas often suggest themselves to us spontaneously, as it were, far
   surpassing in beauty those which arise in the mind upon applying ourselves to any particular subject."

   [If one would keep a journal] "not only would his daily experience be
   greatly increased, since his feelings and ideas would thus be more clearly
   defined, but he would be ready to turn over a new leaf, having carefully
   perused the preceding one, and would not continue to glance carelessly
   over the same page, without being able to distinguish it from a new
   one."

   "Most of us are apt to neglect the study of our own characters, thoughts,
   and feelings, and for the purpose of forming our own minds, look to
   others."

ANNE MORROW LINDBERGH (1906–   ) is an American writer
who is best known for "The Wave of the Future" (1940), a
controversial essay that was regarded as a defense of Fascism. In
1955 she wrote *Gift from the Sea*, which was addressed
especially to women. Her novel *Dearly Beloved* (1962)
comments on marriage, and in *Earth Shine* (1969) she writes of
the launching of the Apollo moon mission. She has also
written several volumes of letters and diaries; in the following
excerpt she tells why her life "does not go well *without* writing."

From

War Within and Without

Anne Morrow Lindbergh

Sunday, June 13th

The children go off after breakfast with C.[1] and with an outdoor
chair I bought for Mrs. L. I go for a short walk and to the trailer.
What bliss. How I love Sunday. No sense of rush, noise, duties,
children. I sink down and go over all that has happened in the last
two weeks. Why is it so vital to do so? What justification have I in
writing in my diary when I might be heaping up pages of a book, as
C. is doing *in his spare time.* Why can I not write as much as he,
when he is holding down a war job as well? It is four children and a
household to run, I explain. But I have people to help. Yes, and they
fight. I sometimes feel it would be better to do it all oneself. (I shall
have to no doubt before long.) Why can't the secretary and the nurse
take that off you? C. asks. Why can't you run your life like a business?
Why can't you be professional? Why can't you work in the house at

From *War Within and Without: Diaries and Letters 1939–1944 of Anne Morrow Lindbergh*,
copyright © 1980, by Anne Morrow Lindbergh. Reprinted by permission of Harcourt Brace
Jovanovich, Inc.
    1. "C." refers to Charles, Anne Morrow Lindbergh's aviator husband. (Editors' note)

8

your writing? Four children—only an excuse? But if you walk away from them and leave them entirely to the nurse you don't know them and their problems. There are so many things only a mother can know or do. Writing comes out of life; life *must* come first.

And yet my life does not go well *without* writing. It is my flywheel, my cloister, my communication with myself and God. It is my eyes to the world, my window for awareness, without which I cannot see anything or walk straight. Writing in a diary is my tool for the development of awareness. It is the crucible through which the rough material of life must pass before I can use it in art. I am always complaining that there is no "craft" to writing, no brush technique, no finger exercises, no going back to the model in clay. But perhaps—for me—writing in a diary is my "craft," a warming-up process for writing. I must do it.

"I have had such a good day!" I say to C. when he comes back. "Oh, how I love Sundays!" "I can see it in you," he says, "but why can't other days be like Sunday—why not Wednesday, for instance?"

He has had a good day, too. The garden chair I bought was a great success! I am so pleased. And the children good.

A sunset walk—the angry crows cawing in a tattered cloud over us as we disturb their roosts. C. and I talk of whether I might take a course in ceramics. I feel a hunger in my hands, for a craft. But would I have time? There is so little now, for my own.

Questions on Meaning

1 Lindbergh says that "writing comes out of life; life *must* come first." How does this explain why she cannot write at the expense of her children?

2 Does her diary entry give any evidence that, as she says, "my life does not go well *without* writing"? Is there evidence that writing does make her life go better?

3 How does her statement "Writing in a diary is my tool for the development of awareness" compare with Thoreau's purpose for keeping a journal?

4 She says that writing in her diary "is the crucible through which the rough material of life must pass before I can use it in art." As a professional writer, she writes in order to write! Cite examples of material in your journal that you could imagine being used as the basis of a formal essay.

Questions on Method

1   Thoreau says that a journal is a "record of our thoughts, feelings, studies, and daily experience." Often, a daily experience is the catalyst for the thoughts and feelings recorded in a journal. To what extent is this true of Lindbergh's journal entry? How does writing about an experience lead to writing about feelings and thoughts?

2   How private do you think Lindbergh believed her diary to be, since she has had all her diaries published? Discuss the extent to which it is possible to be both private and public in writing in a journal.

3   Whereas Thoreau's journal entry is organized like an essay, Lindbergh's is much looser. Which form—highly structured or relatively unstructured—appeals to you? Explain your answer.

Vocabulary and Diction

1   Define "flywheel," "cloister," and "crucible" (2). How do these words serve as appropriate metaphors for writing in a journal?

Writing Topics

1   Write a journal entry using an experience you had during the day as the catalyst for evaluating your feelings and thoughts about a subject.

2   Write a journal entry in which you discuss Lindbergh's statement that "writing comes out of life; life *must* come first."

3   Write a journal entry reacting to Lindbergh's comment that "there are so many things only a mother can know or do."

4   Write a journal entry on "How I love (or hate) Sunday."

From

The Diary of Anaïs Nin

Anaïs Nin

The death of Antonio Francisco Miralles in a hotel room, alone, of asthma. Miralles, my Spanish dancing teacher. 1

Whenever I stepped off the bus at Montmartre, I could hear the music of the merry-go-rounds at the fair, and I would feel my mood, my walk, my whole body transformed by its gaiety. I walked to a side street, knocked on a dark doorway opened by a disheveled concierge, and ran down the stairway to a vast room below street level, a vast cellar room with its walls covered with mirrors. It was the place where the little girls from the Opéra Ballet rehearsed. When I came down the stairway I could hear the piano, feet stamping, and the ballet master's voice. When the piano stopped, there was always his voice scolding, and the whispering of smaller voices. As I entered, the class was dissolving and a flurry of little girls brushed by me in their moth ballet costumes, laughing and whispering, fluttering like moths on their dusty ballet slippers, flurries of snow in the darkness of the vast room, with drops of dew from exertion. I went down with them along the corridors to the dressing rooms. These looked like gardens, with 2 so many ballet skirts, Spanish costumes hanging on pegs. It over-flowed with the smell of cold cream, face powder, cheap cologne.

While they dressed for the street, I dressed for my Spanish 3
dances. Miralles would already be rehearsing his own castanets. The
piano, slightly out of tune, was beginning the dance of Granados.
The floor was beginning to vibrate as other Spanish dancers tried out
their heel work. Tap tap tap tap tap. Miralles was about forty, slender,
erect, not handsome in face but graceful when dancing. His face was
undefined, his features blurred.

I was the favorite. 4

He was like a gentle Svengali, and by his eyes, his voice, his 5
hands, he had the power to make me dance as well as by his ordinary
lessons. He ruled my body with a magnetic rule, master of my dancing.

One day he waited for me at the door, neat and trim. "Will you 6
come and sit at the café with me?"

I followed him. Not far from there was the Place Clichy, always 7
animated, but more so now, as the site of a permanent fair. The
merry-go-rounds were turning swiftly. The gypsies were reading fortunes in little booths hung with Arabian rugs. Workmen were shooting clay pigeons and winning cut glass for their wives. The prostitutes
were enjoying their loitering, and the men were watching them.

My dancing teacher was saying to me: "Anaïs, I am a simple 8
man. My parents were shoemakers in a little village in the south of
Spain. I was put to work in an iron factory where I handled heavy
things and was on the way to becoming deformed by big muscles. But
during my lunch hour, I danced. I wanted to be a dancer and I
practiced every day, every night. At night I went to the gypsies'
caverns, and learned from them. I began to dance in cabarets. And
today, look!" He took out a cigarette case engraved with the names
of all the famous Spanish dancers. "Today I have been the partner
of all these women. If you would come with me, we could be happy.
I am a simple man, but we could dance in all the cities of Europe. I
am no longer young but I have a lot of dancing in me yet. We could
be happy."

The merry-go-round turned and sang, and I imagined myself 9
embarking on a dancing career with Miralles, dancing, which was so
much like flying, from city to city, receiving bouquets, praise in
newspapers, with joyous music at the center always, pleasure as colorful as the Spanish dresses, all red, orange, black and gold, gold and
purple, and red and white.

Imagining . . . like amnesia. Forgetting who I was, and where   10
I was, and why I could not do it. Not knowing how to answer so I
would not hurt him, I said, "I am not strong enough."

"That's what I thought when I first saw you. I thought you   11
couldn't take the discipline of a dancer's life. But it isn't so. You look
fragile and all that, but you're healthy. I can tell healthy women by
their skin. Yours is shining and clear. No, I don't think you have
the strength of a horse, you're what we call a *petite nature*. But you
have energy and guts. And we'll take it easy on the road."

Many afternoons, after hard work, we sat at this little café and   12
imagined what a dancer's life might be.

Miralles and I danced in several places together, at a *haute*   13
couture opening, at a millionaire Brazilian's open house, at a night
club; but when I auditioned for the Opéra, *Amor Brujo*, and was
accepted and would have traveled all over the world, I gave up
dancing [1928].

And Miralles died alone in his hotel room, of asthma. He had   14
been saving his money to retire to his home town, Valencia. He was
good, homely, and would say to me: "You know, I have no vices like
the others. I would be good to you." Just because I listened to his
gaudy stories of a gaudy past, he glowed, he went at his dancing with
renewed vigor, he was rejuvenated, he bought himself a new suit.

For a while, it was as if I had lived in his shabby hotel room   15
with photographs of Spanish dancers pinned to the walls. I knew how
it was in Russia, in music halls all over the world. The odor of the
dancers, of dressing rooms, the pungent atmosphere of rehearsals.
Lola, Alma Viva, L'Argentinita. I would wear bedroom slippers and
flowered kimonos, big Spanish flowered cottons. I would open the
door and my father would be standing there, saying: "Have you
forgotten who you are? You are my daughter, you have forgotten your
class, your name, your true stature in life."

One day I awakened from my amnesia. No longer a dancer.   16
Miralles turned ashen and grey, was snuffed out. He became again an
old, weary dancing teacher.

Questions on Meaning

1   What experience evokes this diary entry?

2 What effect does Nin achieve by contrasting herself with the class of ballet dancers?

3 Nin approaches Miralles from several points of view. How does she visually describe, characterize, and dramatize his life and personality?

4 Why does she frequently describe her relationship with Miralles as one of "amnesia"? What happens to her conception of Miralles once she recovers from her amnesia?

Questions on Method

1 Nin's diary entry has a form very different from that of either Thoreau or Lindbergh in that she tells a story. Why does she choose this method? What effect does it have?

2 Nin vividly describes the people and events. What is the effect of her description, for example, of the ballet dancers as moths and "flurries of snow" and of Spanish dancers as "all red, orange, black and gold, gold and purple, and red and white"?

3 To what extent does Nin's diary entry fulfill Thoreau's expectation that in writing about our experiences we avoid repeating them?

Vocabulary and Diction

1 Make a list of the words Nin uses to convey life and death. What do these contrasting vocabularies contribute to the meaning of her story?

2 Explain the meaning of the following words and phrases used by Nin: disheveled (2), *concierge* (2), castanets (3), Svengali (5), *haute couture* (13).

Writing Topics

1 Write a journal entry in which you re-create an experience. Use description, dialogue, and actions as Nin does. Include the thoughts and feelings the experience evoked for you.

2 Write a journal entry about choosing not to do something you wanted to do because you knew it wasn't right for you.

3 Write a journal entry about someone who had considerable influence on you at one point in your life.

From

The Diary of a Young Girl

Anne Frank

Saturday, 20 June, 1942

I haven't written for a few days, because I wanted first of all to think 1
about my diary. It's an odd idea for someone like me to keep a diary;
not only because I have never done so before, but because it seems
to me that neither I—nor for that matter anyone else—will be interested in the unbosomings of a thirteen-year-old schoolgirl. Still, what
does that matter? I want to write, but more than that, I want to bring
out all kinds of things that lie buried deep in my heart.

There is a saying that "paper is more patient than man"; it came 2
back to me on one of my slightly melancholy days, while I sat chin
in hand, feeling too bored and limp even to make up my mind
whether to go out or stay at home. Yes, there is no doubt that paper
is patient and as I don't intend to show this cardboard-covered notebook, bearing the proud name of "diary," to anyone, unless I find a
real friend, boy or girl, probably nobody cares. And now I come to

the root of the matter, the reason for my starting a diary: it is that I have no such real friend.

Let me put it more clearly, since no one will believe that a girl   3
of thirteen feels herself quite alone in the world, nor is it so. I have darling parents and a sister of sixteen. I know about thirty people whom one might call friends—I have strings of boy friends, anxious to catch a glimpse of me and who, failing that, peep at me through mirrors in class. I have relations, aunts and uncles, who are darlings too, a good home, no—I don't seem to lack anything. But it's the same with all my friends, just fun and joking, nothing more. I can never bring myself to talk of anything outside the common round. We don't seem to be able to get any closer, that is the root of the trouble. Perhaps I lack confidence, but anyway, there it is, a stubborn fact and I don't seem to be able to do anything about it.

Hence, this diary. In order to enhance in my mind's eye the   4
picture of the friend for whom I have waited so long, I don't want to set down a series of bald facts in a diary like most people do, but I want this diary itself to be my friend, and I shall call my friend Kitty.

Questions on Meaning

1 Why does Frank think it is an "odd idea" for someone like her to keep a diary? Why, despite her doubts, does she go ahead and keep a diary?

2 What does the idea of friendship have to do with Frank's motivation for keeping a diary?

3 How close is Frank's purpose for keeping a diary to Thoreau's for keeping a journal or to Scott-Maxwell's (see the next selection) for keeping a notebook?

Questions on Method

1 How well does Frank's entry illustrate her desire to avoid setting down "a series of bald facts" in favor of "unbosoming" or revealing her deepest feelings and thoughts?

2 How uncertain or lacking in confidence is Frank's tone? How certain and self-assured is it? Why does writing in a diary often produce conflicting emotions in the writer? Do any of the other writers in this section reveal a similar conflict?

3   Of all the writers in this chapter, only Frank did not expect to have her journal published. Does her writing indicate that she has a greater sense of privacy than the other writers? Explain.

Vocabulary and Diction

1   In what sense is the word "confidence" at the end of paragraph 3 a pun, a play on words? How does this word convey a double meaning that refers, on the one hand, to Frank's lack of self-assurance and, on the other hand, to Frank's lack of a real friend?

2   What does the phrase "paper is patient" mean? The alliteration of this phrase, the repetition of its initial consonant sounds, adds a touch of poetry to the translation of Frank's entry. How important is the way a piece of writing sounds, compared to the thoughts it expresses, in generating a reader's interest?

Writing Topics

1   Reread a journal entry that you wrote originally with a sense of audience; rewrite it now only for yourself. Compare the two entries. How different are content, attitude (or tone), and style?

2   Write a journal entry about the value you place on your friend. Do you agree with Frank that many people feel they have no "real" friends or that "paper is patient" while people often are not? How does writing a journal offset your need to communicate to friends?

FLORIDA SCOTT-MAXWELL (1883–   ) was taught at home until she was 10; she briefly attended public school in Pittsburgh and then resumed private lessons, beginning a stage career at 16. At 20 she abandoned that pursuit and began writing short stories. In 1910 she married John Maxwell Scott-Maxwell and moved to Scotland. Until 1935 she worked for women's suffrage, wrote plays, and raised a family. Among her books are *Towards Relationships* (1939), *Women and Sometimes Men* (1957), and the plays *The Flash-point* (1914), *They Knew How to Die* (1931), and *Many Women* (1933). In 1933 she began training as an analytical psychologist, studying under Carl Jung. Since then she has practiced in psychology clinics in Scotland and England. In this diary entry she discusses her reactions to getting old.

From

The Measure of My Days

Florida Scott-Maxwell

1   We who are old know that age is more than a disability. It is an intense and varied experience, almost beyond our capacity at times, but something to be carried high. If it is a long defeat it is also a victory, meaningful for the initiates of time, if not for those who have come less far.

2   Being old I am out of step, troubled by my lack of concord, unable to like or understand much that I see. Feeling at variance with the times must be the essence of age, and it is confusing, wounding. I feel exposed, bereft of a right matrix, with the present crime, violence, nihilism heavy on my heart. I weigh and appraise, recoiling, suffering, but very alert. Now that I have withdrawn from the active world I am more alert to it than ever before. Old people have so little personal life that the impact of the impersonal is sharp. Some of us

feel like sounding boards, observing, reading; the outside event startles us and we ask in alarm, "Is this good or bad? To where will it lead? What effect will it have on people, just people? How different will they become?" I fear for the future.

In the past when sorrows, or problems, or ideas were too much   3
for me, I learned to deal with them in a way of my own. At night when I got to bed I lay on my back and gave to their solution what I knew would be many sleepless hours. I would let the problem enter me like a lance piercing my solar plexus. I must be open, utterly open, and as I could stand it the lance went deeper and deeper. As I accepted each implication, opened to my hurt, my protest, resentment and bewilderment the lance went further in. Then the same for others involved—that they did, said, felt, thus and so, then why, face why and endure the lance. As my understanding deepened I could finally accept the truths that lay behind the first truths that had seemed unendurable. At last, the pain of the lance was not there and I was free. No, free is not the right word. My barriers had been lowered and I knew what I had not known before.

Now that I am old something has begun that is slightly the same,   4
enough the same to make me start this note book. When I was sewing, or playing a soothing-boring game of patience, I found queries going round and round in my head and I began to jot them down in this note book which I used to use for sketching. The queries were insistent, and I began a game of asking questions and giving answers. Answers out of what I had read and forgotten, and now thought my own, or out of my recoils and hopes. If the modern world is this, then will it become so and so? My answers must be my own, years of reading now lost in the abyss I call my mind. What matters is what I have now, what in fact I live and feel.

It makes my note book my dear companion, or my undoing. I   5
put down my sweeping opinions, prejudices, limitations, and just here the book fails me for it makes no comment. It is even my wailing wall, and when I play that grim, comforting game of noting how wrong everyone else is, my book is silent, and I listen to the stillness, and I learn.

I am getting fine and supple from the mistakes I've made, but I   6
wish a note book could laugh. Old and alone one lives at such a high moral level. One is surrounded by eternal verities, noble austerities

to scale on every side, and frightening depths of insight. It is inhuman. I long to laugh. I want to be enjoyed, but an hour's talk and I am exhausted.

Questions on Meaning

1 In what ways does Scott-Maxwell feel that old age is both a defeat and a victory?
2 What were her motivations for beginning her "note book"?
3 Why does she describe her "note book" as both her "dear companion" and her "undoing"?

Questions on Method

1 Unlike Thoreau's, Lindbergh's, or Nin's journals, Scott-Maxwell's note book is filled with notes instead of longer, sustained pieces. How effective is her "note" method for fulfilling her purpose in writing?
2 In discussing which topic does Scott-Maxwell generalize about her experience by using the pronoun "we" or "us"? About which topic does she use only the pronoun "I"? What significance can you see in her use of pronouns?

Vocabulary and Diction

1 Scott-Maxwell's language could be considered elegant. Expressions like "the initiates of time" and "troubled by my lack of concord" are not the language of the office or the newspaper. What other such expressions can you find? Does her diction seem appropriate for her subject matter? Explain.
2 Define the following words used by Scott-Maxwell: matrix (2), nihilism (2), supple (6), verities (6), austerities (6).

Writing Topics

1 Write a journal entry or entries composed of a series of notes on one or two topics. Analyze the effect of this style on your journal. What is gained or lost by this method?

2 Scott-Maxwell began her note book as a "game of asking questions and giving answers." Write a journal entry or entries in which you follow this organization.

3 Write in your journal about old age. How do your views of the elderly compare with Scott-Maxwell's?

ALBERT CAMUS (1913–60) was a French novelist, dramatist, essayist, and journalist whose work had a significant impact on his contemporaries. He was a member of the French Resistance movement during World War II and was the editor of *Combat*, an underground publication. Although he has been identified with existentialism, Camus's profound humanism distinguishes him from many existentialist writers. Convinced of the absurdity of life, Camus nevertheless, in his art and in his life, struggled with the paradoxical aspirations of personal freedom and social justice, solitude and solidarity, reason and passion. He was awarded the Nobel Prize in 1957 for his philosophical essays, which include "The Myth of Sisyphus" (1942) and "The Rebel" (1953), and for his fiction, which includes *The Stranger* (1942), *The Plague* (1948), and *The Fall* (1957). He was killed in an automobile accident at the height of his literary career. In the following entry from the first volume of his *Notebooks* he explains why his "deepest joy is to write."

From
Notebooks 1935–1942

Albert Camus

May 1935–September 1937

SEPTEMBER 15

In the cloister of San Francesco in Fiesole there is a little courtyard with an arcade along each side, full of red flowers, sun, and yellow and black bees. In one corner, there is a green water sprinkler, and everywhere the humming of bees. A gentle steam seems to rise from the garden as it bakes in the heat. Sitting on the ground, I think about the Franciscans whose cells I have just visited and whose sources of inspiration I can now see. I feel clearly that if they are right then it is in the same way that I am. I know that behind the wall on which I am leaning there is a hill sloping down toward the town, and the offering of the whole of Florence with all its cypress trees. But this splendor of the world seems to justify these men. I put all my pride in a belief that it also justifies me, and all the men of my race, who know that there is an extreme point at which poverty always rejoins the luxury and richness of the world. If they cast everything off, it is for a greater and not for another life. This is the only meaning which I can accept of a term like "stripping oneself bare." "Being naked" always has associations of physical liberty, of harmony between the hand and the flowers it touches, of a loving understanding between the earth and men who have been freed from human things. Ah, I should become a convert to this if it were not already my religion.

Today, I feel free about the past and about what I have lost. All I want is this compactness and enclosed space—this lucid and patient fervor. And like the warm bread that one kneads and presses I simply want to hold my life between my hands, like the men who knew how to enclose their life between these flowers and these columns. The same is true of those long nights spent on trains, where one can talk to oneself, prepare oneself for life, and feel marvelously patient in taking up ideas again, stopping them in their flight, and then once more moving forward. To lick one's life like a stick of barley sugar, to form, sharpen, and finally fall in love with it, in the same way as one searches for the word, the image, the definitive sentence, the word or image which marks a close or a conclusion, from which one can start out again and which will color the way we see the world. I can easily stop now, and finally reach the end of a year of unrestrained and overstrained life. My effort now is to carry this presence of myself to myself through to the very end, to maintain it whatever aspect my life takes on—even at the price of the loneliness which I now know is so difficult to bear. Not to give way—that is the whole secret. Not to surrender, not to betray. All the violent part of my character helps me in this, carrying me to the point where I am rejoined by my love, and by the furious passion for life which gives meaning to my days.

Every time a man (myself) gives way to vanity, every time he thinks and lives in order to show off, this is a betrayal. Every time, it has always been the great misfortune of wanting to show off which has lessened me in the presence of the truth. We do not need to reveal ourselves to others, but only to those we love. For then we are no longer revealing ourselves in order to seem but in order to give. There is much more strength in a man who reveals himself only when it is necessary. I have suffered from being alone, but because I have been able to keep my secret I have overcome the suffering of loneliness. To go right to the end implies knowing how to keep one's secret. And, today, there is no greater joy than to live alone and unknown. My deepest joy is to write. To accept the world and to accept pleasure—but only when I am stripped bare of everything. I should not be worthy to love the bare and empty beaches if I could not remain naked in the presence of myself. For the first time I can understand the meaning of the word happiness without any ambiguity. It is a little different from what men normally mean when they say: "I am happy."

A certain persistence in despair finally gives birth to joy. And the same men who, in San Francesco, live by the side of these red flowers, keep in their cells a skull to nourish their meditations, seeing Florence from their windows and death on the table before them. And if I now feel that I have come to a turning point in my life, this is not because of what I have won but because of what I have lost. Within me, I feel a deep and intense strength that will enable me to live as I intend. If, today, I feel so distant from everything, it is because I have strength only to love and to admire. Life with its face of tears and sun, life in the salt sea and on warm stones, life as I love and understand it—as I caress it I feel my love and despair gathering strength within me. Today is not like a resting place between "yes" and "no." It is both "yes" and "no." "No," and rebellion against everything which is not tears and sunlight. "Yes" to my life, whose future promise I now feel within myself for the first time. A turbulent, confused year which is coming to an end, and Italy. I am uncertain of the future, but have achieved total liberty toward my past and toward myself. Here lies my poverty, and my sole wealth. It is as if I were beginning the game all over again, neither happier nor unhappier than before. But aware now of where my strength lies, scornful of my own vanities, and filled with that lucid fervor which impels me forward toward my fate.

September 15, 1937

Questions on Meaning

1   What experience evokes the thoughts and feelings of this journal entry?
2   Camus says of the Franciscan monks, "But this splendor of the world seems to justify these men. I put all my pride in a belief that it also justifies me, and all the men of my race, who know that there is an extreme point at which poverty always rejoins the luxury and richness of the world. If they cast everything off, it is for a greater and not for another life." What does he mean in this passage?
3   To what extent do you agree with Camus when he says, "We do not need to reveal ourselves to others, but only to those we love. . . . There is much more strength in a man who reveals himself only when it is necessary"?
4   What connection between man and nature is Camus making when he says, "I should not be worthy to love the bare and empty beaches if I could not remain naked in the presence of myself"?
5   What does Camus mean when he writes that "a certain persistence in despair finally gives birth to joy"?
6   To what extent does this entry fulfill Thoreau's expectation that a journal helps a person "turn over a new leaf, having carefully perused the preceding one, and . . . not continue to glance carelessly over the same page, without being able to distinguish it from a new one"?

Questions on Method

1   Camus begins with a daily experience, as does Lindbergh, and then develops his thoughts and feelings into an essay, as does Thoreau. How effective is his combination of these two methods? In reading the entry, do we lose sight of the experience he is responding to, or are we constantly reminded of the occasion for his ideas?
2   With what methods does Camus attempt to make vivid his description of nature? To what extent does he succeed?
3   What is the effect of Camus's comparing his attitude toward life to holding a loaf of bread and licking a stick of barley sugar?
4   How private do you think Camus intended this notebook entry to be? Does he express thoughts here that, as he says, should not be revealed "to others, but only to those we love"? If so, in your opinion does he lose "strength" by their revelation?

Vocabulary and Diction

1   What is the meaning of the words "lucid" (2), "fervor" (2), and "ambiguity" (3)?

2   Camus says many personal things in an impersonal, philosophical way, such as, "Every time, it has always been the great misfortune of wanting to show off which has lessened me in the presence of truth." Cite other instances of this method. What effect does this way of writing about one's life have? Is it an effective way of writing a journal?

Writing Topics

1   Write a journal entry about an insight you had while visiting an unfamiliar town or city.

2   Write a journal entry discussing your thoughts and feelings about nature or religion.

3   Write an entry in which you express some of your most personal feelings in a general way.

The Journal—Writing Topics

1 Write an essay in which you discuss how Lindbergh's assertion that "writing comes out of life; life *must* come first" applies to the other entries in this chapter.

2 Write an essay on the styles and themes of journal keeping as the writers in this chapter exemplify them. For example, in what order of frequency do the writers select Thoreau's four categories of journal content: "thoughts, feelings, studies, and daily experience"? Do the writers favor writing freely or with careful composition? How do style and content interact? Does one form of style seem more appropriate for one type of content?

3 Read other journal entries in the volume from which one of these entries is taken. Write an essay evaluating the methods and themes of the writer. How well does he or she fulfill the purpose for which the journal was written? For example, do Thoreau's other entries fulfill his stated purpose in writing a journal, that is, "to turn over a new leaf . . . to improve ourselves by reflection"?

4 Lindbergh says that "writing in a diary is my tool for the development of awareness." Choose a theme that emerges from your journal entries, and write an essay evaluating how recording this material has affected your awareness.

5 Choose a recurring theme in your journal entries that you would like to write an essay about, using your journal, therefore, as a "warming-up process for writing," as Lindbergh says. In writing the essay, convey to an audience of your choice the significance the theme has for you and perhaps for it.

TWO
Narration

Narration is storytelling, which answers the question "What happened?" and deals heavily in time and verbs. Narration's purposes run the gamut from relaying information to providing entertainment, ranging from the factual report of an accident or a convention to the escapism of a horror tale or a who-dun-it. In jokes, résumés, medical histories, personal letters, diaries, novels, and newspapers, narrative has been under our very noses from our earliest experience with language.

Narrative is frequently combined with persuasion to make arguments more compelling and with exposition to make explanations clearer and more interesting. The simplest story usually makes a point, at least by implication, and this is where narrative becomes serviceable to exposition. At one end of the spectrum is fiction, where imagination is given free play. At the other end is nonfiction of several kinds: a journalist uses narrative to inform, and the events in a news story allow no admixture of the writer's imagination; the same is true of history, biography, and autobiography, although these often mix narration with interpretation and opinion.

When writing a narrative, you have several choices to make. One of these is point of view, or deciding who the narrator will be. For a story in which you are a participant, the first person will probably seem the natural choice:

> It was early one morning when I went out to chop some wood for the kitchen. I had split hardly a dozen sticks when I turned toward the shed and saw a pair of green eyes staring from a hole in the wall. "Jane, bring me my shotgun," I yelled.

But you could change the perspective or point of view by allowing Jane to tell the story:

> Al had just gone to the woodlot when all of a sudden I heard him yelling for his gun.

Or you might want "green eyes" to be your narrator:

> It's not easy finding shelter in these woods, so when I found an old woodshed I made it my home for the night. Whacks of an ax woke me the next morning, and I peered out a crack between the shingles to see, not five feet away . . .

Or, of course, you could tell the story in the third person:

> Alan Smith paused after chopping half a dozen sticks of firewood to find a pair of green eyes peering out of a hole in the woodshed wall. "Jane," he yelled, "bring me my gun."

Another choice to make regards the speed with which each time sequence should be handled. Will you give equal time to every event or hurry past some unimportant events with a summary, perhaps even skipping some? In a play, so long as a scene is in progress, dramatic time equals real time; the balcony scene in *Romeo and Juliet*, for example, takes as long on stage as it would in real life. If the play covers more than a couple of hours, and the great majority do, the playwright must speed up the clock, and that is one of the purposes of ending one scene and starting another. In the next scene, then, a character relates what, if anything, happened between scenes. The writer of prose narrative has the same choices. In "Hills like White Elephants," whose sole action is a man and a woman talking while they wait for a train to Barcelona, Hemingway speeds up the man's action when he leaves the woman to move the bags:

> He picked up the two heavy bags and carried them around the station to the other tracks. He looked up the tracks but could not see the train. Coming back, he walked through the barroom, where people waiting for the train were drinking. He drank an Anis at the bar and looked at the people. They were all waiting reasonably for the train. He went out through the bead curtain. She was sitting at the table and smiled at him.[1]

This important paragraph omits, among other things, the man's words to the bartender; the word "reasonably" summarizes his complicated attitude toward the *un*reasonable woman whom he may or may not be able to convince to get an abortion.

Here, by contrast, is another scene from the story, narrated in greater detail:

> "What should we drink?" the girl asked. She had taken off her hat and put it on the table.
> "It's pretty hot," the man said.
> "Let's drink beer."
> "Dos cervezas," the man said into the curtain.
> "Big ones?" a woman asked from the doorway.
> "Yes, two big ones."
> The woman brought two glasses of beer and two felt pads. She put the felt pads and the beer glasses on the table and looked at the

---

1. From Ernest Hemingway, *The Short Stories of Ernest Hemingway.* Copyright 1938 by Ernest Hemingway; copyright renewed 1966 by Mary Hemingway. Reprinted with the permission of Charles Scribner's Sons.

man and the girl. The girl was looking off at the line of hills. They were white in the sun and the country was brown and dry.

To present a scene as it happens, you must acquire a good eye for detail and often a good ear for dialogue as well.

Will you tell your story in chronological order or rearrange the sequence in some way? Will you begin at the beginning or somewhere later in the series? You might try experimenting with different arrangements. Suppose you decide to narrate four incidents. You could tell them in chronological order: incident 1, incident 2, incident 3, incident 4; or you could begin with the penultimate incident, flash back to the two earlier ones, and end with the last: incident 3, incident 1, incident 2, incident 4.

Other choices to be made also involve time. You may find it useful to imagine a clock or calendar in your story; you can build to a climax by crowding more and more incidents into a shorter and shorter period of time. Do you want to end with a surprise or to create suspense? A surprise ending is achieved simply by withholding information, but to create suspense you must feed your reader bits of information to awaken his curiosity. Flashbacks are especially useful for creating suspense, leaving unanswered the burning question "What happened next?" while telling what happened earlier. Naturally, transitions, usually involving time order, are all-important, especially if you use flashbacks. Become accustomed to using words and phrases like "earlier," "all at once," "at 3:41 P.M." Dylan Thomas even uses "once below a time."

Writing Narration

1   Choose a point of view that serves your purpose.
2   Choose the organization that best fits your story: (*a*) chronological—begin at the beginning, continue in time order; (*b*) flashback—interrupt your story with earlier incidents.
3   Use dialogue.
4   Alternate in speed between summaries and fully dramatized scenes.
5   Use transitions between incidents and scenes.

PAUL THEROUX (1941–   ) is an American teacher and writer who has taught in many parts of the world, including Uganda and Singapore. His several novels include *Jungle Lovers* (1971) and *Picture Palace* (1978). Among his volumes of nonfiction are *U.S. Napaul* (1973), *The Great Railway Bazaar* (1975), and *The Old Patagonian Express* (1979). In the excerpt that follows, taken from *The Old Patagonian Express*, Theroux recalls an experience that occurred during his stopover in San Salvador.

Soccer in San Salvador

Paul Theroux

The football game that night promised to be one of the best games 1
of the year. El Salvador was playing Mexico at the National Stadium and, as Mexico was scheduled to play in the World Cup in Argentina, it was El Salvador's chance to prove itself.

I had read about Latin American soccer—the chaos, the riots, 2
the passionately partisan crowds, the way political frustrations were ventilated at the stadiums. I knew for a fact that if one wished to understand the British it helped to see a soccer game; then, the British did not seem so tight-lipped and proper. Indeed, a British soccer game was an occasion for a form of gang-warfare for the younger spectators. The muscular ritual of sport was always a clear demonstration of the wilder impulses in national character. The Olympic Games are interesting largely because they are a kind of world war in pantomime.

"Would you mind if I went to the game with you?" I asked 3
Alfredo, a Salvadorean salesman I had met on the train.

Alfredo looked worried. "It will be very crowded," he said. 4
"There may be trouble. It is better to go to the swimming pool
tomorrow—for the girls."

"Do you think I came to El Salvador to pick up girls at a public 5
swimming pool?"

"Did you come to El Salvador to see the football game?" 6

"Yes," I said. 7

The San Salvador railway station was at the end of a torn-up 8
section of road in a grim precinct of the city. My ticket was collected
by a man in a porkpie hat and sports shirt, who wore an old-fashioned
revolver on his hip. The station was no more than a series of cargo
sheds, where very poor people were camped, waiting for the morning
train to Cutuco: the elderly and the very young—it seemed to be the
pattern of victims in Central American poverty. Alfredo had given
me the name of a hotel and said he would meet me there an hour
before kickoff, which was nine o'clock. The games were played late,
he said, because by then it wasn't so hot. But it was now after dark,
and the humid heat still choked me. I began to wish that I had not
left Santa Ana. San Salvador, prone to earthquakes, was not a pretty
place; it sprawled, it was noisy, its buildings were charmless, and in
the glare of headlights were buoyant particles of dust. Why would
anyone come here? "Don't knock it," an American in San Salvador
told me. "You haven't seen Nicaragua yet!"

Alfredo was late. He blamed the traffic: "There will be a million 9
people at the stadium." He had brought along some friends, two boys
who, he boasted, were studying English.

"How are you doing?" I asked them in English. 10

"Please?" said one. The other laughed. The first one said in 11
Spanish, "We are only on the second lesson."

Because of the traffic, and the risk of car thieves at the stadium, 12
Alfredo parked a half mile away, at a friend's house. This house was
worth some study; it was a number of cubicles nailed to trees, with
the leafy branches depending into the rooms. Cloth was hung from
sticks to provide walls, and a strong fence surrounded it. I asked the
friend how long he had lived there. He said his family had lived in
the house for many years. I did not ask what happened when it
rained.

But poverty in a poor country had subtle gradations. We walked 13
down a long hill, toward the stadium, and crossing a bridge I looked

into a gorge, expecting to see a river, and saw lean-tos and cooking fires and lanterns. Who lives there? I asked Alfredo.

"Poor people," he said.

Others were walking to the stadium, too. We joined a large procession of quick-marching fans, and as we drew closer to the stadium they began yelling and shoving in anticipation. The procession swarmed over the foothills below the stadium, crashing through people's gardens and thumping the fenders of stalled cars. Here the dust was deep, and the trampling feet of the fans made it rise until it became a brown fog, like a sepia print of a mob scene, with the cones of headlights bobbing in it. The mob was running now, and Alfredo and his friends were obscured by the dust cloud. Every ten feet, boys rushed forward and shook tickets at me, screaming, "Suns! Suns! Suns!"

These were the touts. They bought the cheapest tickets and sold them at a profit to people who had neither the time nor the courage to stand in a long rowdy line at a ticket window. The seat designations were those usual at a bullfight: "Suns" were the cheapest bleacher seats; "Shades" were more expensive ones under the canopy.

I fought my way through the touts and, having lost Alfredo, made my way uphill to the kettle-shaped stadium. It was an unearthly sight; the crowd of people emerging from darkness into luminous brown fog, the yells, the dust rising, the mountainside smoldering under a sky which, because of the dust, was starless. At that point, I considered turning back; but the mob was propelling me forward toward the stadium, where the roar of the spectators inside made a sound like flames howling in a chimney.

The mob took up this cry and surged past me, stirring up the dust. There were women frying bananas and meat cakes over fires on the walkway that ran around the outside perimeter of the stadium. The smoke from these fires and the dust made each searchlight seem to burn with a smoky flame. The touts reappeared nearer the stadium. They were hysterical now. The game was about to start; they had not sold their tickets. They grabbed my arms, they pushed tickets in my face, they shouted.

One look at the lines of people near the ticket windows told me that I would have no chance at all of buying a ticket legally. I was pondering this question when, through the smoke and dust, Alfredo appeared.

"Take your watch off," he said. "And your ring. Put them in

35

your pocket. Be very careful. Most of these people are thieves. They will rob you."

I did as I was told. "What about the tickets? Shall we buy some 21 Suns from these boys?"

"No, I will buy Shades." 22

"Are they expensive?" 23

"Of course, but this will be a great game. I could never see such 24 a game in Santa Ana. Anyway, the Shades will be quieter." Alfredo looked around. "Hide over there by the wall. I will get the tickets."

Alfredo vanished into the conga line at a ticket window. He 25 appeared again at the middle of the line, jumped the queue, elbowed forward, and in a very short time had fought his way to the window. Even his friends marveled at his speed. He came toward us smiling, waving the tickets in triumph.

We were frisked at the entrance; we passed through a tunnel and 26 emerged at the end of the stadium. From the outside it had looked like a kettle; inside, its shape was more of a salver, a tureen filled with brown screeching faces. In the center was a pristine rectangle of green grass.

It was, those 45,000 people, a model of Salvadorean society. 27 Not only the half of the stadium where the Suns sat (and it was jammed: not an empty seat was visible); or the better-dressed and almost as crowded half of the Shades (at night, in the dry season, there was no difference in the quality of the seats: we sat on concrete steps, but ours, being more expensive than the Suns, were less crowded); there was a section that Alfredo had not mentioned: the Balconies. Above us, in five tiers of a gallery that ran around our half of the stadium, were the Balcony people. Balcony people had season tickets. Balcony people had small rooms, closet-sized, about as large as the average Salvadorean's hut; I could see the wine bottles, the glasses, the plates of food. Balcony people had folding chairs and a good view of the field. There were not many Balcony people—two or three hundred—but at $2000 for a season ticket in a country where the annual per capita income was $373, one could understand why. The Balcony people faced the screaming Suns and, beyond the stadium, a plateau. What I took to be lumpish multicolored vegetation covering the plateau was, I realized, a heap of Salvadoreans standing on top or clinging to the sides. There were thousands of them in this mass, and it was a sight more terrifying than the Suns. They were lighted by the stadium glare; there was a just-perceptible crawling movement among the bodies; it was an anthill.

National anthems were played, amplified songs from scratched records, and then the game began. It was apparent from the outset who would win. Mexico was bigger, faster, and seemed to follow a definite strategy; El Salvador had two ball-hoggers, and the team was tiny and erratic. The crowd hissed the Mexicans and cheered El Salvador. One of the Salvadorean ball-hoggers went jinking down the field, shot and missed. The ball went to the Mexicans, who tormented the Salvadoreans by passing it from man to man, and then, fifteen minutes into the game, the Mexicans scored. The stadium was silent as the Mexican players kissed one another. 28

Some minutes later the ball was kicked into the Shades section. It was thrown back onto the field, and the game was resumed. Then it was kicked into the Suns section. The Suns fought for it. One man gained possession, but he was pounced upon and the ball shot up and ten Suns went tumbling after it. A Sun tried to run down the steps with it. He was caught and the ball wrestled from him. A fight began, and now there were scores of Suns punching their way to the ball. The Suns higher up in the section threw bottles and cans and wadded paper on the Suns who were fighting, and the shower of objects— meat pies, bananas, hankies—continued to fall. The Shades, the Balconies, the Anthill, watched this struggle. 29

And the players watched, too. The game had stopped. The Mexican players kicked the turf, the Salvadorean team shouted at the Suns. 30

Please return the ball. It was the announcer. He was hoarse. *If the ball is not returned, the game will not continue.* 31

This brought a greater shower of objects from the upper seats— cups, cushions, more bottles. The bottles broke with a splashing sound on the concrete seats. The Suns lower down began throwing things back at their persecutors, and it was impossible to say where the ball had gone. 32

The ball was not returned. The announcer repeated his threat. 33

The players sat down on the field and did limbering-up exercises until, ten minutes after the ball had disappeared from the field, a new ball was thrown in. The spectators cheered but, just as quickly, fell silent. Mexico had scored another goal. 34

Soon, a bad kick landed the ball into the Shades. This ball was 35 fought for and not thrown back, and one could see the ball progressing through the section. The ball was seldom visible, but one could tell from the free-for-alls—now here, now there—where it was. The Balconies poured water on the Shades, but the ball was not surrendered. And now it was the Suns' turn to see the slightly better-off Salvadoreans in the Shades section behaving like swine. The announcer made his threat: the game would not resume until the ball was thrown back. The threat was ignored, and after a long time the ref walked onto the field with a new ball.

In all, five balls were lost this way. The fourth landed not far from where I sat, and I could see that real punches were being thrown, real blood spurting from Salvadorean noses, and the broken bottles and the struggle for the ball made it a contest all its own, more savage than the one on the field, played out with the kind of mindless ferocity you read about in books on gory medieval sports. The announcer's warning was merely ritual threat; the police did not intervene—they stayed on the field and let the spectators settle their own scores. The players grew bored: they ran in place, they did pushups. When play resumed and Mexico gained possession of the ball, it deftly moved down the field and invariably made a goal. But this play, these goals—they were no more than interludes in a much bloodier sport which, toward midnight (and the game was still not over!), was varied by Suns throwing firecrackers at each other and onto the field.

The last time play was abandoned and fights broke out among the Suns—the ball bobbing from one ragged Sun to another—balloons were released from the upper seats. But they were not balloons. They were white, blimpy, and had a nipple on the end; first one, then dozens. This caused great laughter, and they were batted from section to section. They were of course contraceptives, and they caused Alfredo no end of embarrassment. "That is very bad," he said, gasping in shame. He had apologized for the interruptions; for the fights; the delayed play. Now this—dozens of airborne rubbers. The game was a shambles; it ended in confusion, fights, litter. But it shed light on the recreations of Salvadoreans. And as for the other thing—the inflated contraceptives—I later discovered that the Agency for International Development's largest Central American family-planning program is in El Salvador. I doubt whether the birthrate has been affected, but children's birthday parties in rural El Salvador must be a great deal of fun, what with the free balloons.

Mexico won the game, six to one. Alfredo said that El Salvador's goal was the best one of the game, a header from thirty yards. So he managed to rescue a shred of pride. But people had been leaving all through the second half, and the rest hardly seemed to notice or to care that the game had ended. Just before we left the stadium I looked up at the anthill. It was a hill once again; there were no people on it, and depopulated, it seemed very small.

Outside, on the stadium slopes, the scene was like one of those lurid murals of hell you see in Latin American churches. The color was infernal, yellow dust sifted and whirled among craterlike pits, small cars with demonic headlights moved slowly from hole to hole like mechanical devils. And where, on the murals, you would see the signs printed and dramatized, the gold lettering saying LUST, ANGER, AVARICE, DRUNKENNESS, GLUTTONY, THEFT, PRIDE, JEALOUSY, USURY, GAMBLING, here, after midnight, were groups of boys lewdly snatching at girls, and knots of people fighting, counting the money they had won, staggering and swigging from bottles, shrieking obscenities against Mexico, thumping the hoods of cars, or duelling with the branches they had yanked from trees and the radio aerials they had twisted from cars. They trampled the dust and howled. The car horns were like harsh moos of pain, and one car was being overturned by a gang of shirtless, sweating youths. Many people were running to get free of the mob, holding hankies over their faces. But there were tens of thousands of people here, and animals, too—maimed dogs snarling and cowering as in a classic vision of hell. And it was hot: dark grimy air that was hard to breathe and freighted with the stinks of sweat; it was so thick it muted the light. It tasted of stale fire and ashes. The mob did not disperse; it was too angry to go home, too insulted by defeat to ignore its hurt. It was loud, and it moved as if thwarted and pushed; it danced madly in what seemed a deep hole.

Alfredo knew a short cut to the road. He led the way through the parking lot and a ravaged grove of trees behind some huts. I saw people lying on the ground, but whether they were wounded or sleeping or dead I could not tell.

I asked him about the mob.

"What did I tell you?" he said. "You are sorry you came, right?"

"No," I said, and I meant it. Now I was satisfied. Travel is pointless without certain risks. I had spent the whole evening scrutinizing what I saw, trying to memorize details, and I knew I would never go to another soccer game in Latin America.

Questions on Meaning

1　Why does Alfredo park his car at a friend's house that is a half mile from the stadium? Why does Theroux feel that this house was "worth some study"?

2　Who are the "touts"? Why does Theroux consider dealing with them? Why does Alfredo choose not to deal with them? In what other ways does Theroux contrast himself to Alfredo?

3　In what ways are the 45,000 people at the game "a model of Salvadorean society"? How many different classes are there? How different are these classes from one another? In what ways are they similar?

4　In paragraph 2 Theroux says, "The muscular ritual of sport was always a clear demonstration of the wilder impulses in national character." What does he mean? What does the soccer game demonstrate about the national character of El Salvador?

5　The author concludes that "travel is pointless without certain risks," but that he "would never go to another soccer game in Latin America." How can you explain the apparent contradiction in his final comments?

Questions on Method

1　Why does Theroux describe in such detail the mobs entering and leaving the stadium? How do his descriptions support his thesis? How do they add suspense to the narrative movement?

2　Theroux uses an extended simile to describe the scene outside the stadium after the game. What does he accomplish by comparing the stadium slopes to one of "those lurid murals of hell you see in Latin American churches?"

3　After narrating in some detail the losses of the first two balls, the author summarizes three more losses in one line: "In all, five balls were lost this way" (36). Why does he change the speed of the action?

4　How important are the dialogues Theroux has with Alfredo? What do they contribute to the narrative movement? What do they reveal about the characters of the two speakers and their countries?

5　In what ways is the image of the dust that hangs over the mobs symbolic?

Vocabulary and Diction

1　Define the following words and phrases used by Theroux: partisan (2), pantomime (2), porkpie hat (8), depending (12), sepia print (15), conga line (25), queue (25), salver (26), tureen (26), jinking (28), header (38), lurid (39), lewdly (39), swigging (39), freighted (39), muted (39).

2   Theroux uses many active verbs such as "swarmed" (15), "crushing" (15), and "thumping" (15) to convey the often frightening movement of the crowd. What other active verbs does he use in this essay?

Writing Topics

1   Using action verbs and dialogue, write about a sports event you witnessed. Expand and contract the action in such a way as to capture the highlights while keeping the less significant aspects of the activity in the background through summary.

2   Narrate an event in such a way that the personalities of the participants are revealed. Use dialogue, active verbs, description of appearance, and dramatization of key actions in conveying the characters' personalities.

3   Write a narrative essay about what it would be like for someone to visit your home town or city for the first time. What experiences might the visitor have? What people might he or she meet? How would these experiences and people make the visitor feel about a place where you feel at home?

4   Write a narration in which the story unfolds mainly through the conversation of two or more characters.

JONATHAN RABAN (1942–   ) is an English writer who is
primarily interested in the social life of large cities, particularly
London, where he has lived since 1965. His writings include
several television plays, as well as many critical essays published
in *New Statesman, London Magazine*, and *Sunday Times*. The
selection "*Qat* Chewing," taken from *Arabia: A Journey through
the Labyrinth* (1979), recounts an incident that introduces us to
aspects of a culture very different from our own.

Qat Chewing

Jonathan Raban

Ali's house was in the center of a warren of junk, sleeping dogs and 1
crumbling mud bungalows. Everything had gone to the color of pie-
crust in the sun: burnt dogs, burnt clay, the burnt-out chassis of
wrecked cars from which every last nut and bolt had been assiduously
beachcombed. Hamud, worried for his springs, inched the car down
a street of boulders and potholes. A lame dog lurched ahead of us.
Too torpid to bother to stop and cock its leg, it leaked as it walked.
Its thin trickle of urine dried the instant that it hit the dust. Hamud
blew his horn at it, but the dog ignored him. It looked as if it didn't
greatly care whether it lived or died. I made some spinsterly English
noises about the miserable state of the animals in the city.

"The government likes to shoot dogs. That is good, I think: to 2
shoot dogs."

We took our bundle of *qat* and crossed the street to Ali's house. 3
A front door opened on a tiny courtyard where the family kept their

two goats and half dozen chickens. A farther door led to the room in which the men lived.

After the desolation of the street outside, the room seemed 4 palatial in its comforts. It was warm and rainbow colored. Squares of brightly patterned dress material had been tacked over the windows to filter the sunlight, which fell in splashes of lemon, red and purple on the carpets and cushions. A cluster of tall brass hookahs occupied the center of the room, and there were silver trays with thermos flasks of coffee and iced water, finger bowls, ears of sweet corn and packs of cigarettes. Beside everyone's cushion were a brass spittoon and a goblet of burning incense. The qat lay in a communal heap. We added our sprigs to this green bonfire, and I was formally introduced to the family.

The bearded grandfather made a little speech of welcome; broth- 5 ers and cousins bowed and shook hands. I was shown to my cushion, and the qat session began.

The solemnity of it, the colored light, the churchy gleam of 6 hammered brass and silver reminded me of a communion service. Hamud taught me how to nip off the topmost leaves from each stalk, chew them, then store them in the pouch of my cheek. Gradually one builds up a fibrous wad of crushed leaves from which one sucks the juice through one's teeth. Qat chewing parches one's throat; one needs drafts of coffee and water every few minutes, and I found that managing this acidic mouthful of dry hedge was difficult enough, without having to undertake the further rigors of making conversation.

Qat is the kind of drug which creeps slowly up on you from 7 behind. I had just decided that it was having no effect on me what-soever when I heard a shrill schoolgirl giggle and realized that I was the one who was giggling. There seemed, in fact, to be two of me. One fellow was crouched in a recess, soberly recording the details of the qat session for his notebook; the other was skittish and voluble. This second man was trying to make a joke in Arabic—an enterprise which struck the first man as so vain and foolhardy that he felt mortified at having to listen to the attempt. The second man's main trouble was that he found it impossible to remember words that he had spoken only a second or two before. He found himself in the middle of a sentence without having the least idea of how he had arrived there or in which direction he was supposed to be going. This did not seem to matter very much, since he appeared to be getting on extremely well with a cousin who was studying "the telegraph."

"You like the *qat?*" Hamud asked. 8

"It doesn't have any effect on me," I said, exchanging clothes 9 with the cousin. He put on my jacket, I put on his tunic. He gave me his belt and dagger. When I tried to fasten the belt around my waist, the two ends were six inches short of each other.

"I am too fat," I said. 10

"All Englishmen are fat," said the cousin, whose own waist 11 cannot have been more than eighteen inches in circumference. He unclipped a small holster from his belt and gave it to me; it contained a Czech automatic pistol with a full clip of slugs and the safety catch off.

"We could go and shoot some dogs," I said. The cousin laughed 12 and put the safety catch on before handing the pistol back to me.

"Let's go and shoot a dog." 13

"You see, you like the *qat*. This is the best *qat* in Yemen." 14

"There's a dog outside. We could shoot that." 15

"This is the first time you eat *qat?*" 16

"It doesn't do anything for me. Why don't we shoot some dogs?" 17

The other me skulked in a corner, watching these goings-on 18 with an expression of detached skepticism. He noted the new telephone standing in a whitewashed alcove. He observed that the cord of the instrument was tied up in a neat loop; it was connected to nothing. If you picked up the receiver, it would be like putting a shell to your ear: you might, with luck, be able to hear the sound of the sea. Some shaky black-and-white pictures were flickering on the portable TV, and a cousin was putting a tape of Arab music into a Hitachi radio-recorder.

I had emptied a whole thermosful of coffee. The grandfather 19 called to the women's quarters for more, and offered me a turn on the hookah. Sucking, chewing, giggling, idly watching the feet of the women passing behind the half-open door which led to their kitchen, I was reduced to a state of contented infantilism.

Another thermos of coffee was brought in by a tiny, scrawny 20 child of three or four. No woman would enter the male quarters when guests were being entertained there, and small children were necessary go-betweens. The little girl went to her grandfather to be cuddled. She had a skin disease of some kind on her face, and looked as if she were on the verge of malnutrition.

My more active self had forgotten his enthusiasm for shooting   21
dogs and was planning a European tour for the cousin. The cousin
had the chance of pursuing his study of the telegraph in Paris: nothing
was actually fixed; as yet he was only a candidate for a scholarship;
but on *qat* he was already there, and we were busy with sights and
itineraries. He was going to be away for three years, and we were
planning trips to London, Florence, Monte Carlo and the Scottish
Highlands. I felt someone jogging my elbow, and found it was myself
again; the skeptic in the corner had detected a flaw in the arrangements.

"What about your wife and your child? Will they go too?"   22
"No, they stay in Sana'a."   23
"But won't you miss them? Is it good to go away for so long   24
when you have a wife and a young child growing up?"
"My mother will look after my wife. She will be quite safe."   25
"But won't you miss her?"   26
"Why? I am only going away for three years." He shrugged. "It   27
is no time."
"When do you leave?"   28
He looked suddenly vague. He tore off another handful of leaves   29
from his branch of *qat* and sat chewing them for a few moments.
"Next month," he said. "Yes. I think I will go to Paris next month."
Ali said, "Perhaps I will go to Paris too. I would like to see the   30
Folies Bergère. In Paris there are many things to do in the nights."
"If you want a night out in Sana'a, what do you do?"   31
"Nothing. There is nothing to do. You cannot go out after ten   32
o'clock. That is the law. There is one cinema. The seats are cracked;
they show the same old film always. Two years ago, I go. Then one
month ago I go again. The people were the same people, they sit in
the same seats, the film is the same film. In Sana'a, they are narrow-
minded, you see. It is not like Paris."
As the afternoon drew on, the rhythm of the *qat* session changed.   33
The manic chatter petered out and everyone in the room became
reflective, slow and inward. The only sounds were the trickle of the
hookah and the footfalls of the women beyond the door. The inside
of my own head was busy with distracted thoughts; it felt like a nest
of cheeping baby birds, but I was in no mood for talking. Nor were
my neighbors. They stretched out vacantly on the cushions, the
pupils of their eyes as big as blackberries, the lumps of *qat* in their
cheeks pulling all the skin on their faces sideways.

The old man was turning the pages of the only book in the   34
room. He spent a long time on each picture, reading the details
carefully as he scanned the page. It wasn't until he shifted his position
that I saw what the book was: a tourist guide to Yemen. The pictures
he was studying so avidly had been printed by the cheapest kind of
color process, and it had given them the livid vigor of very old
Technicolor movies. They showed the streets of Sana'a and the close-
up faces of people who looked exactly like the old man himself.
Perhaps the book was there because it really did include his photo-
graph; or perhaps he liked it because the techniques of photography
had given his own life the interestingly alien glaze of something
fossilized and remote. I would have liked to ask him, but by this time
we were both sealed off from each other in bubbles of deep, drugged
privacy. I would never have found the words I wanted.

Ali said, "You want to go to sleep?" He pointed to a stack of   35
brightly colored mattresses at the far end of the room.

No, I said; I was fine.   36

"This is good *qat*. The best."   37

"Very good—I've enjoyed it very much. I would like to try it   38
again."

He switched up the sound on the television set. There were   39
some pictures of dignitaries accompanied by martial music.

"This is the news . . ."   40

I listened for a mention of *dabbabat* and roadblocks, but there   41
was only a list of tomorrow's official receptions. The minister of
something was going to fly to Riyadh to meet the Saudi minister of
something else. Then the martial music started up again over a jumpy
shot of a man with a bad case of facial warts.

The old man, absorbed in his book, didn't bother to glance up.   42
These announcements were not news—and if there was any news of
importance, it would not come from the television set but be picked
up in the crooked streets of the *souk*.

Hamud and I left. It was already dark, and I felt jittery and on   43
edge. *Qat* produces a hangover which makes one feel altogether too
alert for one's own good. Hamud's unusually careful driving struck me
as dangerously fast and wild. When we reached the Dar Al-Hamd
Palace, I got out my wallet to pay him.

"Please," Hamud said. "Yesterday, we were not friends. Today   44
you are my friend."

"Hamud, really, I would like to pay . . ."   45

"You are my friend now, yes?"   46

"Yes . . ."   47

"Because you are my friend, you give me fifty rials more than 48
what you say yesterday. I think that is right. For friendship."

I gave him the extra fifty thinking it sad that if Hamud had to 49
put a price on his own friendship, he should value it at just $14. Still,
the Yemenis have a reputation for frankness and realism: if they assess
the cost of friendship as half that of whisky, it's highly probable that
they have sound economic reasons for doing so.

Questions on Meaning

1 When does it become apparent that the *qat* is affecting Raban? Why does he at first maintain that it doesn't affect him? Why does a part of Raban continue to watch the *qat* session, as he says in paragraph 18, with "an expression of detached skepticism"? What is skepticism?

2 At the end of the essay Raban says that the Yemenis have a reputation for "frankness and realism." How well does the narrative illustrate whether this reputation is deserved?

3 Why does Raban exchange clothes with the cousin who is studying the telegraph? Does the *qat* have a similar effect on both the "realism" of the Yemenis and the "skepticism" of Raban?

4 How different are the Middle Eastern attitudes of the Yemenis from the Western attitudes of Raban? How different, for example, are their attitudes toward dogs and women?

5 In paragraph 33 Raban says that his head felt "like a nest of cheeping baby birds." What themes of the essay does this simile symbolize?

6 At the end of the essay, Hamud asks Raban for more money than Raban had said he would pay because they have become friends. How does this confusion of cause and effect illustrate the overall effect of the process of *qat* chewing that Raban describes?

Questions on Method

1 In paragraph 7 Raban says that he had trouble talking after chewing the *qat* because he "found it impossible to remember words that he had spoken only a second or two before." Why would Raban have difficulty writing a narration under the influence of *qat*? What other mental processes or patterns of organization does Raban rely on in order to write an effective narration?

2   Raban opens his essay by contrasting the "desolation" of the street outside the house to the "comforts" of the room in which the men lived. How does Raban's opening description prepare us to understand the main theme of the essay?

3   How important is action to Raban's narration? Notice his use of the verbs "inched," "lurched," and "leaked" in paragraph 1. How do these verbs contribute to the reader's appreciation of the action? Select other such active verbs in Raban's essay, and comment on their particular effectiveness.

4   Where in the essay does Raban speed up the action through summary rather than presenting it as it happened through dialogue and detailed description? Why does he accelerate the action at these points?

5   Compare Raban's use of first-person point of view with Theroux's. For what reason does one narrator play a more important role in his narrative than the other?

Vocabulary and Diction

1   In paragraph 19 Raban says that the *qat* had reduced him to "a state of contented infantilism." What does he mean by this phrase? Does the *qat* have a similar effect on the Yemenis? Compare, for example, Raban's interest in the telephone in paragraph 18 to the grandfather's interest in the tourist guide in paragraph 34.

2   What does the adjective "spinsterly," which Raban applies to himself in paragraph 1, indicate about his willingness to question his values? How does the phrase "a shrill schoolgirl giggle," which Raban applies to himself in paragraph 7, clarify the effect of the *qat* on his "spinsterly" attitudes?

3   In what way is the phrase "livid vigor" in paragraph 34 self-contradictory? Can something like the tint of a movie or a bruise on the skin be both livid and vigorous?

4   Define the following words and phrases used by Raban: warren (1), assiduously (1), torpid (1), hookahs (4), skittish and voluble (7), skulked (18).

Writing Topics

1   Narrate an experience you had in another culture or in a place that represented another culture (such as an ethnic neighborhood in an American city, an Indian reservation, or Pennsylvania Dutch country).

Through your use of details, convey how the atmosphere of the place affected your experience.

2   Narrate an experience you had that made you "see double" as the author did in "Qat Chewing"; in other words, report an experience you engaged in that was so strange to you that part of you stood apart and observed the other part of you engaged in the action. Use active verbs in recounting the incident.

Happiness Is a Domestic Bird

Nikos Kazantzakis

It was almost nightfall. The whole day: rain, torrents of rain. 1
Drenched to the bone. I arrived in a little Calabrian village. I had
to find a hearth where I could dry out, a corner where I could sleep.
The streets were deserted, the doors bolted. The dogs were the only
ones to scent the stranger's breath; they began to bark from within
the courtyards. The peasants in this region are wild and misanthropic,
suspicious of strangers. I hesitated at every door, extended my hand,
but did not dare to knock.

O for my late grandfather in Crete who took his lantern each 2
evening and made the rounds of the village to see if any stranger had
come. He would take him home, feed him, give him a bed for the
night, and then in the morning see him off with a cup of wine and
a slice of bread. Here in the Calabrian villages there were no such
grandfathers.

Suddenly I saw an open door at the edge of the village. Inclining 3
my head, I looked in: a murky corridor with a lighted fire at the far

end and an old lady bent over it. She seemed to be cooking. Not a sound, nothing but the burning wood. It was fragrant; it must have been pine. I crossed the threshold and entered, bumping against a long table which stood in the middle of the room. Finally I reached the fire and sat down on a stool which I found in front of the hearth. The old lady was squatting on another stool, stirring the meal with a wooden spoon. I felt that she eyed me rapidly, without turning. But she said nothing. Taking off my jacket, I began to dry it. I sensed happiness rising in me like warmth, from my feet to my shins, my thighs, my breast. Hungrily, avidly, I inhaled the fragrance of the steam rising from the pot. The meal must have been baked beans; the aroma was overwhelming. Once more I realized to what an extent earthly happiness is made to the measure of man. It is not a rare bird which we must pursue at one moment in heaven, at the next in our minds. Happiness is a domestic bird found in our own courtyards.

Rising, the old lady took down two soup plates from a shelf next to her. She filled them, and the whole world smelled of beans. Lighting a lamp, she placed it on the long table. Next she brought two wooden spoons and a loaf of black bread. We sat down opposite each other. She made the sign of the cross, then glanced rapidly at me. I understood. I crossed myself and we began to eat. We were both hungry; we did not breathe a word. I had decided not to speak in order to see what would happen. Could she be a mute, I asked myself—or perhaps she's gone mad, one of those peaceful, kindly lunatics so much like saints.

As soon as we finished, she prepared a bed for me on a bench to the right of the table. I lay down, and she lay down on the other bench opposite me. Outside the rain was falling by the bucketful. For a considerable time I heard the water cackle on the roof, mixed with the old lady's calm, quiet breathing. She must have been tired, for she fell asleep the moment she inclined her head. Little by little, with the rain and the old lady's rhythmical respiration, I too slipped into sleep. When I awoke, I saw daylight peering through the cracks in the door.

The old lady had already risen and placed a saucepan on the fire to prepare the morning milk. I looked at her now in the sparse daylight. Shriveled and humped, she could fit into the palm of your hand. Her legs were so swollen that she had to stop at every step and catch her breath. But her eyes, only her large, pitch-black eyes, gleamed with youthful, unaging brilliance. How beautiful she must have been in her youth, I thought to myself, cursing man's fate, his inevitable deterioration. Sitting down opposite each other again, we drank the milk. Then I rose and slung my carpetbag over my shoulder. I took out my wallet, but the old lady colored deeply.

"No, no," she murmured, extending her hand. 7

As I looked at her in astonishment, the whole of her bewrinkled 8
face suddenly gleamed.

"Goodbye, and God bless you," she said. "May the Lord repay 9
you for the good you've done me. Since my husband died I've never
slept so well."

Questions on Meaning

1 Why does Kazantzakis feel out of place in the Calabrian village? How
   much of his alienation is the effect of his physical discomfort? How much
   is the effect of the "wild and misanthropic" character of the Calabrian
   peasants?

2 What does the title of the essay mean? Why does the narrator contrast
   the happiness people pursue in heaven or in their own minds to what he
   calls in paragraph 3 "earthly happiness"? How would you classify the
   happiness that the old woman feels at the end?

3 Why does the narrator think that the old woman falls asleep so quickly?
   Why are her words in the last paragraph a surprising revelation to him?
   What do you think she meant?

Questions on Method

1 What details most effectively convey to you what Calabria and Calabri-
   ans are like?

2 A narrator must introduce some elements of suspense to keep us interested. In what ways does Kazantzakis create suspense in his essay? How
   do his descriptions of the place function in building suspense? How do
   the actions he narrates help create the tension?

3 In paragraph 4 Kazantzakis says that when the old woman filled the soup
   plates, "the whole world smelled of beans." Is he exaggerating? If so,
   why? How does exaggeration work effectively in the description of the
   old woman in paragraph 6? In what ways can exaggeration be an effective
   device for keeping the reader interested in a narration?

4 What transitional words and phrases does the author use to indicate the
   passage of time? In what part of the sentence do his transitions usually

occur? Which transitions indicate that the narrative is being speeded up? up?

5   Compare Kazantzakis's use of first-person point of view with that of Theroux and Raban. How different is the function of the narrator in each essay?

Vocabulary and Diction

1   In paragraph 4 Kazantzakis compares "peaceful, kindly lunatics" to "saints." Look up the words "lunatic" and "saint." Explain why the comparison is an effective one, given the definitions of these two words.

2   In paragraph 6 Kazantzakis says that man's "fate" is to suffer "inevitable deterioration." According to the author, in what sense is man's deterioration inevitable or fated?

Writing Topics

1   Narrate an experience you had with strangers that either confirmed or upset your expectations about how they would treat you. Use transitional words and phrases to convey the passage of time.

2   How important is physical happiness as compared to mental or spiritual happiness? Narrate an experience that illustrates your opinion.

3   Write a narration in which you exaggerate certain details to hold the reader's interest. You might magnify, as Kazantzakis does, the character or appearance of one of the persons involved in the action, or you might heighten the outcome of the narrative by creating suspense, again as Kazantzakis does, through your description of setting and character.

HANNAH ARENDT (1906–79) fled from Germany to Paris in
1933 and then came to America where she taught at the
University of Chicago, Columbia University, and the
University of California at Berkeley. Her many publications
include *The Origins of Totalitarianism* (1951), *The Life of a
Jewess* (1958), and *Eichmann in Jerusalem* (1963), of which the
following essay is a part. This book caused much controversy,
and perhaps philosopher William Barrett best explains why
when he writes, "Dr. Arendt's mind has always seemed to me
something of an eighth wonder; an erudite and disciplined
thinker, she still retains the ebullient intuition of a woman able
always to come at things from a fresh and unusual angle."

Denmark and the "Final Solution"

Hannah Arendt

The story of the Danish Jews is *sui generis*,[1] and the behavior of the 1
Danish people and their government was unique among all the countries of Europe—whether occupied, or a partner of the Axis,[2] or
neutral and truly independent. One is tempted to recommend the
story as required reading in political science for all students who wish
to learn something about the enormous power potential inherent in
non-violent action and in resistance to an opponent possessing vastly
superior means of violence. To be sure, a few other countries in
Europe lacked proper "understanding of the Jewish question,"[3] and

From *Eichmann in Jerusalem* by Hannah Arendt. Copyright © 1963, 1964 by Hannah
Arendt. Reprinted by permission of Viking Penguin Inc.
    1. Unduplicated, unique. (Editors' note)
    2. Countries aligned with Germany during World War II; Axis originally applied to
Nazi Germany and Fascist Italy, but later extended to include Japan. (Editors' note)
    3. Before the Hitler era the Jews lived mostly peacefully next to their neighbors in their
respective countries; therefore, not many countries could comprehend the fundamental character and meaning of the phrase "Jewish question" in its new application, used by the Germans
for the destruction of European Jewry. (Editors' note)

actually a majority of them were opposed to "radical" and "final" solutions.[4] Like Denmark, Sweden, Italy, and Bulgaria proved to be nearly immune to anti-Semitism, but of the three that were in the German sphere of influence, only the Danes dared speak out on the subject to their German masters. Italy and Bulgaria sabotaged German orders and indulged in a complicated game of double-dealing and double-crossing, saving their Jews by a tour de force of sheer ingenuity, but they never contested the policy as such. That was totally different from what the Danes did. When the Germans approached them rather cautiously about introducing the yellow badge,[5] they were simply told that the King would be the first to wear it, and the Danish government officials were careful to point out that anti-Jewish measures of any sort would cause their own immediate resignation. It was decisive in this whole matter that the Germans did not even succeed in introducing the vitally important distinction between native Danes of Jewish origin, of whom there were about sixty-four hundred, and the fourteen hundred German Jewish refugees who had found asylum in the country prior to the war and who now had been declared stateless by the German government. This refusal must have surprised the Germans no end, since it appeared so "illogical" for a government to protect people to whom it had categorically denied naturalization and even permission to work. (Legally, the prewar situation of refugees in Denmark was not unlike that in France, except that the general corruption in the Third Republic's civil services enabled a few of them to obtain naturalization papers, through bribes or "connections," and most refugees in France could work illegally, without a permit. But Denmark, like Switzerland, was no country *pour se débrouiller.*) The Danes, however, explained to the German officials that because the stateless refugees were no longer German citizens, the Nazis could not claim them without Danish assent. This was one of the few cases in which statelessness turned out to be an asset, although it was of course not statelessness per se that saved the Jews but, on the contrary, the fact that the Danish government had decided to protect them. Thus, none of the prepa-

---

4. "Final solution" was a code name for the liquidation of the Jews in Europe; the German state systematically planned and organized the slaughter of 6 million men, women, and children. (Editors' note)

5. A decree was issued by the German state whereby a yellow Star of David with the inscription *Jude* (Jew) had to be worn by every Jew in European countries in order to differentiate them from the rest of the population. (Editors' note)

ratory moves, so important for the bureaucracy of murder,[6] could be carried out, and operations were postponed until the fall of 1943.

What happened then was truly amazing; compared with what took place in other European countries, everything went topsy-turvy. In August, 1943—after the German offensive in Russia had failed, the Afrika Korps had surrendered in Tunisia, and the Allies had invaded Italy—the Swedish government canceled its 1940 agreement with Germany which had permitted German troops the right to pass through the country. Thereupon, the Danish workers decided that they could help a bit in hurrying things up; riots broke out in Danish shipyards, where the dock workers refused to repair German ships and then went on strike. The German military commander proclaimed a state of emergency and imposed martial law, and Himmler thought this was the right moment to tackle the Jewish question, whose "solution" was long overdue. What he did not reckon with was that— quite apart from Danish resistance—the German officials who had been living in the country for years were no longer the same. Not only did General von Hannecken, the military commander, refuse to put troops at the disposal of the Reich plenipotentiary, Dr. Werner Best; the special S.S. units (*Einsatzkommandos*) employed in Denmark very frequently objected to "the measures they were ordered to carry out by the central agencies"—according to Best's testimony at Nuremberg.[7] And Best himself, an old Gestapo man and former legal adviser to Heydrich,[8] author of a then famous book on the police, who had worked for the military government in Paris to the entire satisfaction of his superiors, could no longer be trusted, although it is doubtful that Berlin ever learned the extent of his unreliability. Still, it was clear from the beginning that things were not going well, and Eichmann's office sent one of its best men to Denmark—Rolf Günther, whom no one had ever accused of not possessing the required "ruthless toughness." Günther made no impression on his

6. To succeed in annihilating the European Jews, the German dictatorship created an entire bureaucratic apparatus, involving the German state and Nazi movement. A special SS unit was selected to serve as an instrument for the actual extermination. (Editors' note)

7. Nuremberg was the city in Germany where the Nazi criminals were brought and tried for war crimes after World War II. (Editors' note)

8. After Nazi succession to power in 1933, Reinhard Heydrich was put in charge of political security, and a year later he was appointed chief of the Gestapo; in 1939 he was chief of the Reich Security Main Office. In 1941 he was appointed by Hitler to deputy protector of Bohemia and Moravia, which were declared a protectorate (an autonomous part of the Reich). In 1942 Heydrich was shot and killed by members of the Czech resistance. (Editors' note)

colleagues in Copenhagen, and now von Hannecken refused even to issue a decree requiring all Jews to report for work.

Best went to Berlin and obtained a promise that all Jews from 3 Denmark would be sent to Theresienstadt[9] regardless of their category—a very important concession, from the Nazis' point of view. The night of October 1 was set for their seizure and immediate departure—ships were ready in the harbor—and since neither the Danes nor the Jews nor the German troops stationed in Denmark could be relied on to help, police units arrived from Germany for a door-to-door search. At the last moment, Best told them that they were not permitted to break into apartments, because the Danish police might then interfere, and they were not supposed to fight it out with the Danes. Hence they could seize only those Jews who voluntarily opened their doors. They found exactly 477 people, out of a total of more than 7,800, at home and willing to let them in. A few days before the date of doom, a German shipping agent, Georg F. Duckwitz, having probably been tipped off by Best himself, had revealed the whole plan to Danish government officials, who, in turn, had hurriedly informed the heads of the Jewish community. They, in marked contrast to Jewish leaders in other countries, had then communicated the news openly in the synagogues on the occasion of the New Year services. The Jews had just time enough to leave their apartments and go into hiding, which was very easy in Denmark, because, in the words of the judgment, "all sections of the Danish people, from the King down to simple citizens," stood ready to receive them.

They might have remained in hiding until the end of the war if 4 the Danes had not been blessed with Sweden as a neighbor. It seemed reasonable to ship the Jews to Sweden, and this was done with the help of the Danish fishing fleet. The cost of transportation for people without means—about a hundred dollars per person—was paid largely by wealthy Danish citizens, and that was perhaps the most astounding feat of all, since this was a time when Jews were paying for their own deportation, when the rich among them were paying fortunes for exit permits (in Holland, Slovakia, and, later, in Hungary) either by bribing the local authorities or by negotiating "legally" with the S.S.,

---

9. Theresienstadt was a Jewish ghetto created in Czechoslovakia, whence the Jews were deported to various death camps in Poland. The Danish Jews were protected by this "important concession" and were not deported for extermination. (Editors' note)

who accepted only hard currency and sold exit permits, in Holland, to the tune of five or ten thousand dollars per person. Even in places where Jews met with genuine sympathy and a sincere willingness to help, they had to pay for it, and the chances poor people had of escaping were nil.

It took the better part of October to ferry all the Jews across the 5 five to fifteen miles of water that separates Denmark from Sweden. The Swedes received 5,919 refugees, of whom at least 1,000 were of German origin, 1,310 were half-Jews, and 686 were non-Jews married to Jews. (Almost half the Danish Jews seem to have remained in the country and survived the war in hiding.) The non-Danish Jews were better off than ever before, they all received permission to work. The few hundred Jews whom the German police had been able to arrest were shipped to Theresienstadt. They were old or poor people, who either had not received the news in time or had not been able to comprehend its meaning. In the ghetto, they enjoyed greater privileges than any other group because of the never-ending "fuss" made about them by Danish institutions and private persons. Forty-eight persons died, a figure that was not particularly high, in view of the average age of the group. When everything was over, it was the considered opinion of Eichmann that "for various reasons the action against the Jews in Denmark has been a failure," whereas the curious Dr. Best declared that "the objective of the operation was not to seize a great number of Jews but to clean Denmark of Jews, and this objective has now been achieved."

Politically and psychologically, the most interesting aspect of 6 this incident is perhaps the role played by the German authorities in Denmark, their obvious sabotage of orders from Berlin. It is the only case we know of in which the Nazis met with *open* native resistance, and the result seems to have been that those exposed to it changed their minds. They themselves apparently no longer looked upon the extermination of a whole people as a matter of course. They had met resistance based on principle, and their "toughness" had melted like butter in the sun, they had even been able to show a few timid beginnings of genuine courage. That the ideal of "toughness," except, perhaps, for a few half-demented brutes, was nothing but a myth of self-deception, concealing a ruthless desire for conformity at any price, was clearly revealed at the Nuremberg Trials, where the defendants accused and betrayed each other and assured the world that they "had always been against it" or claimed, as Eichmann was to do, that their best qualities had been "abused" by their superiors. (In Jerusalem,[10] he accused "those in power" of having abused his "obedience." "The subject of a good government is lucky, the subject of a bad government is unlucky. I had no luck.") The atmosphere had changed, and although most of them must have known that they were doomed, not a single one of them had the guts to defend the Nazi ideology. Werner Best claimed at Nuremberg that he had played a complicated double role and that it was thanks to him that the Danish officials had been warned of the impending catastrophe; documentary evidence showed, on the contrary, that he himself had proposed the Danish operation in Berlin, but he explained that this was all part of the game. He was extradited to Denmark and there condemned to death, but he appealed the sentence, with surprising results; because of "new evidence," his sentence was commuted to five years in prison, from which he was released soon afterward. He must have been able to prove to the satisfaction of the Danish court that he really had done his best.

Questions on Meaning

1   In paragraph 1 Arendt says that the story of the Danish people holds a lesson about "the enormous power potential inherent in non-violent action and in resistance to an opponent possessing vastly superior means of violence." Explain what this lesson means. What parts of the selection best illustrate it?

2   What does Arendt mean when she says that many of the Jews in Denmark were "stateless" refugees? Why was the statelessness of the Jews an asset? What was the "final solution" from which their statelessness, in part, saved the Jews in Denmark? What does Arendt's story stress as being more decisive in saving them?

3   What effect did living in Denmark have on such German officials as General von Hannecken and Dr. Werner Best? Might you classify not only the Jews living in Denmark but also the German officials living there as alienated outsiders? Explain.

4   What is the difference between what Arendt in paragraph 2 calls the "ruthless toughness" of the Germans and what she in paragraph 6 calls the "resistance based on principle" of the Danes? Why does she argue that the toughness of the Germans was "nothing but a myth of self-

10. Eichmann was put on trial in Jerusalem for his Nazi war crimes. (Editors' note)

deception," whereas the resistance of the Danes was open and coura-geous? How do her examples of the defendants' behavior at the Nurem-berg trials and Eichmann's behavior in Jerusalem illustrate her contention about the toughness of the Germans? What examples does she give to support her argument about the courage of the Danes?

Questions on Method

1 Although Arendt tells a story, a narration, she suggests that her purpose is to teach a lesson in political science. How does this purpose affect her tone of voice? How does such a phrase as that beginning paragraph 2, "What happened then was truly amazing," both keep up our interest in the story and sway us toward accepting Arendt's argument? In what way is argumentation an effective technique in both teaching and storytell-ing?

2 Arendt's method of narration is different from Theroux's, Raban's, and Kazantzakis's in both the point of view and the speed with which the event is narrated. What differences can you discern, and why does she use her method?

3 How important is characterization to an effective narration? How big a part does getting us interested in such a character as Dr. Werner Best play both in keeping us interested in the story and in helping us under-stand its main theme? Compare Arendt's characterizations to those of Theroux and Raban.

4 How does Arendt's technique of comparing different forms of behavior increase our understanding of her theme? Focus, for example, on the way she contrasts Danish resistance to the Nazis with Swedish, Italian, and Bulgarian resistance.

5 Discuss Arendt's use of the simile in paragraph 6 that compares the "toughness" of the Nazis to "butter in the sun." Why is this an effective comparison?

Vocabulary and Diction

1 Why does Arendt in paragraph 4 place the word "legally" in quotation marks? Is there a paradox, an absurd contradiction, in applying this word to the Nazi practice of selling exit permits to the Jews in Holland? What other examples of paradox can you point out?

2 Define the following words and phrases used by Arendt: *sui generis* (1),

the Jewish question (1), tour de force (1), yellow badge (1), per se (1), bureaucracy of murder (1), plenipotentiary (2), S.S. (2), gestapo (2).

Writing Topics

1   Have you ever witnessed anti-Semitism or prejudice against some other racial or ethnic group? Narrate an incident that taught you something about prejudice. Write in the third person, as a witness, not as a participant.

2   Is the most courageous response to the violence of others a nonviolent one? Narrate an incident that illustrates either when this holds true or when it can be false. Use the first or third person for your narration.

3   Arendt narrates the story of the Danes in World War II to prove the value of nonviolence. Narrate a historical event, familiar to you, that also demonstrates that nonviolent methods can accomplish a goal effectively. Use the third-person narrative point of view.

DEE BROWN (1908–   ) is an American journalist and novelist whose works reflect his interest in the American frontier. This enthusiasm was fostered by his grandmother, who told him tales of the California Gold Rush and the Civil War. His works include *The Settler's West* (1955), *The Galvanized Yankees* (1963), and *Bury My Heart at Wounded Knee* (1971), from which the selection in this anthology is taken.

The Flight of the Nez Percés

Dee Brown

The whites told only one side. Told it to please themselves. Told much that is not true. Only his own best deeds, only the worst deeds of the Indians, has the white man told.

—YELLOW WOLF OF THE NEZ PERCÉS

The earth was created by the assistance of the sun, and it should be left as it was. . . . The country was made without lines of demarcation, and it is no man's business to divide it. . . . I see the whites all over the country gaining wealth, and see their desire to give us lands which are worthless. . . . The earth and myself are of one mind. The measure of the land and the measure of our bodies are the same. Say to us if you can say it, that you were sent by the Creative Power to talk to us. Perhaps you think the Creator sent you here to dispose of us as you see fit. If I thought you were sent by the Creator I might be induced to think you had a right to dispose of me. Do not misunderstand me, but understand me fully with reference to my affection for the land. I never said the land was mine to do with it as I chose. The one

*who has the right to dispose of it is the one who has created it. I claim a right
to live on my land, and accord you the privilege to live on yours.*
　　　　　—HEINMOT TOOYALAKET (CHIEF JOSEPH) OF THE NEZ PERCÉS

In September, 1805, when Lewis and Clark came down off the 1
Rockies on their westward journey, the entire exploring party was
half-famished and ill with dysentery—too weak to defend themselves.
They were in the country of the Nez Percés, so named by French
trappers, who observed some of these Indians wearing dentalium shells
in their noses. Had the Nez Percés chosen to do so, they could have
put an end to the Lewis and Clark expedition there on the banks of
Clearwater River, and seized their wealth of horses. Instead the Nez
Percés welcomed the white Americans, supplied them with food, and
looked after the explorers' horses for several months while they continued by canoe to the Pacific shore.

Thus began a long friendship between the Nez Percés and white 2
Americans. For seventy years the tribe boasted that no Nez Percé
had ever killed a white man. But white men's greed for land and gold
finally broke the friendship.

In 1855 Governor Isaac Stevens of Washington Territory invited 3
the Nez Percés to a peace council. "He said there were a great many
white people in the country, and many more would come; that he
wanted the land marked out so that the Indians and white men could
be separated. If they were to live in peace it was necessary, he said,
that the Indians should have a country set apart for them, and in
that country they must stay."

Tuekakas, a chief known as Old Joseph by the white men, told 4
Governor Stevens that no man owned any part of the earth, and a
man could not sell what he did not own.

The governor could not comprehend such an attitude. He urged 5
Old Joseph to sign the treaty and receive presents of blankets. "Take
away your paper," the chief replied. "I will not touch it with my
hand."

Aleiya, who was called Lawyer by the white men, signed the 6
treaty, and so did several other Nez Percés, but Old Joseph took his
people back to their home in Wallowa Valley, a green country of
winding waters, wide meadows, mountain forests, and a clear
blue lake. Old Joseph's band of Nez Percés raised fine horses and
cattle, lived in fine lodges, and when they needed anything from the
white men they traded their livestock.

Only a few years after the first treaty signing, government men   7
were swarming around the Nez Percés again, wanting more land. Old
Joseph warned his people to take no presents from them, not even
one blanket. "After a while," he said, "they will claim that you have
accepted pay for your country."[1]

In 1863 a new treaty was presented to the Nez Percés. It took   8
away the Wallowa Valley and three-fourths of the remainder of their
land, leaving them only a small reservation in what is now Idaho.
Old Joseph refused to attend the treaty signing, but Lawyer and
several other chiefs—none of whom had ever lived in the Valley of
Winding Waters—signed away their people's lands. The "thief
treaty," Old Joseph called it, and he was so offended that he tore up
the Bible a white missionary had given him to convert him to Christianity. To let the white men know he still claimed the Wallowa
Valley, he planted poles all around the boundaries of the land where
his people lived.

Not long after that, Old Joseph died (1871), and the chieftain-   9
ship of the band passed to his son, Heinmot Tooyalaket (Young
Joseph), who was then about thirty years old. When government
officials came to order the Nez Percés to leave the Wallowa Valley
and go to Lapwai reservation, Young Joseph refused to listen. "Neither
Lawyer nor any other chief had authority to sell this land," he said.
"It has always belonged to my people. It came unclouded to them
from our fathers, and we will defend this land as long as a drop of
Indian blood warms the hearts of our men."[2] He petitioned the Great
Father, Ulysses Grant, to let his people stay where they had always
lived, and on June 16, 1873, the President issued an executive order
withdrawing Wallowa Valley from settlement by white men.

In a short time a group of commissioners arrived to begin orga-   10
nization of a new Indian agency in the valley. One of them mentioned
the advantages of schools for Joseph's people. Joseph replied that the
Nez Percés did not want the white man's schools.

"Why do you not want schools?" the commissioner asked.   11

"They will teach us to have churches," Joseph answered.   12

"Do you not want churches?"   13

"No, we do not want churches."   14

---

1. Chief Joseph. "An Indian's Views of Indian Affairs." *North American Review*, Vol.
128, 1879, p. 417.
    2. *Ibid.*, p. 418.

"Why do you not want churches?" 15

"They will teach us to quarrel about God," Joseph said. "We do 16
not want to learn that. We may quarrel with men sometimes about
things on this earth, but we never quarrel about God. We do not
want to learn that."[3]

Meanwhile, white settlers were encroaching upon the valley, 17
with their eyes on the Nez Percés land. Gold was found in nearby
mountains. The goldseekers stole the Indians' horses, and stockmen
stole their cattle, branding them so the Indians could not claim them
back. White politicians journeyed to Washington, telling lies about
the Nez Percés. They charged the Indians with being a threat to the
peace and with stealing the settlers' livestock. This was the reverse
of the truth, but as Joseph said, "We had no friend who would plead
our cause before the law council."[4]

Two years after the Great Father promised Wallowa Valley to 18
Joseph's people forever, he issued a new proclamation, reopening the
valley to white settlement. The Nez Percés were given "a reasonable
time" to move to the Lapwai reservation. Joseph had no intention of
giving up the valley of his fathers, but in 1877 the government sent
the One-Armed-Soldier-Chief, General Howard, to clear all Nez
Percés out of the Wallowa area.

In the four years that had passed since Oliver Otis Howard 19
treated Cochise and the Apaches with justice, he had learned that
the Army was not tolerant of "Indian lovers." He came now to the
Northwest country, determined to restore his standing with the military by carrying out his orders swiftly and to the letter. Privately he
told trusted friends that "it is a great mistake to take from Joseph and
his band of Nez Percé Indians that valley." But in May, 1877, he
summoned Joseph to Lapwai for a council which was to set the date
they must surrender their land.

To accompany him to Lapwai, Joseph chose White Bird, Looking 20
Glass, his brother Ollokot, and the Wallowa prophet Toohoolhoolzote. The prophet was a tall, thick-necked, very ugly Indian with a
gift for eloquent rebuttal. "A fugitive from hell," was the way one
white man described him. At the opening of the council, which was
held in a building across from the Fort Lapwai guardhouse, Joseph
presented Toohoolhoolzote as spokesman for the Wallowa Nez Percés.

---

3. U.S. Commissioner of Indian Affairs. Annual Report, 1873, p. 527.
4. Chief Joseph, p. 419.

"Part of the Nez Percés gave up their land," the prophet said. 21
"We never did. The earth is part of our body, and we never gave up
the earth."

"You know very well that the government has set apart a reser- 22
vation, and that the Indians must go on it," Howard declared.

"What person pretended to divide the land and put us on it?" 23
Toohoolhoolzote demanded.

"I am the man. I stand here for the President." Howard was 24
beginning to lose his temper. "My orders are plain and will be executed."

The prophet continued prodding the One-Armed-Soldier-Chief, 25
asking him how the land could belong to white men if it had come
down to the Nez Percés from their fathers. "We came from the earth,
and our bodies must go back to the earth, our mother," he said.

"I don't want to offend your religion," Howard replied testily, 26
"but you must talk about practicable things. Twenty times over I hear
that the earth is your mother and about chieftainship from the earth.
I want to hear it no more, but come to business at once."

"Who can tell me what I must do in my own country?" Too- 27
hoolhoolzote retorted.[5]

The argument continued until Howard felt he must demonstrate 28
his power. He ordered the prophet arrested and taken to the guardhouse, and then he bluntly informed Joseph that the Nez Percés had
thirty days in which to move from the Wallowa Valley to the Lapwai
reservation.

"My people have always been the friends of white men," Joseph 29
said. "Why are you in such a hurry? I cannot get ready to move in
thirty days. Our stock is scattered, and Snake River is very high. Let
us wait until fall, then the river will be low."

"If you let the time run over one day," Howard replied harshly, 30
"the soldiers will be there to drive you onto the reservation, and all
your cattle and horses outside of the reservation at that time will fall
into the hands of the white men."

Joseph knew now that he had no alternative. To defend the 31
valley with less than a hundred warriors was impossible. When he
and his subchiefs returned home they found soldiers already there.
They held a council and decided to gather their stock immediately

5. U.S. Secretary of War. Annual Report, 1877, p. 594. McWhorter, Lucullus V.
Yellow Wolf: His Own Story. Caldwell, Idaho, 1940, p. 39.

for the move to Lapwai. "The white men were many and we could not hold our own with them. We were like deer. They were like grizzly bears. We had a small country. Their country was large. We were contented to let things remain as the Great Spirit made them. They were not, and would change the rivers and mountains if they did not suit them."[6]

Even before they started the long march, some of the warriors [32] began talking of war rather than be driven like dogs from the land where they were born. Toohoolhoolzote, released from prison, declared that blood alone would wash out the disgrace the One-Armed-Soldier-Chief had put upon him. Joseph, however, continued to counsel peace.

To meet General Howard's deadline, they had to leave much of [33] their livestock in the valley, and when they came to Snake River the stream was swirling with melted snow from the mountains. Miraculously they got their women and children across on buffalo-hide rafts without serious accident, but while they were engaged in this task a party of white men came and stole some of their cattle from the waiting herd. Then, when they hurriedly tried to swim their livestock across the river, many animals were lost to the swift-flowing current.

More embittered than ever, the chiefs demanded that Joseph [34] halt the march in Rocky Canyon and hold a council. Toohoolhoolzote, White Bird, and Ollokot spoke for war. Joseph told them it was "better to live at peace than to begin a war and lie dead." The others called him a coward, but he refused to back down.

While they were camped in the canyon, a small band of warriors [35] slipped away one night, and when they returned the Nez Percés could no longer claim that they had never killed a white man. The warriors had killed eleven, in revenge for the theft of their stock and for being driven from their valley.

Like many another peace-loving Indian chief, Joseph was now [36] trapped between the pressures of the white men and the fury of his desperate people. He chose to stay with his people. "I would have given my own life," he said, "if I could have undone the killing of white men by my people. I blame my young men and I blame the white men. . . . I would have taken my people to the buffalo country [Montana] without fighting, if possible. . . . We moved over to

6. Chief Joseph, pp. 420, 423.

White Bird Creek, sixteen miles away, and there encamped, intending to collect our stock before leaving; but the soldiers attacked us, and the first battle was fought." [7]

Although outnumbered two to one, the Nez Percés drew Howard's soldiers into a trap at White Bird Canyon on June 17, turning the attackers' flank, killing a third of them, and routing the remainder. Ten days later the One-Armed-Soldier-Chief brought up heavy reinforcements to do battle again, but the Nez Percés slipped away across the mountains. In a succession of shrewd military actions, Joseph outmaneuvered the pursuing soldiers, severely punished an advance detachment, and then raced to the Clearwater, where Chief Looking Glass was waiting with more warriors. 37

The combined force of Nez Percés now numbered 250 warriors, with 450 noncombatants, their baggage, and two thousand horses. At White Bird Canyon they had captured several rifles and a good supply of ammunition. 38

After withdrawing beyond the Clearwater (where their fathers had welcomed Lewis and Clark as the forerunners of white civilization), Joseph called a council of chiefs. They all knew they could never return to the Valley of Winding Waters or go without punishment to Lapwai. Only one course was left to them—flight to Canada. Sitting Bull of the Sioux had fled to the Grandmother's land, and the American soldiers dared not go there to kill him. If the Nez Percés could reach the Lolo Trail and cross the Bitterroot Mountains, they might be able to escape to Canada. 39

Because they were accustomed to crossing the Bitterroots to hunt in Montana, the Nez Percés quickly outdistanced Howard's baggage-laden army. On July 25 they were filing down the canyon near the mouth of Lolo Creek when their scouts sighted soldiers ahead. The Bluecoats were constructing a log barricade at a narrow place in the pass. 40

Under a white flag, Joseph, Looking Glass, and White Bird rode down to the barricade, dismounted calmly, and shook hands with the commanding officer, Captain Charles Rawn. The chiefs noted that there were about two hundred soldiers in the camp. 41

"We are going by you without fighting, if you will let us," Joseph said to the captain, "but we are going by you anyhow." [8] 42

7. *Ibid.*, p. 425.
8. *Ibid.*, p. 426.

Rawn told Joseph that they could pass only if they gave up their arms. White Bird replied that their warriors would never do that. 43

Knowing that General Howard was approaching from the west and that another large force under Colonel John Gibbon was marching from the east, Captain Rawn decided to stall for time. He suggested that they meet again the next day to discuss arrangements for passage. To this the chiefs agreed, but after two more days of fruitless parleying, the Nez Percé leaders decided they could wait no longer. 44

Early on the morning of July 28, Looking Glass moved the warriors into a screening line among the trees on the upper slope of the canyon. At the same time, Joseph led the noncombatants and livestock up a gulch, climbed to the top of a mountain, and was well around the canyon barricade before Captain Rawn discovered what the Nez Percés were doing. The captain went in pursuit of the Indians, but after a few skirmishes with Joseph's rearguard warriors he decided not to risk a real fight and returned to his now useless barricade. 45

Believing that they had escaped from Howard, and unaware of Gibbon's approaching army, the chiefs decided to move south to the familiar hunting country of the Big Hole. There they could rest their ponies and hunt wild game. If the white men would leave them alone, perhaps they would not have to go to the Grandmother's land and join Sitting Bull. 46

On the night of August 9, the One Who Limps (Colonel Gibbon) brought up a mixed column of local volunteers and mounted infantrymen and concealed them on a hillside overlooking the Nez Percé camp on Big Hole River. As dawn approached, the volunteers asked Gibbon if they should take prisoners during the attack. Gibbon replied that he wanted no Indian prisoners, male or female. The night air was cold, and the men warmed themselves by drinking whiskey. At first daylight several were drunk when Gibbon gave the command to attack. The infantry line began firing volleys, and then charged the Nez Percé tepees. 47

Fifteen-year-old Kowtoliks was asleep when he heard the rattle of rifle fire. "I jumped from my blankets and ran about thirty feet and threw myself on hands and knees, and kept going. An old woman, Patsikonmi, came from the teepee and did the same thing—bent down on knees and hands. She was to my left, and was shot in the breast. I heard the bullet strike. She said to me, 'You better not stay here. Be going, I'm shot.' Then she died. Of course I ran for my life 48 and hid in the bushes. The soldiers seemed shooting everywhere. Through tepees and wherever they saw Indians. I saw little children killed and men fall before bullets coming like rain."[9]

Another teen-age boy, Black Eagle, was awakened by bullets passing through his family tepee. In his fright he ran and jumped into the river, but the water was too cold. He came out and helped save the horses by driving them up a hill and out of sight of the soldiers. [49]

The Indians, meanwhile, had recovered from the shock of the surprise attack. While Joseph directed the rescue of the noncombatants, White Bird deployed the warriors for a counterattack. "Fight! Shoot them down!" he shouted. "We can shoot as well as any of these soldiers."[10] The marksmanship of the Nez Percés, in fact, was superior to that of Gibbon's men. "We now mixed those soldiers badly," Yellow Wolf said. "Scared, they ran back across the river. They acted as if drinking. We thought some got killed by being drunk." [50]

When the soldiers tried to set up a howitzer, the Nez Percés swarmed over the gun crew, seized the cannon, and wrecked it. A warrior fixed his rifle sights on Colonel Gibbon and made him the One Who Limps Twice. [51]

By this time Joseph had the camp in motion, and while a handful of warriors kept Gibbon's soldiers pinned down behind a makeshift barricade of logs and boulders, the Nez Percés resumed flight. They turned southward and away from Canada, because they believed it was the only way left to shake off their pursuers. The warriors had killed thirty soldiers and wounded at least forty. But in Gibbon's merciless dawn attack, eighty Nez Percés had died, more than two-thirds of them women and children, their bodies riddled with bullets, their heads smashed in by bootheels and gunstocks. "The air was heavy with sorrow," Yellow Wolf said. "Some soldiers acted with crazy minds."[11] [52]

The Nez Percé rear guard probably could have starved out Gibbon's barricaded soldiers and killed them all had not General Howard come to the rescue with a fresh force of cavalrymen. Withdrawing hurriedly, the warriors overtook Joseph to warn him that the One-Armed-Soldier-Chief was on their trail again. [53]

9. McWhorter, p. 144.
10. Shields, G. D. *Battle of the Big Hole.* Chicago, 1889, pp. 51–52.
11. McWhorter, pp. 120, 132.

"We retreated as rapidly as we could," Joseph said. "After six days General Howard came close to us, and we went out and attacked him, and captured nearly all his horses and mules."[12] Actually the captured livestock were mostly mules, but they were pack animals which had been carrying Howard's supplies and ammunition. Leaving the soldiers floundering in their rear, the Indians crossed Targhee Pass into Yellowstone Park on August 22.

Only five years earlier the Great Council in Washington had made the Yellowstone area into the country's first national park, and in that summer of 1877 the first adventuresome American tourists were admiring its natural wonders. Among them was none other than the Great Warrior Sherman, who had come out West on an inspection tour to find out how fewer than three hundred Nez Percé warriors, burdened with their women and children, could make fools out of the entire Army of the Northwest.

When Sherman learned that the fleeing Indians were crossing Yellowstone Park almost within view of his luxurious camp, he began issuing urgent orders to fort commanders in all directions to put a network of soldiers around these impudent warriors. Nearest at hand was the Seventh Cavalry, which had been brought back to strength during the year since Custer led it to disaster on the Little Bighorn. Eager to vindicate the regiment's honor by a victory over any Indians willing to fight, the Seventh moved southwestward toward the Yellowstone. During the first week in September Nez Percé scouts and Seventh Cavalry scouts sighted each other's columns almost daily. By clever maneuvering, the Indians shook loose from the Seventh after a skirmish at Canyon Creek, and headed north for Canada. They had no way of knowing, of course, that the Great Warrior Sherman had ordered Bear Coat Miles in a forced march from Fort Keogh, on a course that would cut across their path.

On September 23, after fighting rearguard actions almost daily, the Nez Percés forded the Missouri River at Cow Island Landing. During the next three days scouts reported no sign of soldiers anywhere. On the twenty-ninth, hunters located a small buffalo herd. As they were short of food and ammunition and their horses were badly worn from the fast pace, the chiefs decided to camp in the Bear Paw Mountains. Next day, after filling their empty stomachs on

54

55

56

57

12. Chief Joseph, p. 427.

buffalo meat, they would try to reach the Canadian border in one more long march.

"We knew General Howard was more than two suns back on   58
our trail," Yellow Wolf said. "It was nothing hard to keep ahead of
him." [13]

Next morning, however, two scouts came galloping from the   59
south, shouting, "Soldiers! Soldiers!" While the camp was preparing
to move out, another scout appeared on a distant bluff, waving a
blanket signal—*Enemies right on us! Soon the attack!*.

It was a cavalry charge ordered by Bear Coat Miles, whose Indian   60
scouts a few hours earlier had picked up the trail of the Nez Percés.
Riding with the charging cavalry were the thirty Sioux and Cheyenne
scouts who had been bought by the Bluecoats at Fort Robinson, the
young warriors who had turned their backs on their people by putting
on soldier uniforms—an action which had precipitated the assassi-
nation of Crazy Horse.

The thunder of six hundred galloping horses made the earth   61
tremble, but White Bird calmly posted his warriors in front of the
camp. As the first wave of pony soldiers swept down upon them, the
Nez Percé warriors opened with deadly accurate fire. In a matter of
seconds they killed twenty-four soldiers, wounded forty-two others,
and stopped the charge in a wild scramble of plunging horses and
unsaddled troopers.

"We fought at close range," Chief Joseph said, "not more than   62
twenty steps apart, and drove the soldiers back upon their main line,
leaving their dead in our hands. We secured their arms and ammunition. We lost, the first day and night, eighteen men and three
women." Among the dead were Joseph's brother Ollokot and the
tough old prophet Toohoolhoolzote.

When darkness fell the Nez Percés tried to slip away to the   63
north, but Bear Coat had put a cordon of soldiers completely around
their camp. The warriors spent the night digging entrenchments,
expecting another attack at daylight.

Instead of attacking, however, Bear Coat sent a messenger out   64
with a white flag. The messenger brought a demand for Joseph to
surrender and save the lives of his people. Joseph sent back a reply:
he would think about it and let General Miles know his decision

13. McWhorter, p. 204.

soon. Snow had begun to fall, and the warriors were hopeful that a blizzard might provide an escape screen to Canada.

Later in the day, some of Miles's Sioux scouts rode out under 65 another truce flag. Joseph walked across the battlefield to meet them. "They said they believed that General Miles was sincere and really wanted peace. I walked on to General Miles's tent."

For the next two days Joseph was a prisoner, held by Bear Coat 66 in violation of the flag of truce. During this time Miles brought up artillery and resumed the attack, but the Nez Percé warriors held their ground, and Joseph refused to surrender while he was a prisoner. On both days a bitter cold wind flung showers of snow over the battlefield.

On the third day, Joseph's warriors managed to get him free. 67 They captured one of Miles's officers and threatened to kill him unless the general released their chief. That same day, however, General Howard and his lumbering army arrived to reinforce Miles, and Joseph knew that his dwindling band of warriors was doomed. When Miles sent truce messengers to arrange a battlefield council, Joseph went to hear the general's surrender terms. They were simple and direct: "If you will come out and give up your arms," Miles said, "I will spare your lives and send you to your reservation." [14]

Returning to his besieged camp, Joseph called his chiefs together 68 for the last time. Looking Glass and White Bird wanted to fight on, to the death if necessary. They had struggled for thirteen hundred miles; they could not quit now. Joseph reluctantly agreed to postpone his decision. That afternoon in the final skirmish of the four-day siege, a sharpshooter's bullet struck Looking Glass in the left forehead and killed him instantly.

"On the fifth day," Joseph said, "I went to General Miles and 69 gave up my gun." He also made an eloquent surrender speech, which was recorded in the English translation by Lieutenant Charles Erskine Scott Wood,* and in time it became the most quoted of all American Indian speeches:

Tell General Howard I know his heart. What he told me before I have in my heart. I am tired of fighting. Our chiefs are killed. Looking Glass is dead. Toohoolhoolzote is dead. The old men are all dead. It is the

14. Chief Joseph, pp. 425, 428.
* Lieutenant Wood left the Army not long afterward to become a lawyer and an author of satirical poems and essays. His experiences with Chief Joseph and the Nez Percés influenced his later life; he became an ardent fighter for social justice and a defender of the dispossessed.

young men who say yes or no. He who led on the young men [Ollokot] is dead. It is cold and we have no blankets. The little children are freezing to death. My people, some of them, have run away to the hills, and have no blankets, no food; no one knows where they are— perhaps freezing to death. I want to have time to look for my children and see how many of them I can find. Maybe I shall find them among the dead. Hear me, my chiefs! I am tired; my heart is sick and sad. From where the sun now stands I will fight no more forever.[15]

After dark, while the surrender arrangements were under way, White Bird and a band of unyielding warriors crept through ravines in small groups and started running on foot for the Canadian border. On the second day they were across, and on the third day they saw mounted Indians in the distance. One of the approaching Indians made a sign: *What Indians are you?*   70

Nez Percé, they replied, and asked: *Who are you?*   71

Sioux, was the answer.   72

The next day Sitting Bull took the fugitive Nez Percés into his Canadian Village.[16]   73

For Chief Joseph and the others, however, there was to be no freedom. Instead of conducting them to Lapwai, as Bear Coat Miles had promised, the Army shipped them like cattle to Fort Leavenworth, Kansas. There, on a swampy bottomland, they were confined as prisoners of war. After almost a hundred died, they were transferred to a barren plain in the Indian Territory. As had happened to the Modocs, the Nez Percés sickened and died—of malaria and heartbreak.   74

Bureaucrats and Christian gentlemen visited them frequently, uttering words of sympathy and writing endless reports to various organizations. Joseph was allowed to visit Washington, where he met all the great chiefs of government. "They all say they are my friends," he said, "and that I shall have justice, but while their mouths all talk right I do not understand why nothing is done for my people. . . . General Miles promised that we might return to our own country. I believed General Miles, or *I never would have surrendered.*"   75

He then made an impassioned appeal for justice: "I have heard talk and talk, but nothing is done. Good words do not last long unless they amount to something. Words do not pay for my dead people.   76

15. U.S. Secretary of War. Report, 1877, p. 630.
16. Chief Joseph, p. 432.

They do not pay for my country, now overrun by white men. . . . Good words will not give my people good health and stop them from dying. Good words will not get my people a home where they can live in peace and take care of themselves. I am tired of talk that comes to nothing. It makes my heart sick when I remember all the good words and broken promises. . . . You might as well expect the rivers to run backwards as that any man who was born a free man should be contented when penned up and denied liberty to go where he pleases. . . . I have asked some of the great white chiefs where they get their authority to say to the Indian that he shall stay in one place, while he sees white men going where they please. They cannot tell me.

"Let me be a free man—free to travel, free to stop, free to work, 77 free to trade where I choose, free to choose my own teachers, free to follow the religion of my fathers, free to think and talk and act for myself—and I will obey every law, or submit to the penalty." [17]

But no one listened. They sent Joseph back to Indian Territory, 78 and there he remained until 1885. In that year, only 287 captive Nez Percés were still alive, most of them too young to remember their previous life of freedom, or too old and sick and broken in spirit to threaten the mighty power of the United States. Some of the survivors were permitted to return to their people's reservation at Lapwai. Chief Joseph and about 150 others were considered too dangerous to be penned up with other Nez Percés, whom they might influence. The government shipped them to Nespelem on the Colville Reservation in Washington, and there they lived out their lives in exile. When Joseph died on September 21, 1904, the agency physician reported the cause of death as "a broken heart."

Questions on Meaning

1   What difference in perspective exists between the Nez Percés and the white Americans regarding the possession of land? Why is this central to the Nez Percés problems? How does the discovery of gold intensify the problem?
2   Describe young Joseph. What type of leader is he? Why does he resist the idea of schools for his people?

17. *Ibid.*

3   Describe Oliver Otis Howard. How did he treat the Apaches? With what result? What change occurs in his dealings with the Nez Percés?

4   When ordered to leave the Wallowa Valley, why does Joseph decide not to fight? What pressures are placed on him when some of his warriors first kill white men?

5   What occurs at Lolo Creek? How did you react to the soldiers' behavior during this encounter? Similarly, how did you feel when the soldiers made Joseph a prisoner after sending out a truce flag?

6   What finally precipitates Joseph's surrender? How are he and his tribe treated after he surrenders?

7   Does the essay affect your view of the treatment of American Indians by the U.S. government? In what perspective does the essay place recent Indian land claims?

Questions on Method

1   What is the effect of the introduction? What tone does this first encounter between Lewis and Clark and the Nez Percés establish between whites and Indians?

2   Is the essay written objectively? Are viewpoints of both the Indians and the U.S. government given fair treatment? Explain.

3   What qualities are present in Joseph's surrender speech that would make it the most quoted of all American Indian speeches?

4   What narrative point-of-view technique does Brown use that distinguishes his essay from the other narratives in the chapter? Which essay is most like his? Why did Brown choose this technique? What would have been the effect of a first-person point of view?

5   Although Brown's essay is much longer than most of the narratives here, it does not take much longer to read. Can you account for this? Does it mean his meaning is less complex? Explain.

Vocabulary and Diction

1   What effect does Brown's simplicity of style have on the reader?

2   Explain the meaning of the following words: dentalium (1), testily (26), parleying (44), precipitated (60), cordon (63).

Writing Topics

1 Write a narrative about a historical process with which you are personally familiar, such as the coming of your family to America, the settling of your neighborhood, or the growth of your town or city. Use the third-person pronoun as Brown does. Indicate your attitude toward the event through your retelling rather then by stating it directly.

2 Write a narrative about the treatment your ethnic group has received in America. Make your attitude clear through your narration of the events. Use the third-person pronoun.

3 Narrate the life or part of the life of a public figure whose career you have followed closely. Include in your narration details of the person's activities and speeches, concentrating on those that best reflect the character of the person and the significance of his or her career.

SAM FELDMAN (1914–   ) is a native of New York City. He
terminated his education for economic reasons during the
Depression of the 1930s. In 1940 he was employed by the
Triborough Bridge and Tunnel Authority to collect tolls and to
patrol the newly opened Queens Midtown Tunnel. Except for a
period of almost three years in the Army during World War II,
he continued in this employment, and in 1979 he retired from
the position of superintendent of operations. To continue his
education, he enrolled at Queensborough Community College;
he expects to receive his baccalaureate degree in English from
the City University of New York.

The New Student

Sam Feldman

It was with varied emotions that I resumed my education during the   1
sixth decade of my life, after a lapse of more than forty years. The
happy anticipation of stimulating activities ahead was tinged with the
apprehension of an unknown future within the walls of academe. I
wondered if once again I could adapt to a life-style from which I had
departed so long ago. Would I find the results sufficiently rewarding
to counter the inherent doubts and fears of this new enterprise? With
a somewhat wavering determination, I approached the scene of my
academic trial: an assembly of staid buildings huddled in pedagogical
conference.

As I entered the main gate, I was swept up in a stream of   2
students. Ripples of laughter and babbled words filled the air with
casual disharmony. At a stairway, I was engulfed by a school of biped
salmon struggling upward against a cascade of descending humanity.
A pounding roar reverberated within the narrow enclosure. Reaching
the top of the cataract, I emerged into the placid flow of a corridor:
a lengthy duct bounded by numerically indexed compartments.

I proceeded between the rows of classrooms and soon found the 3
one to which I was assigned. Some fifteen minutes remained before
class time when I entered the room. In the serene and chalk-dusted
atmosphere, I sat alone, pondering my relationship to my new environment until my thoughts were abruptly interrupted by the arrival
of a group of students.

Their spirits were effervescent, their countenances, bright, but 4
their remarks belied their appearance. They expressed loudly voiced
complaints with varying degrees of trepidation. The professor, they
claimed, was notorious for lengthy assignments, frequent tests, and
strict grading. In previous classes, they had been told, those who had
not measured up to his demanding standards had failed. The subject
matter for this course in world literature was extremely difficult, as it
included the inscrutable Kafka, the imponderable Camus, the archa-
ically obscure Shakespeare, and the completely incomprehensible
Milton. Other comments followed, filled with dread and foreboding
of dire consequences to be endured all semester. Yet, all this was
voiced through smiling lips.

I was puzzled by this paradox, and then I suddenly realized what 5
was happening. The students were divesting themselves of their fears
by sharing them among themselves. Repressed within, the dimensions
of their anxieties expanded; but expressed openly and diffused among
the group, the fright diminished and all but disappeared. I wondered
if I had ever done that: how useful it would be to me now! I tried to
remember how I had coped with new experiences in the past with
the hope of resurrecting the process for the present. Then I recalled
an event from my preschool years—the earliest learning experience
in my memory.

I first thought of the street where I spent my childhood as only 6
a playground, but I soon found it also was a school for social conduct
and attitudes. Lessons were not learned from books, however, and
classes were haphazard. The curriculum was a constantly changing ka-
leidoscope of the shifting fragments of emotions, thoughts, and deeds,
drawn from or projected by everyone who came upon the street.

When I was old enough to venture into the street unchaperoned 7
by either my mother or an older sibling, I would eagerly step down
the one flight of stairs, carefully holding the handrail, as I was
constantly reminded to do each time I left our apartment. Pausing at
the top of the stoop, I would survey the sidewalk in front of the row

of buildings, first to the right, the shorter distance to the corner, and then to the lengthier left. Sighting along the line of ornamental iron railings guarding each house, as well as along the curb, I looked where I might find my group of playmates, which could be moved or scattered by a whim like a pool of quicksilver. If not on the walk, they usually would be found "in the middle of the street," as the roadway was called. Unencumbered by moving traffic or parked vehicles, the thoroughfare was as safe as the walk for our sprawling games. The third area of search would be the vast expanse of an empty lot across the street. As yet unlittered by the discards of civilization, this great plain beckoned to youthful adventurers. Finally, I would descend the wooden steps at the side of the building to the alley leading to the backyard. The street, however, was our favorite play area. Mothers also preferred that we stay in the street so that they might crane from their cubicle nests to loudly crow a boy's name and shrilly cackle some urgent message to him.

The residents of the street were immigrants, mostly East European Jews. Family planning was unknown then, and the area was well populated with children. So plentiful were the offspring that individual groups of boys evolved from each building. The accepted social code provided for very little mixing of groups. An outsider might be tolerated occasionally for a short while, but he felt either unwelcome or uncomfortable, and he soon returned to his own environment. 8

Being the youngest among my friends and thereby the last to be enrolled in school, I found myself alone one morning. This provided an opportunity to try something I had been wanting to do by myself, a challenge presented by an inclined cellar door at the corner of the block. By walking up the sloped metal door, I was able to slide down the smooth stone side: an activity I found most exciting. After one such descent, I suddenly became aware of "Bucktooth" Eddie standing next to me. Eddie was several inches taller than I, with about twice my bulk; protruding incisors, which accounted for his nickname, punctured his vapid, rotund face. He was the nemesis of the boys in our block, which he frequently invaded to chase any youngster who happened to be there. Being slothlike in movements, however, he never caught anyone. 9

My reaction to Eddie's presence was one of self-preservation; being unwilling to become his first victim, I ran. I reached the sanctuary of the shadow of my house and, looking back, saw him still 10 standing on the corner. Following the example of my peers, I aimed a stinging insult at the stationary target. It found its mark, for "Bucktooth" lifted his tightly clenched fist as though to crush the affront in his fleshy hand. Unknowingly, we had completed the ritual prescribed by both our factions, thereby contributing toward the continuation of the established relationship.

Sitting in a college classroom over half a century later, I now wondered what would have happened if I had stayed instead of run, offered a sign of friendship instead of insult. He had, after all, committed no hostile act as we stood together. Could we have established a bond of amiability? If so, would it have survived the pressure from our peers, which inevitably would have followed? Another incident, which happened about a year later, now flashed through my mind as an answer to these queries.

At that time, I was seated on the sidewalk curb with two friends when we were approached by two boys whom I recognized as companions of "Bucktooth" Eddie. Each held a handful of stones threateningly. Glaring at us, one demanded, "Are any of you Jews?" Apprehensive, I considered the advisability of discreetly denying my religion. I was startled when one of my companions pointed to me and said, "Yeah, he is." My other friend concurred by his silence. The Judas gemini then walked away, the dull sheen of tarnished silver showing in their shameful, downcast eyes. Stunned by the betrayal, I sat still until I was stirred to action by the invaders' attack. Although I was not struck by the stones, the hurt was more grievous than any that might have been inflicted by a hurled missile.

Such incidents affected, but did not terminate, relations with my false friends. They were part of my group, and I could not abandon a part of the whole. Falseness was merely another condition to be dealt with, stored in memory, and recalled when needed to guide further conduct.

These earliest experiences in learning, I now realize, have had many counterparts over the years. In institutional education as well as in life situations, I have found myself, again and again, a new student facing the unknown and the unexpected. I have encountered other "Bucktooth" Eddies and faithless friends, and designated objectives often have seemed distant and unattainable. Each event, however, has taught me to take care of my own problems. With this accumulated confidence, my doubts and fears now diminished. Once

81

again I was a new student, and, although there might still be new lessons ahead, I was confident that I could achieve my goals.

Questions on Meaning

1 What is the thesis of the essay?
2 How did the younger students rid themselves of their fears on first entering the classroom of a reputedly difficult course?
3 Why does Feldman recall the street where he spent his childhood?
4 What adventure did the author frequently engage in when he was "old enough to venture into the street unchaperoned"?
5 How did the author's experience with his "faithless friends" answer his queries about his treatment of "Bucktooth" Eddie?
6 How does his recalling of those two childhood incidents help the 60-year-old author cope with being a new student?

Questions on Method

1 Four time sequences are narrated here. How does Feldman fuse them into a single essay?
2 The author uses several figures of speech—metaphors and similes—such as "I was engulfed by a school of biped salmon." What other figures of speech can you locate?

Vocabulary and Diction

1 How would you describe Feldman's vocabulary? What effect does it create?
2 Define the following words Feldman uses in his essay: tinged (1), counter (1), pedagogical (1), placid (2), effervescent (4), belied (4), trepidation (4), inscrutable (4), imponderable (4), vapid (9), rotund (9), nemesis (9).

Writing Topics

1 Write an essay on one of the following topics, using the flashback technique. Begin with a scene in the present, one that holds conflict for

you, then recall earlier events. Create suspense by concealing until the end how your conflict is resolved.

a. An educational experience outside school, such as something learned on the streets, in the family, or on a trip.

b. An experience in strange and frightening surroundings.

c. An experience with a bully.

Narration—Writing Topics

For each of the essays below, make the appropriate narrative choices, in terms of point of view, narrative speed, and ordering chronological arrangement.

1 Narrate an experience in which you felt yourself to be an outsider. Discuss the value of the experience to you.

2 The world of adulthood is as strange a place to a child as the worlds visited by Kazantzakis, Theroux, and Raban are to these authors. Write a narration that illustrates the validity of such a comparison.

3 Write an essay about a person who is telling someone else a story. Emphasize the parts of the story that are most effective by describing how they make the listener react.

4 Kazantzakis symbolizes happiness by calling it a "domestic bird." Choose a symbol that represents happiness for you, and write a narration that illustrates its meaning.

5 Write a narration that teaches a lesson or moral. As much as possible, avoid explaining the lesson or moral; instead, let your narration communicate the meaning through your selection of events and details.

6 Narrate a controversial historical event with which you are familiar, either through experience or through research. Do not state your interpretation as Arendt does, but convey it through your choice of events and details as Brown does.

THREE
Description

Whereas narration deals mainly in action and verbs, description seems to give a static word picture, relying primarily on adjectives, nouns, and figures of speech. Perhaps because of this stationary quality, description, more so than exposition, narration, or persuasion, is auxiliary; it seldom stands alone. In fact, unrelieved description soon becomes boring, but put to the service of the other three modes, it increases their clarity and memorability. Consider, for example, the following two versions of a passage from Graham Greene's first autobiography. Most descriptive words and phrases have been deleted from the first. Notice how much more effective the original descriptive passage is. (The italics in the second passage indicate what was deleted from the first.)

1

Now with the revolver in my pocket I thought I had stumbled on the perfect cure. I slipped a bullet into a chamber, and, holding the revolver behind my back, spun the chambers round.

I put the muzzle of the revolver into my ear and pulled the trigger. There was a click, and looking down at the chamber I could see that the charge had moved into the firing position. I was out by one. I remember a sense of jubilation. Life contained a number of possibilities. I went home and put the revolver back in the cupboard.

2

Now with the revolver in my pocket I thought I had stumbled on the perfect cure. *I was going to escape in one way or another, and perhaps because escape was inseparably connected with the Common in my mind, it was there that I went.*

Beyond the Common lay a wide grass ride known for some reason as Cold Harbour to which I would occasionally take a horse, and beyond again stretched Ashridge Park, the smooth olive skin of beech trees and last year's quagmire of leaves, dark like old pennies. Deliberately I chose my ground, I believe without real fear. . . . I slipped a bullet into a chamber and, holding the revolver behind my back, spun the chambers round. *. . .*

I put the muzzle of the revolver into my *right* ear and pulled the trigger. There was a *minute* click, and looking down at the chamber I could see that the charge had moved into the firing position. I was out by one. I remember an *extraordinary* sense of jubilation, *as if carnival lights had been switched on in a dark drab street. My heart knocked in its cage, and* life contained an *infinite* number of possibilities. *It was like a young man's first successful experience of sex—as if among the Ashridge beeches I had passed the test of manhood.* I went home and put the revolver back in the *corner* cupboard.

Description can be classified as objective or subjective. The purpose of objective description is to map out, to locate. Juries and scientists are among those who most value accurate reporting of detail. "What did he look like?" the prosecuting attorney asks. A fair trial may depend on the witness's ability to reproduce in words the victim's appearance detail by detail without prejudice or wishful thinking. A laboratory technician must describe what he sees under a microscope in language stripped of personal and emotional overtones. Where factual word painting is required, objective description is the goal. Here is the description of a whooping crane from *The Audubon Society Field Guide* (1977) that includes size, color (of both mature and immature birds), and voice:

> A very large bird, pure white with jet-black wing tips and red on forehead and cheeks. Immature birds are similar but head and neck are brown. Voice: Trumpetlike call that can be heard for several miles.

The purpose of subjective description, by contrast, is to give an emotional interpretation or to create a mood; this type of description capitalizes on a connotative vocabulary that reveals the writer's values and attitudes. In fiction and even in certain types of biography and journalism (e.g., feature writing), we expect the writer's mental landscape to affect the external scene described; in fact, we expect the two to overlap, outside objects becoming symbols of inner states. T. S. Eliot's name for these symbols, objective correlatives, can hardly be improved on. Almost all description in literature, and much description in nonfiction, is of this impressionistic kind. Consider the connotations, emotional overtones, and figurative language of the second description as opposed to the factual language of the first:

1

My skiff was foundering off the coast of Long Island when the captain of a trawler spotted me, yelled over, and towed me to shore.

2

Amazing grace, how sweet the sound that saved a wretch like me!

If you are writing a subjective description, try to create a dominant mood and choose a vocabulary with the appropriate connotations. Puns and figures of speech can often convey more than literal statement; for example, in the description of a sinister scene the name "creeper" can contribute more than the word "vine." The garden-variety similes of the following description accumulate to form a single, absurdly humorous, impression:

> Her smile is like brandy. Her eyes like blackberries. . . . Her nose is like a little pink potato; her behind is like a juicy pear—yes, the whole

woman is like a strawberry patch. I can see her in front of me, with arms like wonderful cucumbers.

In objective description you can achieve unity by a progression from left to right (or the reverse), from inner to outer (or the reverse), or from least to most important (or the reverse), using transitional words and phrases as you move through these details to indicate your shifting focus. Instead of using a stationary observer, you might employ one who moves through the scene reporting on the various portions as they become visible; this technique is often used to animate long descriptive passages.

Writing Description

1 Select your detail carefully; you can't include everything.
2 In objective description use a step-by-step spatial arrangement or a progression from least to most important (or the reverse).
3 In subjective description choose details and a vocabulary that create a dominant impression.
4 Combine description with narration, exposition, or persuasion.

The Hidden Pool

Rachel Carson

The shore is an ancient world, for as long as there has been an earth 1 and sea there has been this place of the meeting of land and water. Yet it is a world that keeps alive the sense of continuing creation and of the relentless drive of life. Each time that I enter it, I gain some new awareness of its beauty and its deeper meanings, sensing that intricate fabric of life by which one creature is linked with another, and each with its surroundings.

In my thoughts of the shore, one place stands apart for its 2 revelation of exquisite beauty. It is a pool hidden within a cave that one can visit only rarely and briefly when the lowest of the year's low tides fall below it, and perhaps from that very fact it acquires some of its special beauty. Choosing such a tide, I hoped for a glimpse of the pool. The ebb was to fall early in the morning. I knew that if the wind held from the northwest and no interfering swell ran in from a distant storm the level of the sea should drop below the entrance to the pool. There had been sudden ominous showers in the night, with rain like handfuls of gravel flung on the roof. When I looked out into the early morning the sky was full of a gray dawn light but the sun had not yet risen. Water and air were pallid. Across the bay the moon was a luminous disc in the western sky, suspended above the dim line of distant shore—the full August moon, drawing the tide to the low, low levels of the threshold of the alien sea world. As I watched, a gull flew by, above the spruces. Its breast was rosy with the light of the unrisen sun. The day was, after all, to be fair.

Later, as I stood above the tide near the entrance to the pool, 3 the promise of that rosy light was sustained. From the base of the steep wall of rock on which I stood, a moss-covered ledge jutted seaward into deep water. In the surge at the rim of the ledge the dark fronds of oarweeds swayed, smooth and gleaming as leather. The projecting ledge was the path to the small hidden cave and its pool. Occasionally a swell, stronger than the rest, rolled smoothly over the rim and broke in foam against the cliff. But the intervals between such swells were long enough to admit me to the ledge and long enough for a glimpse of that fairy pool, so seldom and so briefly exposed.

And so I knelt on the wet carpet of sea moss and looked back 4 into the dark cavern that held the pool in a shallow basin. The floor of the cave was only a few inches below the roof, and a mirror had been created in which all that grew on the ceiling was reflected in the still water below.

Under water that was clear as glass the pool was carpeted with 5 green sponge. Gray patches of sea squirts glistened on the ceiling and colonies of soft coral were a pale apricot color. In the moment when I looked into the cave a little elfin starfish hung down, suspended by the merest thread, perhaps by only a single tube foot. It reached down to touch its own reflection, so perfectly delineated that there might have been, not one starfish, but two. The beauty of the reflected images and of the limpid pool itself was the poignant beauty of things that are ephemeral, existing only until the sea should return to fill the little cave.

Questions on Meaning

1 In paragraph 2 Carson states her thesis that the cave acquires "some of its special beauty" because one can visit it "only rarely and briefly." Can

you think of other things whose beauty is special because that beauty can be enjoyed only rarely and briefly?

2   What does Carson mean by calling the shore "an ancient world"? In what ways is it, as Carson says in paragraph 2, an "alien" world? Is it paradoxical that this world, despite its alien qualities, gives Carson what she terms in her third sentence a sense of "that intricate fabric of life by which one creature is linked with another, and each with its surroundings"? What links the human race to its surroundings?

Questions on Method

1   How would you classify Carson's tone of voice when she describes "the sense of continuing creation and of the relentless drive of life" she observes in nature? Does she see this drive as healthy or unhealthy?

2   How does the pool, as Carson describes its details, come to symbolize her themes of beauty and of "the intricate fabric of life"?

3   What functions do color, texture, and sound play in her description of the pool?

4   Much of Carson's description is subjective or emotional, but she describes objectively as well. What spatial arrangement does she use in describing the pool?

Vocabulary and Diction

1   In paragraph 3 Carson calls the pool a "fairy" pool. Why does she use this adjective? What other words does she employ to give her picture of the pool a fairy-tale quality? Does Carson romanticize nature in this sense? (Look up the meaning of "romanticize" before answering this question.)

2   Look up the words "poignant" and "ephemeral," which Carson uses in the last sentence. How do these adjectives help suggest that Carson's attitude toward "the relentless drive of life" is more complex than you might have suspected had you read only the essay's first paragraph? How does the adjective "exquisite" in the first sentence of Carson's second paragraph offer a hint of the complexity of her attitude?

3   Define the following words and phrases used by Carson: luminous disc (2), fronds of oarweeds (3), delineated (5).

Writing Topics

1   Describe a place you have visited, either in nature or in a city, that symbolizes something to you about the healthy, creative quality of life.

2   Describe a place as you perceived it when you were feeling particularly romantic, either because you were in love with another person or because you were feeling in love simply with life itself. Redescribe the same place as you perceived it another time, when you were feeling less romantic. Which description is more realistic? How much is a person's perception of nature colored by his or her feelings at a particular moment? Organize your two descriptions so that they illustrate a discussion of this question.

ALFRED KAZIN (1915–   ) is an American literary critic and
teacher. His critical writings include *On Native Grounds* (1942)
and *Contemporaries* (1962). Recently he has been involved in a
study of the literature and films of the Holocaust, and his latest
memoir is *New York Jew* (1979). "Brownsville Food" is taken
from *A Walker in the City* (1951), a series of recollections of his
childhood in Brooklyn.

Brownsville Food

Alfred Kazin

On Belmont Avenue, Brownsville's great open street market, the   1
pushcarts are still lined on each other for blocks, and the din is as
deafening, marvelous, and appetizing as ever. They have tried to tone
it down, the pushcarts are now confined to one side of the street. When
I was a boy, they clogged both sides, reached halfway up the curb to
the open stands of the stores; walking down the street was like being
whirled around and around in a game of blind man's buff. But Belmont
Avenue is still the merriest street in Brownsville. As soon as I walked
into it from Rockaway, caught my first whiff of the herrings and
pickles in their great black barrels, heard the familiarly harsh, mocking cries and shouts from the market women—"*Oh you darlings! Oh
you sweet ones, oh you pretty ones! Storm us! Tear us apart! Devour
us!* "—I laughed right out loud, it was so good to be back among
them. Nowhere but on Belmont Avenue did I ever see in Brownsville
such open, hearty people as those market women. Their shrewd open-
weather eyes missed nothing. The street was their native element;

they seemed to hold it together with their hands, mouths, fists, and knees; they stood up in it behind their stands all day long, and in every weather; they stood up for themselves. In winter they would bundle themselves into five or six sweaters, then putting long white aprons over their overcoats, would warm themselves at fires lit in black oil drums between the pushcarts, their figures bulging as if to meet the rain and cold head-on in defiance.

I could hear them laughing and mock-crying all the way to Stone Avenue, still imploring and pulling at every woman on the street— "*Vayber! Vayber! Sheyne gute vayber! Oh you lovelies! Oh you good ones! Oh you pretty ones! See how cheap and good! Just come over! Just taste! Just a little look! What will it cost you to taste? How can you walk on without looking? How can you resist us? Oh! Oh! Come over! Come over! Devour us! Storm us! Tear us apart! BARGAINS BARGAINS!!*" I especially loved watching them at dusk, an hour before supper, when the women would walk through to get the food at its freshest. Then, in those late winter afternoons, when there was that deep grayness on the streets and that spicy smell from the open stands at dusk I was later to connect with my first great walks inside the New York crowd at the rush hour—then there would arise from behind the great flaming oil drums and the pushcarts loaded with their separate mounds of shoelaces, corsets, pots and pans, stockings, kosher kitchen soap, memorial candles in their wax-filled tumblers and glassware, "chiney" oranges, beet roots and soup greens, that deep and good odor of lox, of salami, of herrings and half-sour pickles, that told me I was truly home.

As I went down Belmont Avenue, the copper-shining herrings in the tall black barrels made me think of the veneration of food in Brownsville families. I can still see the kids pinned down to the tenement stoops, their feet helplessly kicking at the pots and pans lined up before them, their mouths pressed open with a spoon while the great meals are rammed down their throats. "*Eat! Eat! May you be destroyed if you don't eat! What sin have I committed that God should punish me with you! Eat! What will become of you if you don't eat! Imp of darkness, may you sink ten fathoms into the earth if you don't eat! Eat!*"

We never had a chance to know what hunger meant. At home we nibbled all day long as a matter of course. On the block we gorged ourselves continually on "Nessels," Hersheys, gumdrops, polly seeds, nuts, chocolate-covered cherries, charlotte russe, and ice cream. A warm and sticky ooze of chocolate ran through everything we touched; the street always smelled faintly like the candy wholesaler's windows on the way back from school. The hunger for sweets, jellies, and soda water raged in us like a disease; during the grimmest punchball game, in the middle of a fist fight, we would dash to the candy store to get down two-cent blocks of chocolate and "small"—three-cent—glasses of cherry soda; or calling "upstairs" from the street, would have flung to us, or carefully hoisted down at the end of a clothesline, thick slices of rye bread smeared with chicken fat. No meal at home was complete without cream soda, root beer, ginger ale, "celery tonic." We poured jelly on bread; we poured it into the tea; we often ate chocolate marshmallows before breakfast. At school during the recess hour Syrian vendors who all looked alike in their alpaca jackets and black velours hats came after us with their white enameled trays, from which we took *Halvah*, Turkish Delight, and three different kinds of greasy nut-brown pastry sticks. From the Jewish vendors, who went around the streets in every season wheeling their little tin stoves, we bought roasted potatoes either in the quarter or the half— the skins were hard as bark and still smelled of the smoke pouring out of the stoves; apples you ate off a stick that were encrusted with a thick glaze of baked jelly you never entirely got down your throat or off your fingers, so that you seemed to be with it all day; *knishes*; paper spills of hot yellow chick peas. I still hear those peddlers crying up and down the street—"*Arbes! Arbes! Hayse gute árbes! Kinder! Kinder! Hayse gute árbes!*" From the "big" Italians, whom we saw only in summer, we bought watermelons as they drove their great horse-smelling wagons down the street calling up to every window— "Hey you ladies! *Hey ladies! Freschi* and good!" — and from the "small" ones, who pushed carts through the streets, paper cups of shaved ice sprinkled before our eyes with drops of lemon or orange or raspberry syrup from a narrow water bottle.

But our greatest delight in all seasons was "delicatessen"—hot 5 spiced corned beef, pastrami, rolled beef, hard salami, soft salami, chicken salami, bologna, frankfurter "specials" and the thinner, wrinkled hot dogs always taken with mustard and relish and sauerkraut, and whenever possible, to make the treat fully real, with potato salad, baked beans, and french fries which had been bubbling in the black wire fryer deep in the iron pot. At Saturday twilight, as soon as the delicatessen store reopened after the Sabbath rest, we raced into it panting for the hot dogs sizzling on the gas plate just inside the window. The look of that blackened empty gas plate had driven us wild all through the wearisome Sabbath day. And now, as the electric sign blazed up again, lighting up the words JEWISH NATIONAL DELICATESSEN, it was as if we had entered into our rightful heritage. Yet *Wurst* carried associations with the forbidden, the adulterated, the excessive; with spices that teased and maddened the senses to demand more, still more. This was food that only on Saturday nights could be eaten with a good conscience. Generally, we bought it on the sly; it was supposed to be bad for us; I thought it was made in dark cellars. Still, our parents could not have disapproved of it altogether. Each new mouthful of food we took in was an advantage stolen in the battle. The favorite injunction was to *fix yourself*, by which I understood we needed to do a repair job on ourselves. In the swelling and thickening of a boy's body was the poor family's earliest success. "Fix yourself!" a mother cried indignantly to the child on the stoop. "Fix yourself!" The word for a fat boy was *solid*.

Questions on Meaning

1 Kazin's essay appears to be about what he calls in paragraph 3 "the veneration of food in Brownsville families." Why was food so important to the children and parents in Brownsville when Kazin was growing up there? Explain what the phrase "fix yourself" means at the end of the essay.

2 What ethnic group is Kazin describing? At what point in the essay does it become clear that Kazin is describing a particular ethnic group? Is such veneration of food unique to this group, or is it a shared characteristic of many different ethnic groups in America?

3 How important to our understanding of Kazin's theme is the sentence toward the end of the essay, "In the swelling and thickening of a boy's body was the poor family's earliest success." Is this true only of poor families? How much does the theme of poverty account for the richness of detail with which Kazin describes the food he ate as a boy?

Questions on Method

1 Why does Kazin at the start of his essay describe the market women in such detail? How effective is the sales pitch of the women? How do their

words "Devour us! Storm us! Tear us apart!" relate to the theme of the essay?

2 In paragraph 1 Kazin calls Belmont Avenue "the merriest street in Brownsville." Is the tone of his essay essentially merry? How does the sense of urgency about eating, the idea that the children of Brownsville never had a chance "to know what hunger meant," as Kazin says in paragraph 4, affect the merriness of his tone?

3 Why does Kazin begin his essay with the simile that compares walking down Belmont Avenue to "being whirled around and around in a game of blind man's buff"? How accurately does this simile depict Belmont Avenue according to Kazin's literal description?

4 Kazin seems to think that the children's hunger was a sign of good health. At the same time, in paragraph 4 he says that the hunger for sweets raged in them "like a disease." This simile introduces a note of paradox into the essay. Are there other examples of paradox that you can point to in the essay?

5 Although Kazin's description is primarily subjective, he uses some objective description as well. What spatial arrangement does he use in describing the appearance of Belmont Avenue and the market women?

Vocabulary and Diction

1 At the end of paragraph 4 Kazin compares the "big" Italians who sold watermelons from their wagons to the "small" Italians who sold cups of shaved ice from their pushcarts. Why does he place the adjectives "big" and "small" in quotation marks? What does this tell us about the way children perceive the world around them?

2 What does the word "*Wurst*" mean in the middle of paragraph 5? Why did *Wurst* carry associations with "the forbidden, the adulterated, the excessive" in the minds of the children of Brownsville? Is Kazin's description of his feelings about the *Wurst* a good example of an ethnic joke? What is an ethnic joke? Can you find other examples of ethnic humor in Kazin's essay?

3 In the last sentence of Kazin's essay, "The word for a fat boy was *solid*," the word "solid" is a euphemism for the word "fat." What is a euphemism? How does this euphemism clarify the theme of the essay?

4 Define the following words and phrases used by Kazin: shrewd open-weather eyes (1), kosher (2), alpaca (4), velours (4).

Writing Topics

1 Kazin conveys a good deal about his childhood in Brownsville simply by describing Belmont Avenue and its relation to the foods he ate as a child; that is, Kazin characterizes what it was like to live in his neighborhood by describing in detail a part of his experience there. Write an essay employing a similar technique. Describe the overall flavor of your childhood as it relates to the neighborhood in which you grew up by describing in detail one part of your life in one part of that neighborhood.

2 Write an essay that describes your favorite foods. Indicate through your choice of foods who you are and your outlook on life.

3 Write an essay in which you describe something as it is perceived by a small child. Make clear how the child's perception is different from the adult's.

4 Describe the street on which you are living today. Which details are most important to focus on to give the reader the general impression of what life is like in your neighborhood?

CHARLES DARWIN (1809–82) was an English naturalist who expounded the theory of evolution. He studied medicine at Edinburgh University in Scotland. As a naturalist, he sailed on the *Beagle* from 1831 to 1836 on an expedition to South America and Australia. In 1859 he published *Origin of Species*, which is still considered one of the most important books in natural philosophy. In "Tahiti" Darwin focuses on his reactions to the people and the place.

Tahiti

Charles Darwin

At daylight, Tahiti, an island which must for ever remain classical 1 to the voyager in the South Sea, was in view. At a distance the appearance was not attractive. The luxuriant vegetation of the lower part could not yet be seen, and as the clouds rolled past, the wildest and most precipitous peaks showed themselves towards the centre of the island. As soon as we anchored in Matavai Bay, we were surrounded by canoes. This was our Sunday, but the Monday of Tahiti: if the case had been reversed, we should not have received a single visit; for the injunction not to launch a canoe on the Sabbath is rigidly obeyed. After dinner, we landed to enjoy all the delights produced by the first impressions of a new country, and that country the charming Tahiti. A crowd of men, women, and children, was collected on the memorable Point Venus, ready to receive us with laughing, merry faces. They marshalled us towards the house of Mr. Wilson, the missionary of the district, who met us on the road, and gave us a very friendly reception. After sitting a very short time in

"Tahiti" from *Voyage of the Beagle* (1840) by Charles Darwin.

his house, we separated to walk about, but returned there in the evening.

The land capable of cultivation is scarcely in any part more than 2 a fringe of low alluvial soil, accumulated round the base of the mountains, and protected from the waves of the sea by a coral reef, which encircles the entire line of coast. Within the reef there is an expanse of smooth water, like that of a lake, where the canoes of the natives can ply with safety and where ships anchor. The low land which comes down to the beach of coral-sand is covered by the most beautiful productions of the intertropical regions. In the midst of bananas, orange, cocoa-nut, and bread-fruit trees, spots are cleared where yams, sweet potatoes, and sugar-cane, and pine-apples are cultivated. Even the brush-wood is an imported fruit-tree, namely, the guava, which from its abundance has become as noxious as a weed. In Brazil I have often admired the varied beauty of the bananas, palms, and orange-trees contrasted together; and here we also have the bread-fruit, conspicuous from its large, glossy, and deeply digitated leaf. It is admirable to behold groves of a tree, sending forth its branches with the vigour of an English oak, loaded with large and most nutritious fruit. However seldom the usefulness of an object can account for the pleasure of beholding it, in the case of these beautiful woods, the knowledge of their high productiveness no doubt enters largely into the feeling of admiration. The little winding paths, cool from the surrounding shade, led to the scattered houses; the owners of which everywhere gave us a cheerful and most hospitable reception.

I was pleased with nothing so much as with the inhabitants. 3 There is a mildness in the expression of their countenances which at once banishes the idea of a savage; and an intelligence which shows that they are advancing in civilization. The common people, when working, keep the upper part of their bodies quite naked; and it is then that the Tahitians are seen to advantage. They are very tall, broad-shouldered, athletic, and well-proportioned. It has been re-marked, that it requires little habit to make a dark skin more pleasing and natural to the eye of an European than his own colour. A white man bathing by the side of a Tahitian, was like a plant bleached by the gardener's art compared with a fine dark green one growing vigorously in the open fields. Most of the men are tattooed, and the ornaments follow the curvature of the body so gracefully, that they have a very elegant effect. One common pattern, varying in its details, is somewhat like the crown of a palm-tree. It springs from the central line of the back, and gracefully curls round both sides. The simile may be a fanciful one, but I thought the body of a man thus ornamented was like the trunk of a noble tree embraced by a delicate creeper.

Many of the elder people had their feet covered with small 4 figures, so placed as to resemble a sock. This fashion, however, is partly gone by, and has been succeeded by others. Here, although fashion is far from immutable, every one must abide by that prevailing in his youth. An old man has thus his age for ever stamped on his body, and he cannot assume the airs of a young dandy. The women are tattooed in the same manner as the men, and very commonly on their fingers. One unbecoming fashion is now almost universal: namely, shaving the hair from the upper part of the head, in a circular form, so as to leave only an outer ring. The missionaries have tried to persuade the people to change this habit; but it is the fashion, and that is a sufficient answer at Tahiti, as well as at Paris. I was much disappointed in the personal appearance of the women: they are far inferior in every respect to the men. The custom of wearing a white or scarlet flower in the back of the head, or through a small hole in each ear, is pretty. A crown of woven cocoa-nut leaves is also worn as a shade for the eyes. The women appear to be in greater want of some becoming costume even than the men.

Nearly all the natives understand a little English—that is, they 5 know the names of common things; and by the aid of this, together with signs, a lame sort of conversation could be carried on. In returning in the evening to the boat, we stopped to witness a very pretty scene. Numbers of children were playing on the beach, and had lighted bonfires which illumined the placid sea and surrounding trees; others, in circles, were singing Tahitian verses. We seated ourselves on the sand, and joined their party. The songs were impromptu, and I believe related to our arrival; one little girl sang a line, which the rest took up in parts, forming a very pretty chorus. The whole scene made us unequivocally aware that we were seated on the shores of an island in the far-famed South Sea.

Questions on Meaning

1 Darwin begins his essay by telling us that at a distance the appearance of Tahiti is wild and unattractive. What aspects of Tahiti change his

mind about the island's lack of appeal? How common is it for attitudes to differ because of one's proximity to the object or place viewed? Explain.

2   In paragraph 2 Darwin says of the Tahitian woods that "the knowledge of their high productiveness no doubt enters largely into the feeling of admiration." Explain the comparison he sets up between the beauty of an object and its usefulness or productiveness. How does his appreciation of natural beauty compare to Rachel Carson's? How does his description of the natives of Tahiti recall the theme of comparing usefulness and beauty?

3   Discuss Darwin's attitude toward the Tahitian natives. Is he objective and scientific? Does he exhibit emotional or evaluative responses? Find details in the essay to support your answer.

4   Discuss Darwin's development in paragraph 3 of the simile likening the human body to a tree. How does this simile clarify the theme of the essay?

5   How does Darwin's contrast of the civilized and the natural attributes of the natives help us understand a main theme of his essay? How complicated are Darwin's ideas about the values of civilization as compared to the values of nature?

Questions on Method

1   Why does Darwin in paragraph 1 contrast "our Sunday" to "the Monday of Tahiti"? How does this contrast prepare us to understand other contrasts between the white world and that of the natives Darwin describes? Discuss the importance of Darwin's use of the prose pattern of contrast and comparison in organizing his description.

2   Discuss Darwin's description of the geography and plant life of Tahiti. How fragile and delicate does the island appear to be? How strong and healthy or neat and orderly does it seem? Compare his description of Tahiti with Carson's of the pool. Which description is more objective? Explain.

3   Why does Darwin in paragraphs 3 and 4 describe the native practice of tattooing in such detail? How does his description of this detail of Tahitian life work to give us an impression of the quality of native life in general? Discuss the importance of focusing on a few details when you are trying to convey the overall impression of something you have observed. In what way do the other authors in this section use a similar descriptive technique?

Vocabulary and Diction

1   What does the word "classical" mean in Darwin's opening sentence? In what ways is Tahiti well ordered, highly conventionalized, classical?

2   What does the word "impromptu" mean in paragraph 5? How does the final scene in which the native children sing impromptu songs symbolize Darwin's view of Tahiti as a whole? How does the impromptu quality of native life compare to what Darwin in paragraph 1 calls the "rigidly obeyed" religious and social conventions of native life?

3   Define the following words used by Darwin: luxuriant (1), precipitous (1), marshalled (1), bread-fruit (2), brush-wood (2), guava (2), noxious (2), digitated (2), nutritious (2), immutable (4).

Writing Topics

1   Investigate Darwin's theory of natural selection. How well does his description of Tahiti illustrate his theory?

2   Analyze how viewing things scientifically affects a person. In what ways does a scientific perspective increase one's understanding of what is observed? Are there ways such a perspective might limit one's understanding?

3   Analyze the essential characteristics that define a particular group or class in American society—a racial or ethnic group, a political or an age group, an economic class—by focusing on a few details of the group's appearance, behavior, or ideas about life.

4   Describe your school or neighborhood from a scientific point of view as Darwin describes Tahiti. Describe its appearance, activities, and the appearance or fashions of its inhabitants. Try to maintain an anthropologist's objectivity throughout, conveying as little emotion as possible.

LOREN EISELEY (1907–77) was a prolific essayist and poet. He also taught anthropology at the University of Pennsylvania for several years. A philosopher by nature, he was intrigued by the role of fate and its interrelationship with man and nature. His many volumes include *The Immense Journey* (1957), *The Mind of Nature* (1962), and *The Unexpected Universe* (1969). The essay that follows is from *The Immense Journey*.

How Flowers Changed the World

Loren Eiseley

When the first simple flower bloomed on some raw upland late in the   1
Dinosaur Age, it was wind pollinated, just like its early pine-cone
relatives. It was a very inconspicuous flower because it had not yet
evolved the idea of using the surer attraction of birds and insects to
achieve the transportation of pollen. It sowed its own pollen and
received the pollen of other flowers by the simple vagaries of the
wind. Many plants in regions where insect life is scant still follow
this principle today. Nevertheless, the true flower—and the seed that
it produced—was a profound innovation in the world of life.

In a way, this event parallels, in the plant world, what happened   2
among animals. Consider the relative chance for survival of the
exteriorly deposited egg of a fish in contrast with the fertilized egg of
a mammal, carefully retained for months in the mother's body until
the young animal (or human being) is developed to a point where it
may survive. The biological wastage is less—and so it is with the
flowering plants. The primitive spore, a single cell fertilized in the

beginning by a swimming sperm, did not promote rapid distribution, and the young plant, moreover, had to struggle up from nothing. No one had left it any food except what it could get by its own unaided efforts.

By contrast, the true flowering plants (angiosperm itself means 3 "encased seed") grew a seed in the heart of a flower, a seed whose development was initiated by a fertilizing pollen grain independent of outside moisture. But the seed, unlike the developing spore, is already a fully equipped *embryonic plant* packed in a little enclosed box stuffed full of nutritious food. Moreover, by featherdown attachments, as in dandelion or milkweed seed, it can be wafted upward on gusts and ride the wind for miles; or with hooks it can cling to a bear's or a rabbit's hide; or like some of the berries, it can be covered with a juicy, attractive fruit to lure birds, pass undigested through their intestinal tracts and be voided miles away.

The ramifications of this biological invention were endless. 4 Plants traveled as they had never traveled before. They got into strange environments heretofore never entered by the old spore plants or stiff pine-cone-seed plants. The well-fed, carefully cherished little embryos raised their heads everywhere. Many of the older plants with more primitive reproductive mechanisms began to fade away under this unequal contest. They contracted their range into secluded environments. Some, like the giant redwoods, lingered on as relics; many vanished entirely.

The world of the giants was a dying world. These fantastic little 5 seeds skipping and hopping and flying about the woods and valleys brought with them an amazing adaptability. If our whole lives had not been spent in the midst of it, it would astound us. The old, stiff, sky-reaching wooden world had changed into something that glowed here and there with strange colors, put out queer, unheard-of fruits and little intricately carved seed cases, and, most important of all, produced concentrated foods in a way that the land had never seen before or dreamed of back in the fish-eating, leaf-crunching days of the dinosaurs.

That food came from three sources, all produced by the repro- 6 ductive system of the flowering plants. There were the tantalizing nectars and pollens intended to draw insects for pollenizing purposes, and which are responsible also for that wonderful jeweled creation, the hummingbird. There were the juicy and enticing fruits to attract larger animals, and in which tough-coated seeds were concealed, as in the tomato, for example. Then, as if this were not enough, there was the food in the actual seed itself, the food intended to nourish the embryo. All over the world, like hot corn in a popper, these incredible elaborations of the flowering plants kept exploding. In a movement that was almost instantaneous, geologically speaking, the angiosperms had taken over the world. Grass was beginning to cover the bare earth until, today, there are over six thousand species. All kinds of vines and bushes squirmed and writhed under new trees with flying seeds.

The explosion was having its effect on animal life also. Specialized groups of insects were arising to feed on the new sources of food and, incidentally and unknowingly, to pollinate the plant. The flowers bloomed and bloomed in ever larger and more spectacular varieties. Some were pale unearthly night flowers intended to lure moths in the evening twilight, some among the orchids even took the shape of female spiders in order to attract wandering males, some flamed redly in the light of noon or twinkled modestly in the meadow grasses. Intricate mechanisms splashed pollen on the breasts of hummingbirds, or stamped it on the bellies of black, grumbling bees droning assiduously from blossom to blossom. Honey ran, insects multiplied, and even the descendants of that toothed and ancient lizard-bird had become strangely altered. Equipped with prodding beaks instead of biting teeth they pecked the seeds and gobbled the insects that were really converted nectar.

Across the planet grasslands were now spreading. A slow continental upthrust which had been a part of the early Age of Flowers had cooled the world's climates. The stalking reptiles and the leatherwinged black imps of the seashore cliffs had vanished. Only birds roamed the air now, hot-blooded and high-speed metabolic machines.

The mammals, too, had survived and were venturing into new domains, staring about perhaps a bit bewildered at their sudden eminence now that the thunder lizards were gone. Many of them, beginning as small browsers upon leaves in the forest, began to venture out upon this new sunlit world of the grass. Grass has a high silica content and demands a new type of very tough and resistant tooth enamel, but the seeds taken incidentally in the cropping of the grass are highly nutritious. A new world had opened out for the warm-blooded mammals. Great herbivores like the mammoths, horses and bisons appeared. Skulking about them had arisen savage flesh-feeding carnivores like the now extinct dire wolves and the saber-toothed tiger.

Flesh eaters though these creatures were, they were being sus- 10 tained on nutritious grasses one step removed. Their fierce energy was being maintained on a high, effective level, through hot days and frosty nights, by the concentrated energy of the angiosperms. That energy, thirty per cent or more of the weight of the entire plant among some of the cereal grasses, was being accumulated and concentrated in the rich proteins and fats of the enormous game herds of the grasslands.

On the edge of the forest, a strange, old-fashioned animal still 11 hesitated. His body was the body of a tree dweller, and though tough and knotty by human standards, he was, in terms of that world into which he gazed, a weakling. His teeth, though strong for chewing on the tough fruits of the forest, or for crunching an occasional unwary bird caught with his prehensile hands, were not the tearing sabers of the great cats. He had a passion for lifting himself up to see about, in his restless, roving curiosity. He would run a little stiffly and uncertainly, perhaps, on his hind legs, but only in those rare moments when he ventured out upon the ground. All this was the legacy of his climbing days; he had a hand with flexible fingers and no fine specialized hoofs upon which to gallop like the wind.

If he had any idea of competing in that new world, he had better 12 forget it; teeth or hooves, he was much too late for either. He was a ne'er-do-well, an in-betweener. Nature had not done well by him. It was as if she had hesitated and never quite made up her mind. Perhaps as a consequence he had a malicious gleam in his eye, the gleam of an outcast who has been left nothing and knows he is going to have to take what he gets. One day a little band of these odd apes—for apes they were—shambled out upon the grass; the human story had begun.

Apes were to become men, in the inscrutable wisdom of nature, 13 because flowers had produced seeds and fruits in such tremendous quantities that a new and totally different store of energy had become available in concentrated form. Impressive as the slow-moving, dim-brained dinosaurs had been, it is doubtful if their age had supported anything like the diversity of life that now rioted across the planet or flashed in and out among the trees. Down on the grass by a streamside, one of those apes with inquisitive fingers turned over a stone and hefted it vaguely. The group clucked together in a throaty tongue and moved off through the tall grass foraging for seeds and insects. The one still held, sniffed, and hefted the stone he had found. He liked the feel of it in his fingers. The attack on the animal world was about to begin.

If one could run the story of that first human group like a 14 speeded-up motion picture through a million years of time, one might see the stone in the hand change to the flint ax and the torch. All that swarming grassland world with its giant bison and trumpeting mammoths would go down in ruin to feed the insatiable and growing numbers of a carnivore who, like the great cats before him, was taking his energy indirectly from the grass. Later he found fire and it altered the tough meats and drained their energy even faster into a stomach ill adapted for the ferocious turn man's habits had taken.

His limbs grew longer, he strode more purposefully over the 15 grass. The stolen energy that would take man across the continents would fail him at last. The great Ice Age herds were destined to vanish. When they did so, another hand like the hand that grasped the stone by the river long ago would pluck a handful of grass seed and hold it contemplatively.

In that moment, the golden towers of man, his swarming mil- 16 lions, his turning wheels, the vast learning of his packed libraries, would glimmer dimly there in the ancestor of wheat, a few seeds held in a muddy hand. Without the gift of flowers and the infinite diversity of their fruits, man and bird, if they had continued to exist at all, would be today unrecognizable. Archaeopteryx, the lizard-bird, might still be snapping at beetles on a sequoia limb; man might still be a nocturnal insectivore gnawing a roach in the dark. The weight of a petal has changed the face of the world and made it ours.

Questions on Meaning

1   What stages does the author delineate in the process by which "flowers" changed plant life? How did angiosperms change animal life?

2   Why did the human being, "a strange, old-fashioned animal," hesitate to become involved in the changing world? How did flowers eventually change even this creature?

3   Exaggeration is often used to describe the process of evolution, be it a statement that "flowers changed the world," that man descended from

monkeys, or that heaven and earth were created in six days. Why does this subject lend itself to exaggeration, or hyperbole? What other subjects are likewise subject to hyperbole?

Questions on Method

1 Eiseley uses description in the service of his narrative of evolution. At what points in the essay does he describe the visual appearance of evolving life? What spatial arrangement does he use?

2 Eiseley uses many figures of speech to dramatize the story of evolution. In addition to the simile in "All over the world, like hot corn in a popper, these incredible elaborations of the flowering plants kept exploding" (6), he also uses personification, as in "These fantastic little seeds skipping and hopping and flying about" (5). Find other examples of personification in the essay. How are they effective?

3 Eiseley also uses hyperbole or poetic exaggeration. In addition to the title of the essay, what examples of hyperbole does he use in the essay? Why are these figures of speech effective?

Vocabulary and Diction

1 Eiseley was both a poet and an anthropologist. Make one list of the scientific words he uses and a second list of the poetic words. Define unfamiliar words on both lists such as "vagaries" (1), "metabolic" (8), and "prehensile" (11). Is the combination of scientific and poetic language effective? Discuss.

Writing Topics

1 Narrate a process, using description to clarify your narrative at whatever points you think necessary.

2 Describe a scene, a person, or an object using figures of speech—simile, personification, or hyperbole—to enhance your description wherever possible.

RICHARD SELZER (1928–   ) is a fellow of Ezra Stiles College
of Yale University. He teaches surgery at Yale Medical School
and is a frequent contributor to *Harper's, Esquire,* and *Redbook.*
His *Rituals of Surgery,* a collection of short stories, was
published in 1974, and his autobiographical essays, collected in
Mortal Lessons, appeared in 1977. In the following essay from
Mortal Lessons he conveys through the acute perception of a
doctor the alienating experience of being a terminally ill
patient in a typical medical institution.

The Discus Thrower

Richard Selzer

I spy on my patients. Ought not a doctor to observe his patients by   1
any means and from any stance, that he might the more fully assemble
evidence? So I stand in the doorways of hospital rooms and gaze. Oh,
it is not all that furtive an act. Those in bed need only look up to
discover me. But they never do.

From the doorway of Room 542 the man in the bed seems deeply   2
tanned. Blue eyes and close-cropped white hair give him the appearance of vigor and good health. But I know that his skin is not brown
from the sun. It is rusted, rather, in the last stage of containing the
vile repose within. And the blue eyes are frosted, looking inward like
the windows of a snowbound cottage. This man is blind. This man
is also legless—the right leg missing from midthigh down, the left
from just below the knee. It gives him the look of a bonsai, roots and
branches pruned into the dwarfed facsimile of a great tree.

Propped on pillows, he cups his right thigh in both hands. Now   3
and then he shakes his head as though acknowledging the intensity

of his suffering. In all of this he makes no sound. Is he mute as well as blind?

The room in which he dwells is empty of all possessions—no 4
get-well cards, small, private caches of food, day-old flowers, slippers, all the usual kickshaws of the sickroom. There is only the bed, a chair, a nightstand, and a tray on wheels that can be swung across his lap for meals.

"What time is it?" he asks. 5

"Three o'clock." 6

"Morning or afternoon?" 7

"Afternoon." 8

He is silent. There is nothing else he wants to know. 9

"How are you?" I say. 10

"Who is it?" he asks. 11

"It's the doctor. How do you feel?" 12

He does not answer right away. 13

"Feel?" he says. 14

"I hope you feel better," I say. 15

I press the button at the side of the bed. 16

"Down you go," I say. 17

"Yes, down," he says. 18

He falls back upon the bed awkwardly. His stumps, unweighted 19
by legs and feet, rise in the air, presenting themselves. I unwrap the bandages from the stumps, and begin to cut away the black scabs and the dead, glazed fat with scissors and forceps. A shard of white bone comes loose. I pick it away. I wash the wounds with disinfectant and redress the stumps. All this while, he does not speak. What is he thinking behind those lids that do not blink? Is he remembering a time when he was whole? Does he dream of feet? Of when his body was not a rotting log?

He lies solid and inert. In spite of everything, he remains im- 20
pressive, as though he were a sailor standing athwart a slanting deck.

"Anything more I can do for you?" I ask. 21

For a long moment he is silent. 22

"Yes," he says at last and without the least irony. "You can bring 23
me a pair of shoes."

In the corridor, the head nurse is waiting for me. 24

"We have to do something about him," she says. "Every morning 25
he orders scrambled eggs for breakfast, and, instead of eating them, he picks up the plate and throws it against the wall."

"Throws his plate?" 26

"Nasty. That's what he is. No wonder his family doesn't come 27
to visit. They probably can't stand him any more than we can."

She is waiting for me to do something. 28

"Well?" 29

"We'll see," I say. 30

The next morning I am waiting in the corridor when the kitchen 31
delivers his breakfast. I watch the aide place the tray on the stand
and swing it across his lap. She presses the button to raise the head
of the bed. Then she leaves.

In time the man reaches to find the rim of the tray, then on to 32
find the dome of the covered dish. He lifts off the cover and places
it on the stand. He fingers across the plate until he probes the eggs.
He lifts the plate in both hands, sets it on the palm of his right hand,
centers it, balances it. He hefts it up and down slightly, getting the
feel of it. Abruptly, he draws back his right arm as far as he can.

There is the crack of the plate breaking against the wall at the 33
foot of his bed and the small wet sound of the scrambled eggs dropping
to the floor.

And then he laughs. It is a sound you have never heard. It is 34
something new under the sun. It could cure cancer.

Out in the corridor, the eyes of the head nurse narrow. 35

"Laughed, did he?" 36

She writes something down on her clipboard. 37

A second aide arrives, brings a second breakfast tray, puts it on 38
the nightstand, out of his reach. She looks over at me shaking her
head and making her mouth go. I see that we are to be accomplices.

"I've got to feed you," she says to the man. 39

"Oh, no you don't," the man says. 40

"Oh, yes I do," the aide says, "after the way you just did. Nurse 41
says so."

"Get me my shoes," the man says. 42

"Here's oatmeal," the aide says. "Open." And she touches the 43
spoon to his lower lip.

"I ordered scrambled eggs," says the man. 44

"That's right," the aide says. 45

I step forward. 46

"Is there anything I can do?" I say. 47

"Who are you?" the man asks. 48

In the evening I go once more to that ward to make my rounds. 49
The head nurse reports to me that Room 542 is deceased. She has
discovered this quite by accident, she says. No, there had been no
sound. Nothing. It's a blessing, she says.

I go into his room, a spy looking for secrets. He is still there in 50
his bed. His face is relaxed, grave, dignified. After a while, I turn to
leave. My gaze sweeps the wall at the foot of the bed, and I see the
place where it has been repeatedly washed, where the wall looks very
clean and very white.

Questions on Meaning

1 Explain the meaning of the title of the essay. Why is the metaphor an
   appropriate one for this patient?

2 Why does Selzer describe himself as a "spy"? How does his attitude
   toward the patient compare to the attitude of the nurse or the two aides?
   Is he more or less curious about the patient? Is he more or less emotional
   about him? Explain, citing details.

3 To what extent is the patient really "nasty," as the nurse says? Why, for
   example, does the patient keep asking for a pair of shoes? Why does
   Selzer tell us that the patient asks this "without the least irony"?

4 Why does Selzer in paragraph 19 narrate the process by which he treats
   the patient's legs? Compare this to Selzer's narration in paragraph 32 of
   the process the patient goes through to throw his breakfast against the
   wall. How do such elaborate preparations affect our understanding of
   both men?

5 Discuss the comparison Selzer makes in paragraph 2 between the patient's
   "frosted" eyes and the windows of a "snowbound" cottage. How does
   Selzer's description in paragraph 4 of the emptiness of the sickroom
   indicate something about his first impression of the patient's mental
   condition? How does the simile in paragraph 20 that compares the
   patient to "a sailor standing athwart a slanting deck" suggest that Selzer's
   first impression is beginning to change?

6 In paragraph 11 the patient asks Selzer, "Who is it?" The next morning
   he asks, "Who are you?" Why does he repeat the question?

7 Discuss Selzer's final observation about how "clean" and "white" the wall
   looks after the patient has died. How does Selzer's description of the wall
   symbolize his feelings about both the patient and the treatment the
   patient received?

Questions on Method

1   What does Selzer describe objectively in his essay? What effect do these descriptions have on our understanding of the patient's actions? What spatial arrangements does the author use?

2   How does Selzer's scientific method of gathering "evidence" to reach a conclusion lead to his impression of the patient? What role does description play in this evidence?

3   Why is this essay, despite its narrative elements, considered here under "Description," whereas Kazantzakis's essay, which also includes both description and narration, is considered under "Narration"? How do the roles of narration and description differ in the two essays?

Vocabulary and Diction

1   What is a "bonsai" (2)? Does Selzer define the word for you? Is the word an apt description of the patient?

2   What are "kickshaws" (4)? What play on words makes Selzer's use of this word ironic?

3   In paragraph 49 why does the nurse say that "Room 542" is deceased? What does her use of the room number rather than the patient's name indicate about her attitude toward the patient? Why doesn't the patient's name appear at all in the essay?

4   Define the following words and phrases used by Selzer: furtive (1), vile repose (2), dwarfed facsimile (2), glazed fat (19), shard (19).

Writing Topics

1   Have you or has someone you know ever been hospitalized? Describe the character of the treatment received from the hospital staff. Write an essay discussing why people who work in hospitals might often treat patients coldly and distantly.

2   Describe a place where you had an unpleasant experience; use detail sufficient to convey why your surroundings added to the unpleasantness of the experience.

3   Describe a place in such detail that your overall impression of it would be conveyed to a reader. Place your impression at the end of the essay, as does Selzer, rather than at the beginning.

4   Hospital personnel, both doctors and nurses, must pay close attention to a patient's visual appearance as well as to his or her oral complaints or test results. Describe a person's appearance in such detail that his or her state of health will be apparent.

Description—Writing Topics

1 What is the most important difference between the organization of an effective description and the organization of an effective narration? Illustrate your answer by writing an essay that first describes the details of a place you have visited and then tells a story about something that happened there.

2 Describe the flavor of what it is like to live in a certain place so that someone who lives in an entirely different environment can understand your description. To make your essay understandable to such a reader, use metaphors and similes.

3 What part does an author's tone play in affecting our response to his or her descriptions? How do an emotional, lyric tone and a detached, scientific tone differ in focusing a reader's attention and interest on the details of a description? Discuss this question by comparing your response to Kazin's essay with your response to Selzer's or Darwin's essay.

4 Which of the authors in this section do you think has written the most objective description? Write an essay that defends your answer by comparing the description you find most objective to one you find most subjective.

5 Write an essay in which description is used in the service of narration, as Eiseley, Selzer, or Darwin use it. Decide first what event you wish to narrate and then what aspects of the event—places, people, objects—the reader must visualize to understand the actions.

6 Use narration to aid in the description of a place, as Kazin does in "Brownsville Food." Select characteristic incidents whose narration will convey the flavor of the place described.

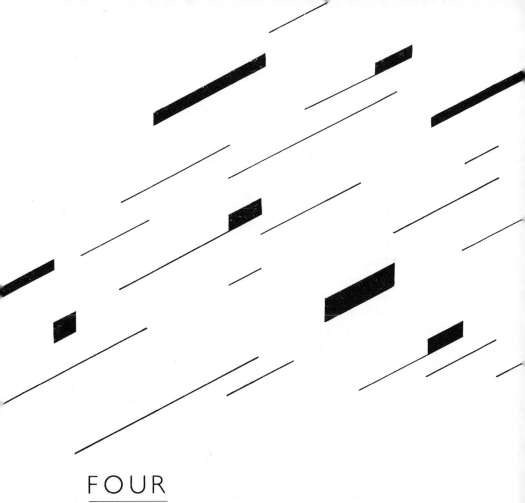

FOUR
Illustration and Example

In a nutshell, exposition consists of progression from the general to the specific (or vice versa), the general being the inclusive, or umbrella, statement. The specific is the particular parts, the details, the things included or implied. The general statement that includes or implies the specifics of a whole paragraph is called the "topic sentence."

Which of these three sentences includes or implies the others?

1   The population of the United States is as mobile as ever.

2   In 1980 the Sun Belt picked up seventeen seats in the House of Representatives.

3   The price of electricity in Atlanta is the lowest in the country.

The answer is statement 1. In fact, the first statement implies many more specifics or details than could be included in a single paragraph; and thus it could be the generalization—called the "thesis"—of a lengthy essay with statements 2 and 3 as topic sentences (lesser generalizations) for paragraphs within that essay. The progression we speak of, then, would consist of the most general, statement 1, leading to the less general (or more specific) statement 2, which in turn would lead to still more specific details, such as "Texas picked up five seats; Georgia, two; and Florida, three."

"Illustration" and "example" are names of two kinds of specifics, an illustration being a longer example with some of the elements of narrative, such as characters and action. As discussed in Chapter 2, stories are frequently told to illustrate a point, or generalization; such stories or illustrations are one kind of "specific," one way to apply a general statement or thesis to a particular set of circumstances. Consider, for example, this story from *The Autobiography of Mark Twain*:

> I was always told that I was a sickly and precarious and tiresome and uncertain child and lived mainly on allopathic medicines during the first seven years of my life. I asked my mother about this, in her old age—she was in her eighty-eighth year—and said:
> "I suppose that during all that time you were uneasy about me?"
> "Yes, the whole time."
> "Afraid I wouldn't live?"
> After a reflective pause—ostensibly to think out the facts—"No—afraid you would."
> It sounds like plagiarism but it probably wasn't.*

The reader of exposition (or nonfiction in general) expects a generalization like "Science has failed us" to be accompanied by a group of specifics such as "Science cannot answer moral questions," "Computers can perform only to the level of their programming," and "Technology has bad side-effects." The purpose of examples and

---

*The Autobiography of Mark Twain. Ed. Charles Neider, Washington Square Press, 1961, p. 12.

illustrations is to interest the reader, to clarify the major points, and to persuade the reader of the truth of the generalizations. The choice of example varies widely in length, number, specificity, familiarity, and so on, depending on the audience and the writer's purpose. But sooner or later the transition from general to specific (or vice versa) must occur. The first excerpt below, from Hannah Arendt's "Denmark and the 'Final Solution,'" is not clear when isolated from the supporting examples she provides later in the text; the second, all examples, is pointless:

> One is tempted to recommend the story [of the Danish Jews] as required reading in political science for all students who wish to learn something about the enormous power potential inherent in non-violent action and in resistance to an opponent possessing vastly superior means of violence.

> Golf is a case in point. Fishing is worse. Sailing is another. People may devote themselves to music.

There are no rules about the number or specificity of examples, but it is probably safe to say the more, the better. Examples, logically, can do no more than indicate a trend or direction (unlike the list of classes in classification, a list of examples need not be exhaustive); but they can also convey the writer's mastery of the subject and sensitivity to the supposed audience and incline the reader to accept the generalizations or conclusions of the essay.

Specificity is relative. The word "specific" is meaningless except in relation to a more inclusive generalization, and what is specific in one context may be general in another. The so-called specific mentioned earlier, "Science cannot answer moral questions," is quite *un*specific when one considers the number of research projects, the number of possible moral questions that societies ask, and the practical implications of both. The writer would probably want to explain *why* science cannot answer moral questions and to give further, more specific examples of scientific research that led to trivial or dangerous results before a convincing level of specificity could be reached.

When writing an essay, in every paragraph you are probably going to be dealing with a topic or subtopic that can be expressed as a general statement (topic sentence). You usually have the choice of beginning with either that topic sentence or the specific examples, and there are advantages to both orders. The generalization-first order is clearer and easier to read because the reader knows exactly what each example is supposed to support or prove; everything falls into place. This order is called deduction. The examples-first order challenges the reader to try to guess what it all adds up to; this is induction, which may make the reader feel included in the thinking process, and it may allow for a dramatic, climactic ending. If your paragraph is long and complex enough, you may want to combine the two orders, beginning with a general statement, going into your examples or illustrations, and returning to a restatement of your topic sentence at the end of the paragraph. Entire essays, as well as single paragraphs, may be developed by both inductive and deductive organization. Whereas many writers begin with an idea and search for examples to support it, other writers, such as scientists, begin with observations of facts (examples) and then formulate a theory about them. As usual, it is helpful to use such transitional words and phrases as "for example" and "finally" to guide the reader.

Developing Essays with Examples and Illustrations

1 Use many examples: the more, the better.
2 Make your examples specific. If possible, make your second and third examples more specific than your first.
3 Experiment with order, choosing from generalization first, examples first, or a combination of the two, depending on your purpose.
4 Use examples and illustrations that are appropriate to your audience.

WOODY ALLEN (1935–   ) was born in Brooklyn and remains a New York City resident. He has made many films, including *Annie Hall*, *Interiors*, and *Manhattan*. He is also the author of *Getting Even* (1971) and *Without Feathers* (1975), both of which reflect his social, satirical wit. This essay, which appeared originally in the *New York Times*, was Allen's advice to 1979 college graduates.

My Speech to the Graduates

Woody Allen

More than any other time in history, mankind faces a crossroads. One path leads to despair and utter hopelessness. The other, to total extinction. Let us pray we have the wisdom to choose correctly. I speak, by the way, not with any sense of futility, but with a panicky conviction of the absolute meaninglessness of existence which could easily be misinterpreted as pessimism. It is not. It is merely a healthy concern for the predicament of modern man. (Modern man is here defined as any person born after Nietzsche's edict that "God is dead," but before the hit recording "I Wanna Hold Your Hand.") This "predicament" can be stated one of two ways, though certain linguistic philosophers prefer to reduce it to a mathematical equation where it can be easily solved and even carried around in the wallet.

Put in its simplest form, the problem is: How is it possible to find meaning in a finite world given my waist and shirt size? This is a very difficult question when we realize that science has failed us. True, it has conquered many diseases, broken the genetic code, and even placed human beings on the moon, and yet when a man of 80 is left in a room with two 18-year-old cocktail waitresses nothing happens. Because the real problems never change. After all, can the human soul be glimpsed through a microscope? Maybe—but you'd definitely need one of those very good ones with two eyepieces. We know that the most advanced computer in the world does not have a brain as sophisticated as that of an ant. True, we could say that of many of our relatives but we only have to put up with them at weddings or special occasions. Science is something we depend on all the time. If I develop a pain in the chest I must take an X-ray. But what if the radiation from the X-ray causes me deeper problems? Before I know it, I'm going in for surgery. Naturally, while they're giving me oxygen an intern decides to light up a cigarette. The next thing you know I'm rocketing over the World Trade Center in bed clothes. Is this science? True, science has taught us how to pasteurize cheese. And true, this can be fun in mixed company—but what of the H-bomb? Have you ever seen what happens when one of those things falls off a desk accidentally? And where is science when one ponders the eternal riddles? How did the cosmos originate? How long has it been around? Did matter begin with an explosion or by the word of God? And if by the latter, could He not have begun it just two weeks earlier to take advantage of some of the warmer weather? Exactly what do we mean when we say, man is mortal? Obviously it's not a compliment.

Religion too has unfortunately let us down. Miguel de Unamuno writes blithely of the "eternal persistence of consciousness," but this is no easy feat. Particularly when reading Thackeray. I often think how comforting life must have been for early man because he believed in a powerful, benevolent Creator who looked after all things. Imagine his disappointment when he saw his wife putting on weight. Contemporary man, of course, has no such peace of mind. He finds himself in the midst of a crisis of faith. He is what we fashionably call "alienated." He has seen the ravages of war, he has known natural catastrophes, he has been to singles bars. My good friend Jacques Monod spoke often of the randomness of the cosmos. He believed everything in existence occurred by pure chance with the possible exception of his breakfast, which he felt certain was made by his housekeeper. Naturally belief in a divine intelligence inspires tranquility. But this does not free us from our human responsibilities. Am I my brother's keeper? Yes. Interestingly, in my case I share that honor with the Prospect Park Zoo. Feeling godless then, what we have done is made technology God. And yet can technology really be the answer when a brand new Buick, driven by my close associate, Nat Persky, winds up in the window of Chicken Delight causing hundreds of customers to scatter? My toaster has never once worked properly in four years. I follow the instructions and push two slices of bread down in the slots and seconds later they rifle upward. Once they broke the nose of a woman I loved very dearly. Are we counting on nuts and bolts and electricity to solve our problems? Yes, the telephone is a good thing—and the refrigerator—and the air conditioner. But not every air conditioner. Not my sister Henny's, for instance. Hers makes a loud noise and still doesn't cool. When the man comes over to fix it, it gets worse. Either that or he tells her she needs a new one. When she complains, he says not to bother him. This man is truly alienated. Not only is he alienated but he can't stop smiling.

The trouble is, our leaders have not adequately prepared us for a mechanized society. Unfortunately our politicians are either incompetent or corrupt. Sometimes both on the same day. The Government is unresponsive to the needs of the little man. Under five-seven, it is impossible to get your Congressman on the phone. I am not denying that democracy is still the finest form of government. In a democracy at least, civil liberties are upheld. No citizen can be wantonly tortured, imprisoned, or made to sit through certain Broadway shows. And yet this is a far cry from what goes on in the Soviet Union. Under their form of totalitarianism, a person merely caught whistling is sentenced to 30 years in a labor camp. If, after 15 years, he still will not stop whistling they shoot him. Along with this brutal fascism we find its handmaiden, terrorism. At no other time in history has man been so afraid to cut into his veal chop for fear that it will explode. Violence breeds more violence and it is predicted that by 1990 kidnapping will be the dominant mode of social interaction. Overpopulation will exacerbate problems to the breaking point. Figures tell us there are already more people on earth than we need to move even the heaviest piano. If we do not call a halt to breeding, by the year 2000 there will be no room to serve dinner unless one is willing to set the table on the heads of strangers. Then they must not move for an hour while we eat. Of course energy will be in short supply and each car owner will be allowed only enough gasoline to back up a few inches.

Instead of facing these challenges we turn instead to distractions

4

5

123

like drugs and sex. We live in far too permissive a society. Never before has pornography been this rampant. And those films are lit so badly! We are a people who lack defined goals. We have never learned to love. We lack leaders and coherent programs. We have no spiritual center. We are adrift alone in the cosmos wreaking monstrous violence on one another out of frustration and pain. Fortunately, we have not lost our sense of proportion. Summing up, it is clear the future holds great opportunities. It also holds pitfalls. The trick will be to avoid the pitfalls, seize the opportunities, and get back home by six o'clock.

Questions on Meaning

1 What is "the predicament of modern man" according to Woody Allen?
2 In paragraph 2 Allen says that despite the great discoveries of science, "the real problems never change." What problems does he mean?
3 According to Allen, why do people feel "godless" or "alienated" today? What is the result of this feeling? Why in paragraph 3 does Allen say about the air conditioner repairman, "Not only is he alienated but he can't stop smiling"? How does this example illustrate something about what Allen considers the "real problems"? How do his other examples of the failure of technology help us understand what these "real problems" are?
4 Why does Allen think, as he states in paragraph 4, that "democracy is still the finest form of government"? How optimistic is Allen about the survival of democracy in the modern world? What examples of threats to the democratic way of life does he offer?
5 What solutions to the modern predicament does Allen suggest in his last paragraph? How important is his sense of humor as a possible solution?

Questions on Method

1 Allen's essay is a parody, a humorous imitation, of the sort of speech given at graduation exercises. In what sense is Allen mocking such serious attempts to discuss modern problems as are exemplified in this section's essays by Lance Morrow and Flora Mancuso Edwards? Compare, for example, the comic quality of Allen's criticism in paragraph 5 or the "permissive" style of American society to the earnest quality of Lance Morrow's criticism in "Back to Reticence!"

2 How satirical is the tone of Allen's parody? In other words, how much is his humor meant as a serious criticism of contemporary problems and failings? Compare Allen's tone to Russell Baker's in "The Paradox of the New Leisure" or to Jonathan Swift's in "A Modest Proposal."

3 Allen uses many standard prose patterns and rhetorical devices to make us laugh. Find examples in his essay of illustration and example, definition, contrast and comparison, cause and effect, parallel phrasing, understatement, and exaggeration. How does he use these to comic effect?

4 Often Allen's punch lines are humorous because they deflate or undercut a serious idea. Discuss Allen's use of the technique of comic deflation. Focus, for example, on such lines as "Let us pray we have the wisdom to choose correctly" (1), "Obviously it's not a compliment" (2), "Particularly when reading Thackeray" (3), "Sometimes both on the same day" (4), "And those films are lit so badly" (5). Can you pick out other examples of comic deflation in the essay?

5 Where in each of his paragraphs does Allen place his generalizations, at the beginning or at the end? How would the effect differ had he used a different arrangement?

Vocabulary and Diction

1 What is "pessimism" (1)? Although Allen asserts that he is not pessimistic, is it possible that his humor masks his pessimism?

2 How does Allen play with the meaning of words for humorous effect? Focus on such examples as the lines in paragraph 4, "Under five-seven, it is impossible to get your Congressman on the phone" and "it is predicted that by 1990 kidnapping will be the dominant mode of social interaction."

3 Define the following words and phrases used by Allen: extinction (1), linguistic philosophers (1), finite (2), ravages (3), wantonly (4), totalitarianism (4), handmaiden (4), exacerbate (4), rampant (5), coherent (5), wreaking (5).

Writing Topics

1 Do you agree with Allen that despite the political, social, and scientific changes that have been experienced throughout history, the "real problems" of life remain much the same today as they were in the past? Write an essay that supports your answer with convincing examples.

2 Drawing on the persuasive technique of illustrations and examples, discuss whether contemporary life is something to feel pessimistic or optimistic about.

3 Try writing a parody of one of the more serious essays in this section using Allen's technique of examples that are comic deflations.

LANCE MORROW was born in Philadelphia and is a graduate of Harvard University. During his journalistic career, he spent several years on the staff of the *Washington Star*. He has published several volumes of poetry and is currently an essay writer for *Time* magazine. In "Back to Reticence!" Morrow advocates departing from the present philosophy of "letting it all hang out" and returning to the decorum of the past.

Back to Reticence!

Lance Morrow

Cultivated to a high degree by art and science, we are civilized to the point where we are overburdened with all sorts of social propriety and decency.

—Immanuel Kant, 1874

1 Jimmy Connors does not labor under Kant's burden. Sometimes when the tennis gets intense, Connors grabs his crotch and shakes it for the crowd. He pelts the linesmen and judges with rotten language. He shoots his finger. The umpire usually responds with the flustered and ineffectual dismay of a curate who has discovered the servants copulating in his study.

2 This sort of court behavior, also indulged in by John McEnroe and Ilie Nastase, is what kindergarten teachers call "age inappropriate." It is punk tennis, the transformation of a formerly pristine game into the moral equivalent of roller derby. The spectacle is symptomatic of something that has befallen the American's idea of how one ought to behave. What would once have been intolerable

and impermissible public conduct has now become commonplace. If it is not exactly accepted, then at least it is abjectly and wearily endured.

Social habit in the U.S. has taken decisive turns toward the awful. Since the end of World War II, Americans have been steadily relinquishing their inhibitions about the social consequences of their actions. They have lost a crucial sense of community, even while highways, jets, satellite TV signals and leisure travel have brought them physically closer together. The social environment has grown polluted along with the natural; a headlong greed and self-absorption have sponsored both contaminations. Somehow, Americans have also misplaced the moral confidence with which to condemn sleaziness and stupidity. It is as if something in the American judgment snapped, and has remained so long unrepaired that no one notices any more.

The daily grind of the offensive is both tiring and obscurely humiliating. It is impossible to watch the nightly news on network television without being treated to a stream of 30-second treatises on hemorrhoids, tampons, feminine deodorant sprays and constipation. "I want to talk to you about diarrhea," says the earnest pitchman. T shirts, sweatshirts and bumper stickers proclaim their aggressive little editorials. Some are mildly funny (a woman's T shirt, for example, that says SO MANY MEN, SO LITTLE TIME). But often they are crude with a faintly alarming determination to affront, even sometimes to menace. They are filled with belligerent scatology. Something or other always SUCKS.

Constitutionally protected grossness—edible underwear, the vibrators in the drugstore window, massage parlors, sex merchandised in its pervasive richness—has spread the pornographic spirit widely. The Twelfth Night Masque, the oldest private subscription ball in Chicago and hitherto a bastion of Midwestern decorum, has suffered a recent rash of crudity. Last year some guests showed up at the ball dressed as hemorrhoids when President Carter was so afflicted; two years before, when the masque theme was "The Father of Our Country," a number of Lake Shore socialites appeared as penises or sperm. No one proposes calling out a SWAT team to deal with this sort of whoopee-cushion wit. It is not sullenly antisocial, like the blaring radios the size of steamer trunks that adolescents haul onto public buses to cook up a small pot of community rage, or the occasional pistols that got waved in gas lines.

Much of today's offensiveness began in the guise of a refreshing   6
virtue: honesty. The doctrine of "letting it all hang out" got propa-
gated in the headlong idealism of the late '60s. The result is a legacy
of insufferable and interminable candor. The idealism has vanished
into the mainstream of the culture or into thin air. We are left with
the residue of bad habits, ugly noises and moral slackness.

As in some burlesque science fiction, the nation seems to have   7
been injected with a truth serum designed to make people bore one
another to death: it has given them a compulsion to confide embarrassing intimacies, has led them on to endless emotional ostentations,
as if, as Saul Bellow once wrote, "to keep the wolf of insignificance
from the door." A man sits down at a New Jersey dinner party, beside
a woman he met half an hour before, and hears in elaborately explicit
detail from soup through coffee, how the woman and her husband
managed to conquer their sexual incompatibility with the help of a
sex therapist. A magazine writer not long ago met the new young
husband of Novelist Erica Jong at a party and realized with a disagreeable little jolt that she knew from Jong's novel *How to Save Your
Own Life* just how large the husband's penis was.

The book racks are filled with volumes of confession and revenge.   8
People rush to destroy their own privacy, possibly judging that loneliness is worse. In the past ten or twelve years everything has tumbled
out of the closet in a heap. Some homosexuals parade themselves like
walking billboards, the placement of the keys and handkerchiefs in
their back pockets acting as a semaphore to signal the specific secrets
of their sexual tastes.

The depressing quality of much American public behavior—from   9
Connors to T shirts—is its edgy meanness. Bad enough that it is
calculatedly cheap. Worse is the stolid nastiness of it, the rock in the
snowball, the compulsion to affront. Even relentless candor—wounding friends or family by telling them their defects in the name of
honesty—is a symptom not only of stupidity but also of unkindness
and buried anger.

There are doubtless profound cultural reasons for such anger: the   10
aggressive self-regard of the era now perhaps passing the centrifugal
individualism, the loss of authority, the sense of alienation from "the
System," a precipitous disenchantment that tended to discredit all

rules, including those of social behavior. It is possible that the price of a certain amount of personal liberty is excess and mess, all the frictions and bad smells generated by social change and people exercising their constitutional rights. Jefferson had an idea that democracy should be genteel, but it did not work out that way. And today, there is no point in growing as mistily sentimental as a Soviet realist hack about the pleasures of right thinking and conformity.

Still, it is possible that the '80s are going to demand some virtues 11
unknown in the '60s and '70s—self-control, self-discipline, stoicism, decorum, even inhibition and a little puritanism. It may be time for a touch of reticence. Coercion cannot produce such attitudes, but the mood of the time may. Americans may find themselves agreeing in some paraphrase of Elihu Root when he walked through a squalid Siberian village as Woodrow Wilson's emissary in the first Soviet revolutionary dawn. "I'm a firm believer in democracy," he said, as he skeptically eyed his surroundings. "But I do not like filth."

Questions on Meaning

1 Explain the opening line of Morrow's essay, "Jimmy Connors does not labor under Kant's burden." How do Morrow's examples of the behavior of tennis players prepare us to understand the thesis of his essay? Where is this thesis stated?

2 In paragraph 3 Morrow says, "The social environment has grown polluted along with the natural; a headlong greed and self-absorption have sponsored both contaminations." Is America's social environment as polluted as Morrow suggests?

3 Explain what Morrow means when he says in paragraph 9 that the grossness and crudity of this behavior are symptoms "not only of stupidity but also of unkindness and buried anger." What do Americans have to be angry about?

4 What "virtues" does Morrow hope will change American social behavior in the 1980s?

Questions on Method

1 In paragraph 5 Morrow contrasts what he calls the "pornographic spirit" of commercials and T-shirt slogans to the more "sullenly antisocial" behavior exemplified by adolescents "blaring" their radios on public

buses. How does this contrast prepare us to understand the more threatening side of American social behavior that Morrow focuses on in paragraphs 9 and 10? What examples of this threatening behavior does he cite?

2   Discuss Morrow's use of the metaphor of pollution throughout his essay. How well do the examples in his fourth and fifth paragraphs illustrate the idea that American social life has become polluted? How does Morrow return to this metaphor again in paragraphs 6 and 10? What other metaphors does Morrow employ to good effect?

3   Morrow uses many examples in support of his argument that our social habits are "awful." A good argument usually includes some recognition of an opposing point of view. Does Morrow anywhere admit that there are some decent social manners? What examples of decent behavior has he excluded?

Vocabulary and Diction

1   Look up the meaning of the word "scatology" (4). How does this word reflect Morrow's theme about the pollution of American social life? What does this word connote or imply about the anger that Morrow thinks lies behind the grossness of social behavior?

2   In paragraph 6 Morrow makes a distinction between two words, "honesty" and "candor," that ordinarily are considered synonyms. Why is it necessary for him to give different connotations to two words that share identical denotations? How do his examples in paragraphs 7 and 8 help us understand how the virtue of honesty turns into the fault of candor? How does Morrow's use of the slang expression "letting it all hang out" convey his disrespect for such candor?

3   Define the following words and phrases used by Morrow: curate (1), punk tennis (2), pristine (2), abjectly (2), treatises (4), bastion (5), centrifugal (10), precipitous disenchantment (10), genteel (10), stoicism (11), decorum (11), squalid (11), emissary (11).

Writing Topics

1   Write an essay about television commercials, citing examples sufficient to indicate a conclusion about American advertisers' perception of the marketplace.

2 Do you agree with Morrow that Americans have taken the idea of "letting it all hang out" too far? Write an essay agreeing or disagreeing with Morrow, making use of illustrative examples.

3 In paragraph 10 Morrow says, "It is possible that the price of a certain amount of personal liberty is excess and mess." Write an essay in which you define what sort of excessive behavior is allowable in maintaining liberty. Cite appropriate examples.

4 Write an essay in which, like Morrow, you attempt to prove a controversial point through sheer number of examples.

RUSSELL BAKER (1925–   ) is a regular columnist for the *New York Times*. He began his career in journalism with the *Baltimore Sun*, and in 1954 he joined the Washington bureau of the *New York Times*. His books include *An American in Washington* (1961), *All Things Considered* (1965), and *Poor Russell's Almanac* (1972). In this essay from the *New York Times* Baker discusses the problems leisure poses for many people.

The Paradox of the New Leisure

Russell Baker

With the onset of the vacation season the real problem of the new   1
leisure becomes obvious. Leisure pastime in this country has become
so complicated that it is now hard work.

Golf is a case in point. A big thing to do with leisure time is to   2
golf it away. All well and good for those who grew up next door to
the golf links, but what of the millions who wasted their muscular
years working up to golfing status and now come to the game unable
to tell a five-iron from a backhand?

It is impossible for them to drop by a golf course, borrow some-   3
body's clubs, and start swinging away. Even on most public courses
one needs an appointment to tee off, and people who hate making
fools of themselves in public often need instruction from a professor.

To golf in style—and style is almost everything in the new   4
leisure—a club membership is *de rigueur*. A golf wardrobe has to be
bought. Clubs, too. And people who hate making fools of themselves
before golf-club salesmen will need preliminary instruction in the

difference between a mashie and a niblick, if that is what they are called.

Fishing is worse. The party who remembers fishing as a time killer performed along creek banks with a length of twine, a beanpole, ten cents' worth of hooks, and a can of worms is in for deep shock at the sporting-goods shop today.

First off, the salesman wants to know what kind of fishing he means to do. Like everything else, today's fishing is for specialists. Admit that you want to put worms on a hook and angle for sunfish and they will rise from their spinners, flies, and four-ply nylon coelacanth casting line and laugh you out of existence.

Modern fishing is as complicated as flying a B-58 to Tacoma. Several years of preliminary library and desk work are essential just to be able to buy equipment without humiliation.

Sailing is another popular time killer, though it is hard to see why, considering all the study and labor it involves. In the first place, it means buying a boat, then finding some place to keep the thing, then finding someone to explain the difference between tacking and keelhauling.

It is also dangerous. Tack when you should be keelhauling, and it may be the end of the new leisure.

People who fear proving themselves inadequate at golf, fishing, and sailing may, of course, devote themselves to the passive culture, music, for example. They soon discover, however, that harmonizing the soul with Berlioz isn't so easy.

The day when a man bought a phonograph, put Berlioz on the turntable, and opened a beer is past. Nowadays he must buy a sound system. It comes in thousands of small electronic parts which must be assembled according to directions in Assyrian.

The object is for each man to build a personal system which will produce a Berlioz purer than any man in the neighborhood has ever heard. The beginner inevitably gets his woofer crossed with his mashie, which produces spinnaker feedback, resulting in excessive bassoon tweeter in the bookcase.

After ruining his first system, the music culturist usually sees the wisdom of a four-year course at the Massachusetts Institute of Technology. This suggests that the sociologists who have been worrying that the decline of work and the increase of leisure may ruin us have been jousting with a straw man.

With its genius for self-adjustment, the society has turned leisure   14
into labor. We are not far from the time when a man after a hard
weekend of leisure will go thankfully off to his job to unwind.

Questions on Meaning

1   According to Baker, what is the "paradox" of the new leisure? Why does
    Baker think Americans no longer know how to relax and enjoy their
    leisure activities?

2   What does Baker mean in paragraph 4 when he writes that "style is
    almost everything in the new leisure"? Can you suggest some popular
    pastimes, other than the examples Baker offers, that have become too
    complex and stylized to deserve being called "leisure" activities?

3   Why does Baker stress in paragraphs 4 and 7 that people need training
    in the activities of the new leisure if they are to avoid making fools of
    or humiliating themselves? How does Baker pick up this idea in para-
    graphs 12 and 13? Does feeling truly relaxed involve feeling free enough
    to let loose and make a fool of oneself?

4   In what way does the new leisure reassure Baker about what he calls in
    paragraph 14 America's "genius for self-adjustment"? How paradoxical
    is Baker's tone of reassurance? How does Baker's final paragraph turn his
    criticism of American attitudes toward leisure into a criticism of Amer-
    ican attitudes toward work?

Questions on Method

1   Baker exaggerates the difficulties of sports and hobbies to make us laugh.
    How much truth is there to his assertion in paragraph 7 that modern
    fishing is "as complicated as flying a B-58 to Tacoma" or to his assertion
    in paragraph 11 that a stereo system "comes in thousands of small
    electronic parts which must be assembled according to directions in
    Assyrian"?

2   What traits of the American character do Baker's examples satirize?
    What do his examples illustrate about the competitiveness of Americans
    or about our fascination with technology? Compare the satirical tone of
    Baker's essay to that of Allen's.

3   Where in his paragraphs are his generalizations placed, at the beginning
    or at the end? What would be the effect were they placed differently?

Vocabulary and Diction

1 How does Baker achieve a comic effect by posing as a man who misunderstands the meaning of words? How humorous is his misuse of "backhand" in paragraph 2 or of "keelhauling" in paragraphs 8 and 9? How does his misuse of words spiral into utter confusion in paragraph 12? In what sense does Baker's confusion over words symbolize a serious theme about the effect of Americans' tendency to overspecialize?

2 What does Baker's use of the term *"de rigueur"* in paragraph 4 suggest about his attitude toward golf? Does his use of this term make golf seem to be a snobbish game?

3 Discuss the different connotations suggested by Baker's use in paragraph 11 of the synonymous terms "phonograph" and "sound system."

Writing Topics

1 Do you agree with Baker that Americans spend their leisure time too seriously? Illustrate your answer with appropriate examples.

2 Write an essay about your favorite sport or hobby. How difficult is it to learn and practice? How expensive is it? Do its difficult or expensive aspects add to or detract from your enjoyment of it? Explain with the use of examples.

3 Baker's title implies that in the past Americans knew how to spend their spare time more simply and enjoyably. Do you agree? What examples can you offer that illustrate the simplicity of leisure pursuits in the past and the sophisticated and complex leisure activities today?

4 Compare the nostalgia for a simpler past that Baker, in his dislike of the complicated present, feels to the nostalgia expressed by Lance Morrow. How nostalgic are Americans in general? Cite three or four extended examples to defend your answer.

TOM WOLFE (1931–   ) is an American journalist and novelist who has worked on the staff of the *Washington Post* and the *New York Herald Tribune*. He is also a frequent contributor to *Esquire* and *Harper's*. His many publications include *The Electric Kool-Aid Acid Test* (1968), *The New Journalism* (1973), *The Painted Word* (1975), and *The Right Stuff* (1979). His essay "In Our Time" (1980) is an excellent example of Wolfe's "supercontemporary" attitudes.

In Our Time

Tom Wolfe

Professor Nkhrani Emu
Chairman, Department of Anthropology
University of Chembuezi
Babuelu, Chembuezi

Most Esteemed Professor:

As you know, dear Sir, our research team is approaching the end of   1
its field study of "The Sexual Mores of the Americans." I hereby
request, most respectfully, that we be granted an extension of the
term of our project and a renewal of funding for this work. It is
impossible for anyone in a society such as ours to envision from afar
the bizarre sexual customs, practices, and rituals to be observed among
the American people.

   In the republic's largest city, New York, the most prestigious   2
form of entertainment takes place in theaters that have been converted to dance halls. Hundreds of young males wearing strap under-

shirts, string vests, and leather garments may be seen dancing with one another to flashing lights and recorded music in a homoerotic frenzy, while prominent citizens, including politicians, lawyers, financiers, and upper-class matrons, as well as every sort of well-known figure in the arts, most of them heterosexual, look on, apparently greatly stimulated by the atmosphere. This is described in the native press as "disco fever."

In fact, the mores that have grown up among the Americans 3 concerning homosexuality are apt to be most baffling to the investigator first arriving from a society such as ours. In the United States it is the homosexual male who takes on the appearance that in our society is associated with heterosexual masculinity. Which is to say, he wears his hair short in a style known as the *crew cut* or *butch cut*; he wears the simple leather jacket, sleeveless shirt, crew sweater, or steel-toed boot of the day laborer, truck driver, soldier, or sailor; and, if he exercises, he builds up the musculature of his upper arms and chest. The heterosexual male, by contrast, wears long hair, soft open-throated shirts that resemble a woman's blouse, necklaces, gold wrist-watches, shapeless casual jackets of a sort worn also by women; and, if he exercises, he goes in for a feminine form of running called *jogging*.

The most popular periodicals in America consist of photographs 4 of young women with gaping pudenda and text of a purportedly serious nature, such as interviews with presidents of the republic(!). These are known as "one-hand magazines."

It is the custom throughout the native schools of America to 5 give *sex education* in the classroom to children by the age of thirteen. The children are taught that sexual intercourse is natural, beautiful, and the highest expression of human love. They are also taught that sexual energy is one of a person's most powerful and creative forces, that it will find expression in some form, that it should not be denied. Yet the Americans are at the same time baffled by the fact that the number of pregnancies out of wedlock among schoolgirls rises continually. In this the Americans are somewhat like the Kombanda tribesmen of our country, who, ignorant of the causal relation of activities separated by time, believe that pregnancy is caused by the sun shining on the bare midsections of females of a certain age. The administrators of the American schools remain bewildered, saying that in the sex-education classes females are given pamphlets clearly outlining birth-control procedures. At the same time, their own records show that only a fraction of American secondary-school graduates can read.

So, most revered Sir, we beseech your support in obtaining for us the resources to complete our work. You will recall, Sir, pointing out to us the importance of Diedrich's discovery of the Luloras, the tribe that made its women climb trees and remain there throughout their menstrual periods. Well, Sir—in all humility!—we are convinced that through our work here we have uncovered a yet more primitive layer in the anthropology of human sexual evolution. 6

> Your worshipful student and friend,
> Pottho Mboti

New York City,
United States of America

Questions on Meaning

1 Who is Pottho Mboti? Why is he writing a letter to Professor Nkhrani Emu?

2 What does Mboti observe about "disco fever"? How astute do you think his observations are?

3 What confuses Mboti when he compares the appearance of homosexual and heterosexual males? How humorous do you find his confusion?

4 What, according to Mboti, is so bizarre about sex education as it is taught in American schools? How are Americans "somewhat like the Kombanda tribesmen" in this respect?

5 Do you think Mboti is correct in believing that his discovery represents "a yet more primitive layer in the anthropology of human sexual evolution" than "Diedrich's discovery of the Luloras"?

Questions on Method

1 Why does Wolfe pretend to be Pottho Mboti? In what way is his essay, like Woody Allen's, an excellent example of parody?

2 Are Wolfe's examples of American sexual customs really as bizarre as he makes them sound? Does Wolfe make them sound strange to make us laugh, or does he make us laugh because he makes us aware of how strange they really are?

3 How satirical is Wolfe's tone? How serious is his criticism of American sexual customs? What other aspects of American culture does he satirize?

4 Which of Wolfe's paragraphs develops inductively, that is, with the generalization placed at the end? How does this paragraph differ in effect from the deductive paragraphs?

5 The entire essay appears to be inductive in that, like scientists, the writer begins with facts (about sexual mores in America) and then comes to a generalization (that our sexual behavior is bizarre). Are any other essays in the chapter inductive, or are all others deductive? Explain.

Vocabulary and Diction

1 Why does Mboti place the phrase in paragraph 4 "one-hand magazines" in quotation marks? How scientific does his language sound here and elsewhere? How much of the essay's humor derives from the contrast between the subject and the language that describes it?

2 Satire often involves exaggeration, which is reflected in the author's choice of words. Define the following words, and explain how they contribute to the satirical intent of the essay: bizarre (1), musculature (3), pudenda (4), purportedly (4), causal (5), beseech (6).

Writing Topics

1 Rewrite Pottho Mboti's letter by inserting your own satirical examples of the sexual mores of Americans.

2 Are the sex education classes taught in American schools helpful or confusing or harmful? Write an essay that backs up your opinion with pertinent examples.

3 Write either a satirical or a straightforward criticism of a set of related American customs or practices that you find somewhat bizarre.

PETE HAMILL (1935–   ) is the author of several novels, collections, and screenplays including "The Gift," *Irrational Ravings*, and *The Invisible City*. Over a twenty-year newspaper career, Hamill was a columnist and reporter for the *New York Post* (1960–74) and the *New York Daily News* (1977–79). His articles have appeared in *Playboy*, the *New York Times*, the *Saturday Evening Post*, the *Village Voice*, *New York*, and several other publications.

Spaldeen Summers

Pete Hamill

Summer, when I was a boy in Brooklyn, was a string of intimacies, 1 a sum of small knowings, and almost none of them cost money. Nobody ever figured out a way to charge us for morning, and morning then was the beginning of everything. I was an altar boy in the years after the war, up in the morning before most other people for the long walk to the church on the hill. And I would watch the sun rise in Prospect Park—at first a rumor, then a heightened light, something unseen and immense melting the hard early darkness; then suddenly there was a molten ball, screened by the trees, about to climb to a scalding noon. The sun would dry the dew on the grass of the park, soften the tar, bake the rooftops, brown us on the beaches, make us sweat, keep us from the tight, small flats of the tenements.

And if dawn was a tremendous overture, endlessly repeated, the 2 days were always improvisations. How did we decide what to do with our time? We didn't; the day decided. The day had its own rhythms.

I don't remember ever drawing up plans, or waiting for some agent of the state to arrive and direct us. Usually, the day would tell us to meet on the corner, with a pink spaldeen and a stickball bat. All through the war, there had been no spaldeens, and the few survivors had been treasured or replaced with those gray furry tennis balls we all despised, because we had never seen tennis played, had no idea what it was about, worshiped no tennis players. When spaldeens returned, stickball entered a golden age. Two blocks away, on 14th Street beside the Minerva Theater, the Tigers played gigantic money games, with pots as large as $300 and audiences jamming the sidewalks. Our games were smaller. We were still amateurs. Literally lovers. Lovers of that simple game with its swift variations on baseball: one strike and you were out, no bases on balls, six men on a team, sewer tops for bases, scoreboards chalked on tar. We made bats from broom handles, and there was an elaborate ritual of transforming broom to bat: clawing away the wire that held the straw by jamming the broom on a picket fence; then burning away the end of the straw; then sanding off splinters and taping the handle. Those brooms made beautiful bats, thin at the handle, thicker at the end. Today, commercially made stickball bats are sold in stores, products of Super Glut; they are terrible bats, as straight and untapered as poles. Playing with them is like playing with a mop handle.

Stickball wasn't always a team game. We played variations called   3
catchaflyerup (or, more literally, catch a fly, you're up), in which a batter kept hitting until someone caught a batted ball on the fly; rolypoly, where you rolled the spaldeen, after it was hit, toward the bat, which lay flat across home plate (if the ball hit the bat, bounced, and the batter missed it, the player who rolled it became the new hitter); and, most simply, tenhitsapiece, in which each batter was allowed to hit ten times. The simpler variations were played early in the morning, before everybody showed up on the court. When there were enough players, we started the full games, with their elaborate, specific ground rules: Off the factory wall was a home run, off the diner was a hindoo (a do-over). Around the city there were dozens of other variations.

We didn't play much baseball because the equipment cost too   4
much money, but we lived and breathed the game. Most of us were Dodger fans, from territorial loyalty, but also because it was one of the greatest of all baseball teams. In all of that neighborhood, I knew

one Giant fan and one guy who unaccountably rooted for the Cincinnati Reds. Nobody rooted for the Yankees.

That was before television's triumph, before so many children 5 were turned into passive slugs, before the relentless tides of Super Glut had jammed or pacified so many imaginations. We didn't have those giant $350 radios you see everywhere now (the radio in our house was shaped like a cathedral, and you had to hold the aerial in the back to hear clearly). But somehow we always knew The Score. Red Barber narrated the Dodger games on WHN, and we would shout into the bars—into Rattigan's, Fitzgerald's, Quigley's, Unbeatable Joe's—"Who's winnin' and who's pitchin' and who got the hits?" We knew; we always knew. The Score was like some insistent melody being played in another room, parallel to our own lives and our own scores.

But we also saw a lot of games at Ebbets Field. The Police 6 Athletic League gave away Knothole Club tickets, and so—reluctantly, fearful of betrayal—we would go into the 72nd Precinct each spring and sign up for the PAL so we could get Dodger tickets. They were almost always in the bleachers, when the worst teams (and poorest draws) were in town against the Dodgers, but we didn't care. There was Dixie Walker, over in right field, and Pete Reiser, playing out the shattered autumn of his career, his brilliant talent broken against the walls of the great field. And Reese, Snider, Billy Cox, Stanky, Furillo, Hodges, and the rest. HIT SIGN WIN SUIT, said Abe Stark's sign under the scoreboard in center; the sign was three feet off the ground, and it would have required three simultaneous outfield coronaries for any batter to bounce a baseball off that sign, but it was a crucial part of the furnishings. And there, jittery and wonderful, dancing off third base, ready to steal home, rattling the pitchers, was Jackie Robinson. That was part of being a Dodger fan then: You were forced to take a moral position. To be a Dodger fan in those days was to endorse the idea that a black man had a right to steal home in the major leagues.

Ebbets Field became our second home. We knew how to scale 7 the fence if there were no PAL tickets; we knew where we could rob programs and scorecards. We developed a variety of techniques for getting in; we had one crippled kid in the neighborhood whom we carried out like a prop, telling the guards he had three days to live, or had been hit by a car driven by a Giant fan, or had been caught

143

in Europe during the war and bombed by the Nazis. The guards always let us in. We knew where to wait for the ballplayers when they came out, and which one signed autographs and which didn't. Tell me I'm fourteen and I'll tell you I just saw Cookie Lavagetto.

We collected baseball picture cards, which came with bubble gum, and there was an elaborate system of games and trading that revolved around the cards. We hated the Yankees so much that we despised the entire league that housed them, so there was no value at all to most players from the American League. If a National League player wasn't a Dodger, he had to be good to be valued; if he was good, we feared him, and that meant we saved Stan Musial, Enos Slaughter, Sal Maglie, Johnny Mize, and, later, Willie Mays.

Because there was no television, we came early to newspapers. They would lie under their two-by-four on Pop Sanew's newsstand: the *News, Mirror, Times, Herald Tribune, Journal-American, World-Telegram, Post,* PM, Brooklyn *Eagle,* and Brooklyn *Times-Union.* In that neighborhood, we thought the *Post* was edited by Joe Stalin, just as other neighborhoods thought that the *Daily News* was edited by Francisco Franco. But we didn't care about any of that. Somehow, with deposits from milk and soda bottles, we bought papers: to read Jimmy Cannon in the *Post,* Frank Graham in the *Journal,* Dan Parker in the *Mirror,* and, most important of all, Dick Young in the *News.* Young was the greatest writer in history, we felt, better than Tommy Holmes or Harold C. Burr in the *Eagle* (which I delivered after school, and had other people deliver when I went to ball games), better than anyone we were forced to read at school. He was always going after the bosses, after Branch Rickey and then after the infamous Walter O'Malley. The dream job was to grow up and be Dick Young.

We would read the papers sitting in doorways on the avenues, memorizing statistics, knowing each minor fluctuation in averages, at bats, strikeouts, or walks. In those days, ERA stood for earned-run average; for some of us it still does. And when we had finished with the sports pages, we would turn to the comics: "Dick Tracy," Milton Caniff's "Terry and the Pirates," and, later, "Steve Canyon," and some of us would cut them out, pasting entire runs of the strips into scrapbooks, making our own comic books. I was probably the only reader of *PM* in that neighborhood, because it carried Crockett Johnson's great comic strip "Barnaby," about a young boy with a fairy godfather named O'Malley who smoked cigars and was a Dodger fan.

Reading the papers, before or after a game, was usually accompanied by eating or drinking Yankee Doodles and Devil Dogs, iced Pepsi, Mission Bell grape, Frank's orange. It seems to me I spent hundreds of hours with seven or eight other guys sucking the air out of empty soda bottles and letting them dangle from my lips. Slowly, gravity would pull the bottles away from our lips, air would leak in, the bottles would disconnect and fall. If you were the last man left, you won the deposit money.

You needed money for soda, spaldeens, comics, and newspapers, but you didn't need money for a lot of other things. You knew that sneakers had to last an entire summer, no matter how worn and disgusting they became, so you learned to bandage them with tape. You would have one pair of roller skates for the season, and one skate key. The skates were the kind that clamped on shoes and had metal wheels. When the wheels began to wear out (developing "skellies"), we took the skates apart, nailed them to two-by-fours, nailed milk boxes to the top of the two-by-fours, and scooter season had begun.

Street games were constant: ringolevio, giant steps, buck buck (how many horns are up?), a bizarre wartime game called concentration camp (Nazis were one team, rounding up the rest of us, and torturing us). Off-the-point and single-double-triple-home-run required spaldeens and were played off stoops; boxball was another variation, as restrained as cricket. Clearly, the spaldeen was at the heart of most of the games, and near the end of the day we would prowl the rooftops looking for balls that had been caught in drains, wedged behind pigeon coops, stuck under slats or behind chimneys. We would boil them to make them clean and to give them more bounce. One day, my brother Tommy boiled a half dozen such balls in a big pot, and they came out pink and glistening. Later on, my mother came home from work, and he made her a cup of tea. She gagged. Tommy hadn't changed the water, and the lovely amber-colored tea tasted of pure spaldeens. The rest of us would have loved the brew.

We played touch football with rolled and taped newspapers. Because of the cost, I didn't hold a real football in my hands until I was sixteen, and I never had a bike. I didn't feel at all deprived. Hockey was played with a puck made of crumpled tin cans, and

11

12

13

14

basketball was a Bronx game. We had no backyard because the house was on an avenue, so there were no pools or hoses to cool us off; we opened the fire hydrants with a wrench and made a spray by holding a wooden slat against the cascading water. There was room to run barefoot in the streets then, because there were almost no cars. Later, when the wars came, they ended the hydrants and ruined the stickball courts and stained the fresh morning air. But we didn't know that would happen. We lived with nouns: marbles, comics, lots, roofs, factories, balls, newspapers, scores. But we were verbs. Verbs to be, and verbs that were active. We didn't know that the nouns contained their own cemeteries.

Coney Island was the great adventure. We went there by trolley car, on a long clacking journey that took us through the last New York farms, with tomato plants ripening on either side of us, figs and dates growing in yards, farmers scratching at spinach fields. I was there the day Luna Park burned down, the giant plumes of smoke billowing into the sky and women crying. And when that old amusement park was gone, we were left with Steeplechase the Funny Place, 31 rides for half a dollar—that and Nathan's, when hot dogs were a dime and never tasted better again anywhere in America. We stayed at Bay 12, near Nathan's, and later moved down to the bay in front of Scoville's, a great Irish summer saloon with umbrellas in the back, where the women sat in summer dresses, and the men bought beer by the pitcher, and the bar smelled of pretzels and suntan oil; and we finished at Bay 22, in front of a place called Oceantide, near Sea Gate.

In memory, we never saw the sand. Every inch was covered with blankets and bodies: glistening young bodies, swollen older bodies of women waddling into the surf, the inaccessible bodies of girls. I would plunge into the unruly sea, thinking of white whales, harpoons, Ahab; of my grandfather Devlin, who had seen Rangoon before his death on the Brooklyn docks, far from his Irish home; of strange continents, exotic cities, women with hot, dark eyes. In Coney Island, I drank my first beer, touched my first female breast, received a wounding kiss from my first great love. Alas and farewell. In my mind, there is always a day when I am under the boardwalk, with the beach suddenly clearing, blankets snatched, books swooped up, as the sky darkens and I am alone, leaning against a coarse concrete pillar, in the rumbling fugue of a summer storm. July is gone. August has almost burnt itself out. And September lies ahead, like a prison sentence.

On those days, careening home on the trolley cars, I would go   17
down to the public library on 9th Street and Sixth Avenue and vanish into books. Or I would walk another block to the RKO Prospect, where my mother was a cashier, and go into the chilly darkness with my brother Tommy. Books made us think; the movies let us dream. One tempered or enriched the other. And both were free. So were the streets. So were we.

That city still exists for me. I live in its ruins. In the mornings   18
of July, I sometimes remember that morning long ago, after Yockomo had been killed by a shot from one of the South Brooklyn Boys, and dawn spilled across the park like blood. I remember the rooftops, pigeons circling against the lucid sky, and the blind semaphore of laundry flapping in the breeze. I'm certain that if I turn on the radio, Red Barber will tell me that Reese is on second, with Furillo batting and Snider in the on-deck circle. If I go out and walk to 13th Street, I can ring the bell and Vito will come down and we'll go up to the Parkside and McAlevey and Horan and Timmy and Duke and Billy and the others will be around, and then we can head for Coney. Or we can walk across the park to Ebbets Field and see the Cardinals. Or we can lie on the fresh cut grass and tell lies about women. I can still do such things. Don't tell me the bells no longer ring. Don't tell me those buildings are no longer there. Don't tell me that I have no right to remember. I only remember life. I will have no memory of dying.

Questions on Meaning

1   Hamill's first sentence is his thesis: "Summer, when I was a boy in Brooklyn, was a string of intimacies, a sum of small knowings, and almost none of them cost money." What illustrations does Hamill cite to support this generalization?

2   What function did the spaldeen play in these summers of the author's childhood?

3   Explain what the author means when he says, "We lived with nouns: marbles, comics, lots, roofs, factories, balls, newspapers, scores. But we were verbs. Verbs to be, and verbs that were active. We didn't know that the nouns contained their own cemeteries."

4   What does the paradoxical last paragraph mean? Explain why the author
     says "That city still exists for me. I live in its ruins."

Questions on Method

1   Hamill uses a great deal of description in illustrating the free pleasures
     of his spaldeen summers. What function do these descriptions fulfill?
2   Why does Hamill include so much detail in each of his illustrations? Are
     they arranged inductively or deductively?
3   Compare Hamill's essay with Kazin's in Chapter 2. Should both have
     been placed in the same chapter? Explain the role of description and of
     example and illustration in each essay.

Vocabulary and Diction

1   Hamill uses adjectives very effectively. List ten of these adjectives and
     discuss why Hamill uses them.

Writing Topics

1   Develop a generalization, or thesis, about your childhood summers, and
     support it with examples or illustrations.
2   Develop Hamill's generalization about pleasures that do not cost money
     into an essay supported by examples or illustrations drawn from your
     experiences.

FLORA MANCUSO EDWARDS is president of Hostos Community College of the City University of New York and has a rich background in bilingual education and curriculum development. Prior to coming to Hostos in March 1979, she held several important positions at La Guardia Community College. Most recently she was associate dean of faculty, supervising all curriculum development for the college. Mancuso Edwards holds a bachelor's degree in romance languages, a master's in comparative romance literature, and a doctorate in linguistics, all from New York University. In the following essay she discusses the plight of the working poor.

Elvira's Story

Flora Mancuso Edwards

Over 150 years ago the English historian Thomas Carlyle had this to say about Victorian society:

> It is not to die, or even to die of hunger, that makes a man wretched; many men have died; all men must die. . . . But it is to live miserable we know not why; to work sore and yet gain nothing; to be heartworn, weary, yet isolated, unrelated, girt in with a cold, universal Laissez-faire.[1]

There are over 4 million people in the United States today who still live miserable and know not why, who still "work sore and yet gain nothing." They are our laboring poor.

Elvira Ramirez is just one example of those who must sell their labor so cheaply that the necessities of life are just barely met. Elvira

1

2

3

"Elvira's Story" by Flora Mancuso Edwards, pp. 71–73 in *The City Today* edited by George L. Groman. Copyright © 1978 by Harper & Row, Publishers, Inc. Reprinted by permission of the publisher.

1. Quoted in Robert Hunter, *Poverty*, ed. Peter d'A. Jones (New York: Macmillan, 1904; Harper & Row, 1965), p. 1.

is a soft-spoken, cheerful, well-mannered woman who works in a luxurious East Side beauty salon doing shampoos and manicures. Her average day is filled by serving New York's well-to-do matrons who spend spring in New York, winter in Miami, and summer on Cape Cod. Elvira listens sympathetically to their problems in getting "reliable help" or to their last-minute preparations for a child's wedding in Switzerland.

For her services and good company she receives $0.25 to $0.50   4 from each one and occasionally $1.00 from a more generous customer. These tips bring up her total salary of $90.00 to approximately $110.00 a week. On this salary, Elvira supports herself, her son, a teen-age daughter, and her mother in a one-bedroom apartment in the Nathan Strauss Housing Projects in the Chelsea section on Manhattan's West Side.

Her apartment is on the third floor of a building whose elevators   5 are as offensive as they are nonfunctioning. Elvira, her mother, her daughter, and her son all used to sleep in one room, but now the boy is older and has inherited the sofa in the living room, which doubles as his bedroom. The apartment has no closets, and there is little room even for the metal Woolworth's wardrobes. The kitchen is so small that there is no place for a table, so when the family must eat together, the sofa is moved and a table set up in the living room.

Elvira receives no health insurance from her job, nor does she   6 receive a vacation or overtime pay. Her mother is only sixty and neither blind nor technically disabled, so she receives no social security or public assistance. Elvira's income—marginal as it may be— is too high for Medicaid, so Elvira works fourteen to sixteen hours a day, six days a week, and prays that no one will get sick. But, because the windows of the third-floor apartment keep getting broken, New York's winter always seems to take its toll in doctor bills, which each year are increasingly hard to pay.

When Elvira was hospitalized several years ago, the Department   7 of Social Services came to her rescue. But it did not take long for Elvira to realize that the benefits came at a high price.

No, the welfare is all waiting with the children crying, waiting outside the office for hours in the freezing cold, sick hungry waiting all day in the clinic, waiting to be looked down on, insulted, and humiliated. No, I'm not earning much more—but it's better than waiting.

God willing, I don't get sick again.[2]

Elvira has no savings and therefore cannot move to larger quar-   8 ters. As it is, rent is her biggest expenditure. Her hopes?

Maybe I go back to the Island when Michele finish school. You know, I guess I didn't do so bad after all. Michele finish fourth in her class. Now she goes to Harpur College. She got a scholarship, you know. I thought when she finish high school she would get a job and help out, but maybe it's better like this. Now she'll be somebody. . . . You know, like a teacher or a nurse or something. That's the most important thing—the kids. Sure I work hard—but the kids—they're going to be something.

Am I poor? No, not really. Really poor people take the welfare. Most of the time we manage to get by.[3]

Elvira receives no benefits, no medical coverage, no public as-   9 sistance. She earns $6,000 a year before taxes. She works harder and longer than most people and earns considerably less. She eats little meat and indulges herself in no luxuries. She does not own a car, goes on no vacations, eats in few restaurants, and buys a minimum of clothing.

Elvira's job is similar to almost one-third of all the jobs in New   10 York, and Elvira is one of 600,000 New Yorkers who live below the poverty line and struggle on day by day, eking out a marginal existence in New York, one of the richest cities in the world.

On a national level, over 4.5 million people (not counting rural   11 sharecroppers) are employed full time and are still poor. In almost half of these families, two people work full time in order to reap the bitter rewards of poverty and want.

2. Personal interviews conducted between May and December 1973.
3. *Ibid.*

151

Questions on Meaning

1 What is the lesson of "Elvira's Story"? About what problem of contemporary life does Dr. Mancuso Edwards teach us?

2 Why does Dr. Mancuso Edwards begin the essay with a quotation from Carlyle? How does our knowledge that people in England 150 years ago suffered in the same way that Elvira suffers today affect our feelings about the quality of life in contemporary America?

3 How "isolated" and "unrelated" does Elvira seem to you? What do you make of her insistence that she is not really poor?

4 In what ways does Elvira's story illustrate the plight of the laboring poor in America? In what ways is this economic class discriminated against by both society and the government? What does such discrimination illustrate about America's economic, social, and political systems?

Questions on Method

1 Whereas the other authors in this section offer numerous short examples to illustrate their points, Dr. Mancuso Edwards relies on one long example. Which method seems a more effective way of illustrating an idea? What do you think is the best method for giving a specific, concrete picture of a general, abstract idea?

2 How does the use that Dr. Mancuso Edwards makes in her third paragraph of comparing Elvira with her customers increase our sympathy for her?

3 Why does the author repeat in paragraph 9 what she already has told us about Elvira's lack of benefits, medical coverage, and public assistance? When can repetition prove an effective writing technique?

4 Elvira's "story" is not a story in a narrative sense. How is it organized?

Vocabulary and Diction

1 What does "Laissez-faire" mean in the quotation from Carlyle? In what sense is Elvira's story an illustration of one price that, however unfairly, is always paid for the personal liberty given to members of a free enterprise system? How would you compare this price to the price Morrow complains about in "Back to Reticence!"?

2 In what sense is Mancuso Edwards's use of the word "reward" in the last sentence ironic? What other ironies in the situation of Elvira and her family does the last sentence refer to?

Writing Topics

1   Elvira says in the quotation in paragraph 8 that she hasn't done so badly in America, because she has given her children the opportunity to "be somebody." In what sense does this make Elvira's story an illustration of the sort of success about which many Americans dream? Write an essay discussing how realistic this American dream of success is today; use examples to support your point.

2   Write an essay in which you illustrate your thesis through one extended example. Do not use a narrative illustration, but instead follow Mancuso Edwards's model of an analytic "story."

Illustration and Example—Writing Topics

1 A theme all the authors in this section focus on is how Americans use their time to educate themselves or earn a living or to relax and enjoy themselves. Write an essay in which you offer a series of short examples of American habits of education, work, and leisure. Think and organize inductively to finally generalize about the quality and characteristics of life in this country.

2 Write an essay that satirizes the failings of an institution, organization, or system in America. Use three or four detailed examples.

3 Write an essay on the political process in America; use the prose patterns of narration and description in developing examples to support your thesis.

4 Use one illustration of American ideas about class as a framework for an essay. Develop inductively a thesis from the lessons your illustration suggests.

5 Using the essays in this chapter as examples and illustrations, write an inductive essay on what contemporary writers think about life in twentieth-century America.

6 Many of the writers in this chapter—Woody Allen, Russell Baker, and Tom Wolfe—use humorous exaggerations to make serious criticisms of the problems and failings of Americans; in other words, they have written satires. Write an essay on the extent to which America is a subject for satire, using illustrations and examples from these essays. Think and organize inductively.

7 Write an essay in which you discuss an issue that concerns Americans today. Work inductively in your first paragraph by giving a series of short examples before introducing your discussion of the problem. Illustrate the problem in greater depth with a single long example developed in the rest of the essay.

FIVE

Definition

To define is to set limits or boundaries and thereby to give shape or meaning. With words, we usually depend on a dictionary to set these limits and provide these meanings, and the basic definition of a word is called a dictionary or formal definition. How does the dictionary define? Here is a dictionary definition of "jujitsu":

A Japanese art of self-defense or hand-to-hand combat based on set maneuvers that force an opponent to use his weight and strength against himself.

As usual, this dictionary definition falls into two parts: placement in a class (or genus) and the differentiation from other members of the same genus. Here the genus is "art of self-defense"; the differentiation is the rest of the definition: "based on set maneuvers that force an opponent to use his weight and strength against himself." Synonyms are another standard feature of dictionary definitions; and derivations from other languages (etymologies) are often included: "ju" derives from the ancient Chinese for "soft" and "yielding" and "jitsu" derives from the ancient Chinese for "art"—we can see just how literal the translation is from Chinese to Japanese to English. Some dictionaries also list antonyms, which define by excluding, or telling what a word does *not* mean. (Jujitsu is *not* karate or judo.) Any formal definition you might write could use any or all of these techniques—putting the word into a genus and differentiating it from other members of the genus and giving synonyms, antonyms, or etymologies. But the use of dictionary definitions is limited for expository purposes because these definitions tend to be objective, short, and noncontroversial and because readers may be insulted or bored if they read definitions of words they already know or can easily look up in a dictionary.

But there are several classes of words—technical, philosophical, scientific, slang, newly coined—whose definition cannot be left to lexicographers; these are words whose definitions are often controversial and must be attempted generation after generation and extended beyond a mere recital of synonyms and etymology. Such words require different, extended definition.

The purpose of extended definition is to carry "limit setting" into the area of explanation or argument; in fact, such discussions, although they may begin with the definition of a key word, usually move quickly to a critique of what is defined. Any extended definition of, say, "liberty," "justice," or "love" soon leaves the dictionary and its methods far behind. Words about which people care deeply (many of them are related to ethics, esthetics, psychology, religion, and politics) invite extended definition. "Superstition" is such a word and such a concept, a touchstone for a world view, around which entire essays might be organized. Other types of word that may require extended definition are coined (or new) words, such as "dystopia" and "freewriting"; words whose meanings have changed, such as "cute" and "holocaust"; and technical words, such as "iatrogenesis."

Extended definition frequently begins with the dictionary definition and expands both the genus (What is an art? Is self-defense

156

an art?) and the differentiation (Is jujitsu superior to karate? Is it superior to Chinese or European forms of self-defense? How can the opponent's strength be used against himself? What are the various holds or stances? How was jujitsu developed?) These expansions require the use of other expository techniques; the questions listed here require contrast, process analysis, description, exemplification, and narration, respectively. An essay on jujitsu might expand to a consideration of many related issues—Japanese character, physical fitness, crime, comparative sociology, history, and so on, using dictionary definition merely as a starting point.

Writing Extended Definition

1 Use extended definition for technical, scientific, philosophical, slang, or newly coined words.
2 Begin with dictionary definition (classification, synonyms, antonyms, etymology).
3 Extend your definition by using other expository modes such as contrast, exemplification, and description.

DAVID HELLERSTEIN (1953–   ) is a graduate of Harvard
College and Stanford Medical School. His essays and fiction
focus primarily on literary and medical topics, and he has a
great interest in the way attitudes toward disease illuminate the
basic assumptions, conflicts, inconsistencies, and apprehensions
of American culture. He was awarded a 1981–82 Pushcart Prize
for an essay published in the *North American Review,* to which
he contributes regularly. A native of Cleveland, he is currently
a Resident in the Department of Psychiatry at the New York
Hospital–Cornell Medical Center in Manhattan.

Cures That Kill

David Hellerstein

Harrison's *Principles of Internal Medicine,* the plump, maroon-bound   1
text that got me through my first clinical years in medical school,
spends all of three paragraphs discussing iatrogenic disease. It defines
iatrogenesis reasonably well: "When the deleterious effects of the
physician's action exceed the advantages that could have been anticipated, one is justified in designating these undesirable effects as
iatrogenic." The author does not imply that the physician must be
negligent or incompetent to create iatrogenic disease. In fact, most
iatrogenic disease today comes from good, or at least well-intentioned,
treatment. One might wish for a more extensive discussion of iatrogenesis as an aspect of contemporary medicine, particularly given the
prominence of iatrogenic diseases; yet Harrison's three paragraphs are
typical of medicine as a whole. Generally one looks in vain for books,
articles, and conferences on iatrogenesis in clinical medicine. Physi-
cian-writers are narrow thinkers, preferring to look at one disease at
a time rather than at trends; toward the future, not the past; at
things, not ideas. Only Ivan Illich, in *Medical Nemesis,* has tried to

formulate an explanation for the wide range of iatrogenic diseases seen today: his analysis, in terms of the "medicalization" of life, spans clinical, social, and cultural iatrogenesis—and goes further in a condemnation of scientific medicine than I think justifiable.

In preparing to write this article, I made a list of iatrogenic 2 illnesses I saw in a little over one year of work at a university and a county hospital. Yet soon after beginning this list I gave up, overwhelmed by sheer numbers. There were innumerable patients with anemia, heart failure, kidney failure, bizarre infections, liver damage, blindness, bleeding from various bodily sites, lung scarring, and so on as a result of treatment with "big gun" antibiotics or anticancer drugs. Many others developed complications from barium enemas, thoracentesis, cardiac catheterization. And on some services, notably hematology and oncology, the majority of my time was spent treating iatrogenic disease.

The few medical studies that have been done on the subject of 3 iatrogenic disease suffer from the same flaw: they rely on self-reporting by physicians. In a British study of general practitioners, one out of forty clinic visits was found to occur as a result of iatrogenic complaints. In an American study, 20 percent of all patients admitted to the hospital suffered one or more iatrogenic "episodes," including drug reactions, negative reactions to diagnostic and therapeutic procedures, and ward accidents (11 percent of mistakes were "medication errors"). As regards death of patients from drug effects, about one out of a thousand patients admitted to the hospital in a third study died as a result of drug treatment; one fourth of these were deemed "avoidable deaths."

None of these studies, however, addresses the problem of what 4 one can do as a doctor to decrease the incidence of iatrogenic disease, much less what a patient can do to avoid unanticipated medical complications, or even death, as a result of hospitalization. When a person becomes ill, he may suddenly be faced with a bewildering range of therapies for his condition, which are in many cases painful or dangerous. His first impulse often is to tell his doctor: "Do what you think is right."

While for many illnesses there is one best treatment, for a large 5 number of others (including treatment for breast cancer, coronary artery disease, gall bladder disease, hypertension, etc.) a wide range of potential treatments is available, each with its advantages and disadvantages. The patient who believes in the myth of medical objectivity, however, expects that since medicine is a science there will be one best treatment for his condition; moreover, he assumes that the doctor, as an objective scientist, will recommend it. He cannot believe that his doctor would recommend an overly dangerous treatment, or that a researcher would subject him to a risky procedure. And the doctor, too, often believes this myth; his training in emotional detachment from patients, his paternalistic habits, and his immersion in medical literature may lead him to extend his scientific authority beyond reasonable limits.

Yet the physician may want to do risky procedures in order to make a diagnosis that will not improve treatment. Or, since success in medicine is generally measured by longevity, he may recommend painful, debilitating therapy. Several recent studies using the technique of utility theory and decision analysis have shown that patients may choose less painful or disfiguring treatments than what doctors would recommend, even if they will not live as long. These preferences are not necessarily irrational or unscientific: they merely reflect different values or a willingness to take fewer risks. Doctors may be willing to accept higher rates of iatrogenic disease than many of their patients; they may take more risks for a higher chance of cure—or for a "definitive diagnosis." At times the interests of M.D.'s and patients *may* be the same, or—in terms of decision-analysis—the two groups may have similar utility curves, but there is no reason to assume this must be always true. And we will see below that the difference in interests between the patient and the medical researcher in the situation of therapeutic research is even greater.

While it may be to the advantage of all concerned for the doctor to guide patients past irrational and childish fears, it is important for patients to continually remind their doctors that longevity is not everything, that dignity and subjective feelings of wellness can be as important as extra years. The patient who says, "Do what you think is right," and thereby throws himself on the mercy of his doctor, may be abdicating the territory of his own preferences, which might be the decisive factor in treatment.

Equally pervasive is the myth of exciting new treatment. The extreme view of it, often quoted, was held by a seventeenth-century French physician who advised other doctors to use new drugs as quickly as possible, since they would soon become useless. Despite scandals over thalidomide, DES, and oral contraceptives, this myth is still sub-scribed to by the general public and the medical community. Gen-erally, it can be stated something like this: "Disease X has always been painful (or debilitating, or fatal), but now we have an exciting new drug (or operation) with which we hope to conquer Disease X forever!" It is buttressed by extravagant claims of popular journalism ("The Miracles of Modern ———" with heart transplantation, mi-crosurgery, Hodgkin's disease treatment, etc. filling the blank), in which the potential benefits of the treatment are advertised as if already realized, and the limitations are summarized in one short paragraph, or ignored. And among medical journals, a similar, if muted, enthusiasm reigns: "Our research group at Hospital Z, with our exciting new treatment, plans to conquer Disease X, within the bounds of randomized clinical trial."

A sophisticated patient will do well to know the limits of such 9 hopeful claims: while the research group may be scientifically respon-sible in their evaluation of a new treatment, in their enthusiasm to succeed they may well minimize potential negative effects of treat-ment or apply it quickly to a wider range of people than can really benefit from it. The patient should keep his desire for cure from obscuring the fact that a new treatment is unevaluated, that there is frequently little reason to believe it will be more effective than existing treatments (no matter how "exciting" the initial trials may have been), and finally, that there are likely to be hidden costs to virtually all new treatments.

When a new drug is released on the general market, the first 10 several thousand (or million) people using it are performing an un-paid, and often unwitting, service to the drug company and the medical profession: they are testing the drug for unknown side effects that might occur too infrequently to be noticed in premarketing testing on animals or humans. Unless a drug induces a high rate of a particular illness, it is unlikely that negative effects will be noticed before general marketing of a drug. Such effects as the possible in-crease in fatal heart attacks from oral antidiabetic agents, or the association of oral contraceptives with uterine cancer, gall bladder disease, and fatal strokes in young women have been discovered after such drugs have been widely marketed and used by large populations. A new drug that is released to general use is therefore likely to have many unknown effects. And even more disturbing are cases of inter-actions between two or more drugs, or between drugs and other modes of therapy—these are much less likely to have been anticipated. When one realizes that whole classes of drugs have moved from being "exciting new drugs" to being deemed "too dangerous for general use" within the span of a few years—oral contraceptives and oral antidiabetic agents are two prominent examples—it is apparent that these hidden costs may be greater than the well-advertised benefits.

Moreover, by taking a historic view, which physicians, with 11
their positivistic and forward-looking habits of mind rarely tend to do, one can see that the much touted "new therapies" of one generation may be laughable in the next. The nineteenth and early twentieth centuries' theories about female complaints arising from slippage of the uterus and the equally pernicious theories of "visceroptosis," prolapse of the abdominal organs, thought to cause a wide variety of complaints, are well known, and the variety of surgical procedures used to remove, reconnect, and tack abdominal organs in various positions remains astonishing. Many of these and similar procedures (removal of the teeth for arthritis, routine tonsillectomies, appendectomies for "chronic appendicitis") were perpetuated because they were never properly scientifically evaluated. Many more useless and potentially dangerous therapies have 12
been promoted, though, by responsible scientists in the interest of research. In the 1950s hundreds of patients received mammary artery ligations purported to improve coronary circulation, a useless operation. The freezing of stomachs for treatment of peptic ulcers, popular in the 1960s, actually caused new ulcers. Even "new and improved" packaging of drugs can have hidden dangers: in the 1960s the use of pressurized inhalers for patients with bronchial asthma caused thousands of sudden deaths. All treatment has risks; one must take risks for cure. The point here is that the myth of the new treatment makes the patient's risks appear much smaller than they most likely are. And bolstered by his own desire for cure, by notices in the press, and by medical hopes for the conquest of disease, the patient may embark on a new form of therapy with completely unrealizable hopes.

Another myth, one fostered by the fledgling work of patient's rights 13
advocates and medical ethicists over the past decade, is the myth of consent. This myth holds that patients become responsible for the direction of their own treatment by the process of informed consent. Before a course of therapy is begun, the patient is supposed to have the potential risks and benefits of several forms of therapy laid out

before him by his physicians, and he will be able to make an informed choice between them, depending on his own values and desires. In the actual workings of a hospital—both in ordinary therapy and in experimental protocols—true informed consent (if such a thing exists) is rarely attained. And in the realm of the law, informed consent protects not the patient's rights to have a say in the making of decisions about his health, but the doctor, who can point to a signature on a consent form and be excused from claims for compensation, as long as no overt malpractice has occurred.

That patients remain far from having a say as to the course of 14 their therapy can be seen from a trivial example: blood drawing. A hospitalized patient, no matter how well he may be, can have blood drawn any number of times per day, any hour of day or night, by any of the physicians responsible for him, whether or not there is any medical indication. A patient who assumes that informed consent implies participation in the making of medical decisions, who then questions the necessity of, or refuses blood drawing, immediately will get in trouble with the hospital staff. He will be labeled as "a crock" or "uncooperative" even if it is at 3 A.M. and blood is being drawn the sixth time that day or because somebody forgot earlier or because an intern wishes to impress his attending physician with his completeness. And in practice, frequently the patient will be forced to have the blood drawn despite his refusal. Granted that very ill patients may need blood drawn more frequently than once or twice a day; most patients do not. Nevertheless, when a patient enters the hospital, he cedes his basic rights to privacy, to the integrity of his own body, and often to the determination of what procedures will be performed on him. Informed consent gives extremely limited protection to the patient and almost none at all against the paternalistic assumption of responsibility for the patient's body made by the medical profession.

I chose this example deliberately because of its triviality and 15 omnipresence in medicine—and because the same structure of power extends to many other procedures, such as the placing of central venous lines, or the performance of thoracenteses or bone marrows— and especially to the dispensing of medications. For all these treatments, the patient is rarely advised of their indications or risks, but merely is told by his doctors, "We're going to do this because it will help you." In these situations the patient is at the mercy of his doctors, not merely because of the power of their specialized knowl-

163

edge (and what they may choose to reveal or conceal), but because the basic structure of the hospital is so powerfully weighted in favor of physicians and against patients, especially those who wish to take an active, knowledgeable role in their therapy. And even in situations where major surgery or chemotherapy is contemplated, the patient will generally find that the major element of decision is being made away from his bedside, and he is lucky if his doctors present him with an actual choice between therapies. The patient is much more likely to be presented with an informed consent form already filled out and a short speech beginning, "We're going to perform this operation on you tomorrow because you need it," and if he is fortunate, ending with, "Any questions?" The patient who wants to know whether a procedure is likely to benefit him (as opposed to the doctor), who wants numbers regarding the risks of various alternatives, who questions whether a particular symptom needs to be treated, is likely to be dealt with as the patient who refuses to have blood drawn: as a troublemaker and a hindrance.

A patient who is injured during the course of participating in a clinical medical experiment, like the patient whose treatment caused leukemia, will discover that informed consent, or lack of it, has little to offer in terms of legal recourse. Legally, compensation is not due the patient who is injured in the course of therapeutic research. My patient, or her family, might sue for compensation for the leukemia she got as a result of the experimental treatment she received, on the grounds that she was never warned she might get leukemia. And she will find that legally she is entitled to nothing; depending on the insurance coverage of the institution in which the research was conducted, or on the generosity of the hospital, she may have medical treatment for her fatal leukemia given gratis. But in fact her consent to participate in that particular experiment on Hodgkin's disease releases the hospital from responsibility for unanticipated negative results. In other words, she agreed that she would bear not only the physical costs but also the financial costs of whatever negative result the experimental treatment may have produced.

16

The burden of this kind of iatrogenic disease—incurred in the course of experimental therapy—falls squarely on the patient. Many people argue that this patient, one participating in therapeutic research, stands to benefit so much from the therapy that compensation is not justified. They would compare it to the case of nontherapeutic

17

experimentation, in which a subject gives of himself altruistically for the cause of scientific progress (whether or not he receives money for participation). Such an injured subject *would* be due compensation. I would argue that there is no significant difference between a patient injured in therapeutic research and a subject injured in nontherapeutic experimentation. Because both subjects are taking risks of unknown magnitude for the general benefit of society, their own possible benefit is incidental.

When a friend of mine discovered that she had breast cancer 18 and underwent a mastectomy, she then had the opportunity of deciding what sort of further therapy she would have. She could have entered a randomized controlled trial at the local university hospital, which was evaluating one standard treatment against a new set of chemotherapeutic agents. She and her husband decided that she would get better treatment from a private oncologist, using the best-known regimen of chemotherapy. Both she and her husband are doctors; yet they chose against participating in a scientific protocol. Why?

I suggest this was because my friends, like many other well- 19 informed patients, understood the risks and costs of participating in a randomized clinical trial and did not think that for them the potential benefits justified participation. Many of these risks and costs develop because the interests of the researcher are further away from the individual patient's best interests than are the private doctor's. Essentially the researcher wants to get a statistically significant difference between two (or more) groups of patients who are randomly selected for these groups, whereas the patient wants the best chance of cure for himself. Of course I do not dispute the role of randomized clinical trials in evaluating new therapies; they are essential. I am merely saying that what is good for the society (scientific progress) and best for the individual (cure) are different things. For the individual patient, participation in an RCT is never the "treatment of choice." In the context of an experiment, the treatment cannot be adjusted to his personal needs. And to find a significant result in the study, a number of subjects may have to suffer significantly. The subject in such a study bears the brunt of possible damages, whereas the general society and the medical profession only gain from the knowledge thus obtained.

The death of my Hodgkin's disease patient from an iatrogenic 20 disease caused by an experimental treatment is one extreme example

165

of this. Her death and the death of other patients like her can lead to improved treatment for other patients. Already the use of combination drug and radiation treatment in Hodgkin's disease has been restricted to situations where the benefits are likely to justify the risks. The subject's sacrifice by failure of a useless therapy, or the creation of iatrogenic illness is one cost of medical progress. When a patient decides to become a subject, he or she is making a sacrifice of substantial magnitude. 被 篷 驗 者

Questions on Meaning

1   What does "iatrogenesis" mean according to Harrison's *Principles of Internal Medicine*? On what basis does Hellerstein quibble with Harrison's definition? What does he think Ivan Illich's discussion adds? What does Hellerstein himself add to the definition of the word?

2   Whether discussing the doctor–patient relationship or the public's attitudes toward medicine in general, Hellerstein implies that people make choices based on a vast mythology about the medical profession. Discuss to what extent people subscribe to these myths.

3   Do you agree with Hellerstein or with the medical profession in the debate over the right of patients injured in therapeutic research to be compensated? What are the issues on both sides?

Questions on Method

1   Hellerstein's definition of "iatrogenesis" proceeds according to several different modes. He begins with an objective description from a medical dictionary and then expands it. What other modes does he use? Is definition his only purpose in writing the essay? Explain.

2   What thematic scheme does he use for organizing his essay?

Vocabulary and Diction

1   It might be accurate to say that Hellerstein is writing for a scientifically sophisticated audience since he does not define much of his medical terminology. Explain what the following words mean: hematology (2), oncology (2), utility curves (6), prolapse (11), ligations (12), protocols (13), venous (15), thoracenteses (15).

Writing Topics

1   Develop the definition of a word by citing examples of it, as Hellerstein defines "iatrogenesis." ·

2   Narrate an incident of iatrogenesis with which you are familiar, showing through your narration which of Hellerstein's myths contributed to the iatrogenic situation.

3   Select a word that needs to be brought to the attention of the public; define it and explain why you think people should know about it.

MARGARET MEAD (1901–78) was among the most widely
recognized of American anthropologists. She won immediate
acclaim for her study of primitive societies in *Coming of Age in
Samoa* (1928). She also taught for many years at Columbia
University and wrote more than twenty books, among the most
recent of which was *Culture and Commitment* (1970). In the
following essay she defines various kinds of superstition.

New Superstitions for Old

Margaret Mead

Once in a while there is a day when everything seems to run smoothly 1
and even the riskiest venture comes out exactly right. You exclaim,
"This is my lucky day!" Then as an afterthought you say, "Knock on
wood!" Of course, you do not really believe that knocking on wood
will ward off danger. Still, boasting about your own good luck gives
you a slightly uneasy feeling—and you carry out the little protective
ritual. If someone challenged you at that moment, you would probably
say, "Oh, that's nothing. Just an old superstition."

But when you come to think about it, what is a superstition? 2

In the contemporary world most people treat old folk beliefs as 3
superstitions—the belief, for instance, that there are lucky and unlucky days or numbers, that future events can be read from omens,
that there are protective charms or that what happens can be influenced by casting spells. We have excluded magic from our current
world view, for we know that natural events have natural causes.

In a religious context, where truths cannot be demonstrated, we 4 accept them as a matter of faith. Superstitions, however, belong to the category of beliefs, practices and ways of thinking that have been discarded because they are inconsistent with scientific knowledge. It is easy to say that other people are superstitious because they believe what we regard to be untrue. "Superstition" used in that sense is a derogatory term for the beliefs of other people that we do not share. But there is more to it than that. For superstitions lead a kind of half life in a twilight world where, sometimes, we partly suspend our disbelief and act as if magic worked.

Actually, almost every day, even in the most sophisticated home, 5 something is likely to happen that evokes the memory of some old folk belief. The salt spills. A knife falls to the floor. Your nose tickles. Then perhaps, with a slightly embarrassed smile, the person who spilled the salt tosses a pinch over his left shoulder. Or someone recites the old rhyme, "Knife falls, gentleman calls." Or as you rub your nose you think, That means a letter. I wonder who's writing? No one takes these small responses very seriously or gives them more than a passing thought. Sometimes people will preface one of these ritual acts—walking around instead of under a ladder or hastily closing an umbrella that has been opened inside a house—with such a remark as "I remember my great-aunt used to . . ." or "Germans used to say you ought not. . . ." And then, having placed the belief at some distance away in time or space, they carry out the ritual.

Everyone also remembers a few of the observances of child- 6 hood—wishing on the first star; looking at the new moon over the right shoulder; avoiding the cracks in the sidewalk on the way to school while chanting, "Step on a crack, break your mother's back"; wishing on white horses, on loads of hay, on covered bridges, on red cars; saying quickly, "Bread-and-butter" when a post or a tree separated you from the friend you were walking with. The adult may not actually recite the formula "Star light, star bright . . ." and may not quite turn to look at the new moon, but his mood is tempered by a little of the old thrill that came when the observance was still freighted with magic.

Superstition can also be used with another meaning. When I 7 discuss the religious beliefs of other peoples, especially primitive peoples, I am often asked, "Do they really have a religion, or is it all just superstition?" The point of contrast here is not between a scientific and magical view of the world but between the clear, theologically

異教徒

defensible religious beliefs of members of civilized societies and what we regard as the false and childish views of the heathen who "bow down to wood and stone." Within the civilized religions, however, where membership includes believers who are educated and urbane and others who are ignorant and simple, one always finds traditions and practices that the more sophisticated will dismiss offhand as "just superstition" but that guide the steps of those who live by older ways. Mostly these are very ancient beliefs, some handed on from one religion to another and carried from country to country around the world.

Very commonly, people associate superstition with the past, with 8 very old ways of thinking that have been supplanted by modern knowledge. But new superstitions are continually coming into being and flourishing in our society. Listening to mothers in the parks in the 1930's, one heard them say, "Now, don't you run out into the sun, or Polio will get you." In the 1940's elderly people explained to one another in tones of resignation, "It was the Virus that got him down." And every year the cosmetics industry offers us new magic— cures for baldness, lotions that will give every woman radiant skin, hair coloring that will restore to the middle-aged the charm and romance of youth—results that are promised if we will just follow the simple directions. Families and individuals also have their cherished, private superstitions. You must leave by the back door when you are going on a journey, or you must wear a green dress when you are taking an examination. It is a kind of joke, of course, but it makes you feel safe.

These old half-beliefs and new half-beliefs reflect the keenness 9 of our wish to have something come true or to prevent something bad from happening. We do not always recognize new superstitions for what they are, and we still follow the old ones because someone's faith long ago matches our contemporary hopes and fears. In the past people "knew" that a black cat crossing one's path was a bad omen, and they turned back home. Today we are fearful of taking a journey and would give anything to turn back—and then we notice a black cat running across the road in front of us.

Child psychologists recognize the value of the toy a child holds 10 in his hand at bedtime. It is different from his thumb, with which he can close himself in from the rest of the world, and it is different from the real world, to which he is learning to relate himself. Psychologists call these toys—these furry animals and old, cozy baby blankets—"transitional objects"; that is, objects that help the child move back and forth between the exactions of everyday life and the world of wish and dream.

Superstitions have some of the qualities of these transitional 11 objects. They help people pass between the areas of life where what happens has to be accepted without proof and the areas where sequences of events are explicable in terms of cause and effect, based on knowledge. Bacteria and viruses that cause sickness have been identified; the cause of symptoms can be diagnosed and a rational course of treatment prescribed. Magical charms no longer are needed to treat the sick; modern medicine has brought the whole sequence of events into the secular world. But people often act as if this change had not taken place. Laymen still treat germs as if they were invisible, malign spirits, and physicians sometimes prescribe antibiotics as if they were magic substances.

Over time, more and more of life has become subject to the 12 controls of knowledge. However, this is never a one-way process. Scientific investigation is continually increasing our knowledge. But if we are to make good use of this knowledge, we must not only rid our minds of old, superseded beliefs and fragments of magical practice, but also recognize new superstitions for what they are. Both are generated by our wishes, our fears and our feelings of helplessness in difficult situations.

Civilized peoples are not alone in having grasped the idea of 13 superstitions—beliefs and practices that are superseded but that still may evoke compliance. The idea is one that is familiar to every people, however primitive, that I have ever known. Every society has a core of transcendent beliefs—beliefs about the nature of the universe, the world and man—that no one doubts or questions. Every society also has a fund of knowledge related to practical life—about the succession of day and night and of the seasons; about correct ways of planting seeds so that they will germinate and grow; about the processes involved in making dyes or the steps necessary to remove the deadly poison from manioc roots so they become edible. Island peoples know how the winds shift and they know the star toward which they must point the prow of the canoe exactly so that as the sun rises they will see the first fringing palms on the shore toward which they are sailing.

This knowledge, based on repeated observations of reliable se- 14 quences, leads to ideas and hypotheses of the kind that underlie scientific thinking. And gradually as scientific knowledge, once developed without conscious plan, has become a great self-corrective system and the foundation for rational planning and action, old magical beliefs and observances have had to be discarded.

But it takes time for new ways of thinking to take hold, and often the transition is only partial. Older, more direct beliefs live on in the hearts and minds of elderly people. And they are learned by children who, generation after generation, start out life as hopefully and fearfully as their forebears did. Taking their first step away from home, children use the old rituals and invent new ones to protect themselves against the strangeness of the world into which they are venturing.   15

So whatever has been rejected as no longer true, as limited, provincial and idolatrous, still leads a half life. People may say, "It's just a superstition," but they continue to invoke the ritual's protection or potency. In this transitional, twilight state such beliefs come to resemble dreaming. In the dream world a thing can be either good or bad; a cause can be an effect and an effect can be a cause. Do warts come from touching toads, or does touching a toad cure the wart? Is sneezing a good omen or a bad omen? You can have it either way— or both ways at once. In the same sense, the half-acceptance and half-denial accorded superstitions give us the best of both worlds.   16

Superstitions are sometimes smiled at and sometimes frowned upon as observances characteristic of the old-fashioned, the unenlightened, children, peasants, servants, immigrants, foreigners or backwoods people. Nevertheless, they give all of us ways of moving back and forth among the different worlds in which we live—the sacred, the secular and the scientific. They allow us to keep a private world also, where, smiling a little, we can banish danger with a gesture and summon luck with a rhyme, make the sun shine in spite of storm clouds, force the stranger to do our bidding, keep an enemy at bay and straighten the paths of those we love.   17

Questions on Meaning

1   In paragraph 4 Mead says that superstitions "belong to the category of beliefs, practices and ways of thinking that have been discarded because they are inconsistent with scientific knowledge." How do the examples she offers of such superstitions help us understand why they are incon-

sistent with scientific knowledge? Discuss the definitions of "scientific knowledge" that Mead offers in paragraphs 11 and 14.

2 In paragraph 7 Mead says that the word "superstition" also is applied to the religious beliefs of uncivilized peoples. Does the use of "superstition" in such cases trivialize these beliefs? Discuss.

3 Why, according to Mead, might even the most civilized person continue to practice some superstitions as if they were what she calls in paragraph 9 "half-beliefs"? In what ways are these half-beliefs comparable to childhood toys or to dreams? What does Mead mean when she says in paragraph 17 that such half-beliefs "give all of us ways of moving back and forth among the different worlds in which we live—the sacred, the secular and the scientific"?

Questions on Method

1 How effectively does Mead use the technique of defining a word by differentiating between what it does and does not mean? Is she right in suggesting in paragraph 1 that people tend to misuse the word "superstition" as a way to avoid admitting how superstitious they really are?

2 How complex is Mead's use of the technique of contrast and comparison? How, for example, does her distinguishing in paragraphs 13 through 15 of a primitive society's "transcendent beliefs," "scientific knowledge," and "old magical beliefs" from one another help us understand that a primitive society is not necessarily classifiable as one that is more superstitious than a developed society?

3 How does Mead's process analysis in paragraph 15 of the way superstitions get carried on from generation to generation help us understand a key value of superstition in even the most advanced society?

4 How accurate is Mead's definition in paragraph 16 of the "world of dreams" as a world where "a cause can be an effect and an effect can be a cause"? Which of her examples makes clear that this unscientific mixup of cause and effect is also a chief characteristic of superstitions?

Vocabulary and Diction

1 What does "protective ritual" mean in paragraph 1? Discuss the ordinarily positive connotations of the word "ritual," or of the word "faith" in paragraph 4, as compared to the ordinarily negative connotations of the word "superstition." In what sense is Mead's essay an attempt to redefine

"superstition" so that the word will share some of the positive connotations of "ritual" or "faith"?

2   What does "transitional objects" in paragraph 10 mean? Does Mead's use of this term from child psychology help us understand better what sort of practices and beliefs should be defined as "superstitions"? When can a technical term prove helpful in giving us a full sense of the meaning of a practice, belief, or way of thinking?

3   Define the following words used by Mead: derogatory (4), tempered (6), urbane (7), supplanted (8), exactions (10), compliance (13), germinate (13), fringing (13), idolatrous (16), potency (16), unenlightened (17).

Writing Topics

1   Write an essay in which you discuss the superstitious qualities of some contemporary ritual, such as a sporting event, a high school prom, or a political election. Do the superstitions associated with such events make these events any less sophisticated or complex? Explain.

2   Mead says in paragraph 9 that we do not always recognize "new superstitions" for what they are. Write an essay in which you identify some examples of such new superstitions.

3   What "private superstitions" (8) do you practice? Write an essay that discusses why such private superstitions are important or helpful to you.

4   Using Mead's technique of defining a word by differentiating between what it does and does not mean, define one of the following: religion, idolatry, dreams. Use the history of the word if it is helpful to do so. Supply examples where appropriate.

JOHN LEONARD (1939–   ) was born in Washington, D.C. He attended Harvard University from 1956 to 1958 and graduated from the University of California at Berkeley in 1962. He began his journalistic career with the *National Review* in Boston and has been book review editor of the *New York Times* since 1971. His publications include *Crybaby of the Western World* (1969) and *This Pen for Hire* (1973). In the following essay he offers his definition of "youth."

Youth

John Leonard

Youth dropped in on us the other night, after dinner. Youth had curly locks, and eyes that had seen the floors of some oceans, and he spoke the latest foreign language: Like, man, you know, laid back. In his steerhide motorcycle jacket with the snap-on lamb collar, his tie-dyed bell-bottom dungarees, his calfskin Wellington boots, Youth was so together that the rest of us felt left out. 1

We were fortunate. Had Youth come by the evening before, he would have caught us playing bridge. The only games one is permitted to play these days are backgammon and aikido. Bridge, in particular, suggests the bourgeois institution of marriage: couples filing two by two onto an Ark with a hole in its hull. If the hard rain of history is falling, Youth will climb into his guitar as though it were a kayak, and go where the water flows. 2

As it was, we were in the company of real people—a novelist, a newspaper reporter, a professor of child psychology, a producer of television documentaries. The conversation was a kind of whittling on our work, to see what shape it might assume, to follow the grain. 3

If we were modest, it was not to the extent of despising ourselves. We felt, on the whole, that we had done more good than harm, at least recently.

Then why did Youth—who chose to sit on a stepladder against the wall, outside our murmuring circle; who gulped from a can of the Uncola as we clutched our brandy snifters; who was innocent of birth and death and Beethoven and Jackie Robinson; who hadn't failed because he hadn't tried, although he was forever promising to get around to it; who seemed to have been sculpted out of a block of vanilla ice cream, no knotholes; on whom advantages fell like leaves off our October—why did Youth make us feel guilty?

He wasn't telling. He just sat. What had he been up to? Well, he had been to California. He was always going to California or the movies. What had he found there? He had found a number of things that knocked him out. He was always being knocked out by things, whereas we had lived our lives trying to roll with the punch; we wobbled. What had knocked him out? Well, it was hard to put into words. Youth was "into actualizing myself." Western psychology and Eastern mysticism had to be reconciled.

Even to look him in the eye, we had to crane our necks, as if hoisting tons of scrap culture—Freud, Marx, Christ, and so on—to the furnace of his opinion. We sought Youth's opinion on every imaginable subject. What a reversal! "A professor," wrote Raymond Aron some years ago, "would have to be very ignorant indeed to be more ignorant than his students, particularly in their first years at university." But according to Youth, feelings were the energy of consciousness. He felt more than we did, so much so that verbalizing about it was, like, nowhere.

My friends aren't stupid. They had heard of est and Esalen, meditation and modern dance, More House and massage, Arica and acupuncture, hypnotism and health foods, tantric yoga and tai chi, Rolfing, Reich, Gestalt, biofeedback, Silva Mind Control, Fischer-Hoffman, Swami Raj-ji. That the brain had two hemispheres didn't surprise them. They wanted, however, to talk about the authoritarian component in the new therapies, the combination of Marine drill instructor and Mary Baker Eddy that was Werner Erhard. What, after all, about Sufism?

Youth, typically, shrugged. Could he, he asked, see the children? Our children had long since been shelved for the night. But Youth liked to rap with kids, who are the ears of Maya. And Youth as usual

served himself, went upstairs. He was back in ten minutes with a
bleary-eyed crew: "They want me to sing," he explained. How do you
argue with vanilla ice cream? He unslung his guitar. We lit a candle.

Youth specialized in a medley of sixties songs— "Blowin' in the
Wind," "We Shall Not Be Moved," "Let the Sun Shine," "Where
Have All the Flowers Gone?," "Hey Jude"—even though he had
been two years old when the sixties started. He could have been
singing about Easter, 1916, or Agincourt, or the burning of the library
in Alexandria. Whereas my friends had been at Berkeley, or in
Mississippi, or thumped on by Chicago cops, before—with children
and hotel reservations—we had marched on Washington by Metroliner.

What could we do? We sang along, and wept. Was it so shameful
that we had gone by Metroliner to protest the war? Ought we forever
apologize for private lives in which we sign our names as often on
checks for worthy and unpopular causes as on petitions against this
or that malfeasance? No. My friends weren't "into actualizing" themselves. They were fussing with the world. They made a distinction.
Unhappy about the world, they would agitate; unhappy about themselves—well, they would change partners or jobs, go into analysis,
drink too much, grapple with God in a dark alley, diet.

But the distinction was crucial. Whether or not feelings are the
energy of consciousness, sometimes when you feel bad you ought to
alter an institution or a policy instead of your consciousness. You
ought to fiddle with social mechanisms instead of the oxygen flow to
your brain. Werner Erhard to the contrary notwithstanding, on occasion everybody *should* feel bad, and a lot of other somebodies are
at fault, and tinkering with the self amounts to criminal stupidity,
and the new therapies add up to nothing more than those old magazine advertisements for techniques to improve your performance at
the piano or in the bed—when the problem may not be music or sex
or you. The problem may be political.

To Youth, one wants to say: Read a book, avoid California,
don't take yourself too seriously, remember that children are easily
pleased, that disappointment is an odds-on favorite to finish first,
that honorable work is not to be sniffed at. We won't say this to
Youth until after he has put down his guitar, because music is the
sort of solvent that makes slush of generation gaps. And what we
would really like to say to Youth is: You are lazy and inexperienced
and self-righteous and naïve, and that perhaps is the only thing for

9

10

11

12

which we can be properly blamed. We won't say these things of course, because if we didn't believe that Youth could improve on us, we would write novels about slitting our own throats. We feel sorry for Youth; he doesn't know any better, or the worst.

Questions on Meaning

1 Leonard seems to be defining the abstract concept of youth by describing his observations of and reactions to the behavior and attitudes of young people he knows. How well does his picture hold up as a definition of youth in general, in any time or place?

2 What does Leonard mean in paragraph 3 by calling the adults in his company "real people"? How does the contrast this suggests between people who are "real" and people who are "unreal" help us understand the attitudes and characteristics of Youth? How "real" or "unreal" is Youth compared to the adults in Leonard's company?

3 In paragraph 4 Leonard asks, "Why did Youth make us feel guilty?" Can you explain why Youth has this effect on the adults? How does the theme of guilt crop up again in paragraphs 6, 10, and 12? Might an apt definition of the word "youth" be "that age group that causes adults to feel guilty"? Explain.

4 How effective is Leonard's protest against his guilt in paragraphs 11 and 12? What does he mean when he says in paragraph 11 that "sometimes when you feel bad you ought to alter an institution or a policy instead of your consciousness"? Is he right in arguing in paragraph 12 that Youth is "lazy and inexperienced and self-righteous and naïve"? Why does he blame adults for Youth's characteristics?

5 In paragraph 12 Leonard says that "music is the sort of solvent that makes slush of generation gaps." What does he mean? How do his examples in paragraph 9 of the songs that Youth sings help us understand the contrast he draws between the generations? In what sense is his essay an act of defining the phrase "generation gap"?

Questions on Method

1 Obviously, Leonard is not interested in giving us a dictionary definition of the word "youth." Where a dictionary defines one word by giving us a series of synonyms for that word, Leonard relies on more complex expository techniques. In what ways does he employ such prose patterns as narration, description, illustration and example, contrast and com-

parison, classification, and cause and effect to create an effective definition?

2   In addition to employing most of the prose patterns discussed in this book, Leonard relies on a number of writing techniques that might be called specialized devices of definition. Pick out examples of Leonard's use of such devices as the following: enumerating the characteristics associated with a word, differentiating between what a word does and does not mean, defining a word by discussing its background, distinguishing a word's significance in different contexts, distinguishing what a word means to different people or at different times.

3   Leonard also employs some poetic devices in his essay. Discuss his use of personification ("Youth dropped in on us the other night, after dinner" [1]), allusion ("an Ark with a hole in its hull" and "the hard rain of history" [2]), metaphor ("The conversation was a kind of whittling on our work" [3], and Youth "seemed to have been sculpted out of a block of vanilla ice cream, no knotholes" [4]), and symbolism (Youth "chose to sit on a stepladder against the wall, outside our murmuring circle" [4], and children are "the ears of Maya" [8]).

4   At the end of the essay Leonard states that he and his company feel "sorry" for Youth. Is his statement believable, or does the tone of the essay make us suspect Leonard's sincerity at the end? What would you say is the dominant tone of Leonard's essay, the primary feeling that he reveals about Youth?

Vocabulary and Diction

1   How does Leonard's use of contemporary slang help him define the word "youth"? Is describing the language a person employs a good means of defining such a person? What effect does Leonard achieve by dropping his use of slang in the last two paragraphs of the essay?

2   How do Leonard's attitudes toward language reveal his attitudes both toward Youth and toward himself and his contemporaries? Why, for example, does he in paragraph 1 call the slang of Youth a "foreign language"? In what sense is the adjective "foreign" a pun?

3   What does the phrase in paragraph 5 "into actualizing myself" mean? Compare Leonard's attitude toward what he calls in paragraph 11 "tinkering with the self" and "the new therapies" to the attitudes of Lance Morrow.

4   Define the following words and phrases used by Leonard: the bourgeois institution of marriage (2), hemispheres (7), Sufism (7), malfeasance (10).

Writing Topics

1 How fair is Leonard's criticism of youth? Are there good things about youth that Leonard ignores? Discuss this issue in a critical essay.

2 Leonard is critical of today's youth for many reasons: their inexperience; their ignorance of the past; their lack of political involvement; their laid-back, "together" attitude. In what sense is Leonard's criticism of youth a criticism of the spirit of the 1980s? Write an essay in which you discuss this issue by defining "the spirit of the 1980s."

3 In paragraph 11 Leonard argues that "on occasion everybody *should* feel bad." Write an essay explaining first why Leonard argues this and then why you agree or disagree.

4 Write an essay in which you define adulthood by personifying this abstract idea and describing the visit that Adult makes to a group of young people.

5 Write an essay in which you define "generation gap." Make use of as many devices of definition as are necessary to convey the meaning of this phrase as fully as possible.

BRUNO BETTELHEIM (1903–   ) is a former professor of psychology at the University of Chicago and now heads the Sonia Shankman Orthogenic School in Chicago. He is well known for his sensitive approach to childhood schizophrenia and autism. He has also written on puberty rites, the dynamics of racial prejudice, and the determinants of concentration-camp survival. His best-known book, *The Informed Heart*, is about the loss of self in modern society. The following definition of the Holocaust is taken from *Surviving and Other Essays* (1979).

The Holocaust

Bruno Bettelheim

賺東西

To begin with, it was not the hapless victims of the Nazis who named   1
their incomprehensible and totally unmasterable fate the "holocaust."
It was the Americans who applied this artificial and highly technical
term to the Nazi extermination of the European Jews. But while the
event when named as mass murder most foul evokes the most immediate, most powerful revulsion, when it is designated by a rare
technical term, we must first in our minds translate it back into
emotionally meaningful language. Using technical or specially created
terms instead of words from our common vocabulary is one of the
best-known and most widely used distancing devices, separating the
intellectual from the emotional experience. Talking about "the holocaust" permits us to manage it intellectually where the raw facts,
when given their ordinary names, would overwhelm us emotionally—
because it was catastrophe beyond comprehension, beyond the limits

of our imagination, unless we force ourselves against our desire to extend it to encompass these terrible events.[1]

This linguistic circumlocution began while it all was only in the 2 planning stage. Even the Nazis—usually given to grossness in language and action—shied away from facing openly what they were up to and called this vile mass murder "the final solution of the Jewish problem." After all, solving a problem can be made to appear like an honorable enterprise, as long as we are not forced to recognize that the solution we are about to embark on consists of the completely unprovoked, vicious murder of millions of helpless men, women, and children. The Nuremberg judges of these Nazi criminals followed their example of circumlocution by coining a neologism out of one Greek and one Latin root: genocide. These artificially created technical terms fail to connect with our strongest feelings. The horror of murder is part of our most common human heritage. From earliest infancy on, it arouses violent abhorrence in us. Therefore in whatever form it appears we should give such an act its true designation and not hide it behind polite, erudite terms created out of classical words.

To call this vile mass murder "the holocaust" is not to give it a 3 special name emphasizing its uniqueness which would permit, over time, the word becoming invested with feelings germane to the event it refers to. The correct definition of "holocaust" is "burnt offering." As such, it is part of the language of the psalmist, a meaningful word to all who have some acquaintance with the Bible, full of the richest emotional connotations. By using the term "holocaust," entirely false associations are established through conscious and unconscious connotations between the most vicious of mass murders and ancient rituals of a deeply religious nature.

Using a word with such strong unconscious religious connota- 4 tions when speaking of the murder of millions of Jews robs the victims of this abominable mass murder of the only thing left to them: their uniqueness. Calling the most callous, most brutal, most horrid, most heinous mass murder a burnt offering is a sacrilege, a profanation of God and man.

---

1. Between the years 1941–45 the Nazi regime planned and executed the unique mass murder of European Jewry. This political ideological task was in accordance with Hitler's orders for the "final solution of the Jewish question"—that is, the elimination of the Jewish people from the European community through a systematic program of murder. Special crematories with gas chambers were erected for the systematic extermination throughout Germany, Poland, and other European countries, where 6 million Jews were gassed. (Editors' note)

Martyrdom is part of our religious heritage. A martyr, burned at 5
the stake, is a burnt offering to his god. And it is true that after the
Jews were asphyxiated, the victims' corpses were burned. But I believe
we fool ourselves if we think we are honoring the victims of systematic
murder by using this term, which has the highest moral connotations.
By doing so, we connect for our own psychological reasons what
happened in the extermination camps with historical events we deeply
regret, but also greatly admire. We do so because this makes it easier
for us to cope; only in doing so we cope with our distorted image of
what happened, not with the events the way they did happen.

By calling the victims of the Nazis "martyrs," we falsify their 6
fate. The true meaning of "martyr" is: "one who voluntarily undergoes
the penalty of death for refusing to renounce his faith" (*Oxford English
Dictionary*). The Nazis made sure that nobody could mistakenly think
that their victims were murdered for their religious beliefs. Renounc-
ing their faith would have saved none of them. Those who had
converted to Christianity were gassed, as were those who were athe-
ists, and those who were deeply religious Jews.[2] They did not die for
any conviction, and certainly not out of choice.

Millions of Jews were systematically slaughtered, as were untold 7
other "undesirables," not for any convictions of theirs, but only
because they stood in the way of the realization of an illusion. They
neither died for their convictions, nor were they slaughtered because
of their convictions, but only in consequence of the Nazis' delusional
belief about what was required to protect the purity of their assumed
superior racial endowment, and what they thought necessary to guarantee them the living space they believed they needed and were
entitled to. Thus while these millions were slaughtered for an idea,
they did not die for one.

Millions—men, women, and children—were processed after they 8
had been utterly brutalized, their humanity destroyed, their clothes
torn from their bodies. Naked, they were sorted into those who were
destined to be murdered immediately, and those others who had a
short-term usefulness as slave labor. But after a brief interval they,
too, were to be herded into the same gas chambers into which the

2. To specify the "undesirable" Jews—or in German terminology, the non-Aryan—a
decree was promulgated in 1933 according to which anyone descending from non-Aryan parents
or grandparents (even if only one parent or grandparent was non-Aryan) was considered a Jew.
The Nazi definition simply meant that a Jew is a Jew is a Jew—that is, down to the third
generation—and eligible for racial persecution. (Editors' note)

others were immediately piled, there to be asphyxiated so that, in their last moments, they could not prevent themselves from fighting each other in vain for a last breath of air.

To call these most wretched victims of a murderous delusion, of   9
destructive drives run rampant, martyrs or a burnt offering is a distortion invented for our comfort, small as it may be. It pretends that this most vicious of mass murders had some deeper meaning; that in some fashion the victims either offered themselves or at least became sacrifices to a higher cause. It robs them of the last recognition which could be theirs, denies them the last dignity we could accord them: to face and accept what their death was all about, not embellishing it for the small psychological relief this may give us.

We could feel so much better if the victims had acted out of   10
choice. For our emotional relief, therefore, we dwell on the tiny minority who did exercise some choice: the resistance fighters of the Warsaw ghetto, for example, and others like them. We are ready to overlook the fact that these people fought back only at a time when everything was lost, when the overwhelming majority of those who had been forced into the ghettos had already been exterminated without resisting. Certainly those few who finally fought for their survival and their convictions, risking and losing their lives in doing so, deserve our admiration; their deeds give us a moral lift. But the more we dwell on these few, the more unfair are we to the memory of the millions who were slaughtered—who gave in, did not fight back—because we deny them the only thing which up to the very end remained uniquely their own: their fate.

Questions on Meaning

1   Why does Bettelheim object to the word "holocaust" as a definition of the "mass murder" of Jews by the Nazis? Is it true, as he asserts in paragraph 1, that whereas the phrase "mass murder most foul" makes us feel an immediate and powerful revulsion, the term "holocaust" is a distancing device used to separate "the intellectual from the emotional experience"? Are there really any words that might make us feel the true horror of the Nazi extermination of European Jews?

2   Discuss the comparison Bettelheim offers in paragraph 2 between the use of the word "holocaust" by Americans and the examples of such "lin-

guistic circumlocution" used by the Nazis and by the Nuremberg judges. How does his example of the Nazi use of the phrase "the final solution of the Jewish problem" help us understand the definition of "linguistic circumlocution"?

3   How fair is it of Bettelheim to apply the phrase "linguistic circumlocution" to the American use of the word "holocaust"? Why, according to Bettelheim, do we use the word "holocaust"?

4   What, according to the third paragraph, are the actual emotional connotations of the word "holocaust"? Why do these connotations lead us to view the European Jews as martyrs?

5   Why is it inappropriate, so far as Bettelheim is concerned, to define the European Jews as martyrs? How does the analysis of why and the description of how the Jews were slaughtered that Bettelheim offers in paragraphs 7 through 9 clarify his objections to the word "martyr"?

Questions on Method

1   Although Bettelheim's essay is concerned with what he feels is the inappropriate use of a particular word, what broader meaning does it imply about the difficulties of definition in general? What general conclusions might you draw from Bettelheim's specific example about the limitations of using any single word to define a complex idea or experience?

2   In paragraph 3 Bettelheim suggests that the act of definition involves giving a "special name" that, over time, becomes "invested with feelings germane to the event it refers to." In what sense is the act of definition as much an act of identifying the definer's subjective thoughts and feelings about something as it is an act of identifying the objective meaning of something? To what extent does this subjective definition apply to the word "holocaust" itself?

3   Might you argue that as Bettelheim differentiates between what "holocaust" actually does and does not mean, and as he discusses the background of the word, he in effect redefines the word so that it begins to represent what he thinks is the true meaning of the event it is supposed to name? Discuss how Bettelheim's use of these writing techniques, as well as such expository techniques as description, contrast and comparison, and cause-and-effect analysis, invests the word "holocaust" with the connotations of emotional horror that he feels it lacks.

Vocabulary and Diction

1 Bettelheim makes a distinction between "ordinary names" that "connect with our strongest feelings" and "technical terms" that fail to make this connection. Might you classify the word "euthanasia" as one of these technical terms? What ordinary words might better define the meaning of "euthanasia"? Can you think of other examples of technical terms that Americans use instead of ordinary names in order to avoid uncomfortable feelings?

2 In what sense are the words "undesirables" in paragraph 7 and "processed" in paragraph 8 good examples of linguistic circumlocution? To what extent do we use these words today to define certain groups of people and how they are treated in America?

Writing Topics

1 In paragraph 2 Bettelheim says that "the horror of murder" is something that arouses "violent abhorrence" in us from earliest infancy, yet his main point is that society conditions us to accept certain kinds of murder. In what ways does such social conditioning involve inappropriately defining certain acts of murder as something else so that we feel them to be less horrible than they actually are? Write an essay in which you discuss the different definitions society gives to murder.

2 What expressions of contemporary jargon—the jargon of commercials, for example, or of slang that is popular among young people today—might you classify as being linguistic circumlocutions? Develop your essay by defining the words and phrases you choose as examples.

3 Write an essay in which you use illustrative examples to define the word "genocide." Does your use of such examples help translate this word into what Bettelheim calls "emotionally meaningful language"?

4 How do Bettelheim's views about our linguistic circumlocution in naming the Holocaust illustrate the validity of John Leonard's argument in "Youth" that "on occasion everybody *should* feel bad"? Explain your answer.

5 How do Bettelheim's views on our lack of courage in naming the Holocaust help us understand more fully Hannah Arendt's admiration expressed in "Denmark and the 'Final Solution'" for the courageous honesty of the Danish people? Write an essay that compares the views of these two authors.

BEN YAGODA is Associate Editor of *New Jersey Monthly* magazine. As a freelance writer, he has been published in *American Heritage, Esquire,* the *New York Times Book Review, Saturday Review, The New Republic,* and other periodicals. He is a 1975 graduate of Yale College.

The Good, the Bad, and the Cute

Ben Yagoda

What do Tony Manero, Rocky Balboa, R2D2 and C3PO, the aliens in "Close Encounters," Annie Hall, Peter Frampton, my 3-year-old cousin and Jimmy Carter have in common? They're cute, that's what. 1

You'll have to take my word about my cousin, and that of a Portland, Ore., woman about the President (she made him blush by telling him recently, "I think you're really cute, I really do"). As for Frampton, a rock writer recently reported: "An editor sent me to a Peter Frampton concert with orders to 'talk to those girls and find out why they like him.' I came back with a notebook in which the word 'cute' was scrawled 452 times." 2

And it seems undeniable that the appeal of the cinematic examples springs from a common source. They are good-hearted, not too bright and, in various ways, ineffectual. Tony and Rocky are tongue-tied, Annie is scatterbrained and the robots and aliens have a hard time getting around. They all represent, it seems to me, a standard of attractiveness that has gained a lamentable ascendancy in America today: the esthetics of cute. 3

Although in nineteenth-century America cute was a synonym 4
for shrewd or clever, it now means, according to my dictionary,
"pleasingly pretty or dainty." The first thing to be called cute in this
sense, I'd be willing to bet, was a baby. I don't know why we find
babies so adorable. Perhaps the attraction evolved so we wouldn't
kick them in the head when they bawled at 3 in the morning and
thereby finish off the species. Whatever the reason, babies definitely
represent the platonic ideal of cute. Other things—dogs, older humans, knickknacks, hats, hair-dos—are called cute insofar as they are
babylike and possess those qualities of softness and inadvertent charm
that knock us out in 2-year-olds.

Cute is not so terrible in itself; it represents, after all, another 5
kind of beauty in the world. But to call someone cute is, in a way,
to insult him: it puts him in the class of toddlers and domestic
animals. Valuing cuteness also means giving short shrift to more
honorable virtues, like intelligence and moral courage, that are self-
conscious, complex, ethically relevant and risky. Esthetically, cute
leads us to overlook the grand in favor of the easily digestible, to
prefer Donny and Marie to Mahler. In general, it reduces the scale
of our sensibilities.

But worst of all is cute's habit of expanding its influence, until 6
it is not merely an esthetic standard, but a principle of behavior.
Some people, in other words, try to be cute, feigning innocence or
helplessness in order to be appealing. They make intentionally silly
jokes, speak in outdated slang, perpetually play the bumpkin. This
preciousness is certainly the low point of cute: it may offer some
momentary charm, but it is really a selling out of the self.

The esthetics of cute have been put to their most widespread 7
use in romantic love. It is a venerable Hollywood dictum that screen
lovers must "meet cute," and so they have—in stalled elevators,
upending each other's cafeteria trays, wearing embarrassing costumes,
and so forth, ad infinitum. The population at large eagerly participates
in this conception of romance, in the idea of love as coincidence and
caprice: after all, cute is America's most popular adjective for sexual
prospects.

Behavior has been affected, too. Men chat up women they are 8
interested in with "lines" that could have been lifted staight from a
'30s comedy, and women respond in kind, with a coquettishness they
have been taught is their chief weapon. The reason for this playacting,

as the geniuses of Hollywood shrewdly realized, is that being cute lets us manage what makes us uncomfortable without really confronting it; it defuses the dangers of love.

Looking to Hollywood again, it's easy to see that more than just 9 love is involved. I am convinced that a major reason for the success of "One Flew Over the Cuckoo's Nest" was the portrayal of the victims of mental illness as cuddly and harmless. Cute old people, spry and feisty, are a cinematic convention that takes the sting out of aging and sells the elderly short. Remember all those comically simple brown-skinned servants? The exotic location films where entire countries were rendered cute?

Viewing foreigners (or anyone) as picturesque robs them of the 10 respect we accord individuals. It leads to travesties like Bloomingdale's theme show, "India: The Ultimate Fantasy," which ignored the dominant characteristics of the fantasized country, horrible poverty. It can be argued, too, that our country's readiness to intervene in Southeast Asia a decade and a half ago was conditioned by our habit of seeing natives as nothing more than lovable and/or inscrutable features of a landscape.

The esthetics of cute can be applied to things as well as people. 11 Consider, for example, the design of franchised fast-food restaurants. When these establishments were first constructed, they resembled tacky spaceships or futuristic factories and thus paid homage to the car culture that spawned them. Today the trend is to make the structures look like suburban homes. Now one can stop for a burger or a pizza in a mock-colonial, mock-Tudor, mock-ranch or mock-Cape Cod joint. This form of cuteness not only plays hooky from the form-reflects-function school of architecture, it also substitutes fraudulent good taste for truthful kitsch.

I sometimes imagine what it would be like if the esthetics of cute 12 took over the whole country. All lettering would be soft and rounded, like a Burger King sign. All men would blush like John Travolta and stumble over words of more than two syllables. All women would wear the Annie Hall look. All advertisements would be self-consciously "wacky." Knickknacks and pets would proliferate. Everybody would dot their i's with circles—or, worse yet, with hearts. Everybody would be a character. And I would move to the Khyber Pass.

Questions on Meaning

1 What characteristics of "cute" does Yagoda enumerate to define the word? How does the background on the meaning of the word that he offers in paragraph 4 help us understand both his definition of and his attitude toward "cute"?

2 Why does Yagoda think, as he says in paragraph 5, that to call someone cute is to insult the person? What does he mean when he says that cuteness is less "complex, ethically relevant and risky" than such virtues as intelligence and moral courage?

3 Yagoda argues that making cuteness an esthetic value, a value of art and beauty, "reduces the scale of our sensibilities." How does his example that contrasts Donny and Marie to Mahler clarify what he means?

4 In what ways has "cute" expanded its influence and become, as Yagoda argues in paragraph 6, more than "merely an esthetic standard"? How do his subsequent examples of the effects that valuing cuteness has had on American behavior in love and politics turn his rather light-hearted criticism into a serious one? Do you agree with his thesis?

Questions on Method

1 How would you describe Yagoda's tone in this essay? Is he cute? Is he satirical? Is he angry?

2 Compare Yagoda's essay with Bettelheim's. To what extent are they concerned with the same issues? How similar are the two writers' attitudes toward their subject matter? How can you account for any differences in tone between their essays?

Vocabulary and Diction

1 What does the phrase "platonic ideal" in paragraph 4 mean? In what sense is Yagoda's use of this term ironic to the point of being sarcastic? What is "sarcasm"? How sarcastic is Yagoda's tone throughout his essay?

2 In what sense does the adverb "shrewdly" in paragraph 8 playfully complicate Yagoda's theme, given the nineteenth-century definition of "cute" that Yagoda offers in paragraph 4?

3 What is the difference between the phrases "fraudulent good taste" and "truthful kitsch," which Yagoda contrasts in paragraph 11? What examples of truthful kitsch can you think of to compare with Yagoda's examples of fraudulent good taste?

4   Define the following words and phrases used by Yagoda: short shrift (5), feigning (6), ad infinitum (7), caprice (7), coquettishness (8), travesties (10), franchised (11), spawned (11), proliferate (12).

Writing Topics

1   To define "cute," Yagoda depends heavily on examples of American popular culture, from the movie and recording industries to Bloomingdale's and Burger King. Are there ways American popular culture illustrates that our fascination with cuteness really reflects our shrewd and clever attributes, our appreciation of the attributes that "cute" represented in the nineteenth century? Discuss this question in an essay that defines the "shrewdness" or "cleverness" of Americans by offering illustrative examples from popular culture.

2   Can "cute" ever be a complimentary term? Discuss the positive values the term connotes that you feel Yagoda ignores?

3   Are the esthetic values by which we judge what is artistic or what is beautiful a good indication of our moral values? Write an essay that defines an important moral value that Americans reveal through their tastes in art and beauty.

4   Write an essay in which you define a word or phrase both by offering examples that enumerate its characteristics and by differentiating it from other, similar terms.

Definition—Writing Topics

1   Most of the authors in this section seem to take an almost superstitious view of the act of definition, regarding a word like "holocaust" or "cute" as almost magical in its capacity to protect us from understanding or feeling the most uncomfortable and upsetting truths. How magical is the act of defining or naming? Discuss the extent to which one of the following words or phrases is a "magical" definition or, in Bettelheim's phrase, a linguistic circumlocution: euthanasia, nuclear incident, enemy, sacrifice, hero, law and order, survivor.

2   Write an essay in which you define a word whose meaning has changed for you over a period of time, by differentiating between what that word means to you now and what it meant to you at the earlier period. What does your changing definition reflect about your own growth? Does the word "freedom," for example, have a different meaning to you now than it had when you were 15?

3   Is the act of definition less a matter of finding the right synonym for a word than it is a matter of offering one's opinion on some subject associated with the word? Discuss this question in an essay that evaluates how opinionated one of the definitions offered in this section is.

4   The fields of medicine, psychology, and sociology are constantly adding new words, such as "iatrogenesis," to the common vocabulary. Choose such a new scientific word with which you are familiar, define it, and discuss the effect the word and its definition have had on society.

5   Some words—liberty, justice, and love, for example—have emotional meanings, meanings beyond the dictionary definition, that may change from century to century. Discuss the current definition of one of these words in an extended definition in which you also contrast its definition today with that of a past age.

SIX

Comparison and Contrast

Comparison is the examination of two or more subjects for the purpose of noting similarities and differences. In expository comparison, specific likenesses and differences are usually examined in detail with the view to making both subjects better known. Comparison is an especially useful mode of organizing expository writing, as it can be adapted to long or short paragraphs or essays. Contrast is a special kind of comparison in which only differences are noted. (Examples of expository comparison are by no means confined to this chapter, but are liberally scattered throughout the book.)

193

A comparison that discusses only similarities is simpler to organize than a comparison that examines both similarities *and* differences. If you write about similarities, you will find yourself using a lot of "both's": both Grant and Lee were expert generals; both Grant and Lee were representative of their region; both Grant and Lee were forgiving to their enemies.

If you want to point out both similarities and differences, it is best to separate the two, for when you come to the differences you will find you have two options: (*a*) organize the material subject by subject, finishing with *x* before moving on to *y*, or (*b*) organize point by point, switching back and forth between *x* and *y* even within the same paragraph. If your composition is divided into many subtopics or if you are dealing with both similarities and differences, the point-by-point method is probably better. Arthur L. Campa's introductory paragraph to "Anglo vs. Chicano: Why?" explains the purpose of his comparison, which is a good way to begin. He then uses paragraph division to show his numerous points of comparison—differences between the mother countries England and Spain, attitudes toward values, motives for colonization, effects of the horse, and so on. The following outlines show at a glance the two ways of organizing Campa's material, the one on the left being his actual choice:

Point by Point	*Subject by Subject*
I. Introduction	I. Introduction
II. Body	II. Body
A. Differences between mother countries	A. Anglo
1. Spain	B. Chicano
2. England	III. Conclusion
B. Different attitudes toward values	
1. Spanish	
2. English	
C. Different motives for colonization	
1. Spanish	
2. English	
D. Different effects of the horse	
⋮	
III. Conclusion	

Note that for every "Anglo point" Campa has a "Chicano point" and that the order of the points remains the same, Spanish (or Chicano) then English (or Anglo). The subject-by-subject method also requires equal and corresponding points for each subject, and consistent ordering of your points is even more important, since the points may be widely separated as they are in the selection from Aristotle's writing.

In "Youth and Old Age" Aristotle juxtaposes two portraits—one of youth, the other of old age—and lets the reader infer most of the differences; he is concerned almost wholly with one point, emotional and mental attitude, so his subject-by-subject method works well.

There is a special kind of comparison called analogy, in which *x* and *y* are necessarily unequal in both interest and importance. An analogy compares a well-known *x* with a less well known *y*, with the sole purpose of teaching what *y* is. Once the reader understands *y*, *x* can be forgotten. C. G. Jung, for example, compares the psyche to an oil well that penetrates stratum after stratum of different rocks and minerals. He is using an analogy to teach, not because he considers the psyche and the oil well to be really comparable, but because he wants to give a picture of the psyche and he believes that most of his readers would know what a geological cross section looks like.

Except in analogy, when we say two things are comparable we mean that they are in the same class—two generals, two athletes, two political philosophies, two countries—and this ensures some similarities between them. In fact, comparison of two logically incomparable things (except for the purposes of analogy) is the basis of such outrageous riddles as "How is a dentist like a parking lot?'" or "How is Los Angeles different from yogurt?" To be worthwhile as an expository mode, comparison must be of two subjects in the same general class, but it must also go beyond the obvious: the fact that Elizabeth I and Mary Stuart were both queens makes them merely comparable—provides a *basis* for comparison—but is too obvious to serve as a worthwhile *point* of comparison. Your points should be significant resemblances or differences that are beyond the obvious.

Transitional words and phrases are especially necessary in writing contrast, since you are continually alternating between points or subjects; get used to providing signals like "yet," "on the other hand," and "finally."

Writing Comparison

1   Explain the purpose of your comparison in your introduction.
2   Decide, primarily by considering the length and complexity of the material, which pattern is clearest, subject by subject or point by point.
3   Choose subjects for comparison that are from the same general class.
4   Use comparison of a well-known subject and an unfamiliar subject (analogy) as a teaching device.
5   Use transitions.

E. B. White (1899–   ) is an American humorist and essayist who began his career as a journalist with the *New Yorker*. He is best known for his children's book *Charlotte's Web*. His several volumes of essays are primarily social commentaries written in witty and succinct prose. In "Education" he contrasts his son's experience in a country school in Maine with his years in a progressive private school in New York City.

Education

E. B. White

I have an increasing admiration for the teacher in the country school 1 where we have a third-grade scholar in attendance. She not only undertakes to instruct her charges in all the subjects of the first three grades, but she manages to function quietly and effectively as a guardian of their health, their clothes, their habits, their mothers, and their snowball engagements. She has been doing this sort of Augean task for twenty years, and is both kind and wise. She cooks for the children on the stove that heats the room, and she can cool their passions or warm their soup with equal competence. She conceives their costumes, cleans up their messes, and shares their confidences. My boy already regards his teacher as his great friend, and I think tells her a great deal more than he tells us.

The shift from city school to country school was something we 2 worried about quietly all last summer. I have always rather favored public school over private school, if only because in public school you meet a greater variety of children. This bias of mind, I suspect, is partly an attempt to justify my own past (I never knew anything but public schools) and partly an involuntary defense against getting kicked in the shins by a young ceramist on his way to the kiln. My wife was unacquainted with public schools, never having been exposed (in her early life) to anything more public than the washroom of Miss Winsor's. Regardless of our backgrounds, we both knew that the change in schools was something that concerned not us but the scholar himself. We hoped it would work out all right. In New York our son went to a medium-priced private institution with semi-progressive ideas of education, and modern plumbing. He learned fast, kept well, and we were satisfied. It was an electric, colorful, regimented existence with moments of pleasurable pause and giddy incident. The day the Christmas angel fainted and had to be carried out by one of the Wise Men was educational in the highest sense of the term. Our scholar gave imitations of it around the house for weeks afterwards, and I doubt if it ever goes completely out of his mind.

His days were rich in formal experience. Wearing overalls and an old sweater (the accepted uniform of the private seminary), he sallied forth at morn accompanied by a nurse or a parent and walked (or was pulled) two blocks to a corner where the school bus made a flag stop. This flashy vehicle was as punctual as death: seeing us waiting at the cold curb, it would sweep to a halt, open its mouth, suck the boy in, and spring away with an angry growl. It was a good deal like a train picking up a bag of mail. At school the scholar was worked on for six or seven hours by half a dozen teachers and a nurse, and was revived on orange juice in midmorning. In a cinder court he played games supervised by an athletic instructor, and in a cafeteria he ate lunch worked out by a dietitian. He soon learned to read with gratifying facility and discernment and to make Indian weapons of a semi-deadly nature. Whenever one of his classmates fell low of a fever the news was put on the wires and there were breathless phone calls to physicians, discussing periods of incubation and allied magic.

In the country all one can say is that the situation is different, and somehow more casual. Dressed in corduroys, sweatshirt, and short rubber boots, and carrying a tin dinner-pail, our scholar departs at crack of dawn for the village school, two and a half miles down the road, next to the cemetery. When the road is open and the car will start, he makes the journey by motor, courtesy of his old man. When the snow is deep or the motor is dead or both, he makes it on hoof. In the afternoons he walks or hitches all or part of the way home in fair weather, gets transported in foul. The schoolhouse is a two-room frame building, bungalow type, shingles stained a burnt brown with weather-resistant stain. It has a chemical toilet in the basement and two teachers above stairs. One takes the first three grades, the other the fourth, fifth, and sixth. They have little or no time for individual instruction, and no time at all for the esoteric. They teach what they know themselves, just as fast and as hard as they can manage. The pupils sit still at their desks in class, and do their milling around outdoors during recess.

There is no supervised play. They play cops and robbers (only 5 they call it "Jail") and throw things at one another—snowballs in winter, rose hips in fall. It seems to satisfy them. They also construct darts, pinwheels, and "pick-up sticks" (jackstraws), and the school itself does a brisk trade in penny candy, which is for sale right in the classroom and which contains "surprises." The most highly prized surprise is a fake cigarette, made of cardboard, fiendishly lifelike.

The memory of how apprehensive we were at the beginning is 6 still strong. The boy was nervous about the change too. The tension, on that first fair morning in September when we drove him to school, almost blew the windows out of the sedan. And when later we picked him up on the road, wandering along with his little blue lunch pail, and got his laconic report "All right" in answer to our inquiry about how the day had gone, our relief was vast. Now, after almost a year of it, the only difference we can discover in the two school experiences is that in the country he sleeps better at night—and *that* probably is more the air than the education. When grilled on the subject of school-in-country *vs.* school-in-city, he replied that the chief difference is that the day seems to go so much quicker in the country. "Just like lightning," he reported.

Questions on Meaning

1   Why does White admire his son's teacher in the country school? How is she different from the teachers in the private school in the city?

2   What is White's attitude toward the private school? How does it compare with his attitude toward public schools?

3   In paragraph 4 White says that education in the country is "somehow more casual." In what ways is country education more casual than city education? Are there ways in which it is less casual?

Questions on Method

1 List the points of difference White's son sees between his private school in the city and his public school in the country. Is there a logic to their order? Does every "city point" have a corresponding "country point"?

2 At the end of paragraph 4 White describes the instruction methods and classroom behavior in the country school. What does this description imply about how education is conducted in a "semi-progressive" private school? Can you pick out other implied contrasts and comparisons in the essay?

3 Why does White contrast the "modern plumbing" in the city school to the "chemical toilet" in the basement of the country school? How does the comparison of these seemingly inconsequential details reflect a major theme of the essay?

4 What do you make of the simile that White offers in paragraph 4, comparing the city school bus to "a train picking up a bag of mail"? In what sense does this simile symbolize the contrasting life-styles of city and country?

5 In paragraph 6 White says that the tension he and his family felt on the first day they drove to the country school "almost blew the windows out of the sedan." Why does he use so exaggerated an image? Compare the exaggerated quality of White's apprehension to the understated quality of his son's laconic report about the first day at the country school. In what sense does this comparison reflect the thesis of the essay?

Vocabulary and Diction

1 Why does White refer to his son as a "third-grade scholar"? How appropriate is the word "scholar" for a third-grader? What point is White making about his attitudes toward education?

2 What does "Augean task" in paragraph 1 mean? To what extent is this classical allusion an exaggerated description of the task facing the country school teacher? What themes of the essay does this allusion reflect?

3 Define the following words and phrases used by White: conceives (1), regimented (2), seminary (3), sallied (3), revived (3), the esoteric (4).

Writing Topics

1 Where White compares two types of school by first describing details of one and then describing related details of the other, sometimes it is more

effective to compare related details point by point. Write an essay in which you make a point-by-point comparison of your high school experience with your college experience.

2   In paragraph 2 White says that the day the Christmas angel fainted was "educational in the highest sense of the term." To what extent is it true that often the most educational moments of a school experience are the unexpected things that occur during extracurricular activities? Discuss this question in an essay that makes full use of the prose patterns of contrast and comparison and illustration and example.

3   Assuming that the teachers and the facilities are of equal quality, does it really matter whether a school's methods are progressive or old-fashioned? Discuss this question, making clear as you do so the differences between a progressive and an old-fashioned education.

4   When White says in paragraph 1 that his son's teacher is "both kind and wise," he implies a certain degree of contrast between these attributes. Write an essay that discusses how difficult it can be to act both kindly and wisely at the same time.

ARISTOTLE (384–322 B.C.) was a Greek philosopher who
defined much of the content of Western thought. He spent
twenty years at Plato's Athenian academy and in later life
established his own institution, the Lyceum, which became a
center for research into every field of inquiry. Of his numerous
works, forty-seven remain, primarily in the form of notes used
in his Lyceum lectures. In the following essay, he draws many
contrasts between youth and age that are still pertinent today.

Youth and Old Age

Aristotle

Young men have strong passions, and tend to gratify them indiscrim-   1
inately. Of the bodily desires, it is the sexual by which they are most
swayed and in which they show absence of self-control. They are
changeable and fickle in their desires, which are violent while they
last, but quickly over: their impulses are keen but not deep-rooted,
and are like sick people's attacks of hunger and thirst. They are hot-
tempered and quick-tempered, and apt to give way to their anger;
bad temper often gets the better of them, for owing to their love of
honor they cannot bear being slighted, and are indignant if they
imagine themselves unfairly treated. While they love honor, they
love victory still more; for youth is eager for superiority over others,
and victory is one form of this. They love both more than they love
money, which indeed they love very little, not having yet learnt what
it means to be without it—this is the point of Pittacus' remark about
Amphiaraus.[1] They look at the good side rather than the bad, not
having yet witnessed many instances of wickedness. They trust others
readily, because they have not often been cheated. They are sanguine;

---

1. Reference unknown.

nature warms their blood as though with excess of wine; and besides that, they have as yet met with few disappointments. Their lives are mainly spent not in memory but in expectation; for expectation refers to the future, memory to the past, and youth has a long future before it and a short past behind it: on the first day of one's life one has nothing at all to remember, and can only look forward. They are easily cheated, owing to the sanguine disposition just mentioned. Their hot tempers and hopeful dispositions make them more courageous than older men are; the hot temper prevents fear, and the hopeful disposition creates confidence; we cannot feel fear so long as we are feeling angry, and any expectation of good makes us confident. They are shy, accepting the rules of society in which they have been trained, and not yet believing in any other standard of honour. They have exalted notions, because they have not yet been humbled by life or learnt its necessary limitations; moreover, their hopeful disposition makes them think themselves equal to great things—and that means having exalted notions. They would always rather do noble deeds than useful ones: their lives are regulated more by moral feeling than by reasoning; and whereas reasoning leads us to choose what is useful, moral goodness leads us to choose what is noble. They are fonder of their friends, intimates, and companions than older men are, because they like spending their days in the company of others, and have not yet come to value either their friends or anything else by their usefulness to themselves. All their mistakes are in the direction of doing things excessively and vehemently. They disobey Chilon's precept[2] by overdoing everything; they love too much and hate too much, and the same with everything else. They think they know everything, and are always quite sure about it; this, in fact, is why they overdo everything. If they do wrong to others, it is because they mean to insult them, not to do them actual harm. They are ready to pity others, because they think every one an honest man, or anyhow better than he is: they judge their neighbour by their own harmless natures, and so cannot think he deserves to be treated in that way. They are fond of fun and therefore witty, wit being well-bred insolence.

Such, then, is the character of the Young. The character of Elderly Men—men who are past their prime—may be said to be formed for the most part of elements that are the contrary of all these.

2. "(Do) nothing in excess."

They have lived many years; they have often been taken in, and often made mistakes; and life on the whole is a bad business. The result is that they are sure about nothing and *under-do* everything. They 'think,' but they never 'know'; and because of their hesitation they always add a 'possibly' or a 'perhaps,' putting everything this way and nothing positively. They are cynical; that is, they tend to put the worse construction on everything. Further, their experience makes them distrustful and therefore suspicious of evil. Consequently they neither love warmly nor hate bitterly, but following the hint of Bias they love as though they will some day hate and hate as though they will some day love.[3] They are small-minded, because they have been humbled by life: their desires are set upon nothing more exalted or unusual than what will help them to keep alive. They are not generous, because money is one of the things they must have, and at the same time their experience has taught them how hard it is to get and how easy to lose. They are cowardly, and are always anticipating danger; unlike that of the young, who are warm-blooded, their temperament is chilly; old age has paved the way for cowardice; fear is, in fact, a form of chill. They love life; and all the more when their last day has come, because the object of all desire is something we have not got, and also because we desire most strongly that which we need most urgently. They are too fond of themselves; this is one form that small-mindedness takes. Because of this, they guide their lives too much by considerations of what is useful and too little by what is noble—for the useful is what is good for oneself, and the noble what is good absolutely. They are not shy, but shameless rather; caring less for what is noble than for what is useful, they feel contempt for what people may think of them. They lack confidence in the future; partly through experience—for most things go wrong, or anyhow turn out worse than one expects; and partly because of their cowardice. They live by memory rather than by hope; for what is left to them of life is but little as compared with the long past; and hope is of the future, memory of the past. This, again, is the cause of their loquacity; they are continually talking of the past, because they enjoy remembering it. Their fits of anger are sudden but feeble. Their sensual passions have either altogether gone or have lost their vigour: consequently they do not feel their passions much, and their actions

3. Bias of Priene; "they treat their friends as probable future enemies and their enemies as probable future friends."

are inspired less by what they do feel than by the love of gain. Hence men at this time of life are often supposed to have a self-controlled character; the fact is that their passions have slackened, and they are slaves to the love of gain. They guide their lives by reasoning more than by moral feeling; reasoning being directed to utility and moral feeling to moral goodness. If they wrong others, they mean to injure them, not to insult them. Old men may feel pity, as well as young men, but not for the same reason. Young men feel it out of kindness; old men out of weakness, imagining that anything that befalls any one else might easily happen to them, which, as we saw, is a thought that excites pity. Hence they are querulous, and not disposed to jesting or laughter—the love of laughter being the very opposite of querulousness.

Such are the characters of Young Men and Elderly Men. People 3 always think well of speeches adapted to, and reflecting, their own character; and we can now see how to compose our speeches so as to adapt both them and ourselves to our audiences.

Questions on Meaning

1 According to Aristotle, what are the basic character traits of youth? Why do young men overdo everything?

2 What does Aristotle mean when he says that the lives of young men "are regulated more by moral feeling than by reasoning"?

3 What are the basic character traits of old age as Aristotle defines them? Why do elderly men underdo everything?

4 What does Aristotle mean when he says that elderly men "love as though they will some day hate and hate as though they will some day love"?

5 In what ways are elderly men more selfish than young men? Why is the pity that old men feel less kind than the pity that young men feel?

6 Why, according to Aristotle, are elderly men "supposed to have a self-controlled character" in contrast to young men? In what way are elderly men, in your opinion, as lacking in self-control as young men?

Questions on Method

1 Aristotle offers one long paragraph that describes numerous characteristics of young men, then a second long paragraph that describes the contrasting characteristics of old men. What effect might Aristotle have

gained had he instead organized a series of short paragraphs in each of which he contrasted one character trait of youth with one corresponding trait of old age?

2   How effectively does Aristotle employ cause-and-effect analysis to explain the differences between youth and old age?

3   Discuss Aristotle's use of the simile of sickness in his third sentence. Where does he make use of this image later in the essay?

4   While Aristotle's overall purpose is to compare young men and elderly men, he also devotes a good deal of the essay to comparisons between the respective characteristics of each age class. Where do you find a "bad" trait canceling out a "good" trait or vice versa? Which subject is left with more "good" traits, the young or the old?

Vocabulary and Diction

1   Aristotle contrasts the sanguine disposition of youth to the cynical disposition of old age. What is a sanguine disposition? What is a cynical disposition? How well does Aristotle define these words for us? Which do you think is more applicable to Aristotle himself?

2   What does the word "loquacity" mean? Why, according to Aristotle, are old men given to loquacity? Why is their loquacity "querulous" rather than "witty"? According to Aristotle, what is "wit"? Is Aristotle a witty writer?

Writing Topics

1   How fair do you think Aristotle's characterization of youth or old age is? How would you characterize them? Write an essay comparing your characterization of either youth or old age with Aristotle's.

2   Do you agree with Aristotle when he says that "we desire most strongly that which we need most urgently"? Write an essay in which you compare your desires with your needs.

3   Do you agree with Aristotle when he says that "we cannot feel fear so long as we are feeling angry"? Write an essay in which you explain your answer.

4   Aristotle tells us experience teaches old men that "most things go wrong, or anyhow turn out worse than one expects." Write an essay in which you compare the validity of such a suspicious or "cynical" view of life to the validity of what Aristotle calls youth's "sanguine" or optimistic view.

5   Write an essay that compares Aristotle's view of youth to John Leonard's.

6 Write an essay that compares Aristotle's view of old age to the impression that E. B. White gives of himself as an old man in "The Sea and the Wind That Blows."

ARTHUR L. CAMPA (1905–   ) was born in Mexico and now
lives in America. He graduated from Columbia University with
a doctorate in Spanish and has taught at several universities,
including the University of New Mexico and the University of
Colorado at Denver. He was a cultural attaché at the U.S.
Embassy in Lima, Peru, from 1955 to 1957. His publications
include several Spanish textbooks as well as more than seventy
monographs, bulletins, and articles on folklore. His interest in
cultural interrelationships is reflected in the essay that follows.

Anglo vs. Chicano: Why?

Arthur L. Campa

The cultural differences between Hispanic and Anglo-American peo- 1
ple have been dwelt upon by so many writers that we should all be
well informed about the values of both. But audiences are usually of
the same persuasion as the speakers, and those who consult published
works are for the most part specialists looking for affirmation of what
they believe. So, let us consider the same subject, exploring briefly
some of the basic cultural differences that cause conflict in the Southwest, where Hispanic and Anglo-American cultures meet.

Cultural differences are implicit in the conceptual content of the 2
languages of these two civilizations, and their value systems stem from
a long series of historical circumstances. Therefore, it may be well to
consider some of the English and Spanish cultural configurations
before these Europeans set foot on American soil. English culture was
basically insular, geographically and ideologically; was more inte-
grated on the whole, except for some strong theological differences;
and was particularly zealous of its racial purity. Spanish culture was

From *Western Review* 9, Spring 1972. © 1972. Reprinted by permission.

peninsular, a geographical circumstance that made it a catchall of Mediterranean, central European and north African peoples. The composite nature of the population produced a market regionalism that prevented close integration, except for religion, and led to a strong sense of individualism. These differences were reflected in the colonizing enterprise of the two cultures. The English isolated themselves from the Indians physically and culturally; the Spanish, who had strong notions about *pureza de sangre* [purity of blood] among the nobility, were not collectively averse to adding one more strain to their racial cocktail. Cortés led the way by siring the first *mestizo* in North America, and the rest of the conquistadores followed suit. The ultimate products of these two orientations meet today in the Southwest.

Anglo-American culture was absolutist at the onset; that is, all 3 the dominant values were considered identical for all, regardless of time and place. Such values as justice, charity, honesty were considered the superior social order for all men and were later embodied in the American Constitution. The Spaniard brought with him a relativistic viewpoint and saw fewer moral implications in man's actions. Values were looked upon as the result of social and economic conditions.

The motives that brought Spaniards and Englishmen to America 4 also differed. The former came on an enterprise of discovery, searching for a new route to India initially, and later for new lands to conquer, the fountain of youth, minerals, the Seven Cities of Cíbola and, in the case of the missionaries, new souls to win for the Kingdom of Heaven. The English came to escape religious persecution, and once having found a haven, they settled down to cultivate the soil and establish their homes. Since the Spaniards were not seeking a refuge or running away from anything, they continued their explorations and circled the globe 25 years after the discovery of the New World.

This peripatetic tendency of the Spaniard may be accounted for 5 in part by the fact that he was the product of an equestrian culture. Men on foot do not venture far into the unknown. It was almost a century after the landing on Plymouth Rock that Governor Alexander Spotswood of Virginia crossed the Blue Ridge Mountains, and it was not until the nineteenth century that the Anglo-Americans began to move west of the Mississippi.

The Spaniard's equestrian role meant that he was not close to   6
the soil, as was the Anglo-American pioneer, who tilled the land and
built the greatest agricultural industry in history. The Spaniard cultivated the land only when he had Indians available to do it for him.
The uses to which the horse was put also varied. The Spanish horse
was essentially a mount, while the more robust English horse was
used in cultivating the soil. It is therefore not surprising that the
viewpoints of these two cultures should differ when we consider that
the pioneer is looking at the world at the level of his eyes while the
caballero [horseman] is looking beyond and down at the rest of the
world.

One of the most commonly quoted, and often misinterpreted,   7
characteristics of Hispanic peoples is the deeply ingrained individualism in all walks of life. Hispanic individualism is a revolt against
the incursion of collectivity, strongly asserted when it is felt that the
ego is being fenced in. This attitude leads to a deficiency in those
social qualities based on collective standards, an attitude that Hispanos do not consider negative because it manifests a measure of
individual freedom. Naturally, such an attitude has no reglas fijas
[fixed rules].

Anglo-Americans who achieve a measure of success and security   8
through institutional guidance not only do not mind a few fixed rules
but demand them. The lack of a concerted plan of action, whether
in business or in politics, appears unreasonable to Anglo-Americans.
They have a sense of individualism, but they achieve it through
action and self-determination. Spanish individualism is based on feeling, on something that is the result not of rules and collective standards but of a person's momentary, emotional reaction. And it is
subject to change when the mood changes. In contrast to Spanish
emotional individualism, the Anglo-American strives for objectivity
when choosing a course of action or making a decision.

The Southwestern Hispanos voiced strong objections to the lack   9
of courtesy of the Anglo-Americans when they first met them in the
early days of the Sante Fe trade. The same accusation is leveled at
the Americanos today in many quarters of the Hispanic world. Some
of this results from their different conceptions of polite behavior.
Here too one can say that the Spanish have no reglas fijas because for
them courtesy is simply an expression of the way one person feels
toward another. To some they extend the hand, to some they bow
and for the more íntimos there is the well-known abrazo. The concepts

of "good or bad" or "right and wrong" in polite behavior are moral considerations of an absolutist culture.

Another cultural contrast appears in the way both cultures share part of their material substance with others. The pragmatic Anglo-American contributes regularly to such institutions as the Red Cross, the United Fund and a myriad of associations. He also establishes foundations and quite often leaves millions to such institutions. The Hispano prefers to give his contribution directly to the recipient so he can see the person he is helping.   10

A century of association has inevitably acculturated both His-panos and Anglo-Americans to some extent, but there still persist a number of culture traits that neither group has relinquished alto-gether. Nothing is more disquieting to an Anglo-American who believes that time is money than the time perspective of Hispanos. They usually refer to this attitude as the "*mañana* psychology." Ac-tually, it is more of a "today psychology," because Hispanos cultivate the present to the exclusion of the future; because the latter has not arrived yet, it is not a reality. They are reluctant to relinquish the present, so they hold on to it until it becomes the past. To an Hispano, nine is nine until it is ten, so when he arrives at nine-thirty, he jubilantly exclaims: "¡Justo!" [right on time]. This may be why the clock is slowed down to a walk in Spanish while in English it runs. In the United States, our future-oriented civilization plans our lives so far in advance that the present loses its meaning. January magazine issues [including ID's] are out in December; 1973 cars have been out since October; cemetery plots and even funeral arrangements are bought on the installment plan. To a person en-grossed in living today the very idea of planning his funeral sounds like the tolling of the bells.   11

It is a natural corollary that a person who is present oriented should be compensated by being good at improvising. An Anglo-American is told in advance to prepare for an "impromptu speech," but an Hispano usually can improvise a speech because "*Nosotros lo improvisamos todo*" [we improvise everything].   12

Another source of cultural conflict arises from the difference between *being* and *doing*. Even when trying to be individualistic, the Anglo-American achieves it by what he does. Today's younger gen-eration decided to be themselves, to get away from standardization, so they let their hair grow, wore ragged clothes and even went barefoot in order to be different from the Establishment. As a result   13 they all ended up doing the same things and created another stereo-type. The freedom enjoyed by the individuality of *being* makes it unnecessary for Hispanos to strive to be different.

In 1963 a team of psychologists from the University of Guada- 14 lajara in Mexico and the University of Michigan compared 74 upper-middle-class students from each university. Individualism and person-alism were found to be central values for the Mexican students. This was explained by saying that a Mexican's value as a person lies in his *being* rather than, as is the case of the Anglo-Americans, in concrete accomplishments. Efficiency and accomplishments are derived char-acteristics that do not affect worthiness in the Mexican, whereas in the American it is equated with success, a value of highest priority in the American culture. Hispanic people disassociate themselves from material things or from actions that may impugn a person's sense of being, but the Anglo-American shows great concern for material things and assumes responsibility for his actions. This is expressed in the language of each culture. In Spanish one says, "*Se me cayó la taza*" [the cup fell away from me] instead of "I dropped the cup."

In English, one speaks of money, cash and all related transactions 15 with frankness because material things of this high order do not trouble Anglo-Americans. In Spanish such materialistic concepts are circumvented by referring to cash as *efectivo* [effective] and when buying or selling as something *al contado* [counted out], and when without it by saying *No tengo fondos* [I have no funds]. This disas-sociation from material things is what produces *sobriedad* [sobriety] in the Spaniard according to Miguel de Unamuno, but in the Southwest the disassociation from materialism leads to *dejadez* [lassitude] and *desprendimiento* [disinterestedness]. A man may lose his life defending his honor but is unconcerned about the lack of material things. *Desprendimiento* causes a man to spend his last cent on a friend, which when added to lack of concern for the future may mean that tomorrow he will eat beans as a result of today's binge.

The implicit differences in words that appear to be identical in 16 meaning are astonishing. Versatile is a compliment in English and an insult in Spanish. An Hispano student who is told to apologize cannot do it, because the word doesn't exist in Spanish. *Apologia* means words in praise of a person. The Anglo-American either apologizes, which is a form of retraction abhorrent in Spanish, or compromises, another concept foreign to Hispanic culture. *Compromiso* means a date, not a compromise. In colonial Mexico City, two hidalgos once entered a narrow street from opposite sides, and when they could not go around, they sat in their coaches for three days until the viceroy ordered them to back out. All this because they could not work out a compromise.

It was that way then and to some extent now. Many of today's   17
conflicts in the Southwest have their roots in polarized cultural differences, which need not be irreconcilable when approached with mutual respect and understanding.

Questions on Meaning

1   What historical differences between England and Spain, according to Campa, account for the differences today between Anglo-American and Hispanic-American cultures?

2   How does the difference that Campa points out in paragraphs 5 and 6 between the English pioneer and the Spanish horseman prepare us to understand the difference between Anglo-American and Hispanic American concepts of individualism?

3   Why, according to Campa, are Anglo-Americans more "pragmatic" than Hispanic-Americans? How is this difference reflected in each culture's attitude toward time?

4   What is the difference Campa points out in paragraph 13 between "being" and "doing"? What effect does the Hispanic emphasis on being have on Hispanic attitudes toward material success?

5   In paragraph 2 Campa states, "Cultural differences are implicit in the conceptual content of the languages of these two civilizations." In what way is Campa's discussion in paragraph 16 of "implicit differences in words that appear to be identical in meaning" an effective summary of the major cultural differences between Anglos and Hispanos? How would you summarize the essential differences between these two groups of people? Do you agree with Campa's conclusion that these differences "need not be irreconcilable"?

Questions on Method

1   How does Campa's organizational method differ from Aristotle's? Why might Campa have organized his comparison differently?

2   Although Campa compares characteristics of each culture, he devotes many more words to explaining Hispanic characteristics than he does to explaining Anglo characteristics. How can you account for this emphasis?

3 How logical and reasonable is Campa's tone? Do you think that his essay would convince both an Anglo-American and a Hispanic American that their cultural characteristics, however different, deserve "mutual respect and understanding"? Are there characteristics of either culture that, as Campa presents them, you find unreasonable and difficult to understand?

Vocabulary and Diction

1 What is the difference between "insular" and "peninsular" in paragraph 2? How do these words of geographical description suggest how geographical differences may either result in or symbolize cultural differences?

2 In what sense is the phrase "*mañana* psychology" in paragraph 11 pejorative or disrespectful? How positive is "today psychology," Campa's alternative phrase?

3 Why does Campa in paragraph 12 place the phrase "impromptu speech" in quotation marks?

4 Define the following words and phrases used by Campa: ideologically (2), zealous (2), *mestizo* (2), conquistadores (2), peripatetic (5), equestrian (5), ingrained (7), the incursion of collectivity (7), *reglas fijas* (7), concerted (8), *íntimos* (9), *abrazo* (9), myriad (10), acculturated (11), corollary (12), compensated (12), personalism (14), impugn (14), circumvented (15), *efectivo* (15), *al contado* (15), *sobriedad* (15), *dejadez* (15), *desprendimiento* (15), versatile (16), retraction (16), abhorrent (16), hidalgos (16), viceroy (16), polarized (17).

Writing Topics

1 Campa's essay focuses on the contrasting values of two of the European-based cultures that meet in the United States. Write an essay on the contrasting values of some of the other cultures in this country. How are the contrasts between Anglos and Hispanos comparable to contrasts that you can point out between Americans from other cultures?

2 In paragraph 11 Campa argues that in America "our future-oriented civilization plans our lives so far in advance that the present loses its meaning." Write an essay in which you compare specific examples of American attitudes toward the past, the present, and the future.

3 Write an essay comparing someone you know who tends to have self-esteem simply because of his or her character and feelings with someone you know who tends to have self-esteem primarily because of his or her accomplishments.

4   One theme of Campa's essay is that the language we use reveals a good deal about the values we live by. Write an essay in which you discuss what the specialized language of a particular cultural activity in America reveals about American values in general. What, for example, does the language of American sportscasters, disc jockeys, or movie heroes reveal about our present-day values?

ALEXANDER PETRUNKEVITCH (1875–1964) was a Russian
zoologist who gained recognition as an authority on spiders. His
several books include *Index Catalogue of Spiders of North, Central
and South America* (1911) and *Principles of Classification* (1952).
He taught for many years at numerous American universities
and in later life was a well-known translator of Russian poetry.
In the following essay he analyzes the characteristics of the
spider and the wasp.

The Spider and the Wasp

Alexander Petrunkevitch

In the feeding and safeguarding of their progeny insects and spiders 1
exhibit some interesting analogies to reasoning and some crass examples of blind instinct. The case I propose to describe here is that
of the tarantula spiders and their arch-enemy, the digger wasps of the
genus Pepsis. It is a classic example of what looks like intelligence
pitted against instinct—a strange situation in which the victim,
though fully able to defend itself, submits unwittingly to its destruction.

Most tarantulas live in the tropics, but several species occur in 2
the temperate zone and a few are common in the southern U.S. Some
varieties are large and have powerful fangs with which they can inflict
a deep wound. These formidable looking spiders do not, however,
attack man; you can hold one in your hand, if you are gentle, without
being bitten. Their bite is dangerous only to insects and small mammals such as mice; for man it is no worse than a hornet's sting.

Tarantulas customarily live in deep cylindrical burrows, from 3
which they emerge at dusk and into which they retire at dawn.

Mature males wander about after dark in search of females and occasionally stray into houses. After mating, the male dies in a few weeks, but a female lives much longer and can mate several years in succession. In a Paris museum is a tropical specimen which is said to have been living in captivity for 25 years.

A fertilized female tarantula lays from 200 to 400 eggs at a time; 4 thus it is possible for a single tarantula to produce several thousand young. She takes no care of them beyond weaving a cocoon of silk to enclose the eggs. After they hatch, the young walk away, find convenient places in which to dig their burrows and spend the rest of their lives in solitude. The eyesight of tarantulas is poor, being limited to a sensing of change in the intensity of light and to the perception of moving objects. They apparently have little or no sense of hearing, for a hungry tarantula will pay no attention to a loudly chirping cricket placed in its cage unless the insect happens to touch one of its legs.

But all spiders, and especially hairy ones, have an extremely 5 delicate sense of touch. Laboratory experiments prove that tarantulas can distinguish three types of touch: pressure against the body wall, stroking of the body hair, and riffling of certain very fine hairs on the legs called trichobothria. Pressure against the body, by the finger or the end of a pencil, causes the tarantula to move off slowly for a short distance. The touch excites no defensive response unless the approach is from above where the spider can see the motion, in which case it rises on its hind legs, lifts its front legs, opens its fangs and holds this threatening posture as long as the object continues to move.

The entire body of a tarantula, especially its legs, is thickly 6 clothed with hair. Some of it is short and wooly, some long and stiff. Touching this body hair produces one of two distinct reactions. When the spider is hungry, it responds with an immediate and swift attack. At the touch of a cricket's antennae the tarantula seizes the insect so swiftly that a motion picture taken at the rate of 64 frames per second shows only the result and not the process of capture. But when the spider is not hungry, the stimulation of its hairs merely causes it to shake the touched limb. An insect can walk under its hairy belly unharmed.

The trichobothria, very fine hairs growing from dislike mem- 7 branes on the legs, are sensitive only to air movement. A light breeze makes them vibrate slowly, without disturbing the common hair. When one blows gently on the trichobothria, the tarantula reacts with a quick jerk of its four front legs. If the front and hind legs are stimulated at the same time, the spider makes a sudden jump. This reaction is quite independent of the state of its appetite.

These three tactile responses—to pressure on the body wall, to moving of the common hair, and to flexing of the trichobothria—are so different from one another that there is no possibility of confusing them. They serve the tarantula adequately for most of its needs and enable it to avoid most annoyances and dangers. But they fail the spider completely when it meets its deadly enemy, the digger wasp Pepsis. 8

These solitary wasps are beautiful and formidable creatures. Most species are either a deep shiny blue all over, or deep blue with rusty wings. The largest have a wing span of about four inches. They live on nectar. When excited, they give off a pungent odor—a warning that they are ready to attack. The sting is much worse than that of a bee or common wasp, and the pain and swelling last longer. In the adult stage the wasp lives only a few months. The female produces but a few eggs, one at a time at intervals of two or three days. For each egg the mother must provide one adult tarantula, alive but paralyzed. The mother wasp attaches the egg to the paralyzed spider's abdomen. Upon hatching from the egg, the larva is many hundreds of times smaller than its living but helpless victim. It eats no other food and drinks no water. By the time it has finished its single Gargantuan meal and become ready for wasphood, nothing remains of the tarantula but its indigestible chitinous skeleton. 9

The mother wasp goes tarantula-hunting when the egg in her ovary is almost ready to be laid. Flying low over the ground late on a sunny afternoon, the wasp looks for its victim or for the mouth of a tarantula burrow, a round hole edged by a bit of silk. The sex of the spider makes no difference, but the mother is highly discriminating as to species. Each species of Pepsis requires a certain species of tarantula, and the wasp will not attack the wrong species. In a cage with a tarantula which is not its normal prey, the wasp avoids the spider and is usually killed by it in the night. 10

Yet when a wasp finds the correct species, it is the other way about. To identify the species the wasp apparently must explore the spider with her antennae. The tarantula shows an amazing tolerance to this exploration. The wasp crawls under it and walks over it without evoking any hostile response. The molestation is so great and 11 so persistent that the tarantula often rises on all eight legs, as if it were on stilts. It may stand this way for several minutes. Meanwhile the wasp, having satisfied itself that the victim is of the right species, moves off a few inches to dig the spider's grave. Working vigorously with legs and jaws, it excavates a hole 8 to 10 inches deep with a diameter slightly larger than the spider's girth. Now and again the wasp pops out of the hole to make sure that the spider is still there.

When the grave is finished, the wasp returns to the tarantula to 12 complete her ghastly enterprise. First she feels it all over once more with her antennae. Then her behavior becomes more aggressive. She bends her abdomen, protruding her sting, and searches for the soft membrane at the point where the spider's legs join its body—the only spot where she can penetrate the horny skeleton. From time to time, as the exasperated spider slowly shifts ground, the wasp turns on her back and slides along with the aid of her wings, trying to get under the tarantula for a shot at the vital spot. During all this maneuvering, which can last for several minutes, the tarantula makes no move to save itself. Finally the wasp corners it against some obstruction and grasps one of its legs in her powerful jaws. Now at last the harassed spider tries a desperate but vain defense. The two contestants roll over and over on the ground. It is a terrifying sight and the outcome is always the same. The wasp finally manages to thrust her sting into the soft spot and holds it there for a few seconds while she pumps in the poison. Almost immediately the tarantula falls paralyzed on its back. Its legs stop twitching; its heart stops beating. Yet it is not dead, as is shown by the fact that if taken from the wasp it can be restored to some sensitivity by being kept in a moist chamber for several months.

After paralyzing the tarantula, the wasp cleans herself by drag- 13 ging her body along the ground and rubbing her feet, sucks the drop of blood oozing from the wound in the spider's abdomen, then grabs a leg of the flabby, helpless animal in her jaws and drags it down to the bottom of the grave. She stays there for many minutes, sometimes for several hours, and what she does all that time in the dark we do not know. Eventually she lays her egg and attaches it to the side of the spider's abdomen with a sticky secretion. Then she emerges, fills the grave with soil carried bit by bit in her jaws, and finally tramples the ground all around to hide any trace of the grave from prowlers. Then she flies away, leaving her descendant safely started in life.

In all this the behavior of the wasp evidently is qualitatively 14 different from that of the spider. The wasp acts like an intelligent animal. This is not to say that instinct plays no part or that she reasons as man does. But her actions are to the point; they are not automatic and can be modified to fit the situation. We do not know for certain how she identifies the tarantula—probably it is by some olfactory or chemo-tactile sense—but she does it purposefully and does not blindly tackle a wrong species.

On the other hand, the tarantula's behavior shows only confu- 15 sion. Evidently the wasp's pawing gives it no pleasure, for it tries to move away. That the wasp is not simulating sexual stimulation is certain because male and female tarantulas react in the same way to its advances. That the spider is not anesthetized by some odorless secretion is easily shown by blowing lightly at the tarantula and making it jump suddenly. What, then, makes the tarantula behave as stupidly as it does?

No clear, simple answer is available. Possibly the stimulation by 16 the wasp's antennae is masked by a heavier pressure on the spider's body, so that it reacts as when prodded by a pencil. But the expla- nation may be much more complex. Initiative in attack is not in the nature of tarantulas; most species fight only when cornered so that escape is impossible. Their inherited patterns of behavior apparently prompt them to avoid problems rather than attack them. For example, spiders always weave their webs in three dimensions, and when a spider finds that there is insufficient space to attach certain threads in the third dimension, it leaves the place and seeks another, instead of finishing the web in a single plane. This urge to escape seems to arise under all circumstances, in all phases of life, and to take the place of reasoning. For a spider to change the pattern of its web is as impossible as for an inexperienced man to build a bridge across a chasm obstructing his way.

In a way the instinctive urge to escape is not only easier but 17 often more efficient than reasoning. The tarantula does exactly what is most efficient in all cases except in an encounter with a ruthless and determined attacker dependent for the existence of her own species on killing as many tarantulas as she can lay eggs. Perhaps in this case the spider follows its usual pattern of trying to escape, instead of seizing and killing the wasp, because it is not aware of its danger. In any case, the survival of the tarantula species as a whole is pro- tected by the fact that the spider is much more fertile than the wasp.

220

Questions on Meaning

1   In paragraph 14 Petrunkevitch says that when a digger wasp attacks a tarantula, the behavior of the wasp is "qualitatively" different from the behavior of the spider. What is the basic difference pointed out by Petrunkevitch?

2   Why, according to paragraph 9, does a mother wasp go "tarantula-hunting"? Describe the sequence of steps the wasp takes to identify, paralyze, and bury the spider. How do scientists know that the spider is not dead, but only paralyzed? What steps in the process does Petrunkevitch admit remain a mystery to scientists?

3   At the end of paragraph 15 Petrunkevitch asks, "What, then, makes the tarantula behave as stupidly as it does?" What possible answers does Petrunkevitch first reject? What answers does he then offer?

Questions on Method

1   Where does Petrunkevitch state his thesis? How does he employ techniques of comparison to support his thesis? List the points about tarantulas that have corresponding "wasp points." Which of these points are used in the later discussion (paragraphs 14 through 17) of instinct versus intelligence? Which method of comparison is used in paragraphs 1 through 14, point by point or subject by subject?

2   Before Petrunkevitch narrates the process of how and why a digger wasp paralyzes a tarantula, he offers a lengthy description of the wasp's victim. Why does his description emphasize the spider's "delicate sense of touch"? How objective is the tone of the description? How objective is the tone of the subsequent narration?

3   In paragraph 16 Petrunkevitch says, "For a spider to change the pattern of its web is as impossible as for an inexperienced man to build a bridge across a chasm obstructing his way." Is there anything about this analogy between a spider and a man that seems to involve specious reasoning, that is, reasoning that sounds logical and fair but may not be so?

4   Why does Petrunkevitch conclude the essay by reminding us that the spider is much more fertile than the wasp?

Vocabulary and Diction

1   How adequate is the definition of "intelligent" behavior that Petrunkevitch offers in paragraph 14?

2   Define the following words and phrases used by Petrunkevitch: progeny (1), genus (1), riffling (5), trichobothria (5), dislike membranes (7), Gargantuan (9), chitinous (9), molestation (11), some olfactory or chemo-tactile sense (14).

Writing Topics

1   Are there times when a person is better off relying on instinct rather than on intelligence? Write an essay in which you compare instinct with intelligence more favorably than Petrunkevitch does.

2   To illustrate the difference between intelligence and instinct, write an essay in which you compare the behavior of two people.

3   The natural process that Petrunkevitch describes presents us, as he says, with a "terrifying sight." Write an essay describing a natural process that presents us, instead, with a calm, peaceful sight. What lesson might you draw about nature out of the contrasting impressions given by these two processes?

4   Write an essay in which you speculate about how someone like Rachel Carson, given her view of nature, might respond to the "terrifying sight" Petrunkevitch describes.

5   Develop an analogy to describe the difference between reasoning intelligence and blind instinct. Write an essay that discusses the degree to which the analogy you develop involves specious reasoning.

RUSSELL BAKER (1925–   ) is a regular columnist for the *New York Times.* He began his career in journalism with the *Baltimore Sun,* and in 1954 he joined the Washington bureau of the *New York Times.* His books include *An American in Washington* (1961), *All Things Considered* (1965), and *Poor Russell's Almanac* (1972). In this essay from the *New York Times* Baker satirizes computer education.

Terminal Education

Russell Baker

Ever since reading about Clarkson College's plan to replace its library 1 with a computer I have been worrying about what college students will do in the spring. I mean, you can't just haul a computer out on the campus and plunk it down under a budding elm and lie there with the thing on your chest while watching the birds at work, can you?

You can do that with a book, and it is one of the better things 2 about going to college. With a computer, though, you've got to have a video terminal, which is basically a television set that rolls little, green, arthritic-looking letters and numbers across a dark screen.

It's not much fun reading a television screen, since, for one 3 thing, the print has a terribly tortured look, as if it had spent four months in a Savak cellar, and since, for another, you always expect it to be interrupted by a commercial. Which is neither here nor there, of course, since this kind of reading is not supposed to convey pleasure, but information.

The difficulty is that you can't take your television screen out 4
under the elm tree and plug it into the computer—the information
bank or the information center or the information conveyor, or
whatever they choose to call it—since (1) television screens are
expensive and fragile and no college president in his right mind is
going to let students expose them to ants, dew and tree sap, and since
(2) colleges aren't going to shortchange the football team to pay for
installing electrical outlets in the tree trunks.

What this means for college students of the future—and Clark- 5
son's electronic library is the library of the future, make no mistake—
what it means is that students are going to be spending their springs
sitting alone in stale air staring at television screens.

Give them a six-pack of beer or a glass of bourbon, you might 6
say, and you have the ideal training program for American adult
home life, which, one supposes, they will still be expected to undertake once they leave college stuffed with information. All I can say
is: What does this have to do with education?

The answer comes from Dr. Walter Grattidge, director of Clark- 7
son's new Educational Resources Center—Clarkson's term, not mine.
"Education," he told a New York Times reporter, "is basically an
information-transfer process." At the risk of sounding somewhat snap-
pish, I say, "Fie, Dr. Grattidge! Fie!"

"Information-transfer process" indeed. Education is not like a 8
decal, to be slipped off a piece of stiff paper and pasted on the back
of the skull. The point of education is to waken innocent minds to
a suspicion of information.

An educated person is one who has learned that information 9
almost always turns out to be at best incomplete and very often false,
misleading, fictitious, mendacious—just dead wrong. Ask any seasoned cop or newspaper reporter. Ask anybody who has ever been
the defendant in a misdemeanor trial or the subject of a story in a
newspaper.

Well, let's grant that Dr. Grattidge's opinion about being "ba- 10
sically an information-transfer process" is only 80 percent baloney. If
you're going to learn the importance of mistrusting information,
somebody first has to give you some information, and college is a
place where people try to do this, if only so the professors can find
out how gullible you are.

Knowing that, they can then begin to try to teach you to ask a 11
few questions before buying the Brooklyn Bridge or the newest theory

about the wherefore of the universe. I'm talking about the good professors now, not the ones who spend all their time compiling fresh information to be transferred to the book-buying public. Even the good professors, however, rarely have enough time to teach the whole student body the art of doubting, which leads to the astonishing act of thinking.

This is why so much of whatever educating happens at college 12 happens in places like the grass under the elm where somebody has gone to read a book, just because it seems like a nicer place to read than the library, and has become distracted by the shape of the clouds, or an ant on the elbow, or an impulse to say to the guy or the girl crossing the quadrangle, "Let's chuck the books for a while and get a beer."

If the time is autumn, and the campus has an apple tree, who 13 knows? Maybe somebody half asleep in an informational-transference volume will look up, see an apple fall and revolutionize science. Not much chance of that happening if you're sitting in a room staring at a TV screen plugged into the Educational Resources Center, is there?

In there you are just terribly alone, blotting up information from 14 a machine which, while very, very smart in some ways, has never had an original thought in its life. And no trees grow, and no apples fall.

Questions on Meaning

1 Why is Baker worried about what college students will do in the spring?
2 What does Baker dislike about computers as educational tools? Why does he prefer learning from books?
3 What does Baker mean when he writes in paragraph 8 that "the point of education is to waken innocent minds to a suspicion of information"? How does his view of education's purpose contrast with that of Dr. Grattidge?
4 What is an educated person, according to Baker? Why is a person more likely to become educated, in Baker's sense of the word, by sitting under an apple tree than by sitting in a library?

Questions on Method

1 How much does Baker exaggerate when he contrasts books with computers as learning tools? List the differences, as Baker sees them, between books and computers. Do the points correspond logically? Are books and computers comparable? Why?
2 What attitude does Baker's tone convey?
3 In paragraph 11 Baker claims that "the art of doubting" leads to "the astonishing act of thinking." How valid is Baker's cause-and-effect analysis here and elsewhere in the essay?
4 In paragraph 3 Baker says that the reading one does in a library is "not supposed to convey pleasure, but information." Does Baker himself believe that there are two contrasting types of reading? How does understanding Baker's attitude toward this contrast clarify our understanding of his thesis?

Vocabulary and Diction

1 Explain the pun in Baker's title.
2 Why does Baker object to the phrase "information-transfer process" as a definition of education? Do you share his objection?
3 How objective is Baker's definition of "video terminal" in paragraph 2?

Writing Topics

1 Write an essay in which you contrast the benefits or gains to the possible damages or losses that result from the use of computers in education, business, government, sports, or some other field with which you are familiar.
2 How much education at college does go on, as Baker says, "in places like the grass under the elm where somebody has gone to read a book"? Compare two educational experiences that you have had, one inside the classroom or library, one outside.
3 Do you agree with Baker when he charges that "information almost always turns out to be at best incomplete and very often false"? Write an essay explaining your answer.
4 Write an essay that compares Baker's attitudes toward education with the attitudes of E. B. White.

Comparison and Contrast—Writing Topics

1   Write an essay in which you compare the advantages and the disadvantages of each of the two major organizational methods used by the authors in this chapter. When is it more advantageous to organize a comparison by first discussing one set of details, then discussing a contrasting set of details? When is it more advantageous to first compare one detail to a contrasting detail, then a second detail to a second contrasting detail, and so on?

2   Which of the authors in this chapter do you find to be the most objective in comparing the relative attributes of two different points of view? Which do you find to be the least objective, the most slanted or biased? Write an essay that explains your answer.

3   Write an essay that compares the views two people who differ in age, personality, or background take toward a controversial subject.

4   Is there a difference between being educated and being intelligent? Write an essay comparing these two concepts.

5   Write an essay in which a contrast between two animals illustrates by way of analogy a significant difference in two types of human behavior.

SEVEN

Classification

Classification, like sorting clothes or silverware, is an act of organizing. The yellow pages, classified ads, and catalogs and indexes of all kinds use classification to bring order to a subject or a set of things by showing the relationship of parts to the whole and to one another. Classification is one of the best ways to understand and explain a subject.

When making a classification, you are asking the question "What kinds of x are there?" and are grouping these kinds on the basis of resemblances and differences. Classification, indeed, can be viewed as a special application of comparison and contrast. For example, in the system devised by the botanist Charles Linnaeus all plants and animals have two names, the first being the name of the genus; the second, of the species. Thus similarity gives to all carnations the common name *Dianthus,* and the differences among carnations are accounted for by the names *Dianthus prolifer, Dianthus barbatus, Dianthus deltoides,* and many more. (A good classification would never include the phrase "and many more" or the abbreviation "etc.," for a classification must be a complete list of classes.) The members of a class, therefore, are all alike in some one way, and that way (or basis of classification) must be applied throughout the system. If you have a choice of several bases of classification, choose the one that fits your purpose for making a classification. Linnaeus' basis—structure or morphology rather than, say, appearance—allows for the widest application to a continually growing field of knowledge, which was his main purpose. But plants can also be classified according to their food value, their medical use, their scent, their environment, their mythological associations, and so on.

Suppose your purpose—more modest than Linnaeus'—is to persuade the local school board to spend more money on certain sports. You might begin by classifying them, using as your basis of classification the objective you want to promote. Some possible bases might be (*a*) popularity with townspeople and alumni, (*b*) local traditions, (*c*) age at which the sport can be played, (*d*) number of players required, and (*e*) cost. You can see what a different classification each basis would produce. Your choice would finally have to depend on your purpose for making the classification—for example, to convince the board to budget more money for lifelong sports like tennis and swimming. Having chosen the basis, you would include every sport that fits your classes and exclude all others; you would choose and label your classes so that a sport fits into only one class. You could not divide sports into the categories of soccer, basketball, and tennis because your system would be incomplete. You could not divide sports into winter, summer, and team because some sports would fit into two classes, making the division meaningless.

Not every subject can be easily classified, and many bases of classification do not provide clear-cut classes. One of the bases for classifying sports noted above, cost, will not provide clear-cut classes: is a sport that uses $100 worth of equipment different in kind from one that uses $101 worth? The color red shades imperceptibly into reddish orange; the compass direction west into west-northwest and northwest; and middle-class, into lower middle-class. In a continuum or spectrum the basis of classification becomes more important than the classes because instead of absolute and fixed classes we have trends or tendencies toward one or the other end of the spectrum. More of our classes than we often realize are arbitrary points on a continuum— "the Middle Ages," "animal," "person." If you find it difficult to answer the question "What kinds of person are there?" you may have to settle for a spectrum on which people "tend" toward one pole or the other rather than for a set of absolute classes into which they fit. Even so, if you can devise such a spectrum, you will have brought some order to the subject.

Having devised a system, use other expository modes to develop it, such as explaining your purpose and the basis of classification, defining class names, and perhaps comparing your system to less adequate ones. Narration and description may also come to your aid.

Writing Classification

1 Choose a basis of classification that serves your purpose.
2 Provide only one class for every part.
3 Develop your outline with examples, description, definition, process analysis, cause and effect, and so on.

JAMES DAVID BARBER (1930–   ) is a professor of political
science at Duke University and a frequent guest lecturer at
colleges throughout the country. He has written many essays for
both scholarly and popular periodicals and has edited *Race for
the Presidency* (1978) and *The Pulse of Politics* (1980). In the
following essay, taken from *The Presidential Character*, he
classifies four types of President.

Four Types of President

James David Barber

Who the President is at a given time can make a profound difference   1
in the whole thrust and direction of national politics. Since we have
only one President at a time, we can never prove this by comparison,
but even the most superficial speculation confirms the commonsense
view that the man himself weighs heavily among other historical
factors. A Wilson re-elected in 1920, a Hoover in 1932, a John F.
Kennedy in 1964 would, it seems very likely, have guided the body
politic along rather different paths from those their actual successors
chose. Or try to imagine a Theodore Roosevelt ensconced behind
today's "bully pulpit" of a Presidency, or Lyndon Johnson as President
in the age of McKinley. Only someone mesmerized by the lures of
historical inevitability can suppose that it would have made little or
no difference to government policy had Alf Landon replaced FDR in
1936, and Dewey beaten Truman in 1948, or Adlai Stevenson reigned
through the 1950s. Not only would these alternative Presidents have
advocated different policies—they would have approached the office

from very different psychological angles. It stretches credibility to think that Eugene McCarthy would have run the institution the way Lyndon Johnson did.

The first baseline in defining Presidential types is *activity-passivity.* 2
How much energy does the man invest in his Presidency? Lyndon Johnson went at his day like a human cyclone, coming to rest long after the sun went down. Calvin Coolidge often slept eleven hours a night and still needed a nap in the middle of the day. In between the Presidents array themselves on the high or low side of the activity line.

The second baseline is *positive-negative affect* toward one's activ- 3
ity—that is, how he feels about what he does. Relatively speaking, does he seem to experience his political life as happy or sad, enjoyable or discouraging, positive or negative in its main effect. The feeling I am after here is not grim satisfaction in a job well done, not some philosophical conclusion. The idea is this: is he someone who, on the surfaces we can see, gives forth the feeling that he has *fun* in political life? Franklin Roosevelt's Secretary of War, Henry L. Stimson, wrote that the Roosevelts "not only understood the *use* of power, they knew the *enjoyment* of power, too. . . . Whether a man is burdened by power or enjoys power; whether he is trapped by responsibility or made free by it; whether he is moved by other people and outer forces or moves them—that is the essence of leadership."

The positive-negative baseline, then, is a general symptom of 4
the fit between the man and his experience, a kind of register of *felt* satisfaction.

Why might we expect these two simple dimensions to outline 5
the main character types? Because they stand for two central features of anyone's orientation toward life. In nearly every study of personality, some form of the active-passive contrast is critical; the general tendency to act or be acted upon is evident in such concepts as dominance-submission, extraversion-introversion, aggression-timidity, attack-defense, fight-flight, engagement-withdrawal, approach-avoidance. In everyday life we sense quickly the general energy output of the people we deal with. Similarly we catch on fairly quickly to the affect dimension—whether the person seems to be optimistic or pessimistic, hopeful or skeptical, happy or sad. The two baselines are clear and they are also independent of one another: all of us know people who are very active but seem discouraged, others who are quite passive but seem happy, and so forth. The activity baseline

refs to what one does, the affect baseline to how one feels about what he does.

Both are crude clues to character. They are leads into four basic character patterns long familiar in psychological research. In summary form, these are the main configurations: 6

Active-positive: There is a congruence, a consistency, between much activity and the enjoyment of it, indicating relatively high self-esteem and relative success in relating to the environment. The man shows an orientation toward productiveness as a value and an ability to use his styles flexibly, adaptively, suiting the dance to the music. He sees himself as developing over time toward relatively well-defined personal goals—growing toward his image of himself as he might yet be. There is an emphasis on rational mastery, on using the brain to move the feet. This may get him into trouble, he may fail to take account of the irrational in politics. Not everyone he deals with sees things his way and he may find it hard to understand why. 7

Active-negative: The contradiction here is between relatively intense effort and relatively low emotional reward for that effort. The activity has a compulsive quality, as if the man were trying to make up for something or to escape from anxiety into hard work. He seems ambitious, striving upward, power-seeking. His stance toward the environment is aggressive and he has a persistent problem in managing his aggressive feelings. His self-image is vague and discontinuous. Life is a hard struggle to achieve and hold power, hampered by the condemnations of a perfectionistic conscience. Active-negative types pour energy into the political system, but it is an energy distorted from within. 8

Passive-positive: This is the receptive, compliant, other-directed character whose life is a search for affection as a reward for being agreeable and cooperative rather than personally assertive. The contradiction is between low self-esteem (on grounds of being unlovable, unattractive) and a superficial optimism. A hopeful attitude helps dispel doubt and elicits encouragement from others. Passive-positive types help soften the harsh edges of politics. But their dependence and the fragility of their hopes and enjoyments make disappointment in politics likely. 9

234

Passive-negative: The factors are consistent—but how are we to account for the man's *political* role-taking? Why is someone who does little in politics and enjoys it less there at all? The answer lies in the passive-negative's character-rooted orientation toward doing dutiful service; this compensates for low self-esteem based on a sense of uselessness. Passive-negative types are in politics because they think they ought to be. They may be well adapted to certain nonpolitical roles, but they lack the experience and flexibility to perform effectively as political leaders. Their tendency is to withdraw, to escape from the conflict and uncertainty of politics by emphasizing vague principles (especially prohibitions) and procedural arrangements. They become guardians of the right and proper way, above the sordid politicking of lesser men.

Active-positive Presidents want most to achieve results. Active-negatives aim to get and keep power. Passive-positives are after love. Passive-negatives emphasize their civic virtue. The relation of activity to enjoyment in a President thus tends to outline a cluster of characteristics, to set apart the adapted from the compulsive, compliant, and withdrawn types.

The first four Presidents of the United States, conveniently, ran through this gamut of character types. (Remember, we are talking about tendencies, broad directions; no individual man exactly fits a category.) George Washington—clearly the most important President in the pantheon—established the fundamental legitimacy of an American government at a time when this was a matter in considerable question. Washington's dignity, judiciousness, his aloof air of reserve and dedication to duty fit the passive-negative or withdrawing type best. Washington did not seek innovation, he sought stability. He longed to retire to Mount Vernon, but fortunately was persuaded to stay on through a second term, in which, by rising above the political conflict between Hamilton and Jefferson and inspiring confidence in his own integrity, he gave the nation time to develop the organized means for peaceful change.

John Adams followed, a dour New England Puritan, much given to work and worry, an impatient and irascible man—an active-negative President, a compulsive type. Adams was far more partisan than Washington; the survival of the system through his Presidency demonstrated that the nation could tolerate, for a time, domination by one of its nascent political parties. As President, an angry Adams brought the United States to the brink of war with France, and presided over the new nation's first experiment in political repression: the Alien and Sedition Acts, forbidding, among other things, unlawful combinations "with intent to oppose any measure or measures of the government of the United States," or "any false, scandalous, and malicious writing or writings against the United States, or the President of the United States, with intent to defame . . . or to bring them or either of them, into contempt or disrepute."

Then came Jefferson. He too had his troubles and failures—in the design of national defense, for example. As for his Presidential character (only one element in success or failure), Jefferson was clearly active-positive. A child of the Enlightenment, he applied his reason to organizing connections with Congress aimed at strengthening the more popular forces. A man of catholic interests and delightful humor, Jefferson combined a clear and open vision of what the country could be with a profound political sense, expressed in his famous phrase, "Every difference of opinion is not a difference of principle."

The fourth President was James Madison, "Little Jemmy," the constitutional philosopher thrown into the White House at a time of great international turmoil. Madison comes closest to the passive-positive, or compliant, type; he suffered from irresolution, tried to compromise his way out, and gave in too readily to the "warhawks" urging combat with Britain. The nation drifted into war, and Madison wound up ineptly commanding his collection of amateur generals in the streets of Washington. General Jackson's victory at New Orleans saved the Madison administration's historical reputation; but he left the Presidency with the United States close to bankruptcy and secession.

These four Presidents—like all Presidents—were persons trying to cope with the roles they had won by using the equipment they had built over a lifetime. The President is not some shapeless organism in a flood of novelties, but a man with a memory in a system with a history. Like all of us, he draws on his past to shape his future. The pathetic hope that the White House will turn a Caligula into a Marcus Aurelius is as naive as the fear that ultimate power inevitably corrupts. The problem is to understand—and to state understandably—what in the personal past foreshadows the Presidential future.

Questions on Meaning

1   In what two ways does the President affect history? Which of these two does Barber focus on as a means of classifying different Presidential types?

2   What are the two "baselines" Barber uses to define Presidential types? Why, according to paragraph 5, should we expect these two baselines "to outline the main character types"?

3   What are the "four basic character patterns" Barber summarizes in paragraphs 7 through 10?

4   What does Barber mean by concluding that it is as naive to hope "that the White House will turn a Caligula into a Marcus Aurelius" as it is to fear "that ultimate power inevitably corrupts"? How predictable, according to Barber, is any President's performance if we understand that President's past?

Questions on Method

1   How effectively do the examples Barber cites in paragraphs 12 through 15 help us to understand his classification system?

2   How arbitrary is it of Barber to employ a general system for classifying human personality types specifically to classify Presidential types? Does Barber have a good reason for using a general system?

3   Do you agree with Barber's doubts, expressed in his second sentence, about the possible effectiveness of using comparison to prove that the President's personality makes a difference in national politics? Why does Barber say that in this case comparison is an inappropriate method? How does Barber, nevertheless, make effective use of it?

Vocabulary and Diction

1   What does the phrase "compulsive quality" in paragraph 8 mean? Is there any way the act of classification itself partakes of a compulsive quality? How well does Barber define the other terms from psychology that he employs?

2   Why does Barber italicize the word "felt" in paragraph 4? How does this help us understand what he means by "affect dimension"?

3   Define the following words and phrases used by Barber: ensconced (1), configurations (6), congruence (7), the irrational (7), discontinuous (8), elicits (9), gamut (12), pantheon (12), judiciousness (12), integrity (12),

irascible (13), partisan (13), nascent (13), political repression (13), defame (13), the Enlightenment (14).

Writing Topics

1 Write an essay in which you classify, according to Barber's system, the men who have been President in your lifetime. Explain fully why you classify each President as you do.

2 Write an essay applying Barber's system of classification to some profession other than politics.

3 In what ways does Barber's system strike you as being a more effective way of classifying Presidents than the traditional classification according to political parties? What variables or baselines other than Democrat or Republican does the traditional system employ? Write an essay that compares the way each system would classify two Presidents who common sense tells you are very different from each other.

4 In paragraph 3 Barber quotes Henry L. Stimson's definition of "the essence of leadership" as "the *enjoyment* of power." Write an essay explaining whether you find this a good definition and why.

5 Write an essay in which you argue that one President was the greatest leader America has had, explaining clearly what criteria you used to decide who the greatest leader was.

6 Write an essay in which you argue that one President was the worst leader America has had.

ALVIN TOFFLER (1928–   ), after several years as a free-lance writer and an editor of *Fortune,* wrote *Future Shock* in 1970. It became an immediate best seller and made the subject and the author famous. His most recent study, *The Third Wave,* was published in 1980. The analysis of human relationships that follows was first published in *Future Shock.*

The Duration of Human Relationships

Alvin Toffler

Sociologists like Wirth have referred in passing to the transitory 1 nature of human ties in urban society. But they have made no systematic effort to relate the shorter duration of human ties to shorter durations in other kinds of relationships. Nor have they attempted to document the progressive decline in these durations. Until we analyze the temporal character of human bonds, we will completely misunderstand the move toward superindustrialism.

For one thing, the decline in the *average* duration of human 2 relationships is a likely corollary of the increase in the number of such relationships. The average urban individual today probably comes into contact with more people in a week than the feudal villager did in a year, perhaps even a lifetime. The villager's ties with other people no doubt included some transient relationships, but most of the people he knew were the same throughout his life. The urban man may have a core group of people with whom his interactions are sustained over long periods of time, but he also interacts with hundreds, perhaps thousands of people whom he may see only once or twice and who then vanish into anonymity.

All of us approach human relationships, as we approach other 3 kinds of relationships, with a set of built-in durational expectancies. We expect that certain kinds of relationships will endure longer than others. It is, in fact, possible to classify relationships with other people in terms of their expected duration. These vary, of course, from culture to culture and from person to person. Nevertheless, throughout wide sectors of the population of the advanced technological societies something like the following order is typical:

Long-duration relationships. We expect ties with our immediate 4 family, and to a lesser extent with other kin, to extend throughout the lifetimes of the people involved. This expectation is by no means always fulfilled, as rising divorce rates and family break-ups indicate. Nevertheless, we still theoretically marry "until death do us part" and the social ideal is a lifetime relationship. Whether this is a proper or realistic expectation in a society of high transience is debatable. The fact remains, however, that family links are expected to be long term, if not lifelong, and considerable guilt attaches to the person who breaks off such a relationship.

Medium-duration relationships. Four classes of relationships fall 5 within this category. Roughly in order of descending durational expectancies, these are relationships with friends, neighbors, job associates, and co-members of churches, clubs and other voluntary organizations.

Friendships are traditionally supposed to survive almost, if not 6 quite, as long as family ties. The culture places high value on "old friends" and a certain amount of blame attaches to dropping a friendship. One type of friendship relationship, however, acquaintanceship, is recognized as less durable.

Neighbor relationships are no longer regarded as long-term com- 7 mitments—the rate of geographical turnover is too high. They are expected to last as long as the individual remains in a single location, an interval that is growing shorter and shorter on average. Breaking off with a neighbor may involve other difficulties, but it carries no great burden of guilt.

On-the-job relationships frequently overlap friendships, and less 8 often, neighbor relationships. Traditionally, particularly among white-collar, professional and technical people, job relationships were supposed to last a relatively long time. This expectation, however, is also changing rapidly, as we shall see.

Co-membership relationships—links with people in church or   9
civic organizations, political parties and the like—sometimes flower into friendship, but until that happens such individual associations are regarded as more perishable than either friendships, ties with neighbors or fellow workers.

Short-duration relationships. Most, though not all, service rela-   10
tionships fall into this category. These involve sales clerks, delivery people, gas station attendants, milkmen, barbers, hairdressers, etc. The turnover among these is relatively rapid and little or no shame attaches to the person who terminates such a relationship. Exceptions to the service pattern are professionals such as physicians, lawyers and accountants, with whom relationships are expected to be somewhat more enduring.

This categorization is hardly airtight. Most of us can cite some   11
"service" relationship that has lasted longer than some friendship, job or neighbor relationship. Moreover, most of us can cite a number of quite long-lasting relationships in our own lives—perhaps we have been going to the same doctor for years or have maintained extremely close ties with a college friend. Such cases are hardly unusual, but they are relatively few in number in our lives. They are like long-stemmed flowers towering above a field of grass in which each blade represents a short-term relationship, a transient contact. It is the very durability of these ties that makes them noticeable. Such exceptions do not invalidate the rule. They do not change the key fact that, across the board, the *average* interpersonal relationship in our life is shorter and shorter in duration.

Questions on Meaning

1   Why, according to Toffler, is the "*average* interpersonal relationship" of shorter duration in today's societies than it was in earlier societies? Of what is the transitory nature of such relationships a corollary?

2   Is it true, as Toffler asserts, that because we expect certain kinds of relationship to last longer than others, we feel guilty about ending these relationships? What relationships, according to Toffler, do we expect to last longest?

3   What relationships does Toffler classify as medium-duration relationships? What does he mean when he says in paragraph 7 that "breaking off with a neighbor may involve other difficulties, but it carries no great burden of guilt"?

4   What relationships does Toffler classify as short-duration relationships? Is it true, as he says in paragraph 10, that "little or no shame attaches to a person who terminates such a relationship"?

Questions on Method

1   Why does Toffler make the basis of his classification system what he calls in paragraph 1 "the temporal character of human bonds"? In what ways is his categorization, as he admits in paragraph 11, "hardly airtight"?

2   How effective is the image Toffler offers describing transient relationships as blades of grass? To what extent does it exaggerate the difference between such relationships and those longer-term relationships that Toffler compares to long-stemmed flowers?

Vocabulary and Diction

1   In paragraph 3 Toffler says that all of us approach human relationships with "a set of built-in durational expectancies." What, expressed simply, does this phrase mean? What tone is lent to the essay by Toffler's use of such diction from the field of sociology?

2   In paragraph 6 Toffler says, "One type of friendship relationship, however, acquaintanceship, is recognized as less durable." How adequate is Toffler's definition of the word "acquaintanceship"?

Writing Topics

1   Write an essay in which you classify your relationships with people according to something other than the length of time you expect each type of relationship to last.

2   In paragraph 4 Toffler questions whether it is realistic to expect marriage to last a lifetime in "a society of high transience." Write an essay discussing whether it is unrealistic to expect marriage to last a lifetime in modern American society. What expectations do people have about marriage today? What expectations should they have?

242

3   Write an essay comparing three people with whom you have relationships, one with whom you have what Toffler would classify as a long-duration relationship, one with whom you have a medium-duration relationship, and one with whom you have a short-duration relationship. Are there any ways you consider the second and third relationships equally or more valuable than the first relationship?

4   How would you classify Toffler's view of the transience of the average interpersonal relationship today? Would you say that Toffler is realistic, objective, or scientific? Would you call him pessimistic or cynical? Compare your own view on this subject to Toffler's.

KENNETH H. COOPER spent several years as a physician in the U.S. Air Force. In his book *Aerobics* (1968), from which the following essay is taken, he discusses how to increase the oxygen capacity of the body through exercise.

How Fit Are You?

Kenneth H. Cooper

I was visiting a colleague who was testing volunteers for a special 1 project that would require men in the best possible condition. I passed three of the volunteers in the hall. Two had normal builds, but the third was definitely muscular.

"Which of the three do you think will get our recommendation?" 2 my friend asked, tossing their medical records across the desk. I skimmed over the physiological data until I came to the slot where it asked, "Regular exercise?"

One wrote, candidly, "None." 3

The second, "Nothing regular. Just ride my bike to the base and 4 back every day. About three miles one way."

The third, "Isometrics and weight lifting, one hour a day, five 5 days a week." The muscular one!

I glanced back over each of the records. All pilots, all in their 6 early 30s, none with any history of illness.

"Well?" asked my friend. 7

"I'd bet on the cyclist."   8

"Not the weight lifter?"   9

"Not if that's all he does."   10

My friend smiled. "I think you're right."   11

Next day he proved it. The three came back for their treadmill   12
tests and the nonexerciser and the weight lifter were completely
fatigued within the first five minutes. The cyclist was still going strong
10 minutes later, running uphill at a 6½ mph clip. He was recommended for the project. The other two weren't.

This story, when I use it in my lectures, always surprises people.   13
The nonexerciser they can believe. The cyclist, maybe. But the
weight lifter, or anyone who does strictly isometrics or calisthenics,
they all *look* in such good condition!

In my business, looks are deceitful. Some exceptionally physi-   14
cally fit men tested in our laboratory were middle-aged types with
slight builds, including an occasional one with a paunch. Some of
the most unfit we've ever seen were husky young men with cardiac
conditions.

If this shatters any illusions about slim waistlines and large biceps   15
being the key to good health, I'm sorry. They're not a deterrent, but
they're no guarantee either. They're mostly a byproduct. The real key
is elsewhere.

Take those three volunteers. By ordinary standards, all three   16
should have been accepted. None of them had any physical defects,
or ever had any. Why the discrimination?

For special projects, the military services can afford to be dis-   17
criminate. They can afford to classify the physically fit into their
three classic categories and choose only the most fit.

The nonexerciser represents passive fitness. There's nothing   18
wrong with him—not yet anyway—but there's nothing really right
with him either. If he's lucky, he can coast like that for years. But,
without any activity, his body is essentially deteriorating.

The weight lifter, or those who emphasize isometrics or calis-   19
thenics, represent muscular fitness. These types, who have the right
motives but the wrong approach, are stuck with the myth that muscular strength or agility means physical fitness. This is one of the
great misconceptions in the field of exercise. The muscles that show—
the skeletal muscles—are just one system in the body, and by no
means the most important. If your exercise program is directed only
at the skeletal muscles, you'll never achieve real physical fitness.

The cyclist, whether he knew it or not, had found one of the 20
most basic means to overall fitness. . . . By riding three miles to
work, six miles round trip, he was earning more than enough points
to answer the question, "How much exercise?" and he proved it on
the treadmill.

The cyclist represents the third, and best, kind of fitness, overall 21
fitness. We call it endurance fitness, or working capacity, the ability
to do prolonged work without undue fatigue. It assumes the absence
of any ailment, and it has little to do with pure muscular strength or
agility. It has very much to do with the body's *overall* health, the
health of the heart, the lungs, the entire cardiovascular system and
the other organs, *as well as* the muscles.

Questions on Meaning

1   In paragraph 14 Cooper says that in his business "looks are deceitful."
    What does he mean?
2   What are the "three classic categories" into which, according to Cooper,
    the military services classify the physically fit?
3   Why does Cooper in paragraph 18 say about the nonexerciser that,
    although there is nothing wrong with him, "there's nothing really right
    with him either"?
4   What misconception does Cooper in paragraph 19 say the weight lifter
    bases his exercise program on?
5   What "physiological" traits must one have in order to be classified in
    the same category as the cyclist?

Questions on Method

1   To what extent is Cooper's system of classification less arbitrary and more
    objective than the systems of the other authors in this chapter?
2   How completely do Cooper's categories account for all types of physical
    fitness? Can you think of any type that Cooper's system would not be
    able to classify?
3   Cooper uses the prose patterns of classification and narration to make a
    convincing argument. What lesson does he wish to teach? In what way
    does his use of classification make his argument more convincing than
    it would have been had he used only narration?

Vocabulary and Diction

1   In what ways does Cooper redefine "physically fit" for us? Might it be possible to classify Cooper's essay as an essay of definition?

Writing Topics

1   How do American health habits, our habits of eating and exercise and recreation, reflect what Cooper calls "the myth that muscular strength or agility means physical fitness"? Are there other aspects of American culture that also reflect this myth? Answer these questions, and then write an essay analyzing how physically fit Americans are.

2   To what extent do people seek what Cooper calls "muscular fitness" for reasons other than good health? Write an essay in which you analyze the different reasons people might try to look as though they are in good condition. See if you can develop a system for classifying different types of body builder.

3   Write an essay in which you describe the healthiest person you know. Proceed to classify the health of other acquaintances according to how they compare with the first person you described.

Of Studies

Francis Bacon

Studies serve for delight, for ornament, for ability. Their chief use 1
for delight is in privateness and retiring; for ornament, is in discourse;
and for ability, is in the judgment and disposition of business; for
expert[1] men can execute, and perhaps judge of particulars, one by
one; but the general counsels, and the plots and marshaling of affairs
come best from those that are learned. To spend too much time in
studies is sloth; to use them too much for ornament is affectation; to
make judgment wholly by their rules is the humor[2] of a scholar. They
perfect nature, and are perfected by experience; for natural abilities
are like natural plants, that need pruning by study; and studies themselves do give forth directions too much at large,[3] except they be
bounded in by experience. Crafty men contemn studies, simple men
admire them, and wise men use them; for they teach not their own
use; but that is a wisdom without them and above them, won by
observation. Read not to contradict and confute, nor to believe and
take for granted, nor to find talk and discourse, but to weigh and

---

1. Experienced. (Editors' note)
2. Inclination. (Editors' note)
3. Too general. (Editors' note)

consider. Some books are to be tasted, others to be swallowed, and some few to be chewed and digested; that is, some books are to be read only in parts; others to be read but not curiously, and some few to be read wholly, and with diligence and attention. Some books also may be read by deputy, and extracts made of them by others; but that would be only in the less important arguments and the meaner sort of books; else distilled books are, like common distilled waters, flashy[4] things. Reading maketh a full man; conference a ready man; and writing an exact man. And, therefore, if a man write little, he had need have a great memory; if he confer little, he had need have a present wit; and if he read little, he had need have much cunning, to seem to know that he doth not. Histories make men wise; poets, witty; the mathematics, subtle; natural philosophy, deep; moral, grave; logic and rhetoric, able to contend: *Abeunt studia in mores!*[5] Nay, there is no stand[6] or impediment in the wit but may be wrought out by fit studies; like as diseases of the body may have appropriate exercises. Bowling is good for the stone and reins,[7] shooting for the lungs and breast, gentle walking for the stomach, riding for the head, and the like. So if a man's wit be wandering, let him study the mathematics; for in demonstrations, if his wit be called away never so little, he must begin again. If his wit be not apt to distinguish or find differences, let him study the schoolmen; for they are *cymini sectores!*[8] If he be not apt to beat over[9] matters, and to call up one thing to prove and illustrate another, let him study the lawyers' cases. So every defect of the mind may have a special receipt.

Questions on Meaning

1 What, according to Bacon, are the three reasons that people study? What are the three reasons that some spend more time studying than they should?

2 Explain Bacon's observation that studies "perfect nature, and are perfected by experience." What is the relationship, as Bacon develops it,

---

4. Tasteless, flat. (Editors' note)
5. "Studies develop into habits." (Editors' note)
6. Obstacles. (Editors' note)
7. Testicles and kidneys. (Editors' note)
8. Hairsplitters. (Editors' note)
9. Thrash. (Editors' note)

between the knowledge that someone gains from study and the knowledge that someone gains from experience?

3　What are the reasons Bacon gives for reading? What general effect does reading have on a person compared to the general effect of conference or writing? How does Bacon classify the different types of effect that different types of reading have?

Questions on Method

1　An epigram is a witty, terse saying. List the epigrams you find in this classification. How many of them come in threes? What percentage of this classification consists of epigrams? Is this a convincing method of classifying? Which is more convincing, Bacon's method or Barber's?

2　Why does Bacon first classify books according to how they should be read, then according to why they should be read?

Vocabulary and Diction

1　In his second sentence Bacon contrasts "expert" with "learned." What does Bacon mean by the adjectives? In what way may the expert person become too crafty while the learned one may become too simple?

2　Define the following words and phrases used by Bacon: ornament, disposition, sloth, affectation, contemn, confute, diligence, distilled, subtle, grave, rhetoric.

Writing Topics

1　Bacon says, "*Abeunt studia in mores,*" that is, "Studies develop into habits." Do you agree with Bacon's theory that different classes of study help us develop or train different mental habits or skills? Write an essay in which you classify different subjects you have studied according to the type of mental skill each subject stressed.

2　How would you classify American attitudes toward study today? Do Americans tend to view study too pragmatically, simply as a means to a practical or useful end? Discuss this issue in an essay that classifies various attitudes one might take toward one's studies.

3　Write an essay in which you classify different types of wisdom or knowledge according to the way such knowledge is learned or used.

4　Write an essay that compares Bacon's attitude toward experience with the attitude Aristotle expresses in "Youth and Old Age."

R. D. Rosen (1949–   ) is a teacher and writer whose publications include *Psychobabble: Fast Talk and Quick Cure in the Era of Feeling* (1977). He is also a frequent contributor to periodicals such as *New Times* and *New Republic.* In the following essay from *Psychobabble* Rosen discusses the debasement of language in the 1970s.

Psychobabble

R. D. Rosen

While having drinks recently with a young woman I had not seen for some time, I asked how things were going and received this reply: "I've really been getting in touch with myself lately. I've struck some really deep chords." I recoiled slightly at the grandeur of her remarks, but she proceeded, undaunted, to reel out a string of broad psychological insights with an enthusiasm attributable less to her Tequila Sunrises than to the confessional spirit that is sweeping America.

I could not help thinking that I disappointed her with my inability to summon more lyricism and intensity in my own conversation. Now that reticence has gone out of style, I sensed an obligation to reciprocate her candor but couldn't bring myself to use the popular catch phrases of revelation. Would she understand if I said that instead of striking deep chords I had merely tickled the ivories of my psychic piano? That getting my head together was not exactly the way in which I wanted to describe what was going on above my neck? Surely it wouldn't do any good if I resorted to more precise, but

251

pompously clinical, language and admitted that I was well on my way to resolving my attitude toward my own maternal introject.

"Whenever I see you," she said brightly, "it makes me feel very 3 good inside. It's a real high-energy experience."

So what was wrong with me that I couldn't feel the full voltage 4 of our meeting? Unable to match her incandescence, I simply agreed, "Yes, it's good to see you, too," then fell silent.

Finally she said, her beatific smile widening, "But I can really 5 dig your silence. If you're bummed out, that's OK."

If anything characterizes the cultural life of the Seventies in 6 America, it is an insistence on preventing failure of communication. Everything must now be spoken. The Kinsey Report, Masters and Johnson, *The Joy of Sex* and its derivatives; The *Playboy* Advisor, the Penthouse Forum, *Oui*'s Sex Tapes; contraception; Esalen and the human potential movement; the democratization of psychotherapy—all these various oils have helped lubricate the national tongue. It's as if the full bladder of civilization's squeamishness has finally burst. The sexual revolution, this therapeutic age, has culminated in one profuse, steady stream of self-revelation, confessed profligacy and publicized domestic trauma.

It seems that almost everybody belongs to the Cult of Candor 7 these days, and that everyone who does speaks the same dialect. Are you relating? Good. Are you getting in touch with yourself? Fine. Gone through some heavy changes? Doing your own thing? (Or, are you, by some mistake, doing someone else's?) Is your head screwed on straight? Are you going to get your act together, or just your shit? Are you mind-fucked, or just engaging in mental foreplay?

One hears it everywhere, like endless panels of a Feiffer cartoon. 8 In restaurants distraught lovers lament, "I wish I could get into your head." A man on a bus says to his companion, "I just got back from the coast. What a different headset!" The latest reports from a corrupt Esalen provide us with new punch lines: A group leader there intones that "it's beautiful if you're unhappy. Go with the feeling . . . You gotta be you 'cause you're you and you gotta be, and besides, if you aren't gonna be you who else's gonna be you, honey. . . . This is the Aquarian Age and the time to be oneself, to love one's beauty, to go with one's process."

Are you sufficiently laid back to read this article? Will it be a 9 heavy experience, or merely the mock?

It's time we lend a name to this monotonous patois, this psy- 10
chological patter, whose concern is to faithfully catalog the ego's
condition: Psychobabble. As Psychobabble begins to tyrannize con-
versations everywhere, it is difficult to avoid, and there is an embarrassment involved in not using it in the presence of other Psychobabblers that is akin to the mild humiliation experienced by American
tourists in Paris who cannot speak the native language. It is now
spoken by magazine editors, management consultants, sandal makers,
tool and die workers and Ph.D.s in clinical psychology alike. What
the sociologist Philip Rieff in the mid-Sixties called "Psychological
Man," that mid-20th century victim of his own interminable intro-
spection, has become Psychobabbler, the victim of his own inability
to describe human behavior with anything but platitudes.

Psychobabble seems to have emerged toward the end of the 11
Sixties, distilled from the dying rad/lib dialects of political activism
and the newly thriving language of the human potential movement
with its Fritz Perls of wisdom. Activism was acquiring more and more
of a therapeutic cast, and the radical battles, once fought exclusively
in the real political world, were now being enacted in the individual
psyche. T-groups, encounter groups, sensitivity training, group
gropes, drama and primal therapies all helped shape the trend. Two
years ago, when Jerry Rubin proclaimed in *Psychology Today* that he
was going back to his body, where the real wars of liberation were
taking place, those who hadn't already preceded him now clamored
to trade in their political critiques for therapeutic ideals. The disaf-
fected were saying "Off the pigs" one day and "Man, I really feel
tense, don't mess with my head" the next.

Of course, this is not the first time in our history that psycho- 12
logical ideas have dominated national conversation. The old Psychobabble, however, was really just the wholesale use of Freudian
terms, less banter than a sort of intellectual one-upmanship. In post–
World War II America, Freudian terminology was embraced by liberal
magazines, novelists and enough of the middle class so that the
growing demand for psychoanalysis easily outdistanced the supply of
doctors.

As one Boston psychoanalyst, who has practiced for over 30 13
years, says, "After the war, everyone was talking simplistically about
the Oedipus complex. It was the rage. Everyone had the idea that
knowledge itself would make you free." Now he has to listen to the
new Psychobabble. A social worker patient in his 30s, himself a group

leader, eagerly responded at the beginning of therapy to each interpretation his analyst made by saying, "I hear you, I hear you."

"I'm sorry," said the doctor, "I didn't know you were a little 14
deaf."

"I'm not. I *hear* you. It means I comprehend." 15

"Well, *what* do you comprehend?" 16

The patient paused. "Jesus," he replied, "I don't know." 17

Psychobabble, the psychoanalyst says, "is just a way of using 18
candor in order not to be candid." The dangers of the old Psychobabble were remarked upon as early as 1929 in an article by Joseph
Jastrow in *The Century* entitled "The Freudian Temper and Its Menace to the Lay Mind." In it, Jastrow quotes a Boston analyst, Dr.
Myerson of Beacon Street: "Everybody talks glibly of repression,
complexes, sublimation, wish fulfillment and subconsciousness as if
they really understood Freud and what he was talking about. Gentle
reader, let me say this, that with the exception of a few professional
philosophers, psychologists, psychiatrists and psychoanalysts, I have
not met a dozen people who knew more than the terms of Freud."

The new Psychobabblers, however, don't even seem to know 19
the terms—of Freud, Jung, Adler, or any body of psychological
thought. Their language seems to free-float in some linguistic atmosphere, a set of repetitive verbal formalities that kills off the very
spontaneity, candor and understanding it pretends to promote. It's
an idiom that reduces psychological insight and therapeutic processes
to a collection of standardized insights, that provides only a limited
lexicon to deal with an infinite variety of problems. "Uptight" is a
word now used to describe an individual who is experiencing anything
from mild uneasiness to a clinical depression. To ask someone why
he or she refers to another as being "hung-up" produces a reply along
the lines of: *"Why?* Man, he's just *hung-up."* Oddly, those few psy-
chiatric terms borrowed by Psychobabble are used recklessly. One is
no longer fearful: one is *paranoid.* The adjective is applied to the
populace with a generosity that must confuse real clinical paranoiacs.
Increasingly, people describe their moody friends as *manic-depressives*
and almost anyone you don't like is psychotic, or at least *schizzed-out.*

The Cult of Candor, and particularly its language, Psychobabble, 20
is a feature of contemporary decorum, a form of *politesse,* a signal to
others that one is ready to talk a certain kind of turkey, to engage in
real dialogue. And real dialogue, it turns out, is often no more than
a monologue. When I asked a man to whom I had just been intro-

duced at a party recently, "How do you do?" he responded by describing, with an utter disrespect for brevity, his relationship with his wife. Confession is the new handshake.

If Psychobabble were a question of language alone, the worst 21 one could say about it is that it is just another example of the corrosion and unimaginativeness of spoken English. But the prevalence of Psychobabble reflects more than a mere "loss for words." It indicates that, in an era when the national gaze has turned inward, and in a country that needs therapy perhaps more than any other, Americans still have enormous difficulty in understanding the depth of their psychological problems, perhaps even in understanding that psychological problems *have* depth.

Questions on Meaning

1   Why does Rosen use the phrase "the Cult of Candor" to characterize American cultural life in the 1970s?
2   What is Psychobabble, and how did it develop?
3   In what ways does the present form of Psychobabble compare with what Rosen in paragraph 12 calls the "old Psychobabble"?
4   What does Rosen dislike about Psychobabble? What does he fear its prevalence indicates about the psychological problems of Americans?

Questions on Method

1   What general characteristics does Rosen focus on in order to classify someone's speech as Psychobabble?
2   What does the example Rosen offers in paragraphs 13 through 17 of the social worker's Psychobabble illustrate about this social phenomenon?
3   What is the dominant tone of the essay? Is it more humorous or more serious? How does the tone of paragraphs 1 through 9 convey Rosen's feelings about Psychobabble? Does the tone change noticeably in the second half of the essay?
4   What other, more respectable classes of language does Rosen's criticism of Psychobabble imply? Can you think of a neutral name for Psychobabble, one without derogatory connotations? How many kinds of language can you think of? How many do you use?

255

Vocabulary and Diction

1 Are any of the phrases that Rosen classifies as Psychobabble common to your speech? Do they mean more when you use them?

2 Define the following words and phrases used by Rosen: maternal introject (2), incandescence (4), profligacy (6), trauma (6), the mock (9), patois (10), banter (12), Oedipus complex (13), glibly (18), repression, complexes, sublimation, wish fulfillment and subconsciousness (18), lexicon (19), *politesse* (20).

Writing Topics

1 Rosen says that the Psychobabbler is "the victim of his own inability to describe human behavior with anything but platitudes." Write an essay in which you compare the platitudes used by Psychobabblers to the platitudes used by other culturally identifiable groups such as politicians, sports figures, entertainers, advertisers, or teachers. What are the primary characteristics of a phrase of speech that make it classifiable as a platitude?

2 What type of writer is Rosen? Can you categorize writers, divide them into distinct classifications? Write an essay in which you set up a system for classifying different types of writer, then explain which type Rosen is according to your system.

3 Rosen obviously disliked the 1970s in America. How did you feel about them? Write an essay in which you classify the 1970s from your point of view.

4 Do you agree with Rosen that America is "a country that needs therapy perhaps more than any other"? Write an essay arguing that Rosen is either right or wrong.

Classification—Writing Topics

1   How much does the act of classification require the ability to contrast and compare? Devise a system for classifying something with which you are familiar—the records in your record collection, for example—then write an essay that explains what sort of contrast and comparison you made to devise your system.

2   Write an essay in which you compare the system of classification presented in this chapter that seems to you the least arbitrary with the one that seems to you the most arbitrary.

3   Pick any essay in this chapter and devise a different system from the one used by its author to classify its subject matter. Can you devise a more comprehensive system, a system that better accounts for all the differences among the parts or types into which the subject can be divided?

4   A gourmand might well devise a different system for classifying restaurants than would a dieter or a business executive. Pick a subject about which people with differing interests are likely to have differing views, then write an essay that describes the systems that might be devised to classify the parts of the subject.

5   Devise a system for classifying the teachers at your school, a system that would help students decide whether to take a course with a particular teacher. Write an essay that explains how your system would work.

6   Although America is supposed to be the great melting pot, its people are divided into social classes. Write an essay in which you identify different types of American according to social class.

7   Write an essay classifying the members of a profession in America. Set up a system for categorizing different types of doctor, for example, or blue-collar worker, sports star, business figure, or actor.

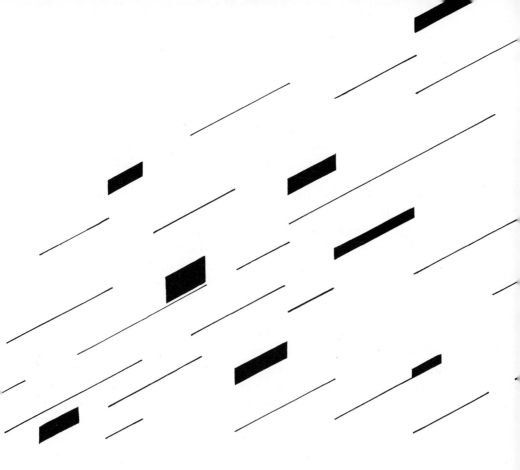

EIGHT

Process Analysis

Process analysis is one of the most common and practical kinds of exposition. It explains how to do something or how something is or was done. It has many purposes; everybody who does anything or tries to teach another person how to do something uses process analysis sooner or later. Success in a profession or career is usually measured by one's success at performing a process or set of processes—a secretary's success at taking shorthand, a doctor's at diagnosing, a salesperson's at selling. To increase one's proficiency or to teach others, it is usually necessary to analyze this process, dividing it into its constituent steps.

Like narration, process analysis consists of a series of incidents or steps in time, with the difference that "getting there is *not* half the fun"; in process analysis what counts is crossing the finish line, especially in the more practical how-to-do-it (rather than the how-it-was-done) analysis. The how-to-do-it essay is also like cause-and-effect exposition (see Chapter 9) in that it uses a sequence that theoretically can always be repeated to produce the same result.

You have had to learn step by step many processes that you now perform automatically and so take for granted, such as tying your shoes, reading, cooking, swimming, or driving. To analyze these processes so that you can improve your own performance or teach them to another person, you have to try to recover some of your naiveté and relive those learning experiences so that you can divide the process into its simplest steps. That is the pattern for any process analysis. The structure should be chronological where possible, isolating one step from another and isolating smaller processes (driving a car) from larger ones to which they have become attached (maintaining, buying, selling, racing, chauffeuring a car). Later in your essay you can show how the smaller processes link up with the larger ones. Imagine that you are writing one chapter in a textbook and that you will not be on hand to answer your students' questions. Assume an audience of beginners; explain terminology; describe equipment, tools, and parts; include diagrams where appropriate; give a reasonable estimate of the cost in time, training, and money.

Sometimes you may be called upon to analyze a set of processes only some of whose components can be explained: there are mysteries to managing an office and writing a novel that cannot be reduced to steps. Isolating the explainable from the unexplainable is an essential step in analysis; admit the limits of your knowledge. The fact that some of the most important processes are complex and imperfectly understood (especially those that involve the human being) has never prevented writers—and should not prevent you—from attempting to analyze them: how to land a job, how to succeed with the opposite sex, how to invest, how to avoid war, how to lose weight, how to interpret dreams, how to write an essay. Often the analyzer can only give pointers, indicate a direction, and hope that his or her directions find a receptive audience. Suppose, for example, you want to explain how to write an expository essay. You start by dividing the process into steps:

1 Choose a topic.
2 Limit the topic.
3 Make an outline.
4 Write a first draft.
5 Revise what you have written.

You soon find that each step assumes too much knowledge, leaving out too many intervening steps. So you break down these steps into smaller ones. Although each step may seem endlessly divisible, the time comes when you must stop and trust to your reader's good sense.

Make your analysis as specific, practical, and interesting as possible; give a set of clear steps and use other expository modes such as exemplification, definition, and comparison to expand these steps and appeal to the reader's reason, imagination, and ambition to succeed.

Writing Process Analysis

1 Break down the process into clear, chronological steps.
2 Use transitional words and phrases between steps.
3 Explain unfamiliar terminology or equipment. If you write for a general audience, risk including too much detail rather than too little.
4 If the subject is complex, indicate the time and training necessary to follow your directions.
5 Show how your process links up with others to form a larger process.

ARTHUR ASHE and CLARK GRAEBNER were both members of the U.S. tennis team that won the Davis Cup from Australia in 1968. They later coauthored a book on tennis, *Your Serve.* In this excerpt from that work they describe the process involved in serving.

The Serve

Arthur Ashe and Clark Graebner

The serve is the most important single shot in tennis. It is the one shot you can practice by yourself any time without need of someone else. Master the serve and you have taken a big step toward being a winning player.

The beginner should hold his racket with a forehand grip. Advanced players use the backhand grip to serve, and you will too eventually, but for the time, the forehand grip will be easier. You should develop a smooth flowing serving stroke before attempting to use the backhand grip.

When you step up to the baseline to serve, your body should be sideways to the net and your feet should be spread perhaps 12 to 18 inches apart. When you serve in the forehand court (the one to your left as you face the net), your left toe should be about an inch behind the baseline, your left heel about six inches behind it. In other words, your feet are not parallel to the baseline. When you serve, your left foot should not touch the line, nor should your right foot step into the court until your racket has made contact with the ball. Otherwise it is a footfault and the penalty is the same as if you hit your serve into the net.

From *Your Serve* by Arthur Ashe and Clark Graebner. Copyright © 1972 by Grow Ahead Press. Reprinted by permission.

Essentially, the serving motion is the same as the ball throwing   4
motion. Pretend the racket is a ball and "throw" it toward the service
area. The first motion you make backward transfers your weight to
your back foot. As you swing the racket forward, the weight is
transferred to the forward foot. At no point during the serve should
your arm stop moving; it is all one continuous motion.

A vital part of the serve is the toss of the ball. The object is to   5
place the ball in air exactly where you want to hit it. You get two
serves, but there is no reason why you should have to hold two balls
at once. That's what pockets are made for. The ball should be held
in the fingers of the left hand, never in the palm. The left hand starts
at the waist, rises slowly and straightens. You should release the ball
only when the arm is fully extended. It should be thrown just to the
point where it will meet the center of the racket when the right arm
is fully extended. If you can achieve a perfect toss, the rest should
come easily. Keep this in mind. There is no rule in tennis that says
you must hit the ball once you toss it. If by chance you make a bad
toss, say, too far behind you, stop in mid-swing and start over again.
After apologizing to your opponent, of course.

Here is a suggestion: since the fun of tennis is to be able to get   6
the ball into play as soon as possible you may enjoy learning to serve
more if you start, not from the baseline, but from the service line.
Once you start putting the ball into the service court from close
range, keep moving back until at last you are on the baseline.

Once you have learned how to serve, how to hit the ball into   7
the court, you can try a few variations. There are, basically, three
serves—the slice, twist and flat, sometimes known as cannonball.
The slice is the basic delivery for all players, whether beginners or
advanced. The racket face sweeps across the side of the ball furthest
from you (the three o'clock side) instead of striking directly behind
it, and causes the ball to move from your opponent's left to his right.
The flat serve has almost no spin and no chance of going in unless
you are six feet tall. The flat serve moves in a straight line from the
middle of the racket down to the court, but in the process it must,
of course, cross the net. Tall players can do this, but shorter ones
need spin to give the ball a curved trajectory.

The twist is good only if served well. Otherwise it will provide   8
a set-up for the receiver. It must be deep and it must have a high
kick to the backhand side. You can put twist on the ball by tossing
it slightly behind your head (instead of in front on the slice), then

bringing the racket across it from left to right. Don't try this one until you can put your regular serve into play consistently.

Questions on Meaning

1   According to Ashe and Graebner, what are the four basic steps that must be learned to serve a tennis ball correctly?
2   What are the differences among the three basic types of serve described by Ashe and Graebner? Why is the slice the most basic? Why are the flat and the twist more difficult?

Questions on Method

1   In what sense do Ashe and Graebner explain each step of the serve as a separate process? Is their explanation about how to position your feet, for example, or about how to toss the ball a fully detailed process analysis by itself? How do they make it clear that the ball must be tossed at the same time that the racket swing is in progress?
2   In paragraph 2 Ashe and Graebner assume that their reader is already familiar with the difference between a forehand and a backhand grip. What other knowledge about tennis do the authors assume their readers possess?
3   How does the analogy drawn in paragraph 4 between throwing the ball and swinging the racket help increase your understanding of how to achieve a proper serving motion? Where else might the authors have made instructive use of analogy?

Vocabulary and Diction

1   How well do Ashe and Graebner define such tennis terms as "forehand court" and "footfault"? Are there terms specific to their field that they use without offering any definition for the reader?

Writing Topics

1   Write a process analysis that instructs the reader how to do something you do well. Attempt to organize your essay in a step-by-step sequence, as Ashe and Graebner do, and still make it clear when more than one step must be performed at the same time.

LEWIS THOMAS (1913–   ) is a physician and researcher as well as director of the Memorial Sloane-Kettering Cancer Center. He published his first book, *Lives of a Cell,* in 1974, which resulted in his wide acclaim as an essayist. In addition to writing frequently for the *New England Journal of Medicine,* Thomas has published a second essay collection, *The Medusa and the Snail* (1974–79), from which the following essay is taken.

On Transcendental Metaworry (TMW)

Lewis Thomas

It is said that modern, industrialized, civilized human beings are 1
uniquely nervous and jumpy, unprecedentedly disturbed by the future, despaired by the present, sleepless at memories of the recent past, all because of the technological complexity and noisiness of the machinery by which we are surrounded, and the rigidified apparatus of cold steel and plastic which we have constructed between ourselves and the earth. Incessant worry, according to this view, is a modern invention. To turn it off, all we need do is turn off the engines and climb down into the countryside. Primitive man, rose-garlanded, slept well.

I doubt this. Man has always been a specifically anxious creature 2
with an almost untapped capacity for worry; it is a gift that distinguishes him from other forms of life. There is undoubtedly a neural center deep in the human brain for mediating this function, like the centers for hunger or sleep.

Prehistoric man, without tools or fire to be thinking about, must   3
have been the most anxious of us all. Fumbling about in dimly lit
caves, trying to figure out what he ought really to be doing, sensing
the awesome responsibilities for toolmaking just ahead, he must have
spent a lot of time contemplating his thumbs and fretting about them.
I can imagine him staring at his hands, apposing thumbtips to each
fingertip in amazement, thinking, By God, that's something to set us
apart from the animals—and then the grinding thought, What on
earth are they for? There must have been many long, sleepless nights,
his mind all thumbs.

It would not surprise me to learn that there were ancient prefire   4
committees, convened to argue that thumbs might be taking us too
far, that we'd have been better off with simply another finger of the
usual sort.

Worrying is the most natural and spontaneous of all human   5
functions. It is time to acknowledge this, perhaps even to learn to do
it better. Man is the Worrying Animal. It is a trait needing further
development, awaiting perfection. Most of us tend to neglect the
activity, living precariously out on the thin edge of anxiety but never
plunging in.

For total immersion in the experience of pure, illuminating   6
harassment, I can recommend a modification of the technique of
Transcendental Meditation, which I stumbled across after reading an
article on the practice in a scholarly magazine and then trying it on
myself, sitting on an overturned, stove-in canoe under a beech tree
in my backyard. Following closely the instructions, I relaxed, eyes
closed, breathing regularly, repeating a recommended mantra, in this
instance the word "oom," over and over. The conditions were suitable
for withdrawal and detachment; my consciousness, which normally
spends its time clutching for any possible handhold, was prepared to
cut adrift. Then, suddenly, the telephone began to ring inside the
house, rang several times between breathed "oom"s, and stopped. In
the instant, I discovered Transcendental Worry.

Transcendental Worry can be engaged in at any time, by anyone,   7
regardless of age, sex, or occupation, and in almost any circumstance.
For beginners, I advise twenty-minute sessions, in the morning before
work and late in the evening just before insomnia.

What you do is sit down someplace, preferably by yourself, and   8
tense all muscles. If you make yourself reasonably uncomfortable at

the outset, by sitting on a canoe bottom, say, the tension will come naturally. Now close the eyes, concentrate on this until the effort causes a slight tremor of the eyelids. Now breathe, thinking analytically about the muscular effort involved; it is useful to attempt breathing through one nostril at a time, alternating sides.

Now, the mantra. The word "worry," repeated quite rapidly, is 9 itself effective, because of the allusive cognates in its history. Thus, intruding into the recitation of the mantra comes the recollection that it derives from the Indo-European root *wer,* meaning to turn or bend in the sense of evading, which became *wyrgan* in Old English, meaning to kill by strangling, with close relatives "weird," "writhe," "wriggle," "wrestle," and "wrong." "Wrong" is an equally useful mantra, for symmetrical reasons.

Next, try to float your consciousness free. You will feel something 10 like this happening after about three minutes, and, almost simultaneously with the floating, yawing and sinking will begin. This complex of conjoined sensations becomes an awareness of concentrated, irreversible trouble.

Finally you will begin to hear the *zing,* if you are successful. This 11 is a distant, rhythmic sound, not timed with either the breathing or the mantra. After several minutes, you will discover by taking your pulse that the *zing* is synchronous, and originates somewhere in the lower part of the head or perhaps high up in the neck, presumably due to turbulence at the bend of an artery, maybe even the vibration of a small plaque. Now you are In Touch.

Nothing remains but to allow the intensification of Transcen- 12 dental Worry to proceed spontaneously to the next stage, termed the Primal Wince. En route, you pass through an almost confluent series of pictures, random and transient, jerky and running at overspeed like an old movie, many of them seemingly trivial but each associated with a sense of dropping abruptly through space (it is useful, here, to recall that "vertigo" also derives from *wer*). You may suddenly see, darting across the mind like a shrieking plumed bird, a current electric-light bill, or the vision of numbers whirring too fast to read on a gasoline pump, or the last surviving humpback whale, singing a final song into empty underseas, or simply the television newscast announcing that détente now signifies a Soviet-American Artificial-Heart Project. Or late bulletins from science concerning the pulsing showers of neutrino particles, aimed personally by collapsing stars, which cannot be escaped from even at the bottom of salt mines in South Dakota. Watergate, of course. The music of John Cage. The ascending slopes of chalked curves on academic blackboards, interchangeably predicting the future population of pet dogs in America, rats in Harlem, nuclear explosions overhead and down in salt mines, suicides in Norway, crop failures in India, the number of people at large. The thought of moon gravity as a cause of baldness. The unpreventability of continental drift. The electronic guitar. The slipping away of things, the feel of rugs sliding out from under everywhere. These images become confluent and then amorphous, melting together into a solid, gelatinous thought of skewness. When this happens, you will be entering the last stage, which is pure worry about pure worry. This is the essence of the Wisdom of the West, and I shall call it Transcendental Metaworry (TMW).

Now, as to the usefulness of TMW. First of all, it tends to fill   13
the mind completely at times when it would otherwise be empty. Instead of worrying at random, continually and subliminally, wondering always what it is that you've forgotten and ought to be worrying about, you get the full experience, all in a rush, on a schedule which you arrange for yourself.

Secondly, it makes the times of the day when there is really   14
nothing to worry about intensely pleasurable, because of the contrast.

Thirdly, I have forgotten the third advantage, which is itself one   15
less thing to worry about.

There are, of course, certain disadvantages, which must be faced   16
up to. TMW is, admittedly, a surrogate experience, a substitute for the real thing, and in this sense there is always the danger of overdoing it. Another obvious danger is the likely entry of technology into the field. I have no doubt that there will soon be advertisements in the back pages of small literary magazines, offering for sale, money back if dissatisfied (or satisfied), electronic devices encased in black plastic boxes with dials, cathode screens, earphones with simulated sonic booms, and terminals to be affixed at various areas of the scalp so that brain waves associated with pure TMW can be identified and volitionally selected. These will be marketed under attractive trade names, like the Angst Amplifier or the Artificial Heartsink. The thought of such things is something else to worry about, but perhaps not much worse than the average car radio.

Questions on Meaning

1 According to Thomas, why is it said that worry is "a modern invention"? Why does Thomas disagree?

2 How did Thomas stumble across the technique of Transcendental Metaworry? Why does he recommend such a "total immersion in the experience of pure, illuminating harassment"?

3 What steps must one perform before hearing what Thomas refers to in paragraph 11 as "the *zing*"? Once one is "In Touch," what sort of thoughts and images are experienced en route to entering "the last stage"? What happens during this last stage?

4 In what ways, according to Thomas, is TMW useful? What are its disadvantages?

Questions on Method

1 Like Woody Allen's "My Speech to the Graduates," "On Transcendental Metaworry" is a parody. What sort of serious process analysis is Thomas mocking in his essay?

2 A parody's humor often derives from the way the parodist undercuts or reverses our usual expectations and standards of judgment. How does Thomas's parody do this?

3 In paragraph 12 Thomas offers a long list of examples of thoughts and images that dart across the mind as one slips into a state of pure TMW. How satirical are these examples? Where else does the humor of the essay become satirical?

Vocabulary and Diction

1 In what sense is the phrase "his mind all thumbs," at the end of paragraph 3, a pun? What sort of word game does Thomas play by using such phrases as "Primal Wince" in paragraph 12 and "Angst Amplifier" or "Artificial Heartsink" in paragraph 16?

2 In paragraph 9 Thomas offers an etymology of the word "worry." What is an etymology? Consult the Oxford English Dictionary to determine how accurate the etymology of "worry" offered by Thomas is.

3 Define the following words and phrases used by Thomas: neural center (2), apposing (3), stove-in (6), mantra (6), allusive cognates (9), yawing

(10), synchronous (11), plaque (11), confluent (12), neutrino (12), collapsing stars (12), continental drift (12), amorphous (12), gelatinous (12), skewness (12), subliminally (13), surrogate (16), cathode screens (16).

Writing Topics

1 Compare the view of modern life offered by Thomas to that offered by Woody Allen. How seriously do you take the worry about life that each of them expresses?

2 Is it possible that worrying can be beneficial at times? Write an essay that describes seriously a way to use worry to one's benefit.

3 Write an essay in which you describe a process that you perform in order to relax. Does the way you relax reveal anything about your philosophy of life, about what things in life you consider important and valuable?

4 Try writing a parody of some process that you think people perform either too seriously or not seriously enough.

LEO ROSTEN (1908–   ) was born in Poland and came to
America at the age of 2. He graduated with a doctorate in
political science from the University of Chicago and taught at
several universities, including Stanford and Columbia. His many
publications include *The Joys of Yiddish* (1968), *The Power of
Positive Nonsense* (1977), and *Passions and Prejudice* (1978). In
the following essay, portraying his childhood English teacher
Miss O'Neill, he analyzes the techniques that made her a fine
teacher.

Dear Miss O'Neill

Leo Rosten

On the hellish hot days (and the only city more hellish than   1
Chicago, where this happened, is Bombay), Miss O'Neill would lift
her wig and gently scratch her pate. She did it absently, without
interrupting whatever she was saying or doing.

We always watched this with fascination. Miss O'Neill was our   2
7th-grade teacher, and it was the consensus of my more sophisticated
peers that Miss O'Neill had, until very recently, been a nun. That
was the only way they could explain the phenomenal fact of her
baldness. Miss O'Neill, they whispered, had left her holy order for
heartrending reasons, and the punishment her superiors had decreed
was that she become a slave in the George Howland Elementary
School on 16th Street.

We never knew Miss O'Neill's first name (teachers never had a   3
first name), and when my mother once asked me how old she was,
I answered, "Oh, she's *old.*" All teachers are *old.* And "old" meant
at least 30, even 40—which, to an 11-year-old, is as decrepit and
remote and meaningless as, say 60 or 70, though not 100.

Miss O'Neill was dumpy, moonfaced, sallow-skinned, colorless, 4
and we loathed her as only a pack of West Side barbarians could
loathe a teacher of arithmetic. She did not teach arithmetic—but
that is how much all of us hated her.

She was our English teacher, a 33rd-degree perfectionist who 5
drilled us, endlessly, mercilessly, in spelling and grammar and diction
and syntax. She had a hawk's eye for a dangling participle or an
upright non sequitur, a "not *quite* right" word or a fruity solecism.
(Did you know that "solecism" comes from the contempt of Greek
patricians for the dialect that thrived in Soloi?) Whenever any of us
made an error in composition *or* recitation, Miss O'Neill would send
the culprit to the blackboard to "diagram" the sentence! That was
the torture we most resented.

We had to designate the function of every word and phrase and 6
clause; we had to describe how each part of every sentence worked;
we had to explain how the parts fit together, and how they mesh and
move to wheel out meaning. Before our whole runny-nosed congre-
gation, an innocent child had himself or herself to locate an error,
identify a malfunction, explain the *reason* for the correction. Miss
O'Neill impassively awaited. She waited as if she could sit there until
Gabriel blew his kazoo, as our devastating humor had it. And if the
offered correction was itself wrong, Miss O'Neill compounded her
discipline by making the errant urchin diagram *that* on the board,
instructing him to persevere.

Some kids would break into a sweat as they floundered around 7
failing to hit the bull's-eye, praying that Miss O'Neill would end their
agony by the generous gift of the one good and true answer. But that
Miss O'Neill rarely proffered. Instead, she would turn her inquisition
from the pupil at the blackboard to the helots in the chairs. "Well,
class? . . . Jacob, do *you* know the answer? . . . No? . . . Shirley?
. . . Harold? . . . Joseph?" So heartless and unyielding was her
method.

Each day, as we poured out of George Howland like Cheyennes 8
en route to a scalping, we would pause briefly to pool our misery and
voice our rage over the fate that had condemned us to such an
abecedarian. Had we known Shakespeare, we would have added one
word to Hamlet's brutal advice to Ophelia, making it, with feeling,
"Get thee back to a nunnery."

Miss O'Neill never raised her voice, never lost her patience, 9
never got angry. What was even more surprising, she never had to

punish or even threaten our most ingenious troublemakers. For some reason we never discovered, the small impertinences and sly infractions and simulated incomprehensions with which we shrewdly persecuted our other teachers never seemed to get anywhere in the tight, shipshape world of Miss O'Neill's classroom.

I say that my comrades and I hated Miss O'Neill—but that is   10
not entirely true. I only pretended to hate her. In our sidewalk conclaves, when we chortled over the latest tour de force of Douglas Fairbanks, or mourned the defeat of the noble Cubs by the disgusting White Sox, or matched extravagances about what we would do if we found *ten million dollars,* or imagined the possible surrender of one or another maiden to our lascivious fumblings, I, too, would howl about Miss O'Neill's tyranny, cursing her adamantine ways as fervently as any of my companions. So strong is the desire of a boy to "belong," to be no different from even the grubbiest of his fellows.

But secretly, my respect for Miss O'Neill—nay, my affection—   11
increased week by week. For I was exhilarated by what I can only call the incorruptibility of her instruction. I found stirring within myself a sense of excitement, of discovery, a curious quickening of the spirit that attends initiation into a new world. Though I could not explain it in these words, and would have scorned the Goody-Two-Shoes overtone, I felt that Miss O'Neill was leading me not through the irksome labyrinth of English but into a sunlit realm of order and meaning. Her iron rules, her crisp strictures, her constant corrections were not, to me, the irritating nit picking they were to my buddies. They were sudden flashes of light, glimpses of the magic hidden within prose, intoxicating visions of that universe that awaits understanding. It was as if a cloak of wonder had been wrapped around the barren bones of grammar. For it was not grammar or diction or syntax that Miss O'Neill, whether she knew it or not, was introducing me to. She was teaching what earlier generations so beautifully called "right reason."

The most astonishing thing about Miss O'Neill was that she   12
proceeded on the sanguine assumption that she could actually teach a pack of potential roller-skate-derby fans how to write, clear, clean, correct sentences, organized in clear, clean, correct paragraphs—in their native tongue.

I do not think Miss O'Neill had the slightest awareness of her   13
hold and influence on me. Nor was she especially interested in me. She never betrayed an inkling of preference or favoritism for any of

her captive flock. Nor was she interested in the high, immortal reaches of the language whose terrain she so briskly charted. She was a technician, pure and simple—efficient, conscientious, immune to the malarky some pupils resorted to. Nothing derailed Miss O'Neill from professionalism.

And that is the point. Miss O'Neill did not try to please us. She 14 did not even try to like us. She certainly made no effort to make us like her. She valued results more than affection, and respect more than popularity. Not endowed with loving or lovable qualities, she did not bother regretting it, or denying it, or trying to compensate for it. She went about her task with no concessions to the we're-all-friends or think-of-me-as-your-pal gambits. She used the forthright "I want" or "You go" instead of the repulsive "Shall we?" Alien to humor or affection, she concentrated on nothing more than transmission of her knowledge and her skill.

I think Miss O'Neill knew what the evangelists of "progressive" 15 education are bound to rediscover: that the young prefer competence to "personality" in a teacher, and certainly to camaraderie; that a teacher need be neither an ogre or a confidant; that what is hard to master gives children special rewards (pride, self-respect, the gratifications of succeeding) precisely because difficulties have been conquered; that there may indeed be no easy road to learning some things, and no "fascinating" or "fun" way of learning some things really well.

I do not know whether Miss O'Neill infected anyone else in my 16 7th grade with passion for, or even an abiding interest in, English. To me, she was a force of enlightenment.

She has long since shucked her travail among the West Side 17 aborigines. Perhaps she has departed this baffling world to don wings—and, I hope, golden locks, to replace her wig under whose gauzy base she scratched relief from itching. If she is still alive, she must be in her dotage. And if she is among us still, I hope she somehow gets word of these long-belated thanks for a job supremely done. I have never forgotten what she taught.

To this day, whether I am wrestling an intransigent sentence, 18 or stand glazed before a buck-passing phrase whose improvement eludes me, or flagellate myself for some inspiration that might light up the drab texture of tired prose, whether I am winded by a rodomontade clause in Shaw or knocked cold by a tortured sentence in Talcott Parsons, I find myself thinking of Miss (What-oh-what?)

O'Neill—and, sighing, take a sheet of paper and diagram the English until I know—and know *why*—it is right or wrong, or how it can be swept clean of that <u>muddleheadedness</u> that plagues us all.

Questions on Meaning

1   What did Miss O'Neill teach her seventh-grade English class? How did she go about doing it? Was her "method" really "heartless and unyield-ing," as Rosten says in paragraph 7?

2   What were Miss O'Neill's pupils like? Do they seem like typical 11-year-old children? How did they feel about Miss O'Neill? How was Rosten, as a boy, different from the other boys?

3   Why did the "more sophisticated" among Rosten's peers believe that Miss O'Neill had been a nun? What does Rosten mean in paragraph 13 when he writes that she was a "technician, pure and simple"?

4   What are the "small impertinences," "sly infractions," and "simulated incomprehensions" that seventh-graders resort to when they want to give a teacher a hard time? Why did Miss O'Neill's technique, as Rosten says in paragraph 9, keep even the "most ingenious troublemakers" in line?

5   In paragraph 14 Rosten says that Miss O'Neill had neither loving nor lovable qualities. How has his previous description of her and the process by which she taught made this clear? What admirable qualities did she have, and how were these reflected in her relationship with her students? What lesson does Rosten draw, out of his memory of this relationship, for those whom he calls in paragraph 15 "the evangelists of 'progressive' education"?

Questions on Method

1   Why does Rosten write an essay about how his seventh-grade teacher taught? What sort of argument does he wish to make? Where does his tone become most argumentative?

2   List the steps in the process of teaching grammar as Miss O'Neill prac-ticed it ([6] and [7]). What general methods did she apply to teaching? Could another teacher use Rosten's analysis to repeat this process, that is, to imitate Miss O'Neill's methods? Why or why not?

3   Aside from an argumentative tone, what tones does Rosten employ throughout the essay? Where is he most analytical? Where is he most humorous? How would you characterize the tone of the last two para-

graphs? What attitudes do Rosten's tones convey about teaching and learning?

Vocabulary and Diction

1   What does Rosten mean in paragraph 11 when he writes that Miss O'Neill introduced him, not to grammar or diction or syntax, but to "right reason"? To what extent does his last paragraph help you to understand what he means by "right reason"?

2   In paragraph 6 Rosten writes that Miss O'Neill would wait for a correct answer "as if she could sit there until Gabriel blew his kazoo, as our devastating humor had it." What is a kazoo? Is there much humor in associating this instrument with Gabriel? What effect does Rosten achieve by calling the humor of himself and his peers "devastating"?

3   Define the following words and phrases used by Rosten: pate (1), moon-faced (4), diction and syntax (5), dangling participle (5), non sequitur (5), solecism (5), Greek patricians (5), errant urchin (6), helots (7), pool (8), abecedarian (8), chortled (10), lascivious fumblings (10), adamantine (10), Goody-Two-Shoes overtone (11), irksome labyrinth (11), sanguine (12), gambits (14), camaraderie (15), ogre (15), shucked (17), don (17), flagellate (18), rodomontade clause (18).

Writing Topics

1   Rosten argues that there may be "no easy road to learning some things, and no 'fascinating' or 'fun' way of learning some things really well." Do you agree? Write an essay in which you describe a difficult process that you went through to learn something that couldn't be learned in a fascinating or fun way.

2   Write an essay that discusses the validity of Rosten's claim that "the young prefer competence to 'personality' in a teacher, and certainly to camaraderie." Is it true, as Rosten suggests, that teachers today are too easy on students, that they are more concerned with making friends with their students than with making their students try to master hard lessons?

3   How would you compare Rosten's attitude toward education with E. B. White's in "Education"? Write an essay that accounts for the differences in their attitudes.

4   As Woody Allen does in "My Speech to the Graduates," Rosten uses humor to help persuade us to share his point of view. Compare the extent to which each author lets his humor do his arguing for him.

5   Write an essay that describes an educational process to which you were subjected as a child and toward which your feelings have changed, either in a positive or a negative way, now that you are older.

6   Write an essay that describes the process by which you taught someone to do or understand something he or she did not understand or know how to do.

7   Write an essay in which you analyze why school is not more fun than it is.

DAVIDYNE MAYLEAS is a free-lance writer and co-author with
Tom Jackson of *The Hidden Job Market: A System to Beat the
System* (1976). She is also the author of *Rewedded Bliss: Love,
Alimony, Incest, Ex-Spouses and Other Domestic Blessings* (1977).

How to Land the Job You Want

Davidyne Mayleas

Louis Albert, 39, lost his job as an electrical engineer when his   1
firm made extensive cutbacks. He spent two months answering classified ads and visiting employment agencies—with zero results. Albert
might still be hunting if a friend, a specialist in the employment field,
had not shown him how to be his own job counselor. Albert learned
how to research unlisted openings, write a forceful résumé, perform
smoothly in an interview, even transform a turndown into a job.

 Although there seemed to be a shortage of engineering jobs,   2
Albert realized that he still persuaded potential employers to see him.
This taught him something—that his naturally outgoing personality
might be as great an asset as his engineering degree. When the
production head of a small electronics company told him that they
did not have an immediate opening, Albert told his interviewer,
"You people make a fine product. I think you could use additional
sales representation—someone like me who understands and talks
electrical engineer's language, and who enjoys selling." The inter-

viewer decided to send Albert to a senior vice president. Albert got a job in sales.

You too can be your own counselor if you put the same vigorous effort into *getting* a job as you would into *keeping* one. Follow these three basic rules, developed by placement experts:

1. FIND THE HIDDEN JOB MARKET. Classified ads and agency listings reveal only a small percentage of available jobs. Some of the openings that occur through promotions, retirements and reorganization never reach the personnel department. There are three ways to get in touch with this hidden market:

Write a strong résumé with a well-directed cover letter and mail it to the appropriate department manager in the company where you'd like to work. Don't worry whether there's a current opening. Many managers fill vacancies by reviewing the résumés already in their files. Dennis Mollura, press-relations manager in the public-relations department of American Telephone and Telegraph, says, "In my own case, the company called me months after I sent in my résumé."

Get in touch with people who work in or know the companies that interest you. Jobs are so often filled through personal referral that Charles R. Lops, executive employment manager of the J.C. Penney Co., says, "Probably our best source for outside people comes from recommendations made by Penney associates themselves."

"Drop in" on the company. Lillian Reveille, employment manager of Equitable Life Assurance Society of the United States, reports: "A large percentage of the applicants we see are 'walk-ins'—and we do employ many of these people."

2. LOCATE HIDDEN OPENINGS This step requires energy and determination to make telephone calls, see people, do research, and to keep moving despite turndowns.

Contact anyone who may know of openings, including relatives, friends, teachers, bank officers, insurance agents—anyone you know in your own or an adjacent field. When the teachers' union and employment agencies produced no teaching openings, Eric Olson, an unemployed high-school math instructor, reviewed his talent and decided that where an analytical math mind was useful, there he'd find a job. He called his insurance agent, who set up an interview with the actuarial department of one of the companies he represented. They hired Olson.

279

It's a good idea to contact not only professional or trade associations in your field, but also your local chamber of commerce and people involved in community activities. After Laura Bailey lost her job as retirement counselor in a bank's personnel department, she found a position in customer relations in another bank. Her contact: a member of the senior-citizens club that Mrs. Bailey ran on a volunteer basis. 10

Use local or business-school libraries. Almost every field has its own directory of companies, which provides names, addresses, products and/or services, and lists officers and other executives. Write to the company president or to the executive to whom you'd report. The vice president of personnel at Warner-Lambert Co. says, "When a résumé of someone we could use—now or in the near future—shows up 'cold' in my in-basket, that's luck for both of us." 11

Consult telephone directories. Sometimes the telephone company will send you free the telephone directories of various cities. Also, good-sized public libraries often have many city directories. Fred Lewis, a cabinet maker, checked the telephone directories of nine different cities where he knew furniture was manufactured. At the end of five weeks he had a sizable telephone bill, some travel expenses—and ten interviews which resulted in three job offers. 12

3. AFTER YOU FIND THE OPENING, GET THE JOB. The applicants who actually get hired are those who polish these six job-getting skills to perfection. 13

Compose a better résumé. A résumé is a self-advertisement, designed to get you an interview. Start by putting yourself in an employer's place. Take stock of your job history and personal achievements. Make an inventory of your skills and accomplishments that might be useful from the employer's standpoint. Choose the most important and describe them in words that stress accomplishments. Avoid such phrases as "my duties included . . ." Use action words like planned, sold, trained, managed. 14

Ask a knowledgeable business friend to review your résumé. Does it stress accomplishment rather than duties? Does it tell an employer what you can do for him? Can it be shortened? (One or two pages should suffice.) Generally, it's not wise to mention salary requirements. 15

Write a convincing cover letter. While the résumé may be a copy, the cover letter must be personal. Sy Mann, director of research for 16

Aceto Chemical Co., says: "When I see a mimeographed letter that states, 'Dear Sir, I'm sincerely interested in working for your company,' I wonder, 'How many other companies got this valentine?'" Use the name and title of the person who can give you the interview, and be absolutely certain of accuracy here. Using a wrong title or misspelling a prospective employer's name may route your correspondence directly to an automatic turndown.

Prepare specifically for each interview. Research the company thoroughly; know its history and competition. Try to grasp the problems of the job you're applying for. For example, a line in an industry journal that a food company was "developing a new geriatric food", convinced one man that he should emphasize his marketing experience with vitamins rather than with frozen foods. 17

You'll increase your edge by anticipating questions the interviewer might raise. Why do you want to work for us? What can you offer us that someone else cannot? Why did you leave your last position? What are your salary requirements? 18

An employer holds an interview to get a clearer picture of your work history and accomplishments, and to look for characteristics he considers valuable. These vary with jobs. Does the position require emphasis on attention to detail or on creativity? Perseverance or aggressiveness? Prior to the interview decide what traits are most in demand. And always send a thank-you note immediately after the interview. 19

Follow up. They said you would hear in a week: now it's two. Call them. Don't wait and hope. Hope and act. 20

Supply additional information. That's the way Karen Halloway got her job as fashion director with a department store. "After my interview I sensed that the merchandise manager felt I was short on retail experience. So I wrote to him describing the 25 fashion shows I'd staged yearly for the pattern company I'd worked for." 21

Don't take no for an answer. Hank Newell called to find out why he had been turned down. The credit manager felt he had insufficient collection experience. Hank thanked him for his time and frankness. The next day, Hank called back saying, "My collection experience is limited, but I don't think I fully emphasized my training in credit checking." They explored this area and found Hank still not qualified. But the credit manager was so impressed with how well Hank took criticism that when Hank asked him if he could suggest other employers, he did, even going so far as to call one. Probing for leads 22

281

when an interview or follow-up turns negative is a prime technique for getting personal referrals.

The challenge of finding a job, approached in an active, orga- 23 nized, realistic way, can be a valuable personal adventure. You can meet new people, develop new ideas about yourself and your career goals, and improve your skills in dealing with individuals. These in turn can contribute to your long-term job security.

Questions on Meaning

1 Why, according to Mayleas, should you not rely on classified ads and agency listings looking for a job? What steps should you take to find the hidden job market?

2 Once you find this hidden job market, what steps will help you locate job openings?

3 What are the six job-getting skills that Mayleas suggests will help you get a job once you have found an opening? How important is it in each of these steps to understand the prospective employer's standpoint?

4 In her last paragraph Mayleas says that through the challenge of finding a job, you can "develop new ideas about yourself and your career goals." What steps in the process of finding a job, as Mayleas describes this process, are most likely to stimulate you to develop new ideas about yourself? What did Louis Albert, in the opening example, discover about himself?

Questions on Method

1 In what sense is the process Mayleas describes a small part of a much larger one?

2 Is there any need for Mayleas to present her first two "rules" as separate steps in an apparently sequential process? Is there really any difference between finding the hidden job market and locating hidden openings?

3 Mayleas offers numerous examples to illustrate her points. Which of her examples, practically speaking, help you better understand how you might go about performing the step in the process they are meant to illustrate?

4 Just how much practical help does Mayleas offer someone who is looking for a job?

Writing Topics

1   Describe the process you went through to land a job. How many of the steps that Mayleas advises a job seeker to take did you take? Are there steps you took that Mayleas doesn't mention?

2   Like Ashe and Graebner, Mayleas writes a "practical" process analysis. In each essay the tone is matter-of-fact, suggesting that if the steps of the process are followed a certain result will be achieved. Write an essay in which you discuss why the directions Mayleas offers may not be as easy to follow as her tone suggests. Compare the essay by Mayleas in this sense to the essay by Ashe and Graebner.

JONATHAN MILLER (1934–   ) is a British stage and film
director as well as a physician. He has produced several plays in
London and coauthored and directed *Beyond the Fringe* (1961–
1964). His book *The Body in Question* is based on his experience
as a doctor in a London hospital. In this essay on "patients'
rites" he compares how people react to illness as opposed to
health.

Patients' Rites

Jonathan Miller

At one time or another we have all been irked by aches and pains.   1
We have probably noticed alterations in weight, complexion and
bodily function, changes in power, capability and will, unaccountable
shifts of mood. But on the whole we treat these like changes in the
weather: as part and parcel of living in an imperfect world. The
changes they cause in our behaviour are barely noticeable—not in-
convenient enough to interfere with our routine. We may retreat a
little, fall silent, sigh, rub our heads, retire early, drink glasses of
water, eat less, walk more, miss a meal here and there, avoid fried
foods, and so on and so on. But sometimes the discomfort, alarm,
embarrassment or inconvenience begin to obstruct the flow of ordinary life; in place of modest well-being, life becomes so intolerably
awkward, strenuous or frightening that we fall ill.

　　Falling ill is not something that happens to us, it is a choice we   2
make as a result of things happening to us. It is an action we take
when we feel unacceptably odd. Obviously, there are times when this
choice is taken out of the victim's hands: he may be so overwhelmed

by events that he plays no active part in what happens next and is brought to the doctor by friends or relatives, stricken and helpless. But this is rare. Most people who fall ill have chosen to cast themselves in the role of patient. Viewing their unfortunate situation, they see themselves as sick people and begin to act differently.

Usually this is a prelude to seeking expert advice, but falling ill 3 can sometimes be performed as a solo act. In New Guinea, for example, the decision to fall ill is almost invariably followed by a consistent and easily recognised form of behaviour. The sufferer withdraws from the community and retires into his hut: he strips himself naked, smears himself with ash and dust, and lies down in the darkness. He also changes his tone of voice: when his friends and relatives make solicitous enquiries, he answers them in a quavering falsetto.

Such people are not merely suffering illness: they are performing 4 it, thereby announcing both to themselves and to the community that they are sick people in need of care and attention. In New Guinea this is such a well-recognized form of behaviour that one is tempted to regard it as a formal ritual. Something similar, however, can often be found in more sophisticated communities. When someone falls ill but is not yet ready to summon expert help, he usually takes care to advertise his condition through the medium of a performance. In fact, such a performance is often demanded of him by those with whom he lives. Someone who takes to his bed when he has a sick headache, for instance, is not entirely prompted by the need for relief. It is a way of boosting his credibility as a sick person, and it may be the only way of getting the attention and concern which he thinks he deserves. In fact, the patient may have to abstain from activities he is quite capable of performing, if only to convince those around him that there is a good reason for his staying away from work.

A patient, then, is a special sort of person, rather like a recruit 5 or a convert or a bride. By taking on the role of patient you change your social identity, turning yourself from someone who helps himself into someone who accepts the orders, routine and advice of qualified experts. You submit to the rules and recommendations of a profession, just as a novice submits to the rules and recommendations of his or her chosen order. Ordinary life is full of such voluntary transitions—changes of social role or status which are accompanied by corresponding changes in obligation and expectation. Whenever these take place, they are accompanied by rituals which mark the event and make it clearly recognisable to all who are involved. The anthropologists have called these 'rites of passage', symbolic actions which represent and dramatise significant changes in social status: they include baptisms, immersions, confirmations, all sorts of melodramatic initiations and humiliating ordeals, such as strippings, shavings, scarrings. Whenever we cross a threshold from one social role to another we take pains to advertise the fact with ceremonies which represent it in terms of vivid and memorable images.

The idea of 'rites of passage' was first introduced by the French anthropologist Arnold Van Gennep in 1909. Van Gennep insisted that all rituals of 'passing through' occurred in three successive phases: a rite of separation, a rite of transition and a rite of aggregation. The person whose status is to be changed has to undergo a ritual which marks his departure from the old version of himself: there has to be some act which symbolises the fact that he has rid himself of all his previous associations. He is washed, rinsed, sprinkled or immersed, and, in this way, all his previous obligations and attachments are symbolically untied and even annihilated. This stage is followed by a rite of transition, when the person is neither fish nor fowl; he has left his old status behind him but has not yet assumed his new one. This liminal condition is usually marked by rituals of isolation and segregation—a period of vigil, mockery perhaps, fear and trembling. There are often elaborate rites of humiliation—scourging, insults, and darkness. Finally, in the rite of aggregation, the new status is ritually conferred: the person is admitted, enrolled, confirmed and ordained.

This idea can be applied to the process of becoming a patient. The fact that most of the procedures involved have a rational and practical explanation doesn't prevent them from playing a very important symbolic role as well. Although one can readily understand most of what happens to someone on entering hospital in utilitarian terms, there is no doubt that both the patient and the doctor experience some of these manoeuvres as symbolic transformations. Once someone has chosen to fall ill he has to apply for the role of patient: he auditions for the part by reciting his complaint as vividly and as convincingly as he can. This can also be seen in terms of religious confirmation: the candidate submits himself to a formal questionnaire in order to satisfy the examiner that he is a suitable person to be enrolled. If he passes the preliminary test he has to undertake the initial rites of separation. He is undressed, washed, and until quite recently, he often had to submit himself to a cleansing enema. Then come the rites of transition. No longer a person in the ordinary world, he is not yet formally accepted by his fellow patients—anxious and isolated in his novice pyjamas, he awaits the formal act of aggregation. He is introduced to the ward sister, hands over his street clothes, submits to a questionnaire by the houseman and registrar. Dressed with all the dignified credentials of a formally admitted patient, he awaits the forthcoming event.

Questions on Meaning

1 What does Miller mean when he says, at the start of the second paragraph, "Falling ill is not something that happens to us, it is a choice we make as a result of things happening to us"? When and why, according to Miller, do people choose to "cast themselves in the role of patient"?

2 How fair is the distinction Miller makes between "suffering" and "performing" illness? To what extent is it true that people often act sicker than they feel? Why do they act this way?

3 Explain in your own words the three phases of a rite of passage. Do you agree with Miller's analysis of the process by which one enters a hospital as a symbolic rite of passage?

Questions on Method

1 What sort of process is Miller analyzing in this essay—physiological, psychological, sociological, or some other kind?

2 Paragraph 6 analyzes the steps in a typical rite of passage so that a comparison can be made in paragraph 7 between the ritual and the process of becoming a patient. In parallel columns list the steps in both processes and evaluate their similarity. Is this comparison an analogy?

3 In paragraph 5 Miller draws an analogy between a patient and "a recruit or a convert or a bride." What similarity that these otherwise different roles have in common is Miller's analogy intended to help us understand? How does Miller extend his analogy of a patient and a religious convert in the following paragraphs? How effective is Miller's extended analogy in helping clarify his thesis?

4 In paragraph 7 Miller, referring to the process of becoming a patient in a hospital, argues, "The fact that most of the procedures involved have

a rational and practical explanation doesn't prevent them from playing a very important symbolic role as well." In what sense is Miller here anticipating and countering the major criticism that might be leveled against his thesis? How would you describe his tone in this sentence? How effectively does he argue his case here and elsewhere in the essay?

Vocabulary and Diction

1 How accurate is Miller's definition in paragraph 5 of a "patient" as someone who seeks the help of others rather than helping himself? Can you think of examples of patients who, on the contrary, are dedicated to helping themselves?

2 In what sense is the clause in the last sentence of paragraph 5, "we take pains," a pun? How does this play on words help emphasize Miller's comparison between the rite of becoming a patient and more traditional rites of passage?

3 Define the following words and phrases used by Miller: solicitous enquiries (3), quavering falsetto (3), credibility (4), novice (5), voluntary transitions (5), immersions (5), melodramatic initiations (5), vigil (6), liminal condition (6), utilitarian (7).

Writing Topics

1 Write a detailed description of the process you go through to make yourself feel better when you are suffering from a cold or a mild case of flu.

2 Have you ever gone through a rite of passage? Write an essay describing the process as you experienced it.

3 Write an essay in which you compare the description Miller offers of what goes on in a hospital with the description Richard Selzer offers in "The Discus Thrower."

4 Write an essay explaining something that is difficult to understand by drawing an extended analogy between it and something that is easier to understand. For example, one might explain a toothache to a child by drawing a detailed analogy between the way sugar corrodes a tooth and the way rust corrodes a piece of metal. How far can you extend your analogy before it begins to give a false impression of the subject you are trying to explain?

Process Analysis—Writing Topics

1   Write an essay in which you narrate a step-by-step process you perform regularly; include descriptions of how you feel and what you think about as you perform each step.

2   Describe how you were taught to write in grammar school and high school. Use your description as part of an essay that explains what you think would be the most effective way to learn how to write well.

3   Write an essay about how you might make what seems like an unnecessarily complicated process more efficient and easier to get through. Choose, for example, the process of electing a new President. Imagine that your audience is European.

4   Write an essay in which you compare different techniques used to attain the same general results, such as the different ways that men try to pick up women (or vice versa).

5   Analyze your studying process. How effective or ineffective is it, and why? Imagine you are addressing an audience of veterans returning to school, and pitch your analysis to their interests.

6   Analyze the thought process you went through in making an important decision. Explain how and why one step of thought led to the next and so on until you reached your final decision. Did this process lead to a repeatable or teachable method? Explain it. What audience might find this method useful? Try to appeal to this audience.

7   Write an essay in which you explain how to do something that most people do not understand, drawing an analogy between this process and a process about which most people have a fairly clear understanding. For example, you might explain how to go about choosing a wife or husband by drawing an analogy between this process and the process of choosing a new car.

NINE
Cause and Effect

Why do I hate my job? What is causing our current double-digit inflation? Why didn't the American automobile industry predict the current market for small cars? Why is Iran anti-American? What is the effect of the Massachusetts handgun law? What caused the robbery? Narration asks, "What happened?" Cause-and-effect exposition asks, "Why did it happen?" A great deal of exposition is organized around the answer to this question.

The structure of cause-and-effect exposition, like that of narration and process analysis, is a series or sequence in time whose last event or condition, the effect, could not occur without the preceding ones. In narration the fact of preceding and following does not necessarily prove causality although there is often a strong presumption of causality even when it is not clearly stated. "The king died and the queen died," which is simple narration, could be taken to imply that one death caused the other; but "The king died and the queen died of grief" clearly adds causality to the narration. Mere sequence, however, often does not establish causality until a pattern has been observed. If you get an upset stomach after a first, second, and third meal at which eggplant was the only common dish, you might conclude that eggplant caused your trouble. The misconception that mere sequence establishes causality is called the *post hoc ergo propter hoc* fallacy. This Latin phrase means "*y* follows and is therefore caused by *x*." But it takes more than preceding—going before—to make *x* a cause of *y*.

Before the rise of science in the seventeenth century, Authority was regarded as the single best source of answers to questions of causality: ask Aristotle, ask Galen, ask St. Thomas, ask Scaliger. One turned to the theologian or philosopher. Today Authority itself must prove its credentials; we now think that the discovery of causes involves what is called scientific method, a combination of thinking (careful formulation of questions, establishment of hypotheses) and observation under controlled circumstances, the conclusion to be expressed wherever possible in mathematical terms.

The last event or condition in a causal series is, as we said, the effect. The immediately preceding events or conditions are the "immediate" causes; if one immediate cause can alone produce the effect, it is called "sufficient," which is difficult to isolate. Conditions or events at the beginning of the series are "remote" or "contributing" causes, and they may be numerous.

In answering the question "What caused the robbery?" you would find a series of earlier events or conditions among which might be poorly lighted streets and yards, unlocked doors or windows, accessible fire escapes, an ineffective police and court system, high unemployment, drug use, and so on, some of which may have been recently aggravated or exacerbated, and you would certainly hope to find an immediate cause called "the perpetrator." To avoid beginning too early in a potentially endless series, you must keep in mind the question "What had to happen for the robbery to occur?"

Cause-and-effect exposition can answer the corollary question, "What is the effect of *x*?" You can ask, "What is the *effect* of the robbery?" (or, what amounts to the same thing, "What did the robbery cause?"). Now the series begins with robbery and ends with later events or conditions: fear, anger, increased insurance costs, deterioration of a neighborhood, purchase of a burglar alarm, and so on. To keep the series from growing unmanageably long, keep in mind the question "What would not have happened if the robbery had not happened?"

Cause-and-effect exposition requires rigorous thinking and an awareness of the pitfalls of language. Examine the language of your questions. The words they are phrased in will determine to a large extent how they are answered. Questions often hide preconceived notions that may be erroneous. "Why are Iranians anti-American?," for example, bristles with preconceptions: Iranians are anti-American; Iranians are all alike; the Iranian attitude toward the United States is different from the Iranian attitude toward other countries; attitudes are fixed and unchanging; and so on. In presenting your case for cause and effect, support your conclusions with proof or evidence. Use statistics, reports, or your own and the authoritative experience of others. Don't expect to be believed merely because you say something is the cause. Use any of the expository modes—exemplification, comparison, definition, and so forth—and narration and description to help you present your case.

Writing Cause-and-Effect Exposition

1   Distinguish between causality and mere sequence.
2   Identify various kinds of cause: sufficient, immediate, contributing, remote.
3   Provide proof.

E. B. WHITE (1899–   ) is a graduate of Cornell
University. He spent many years on the editorial staff of the
New Yorker, contributing verse, editorials, and satirical essays.
He has received many academic honors and literary prizes. His
publications include several collections of short stories, letters,
and essays. His incisive wit and individualistic style are perhaps
most evident in his essays, two of which are included in this
anthology. In "The Sea and the Wind That Blows" White
distinguishes his emotional reaction to the sea from his
intellectual response.

The Sea and
the Wind That Blows

E. B. White

Waking or sleeping, I dream of boats—usually of rather small 1
boats under a slight press of sail. When I think how great a part of
my life has been spent drumming the hours away and how much of
this total dream life has concerned small craft, I wonder about the
state of my health, for I am told that it is not a good sign to be always
voyaging into unreality, driven by imaginary breezes.

I have noticed that most men, when they enter a barber shop 2
and must wait their turn, drop into a chair and pick up a magazine.
I simply sit down and pick up the thread of my sea wandering, which
began more than fifty years ago and is not quite ended. There is
hardly a waiting room in the East that has not served as my cockpit,
whether I was waiting to board a train or to see a dentist. And I am
usually still trimming sheets when the train starts or the drill begins
to whine.

If a man must be obsessed by something, I suppose a boat is as 3 good as anything, perhaps a bit better than most. A small sailing craft is not only beautiful, it is seductive and full of strange promise and the hint of trouble. If it happens to be an auxiliary cruising boat, it is without question the most compact and ingenious arrangement for living ever devised by the restless mind of man—a home that is stable without being stationary, shaped less like a box than like a fish or a bird or a girl, and in which the homeowner can remove his daily affairs as far from shore as he has the nerve to take them, close-hauled or running free—parlor, bedroom, and bath, suspended and alive.

Men who ache all over for tidiness and compactness in their lives often find relief for their pain in the cabin of a thirty-foot sailboat at anchor in a sheltered cove. Here the sprawling panoply of The Home is compressed in orderly miniature and liquid delirium, suspended between the bottom of the sea and the top of the sky, ready to move on in the morning by the miracle of canvas and the witchcraft of rope. It is small wonder that men hold boats in the secret place of their mind, almost from the cradle to the grave.

Along with my dream of boats has gone the ownership of boats, a long succession of them upon the surface of the sea, many of them makeshift and crank. Since childhood I have managed to have some sort of sailing craft and to raise a sail in fear. Now, in my seventies, I still own a boat, still raise my sail in fear in answer to the summons of the unforgiving sea. Why does the sea attract me in the way it does? Whence comes this compulsion to hoist a sail, actually or in dream? My first encounter with the sea was a case of hate at first sight. I was taken, at the age of four, to a bathing beach in New Rochelle. Everything about the experience frightened and repelled me: the taste of salt in my mouth, the foul chill of the wooden bathhouse, the littered sand, the stench of the tide flats. I came away hating and fearing the sea. Later, I found that what I had feared and hated, I now feared and loved.

I returned to the sea of necessity, because it would support a boat; and although I knew little of boats, I could not get them out of my thoughts. I became a pelagic boy. The sea became my unspoken challenge: the wind, the tide, the fog, the ledge, the bell, the gull that cried help, the never-ending threat and bluff of weather. Once having permitted the wind to enter the belly of my sail, I was not able to quit the helm; it was as though I had seized hold of a high-tension wire and could not let go.

I liked to sail alone. The sea was the same as a girl to me—I did 7
not want anyone else along. Lacking instruction, I invented ways of
getting things done, and usually ended by doing them in a rather
queer fashion, and so did not learn to sail properly, and still cannot
sail well, although I have been at it all my life. I was twenty before
I discovered that charts existed; all my navigating up to that time
was done with the wariness and the ignorance of the early explorers.
I was thirty before I learned to hang a coiled halyard on its cleat as
it should be done. Until then I simply coiled it down on deck and
dumped the coil. I was always in trouble and always returned, seeking
more trouble. Sailing became a compulsion: there lay the boat, swinging to her mooring, there blew the wind; I had no choice but to go.
My earliest boats were so small that when the wind failed, or when
I failed, I could switch to manual control—I could paddle or row
home. But then I graduated to boats that only the wind was strong
enough to move. When I first dropped off my mooring in such a boat,
I was an hour getting up the nerve to cast off the pennant. Even now,
with a thousand little voyages notched in my belt, I still feel a
memorial chill on casting off, as the gulls jeer and the empty mainsail
claps.

Of late years, I have noticed that my sailing has increasingly 8
become a compulsive activity rather than a simple source of pleasure.
There lies the boat, there blows the morning breeze—it is a point of
honor, now, to go. I am like an alcoholic who cannot put his bottle
out of his life. With me, I cannot not sail. Yet I know well enough
that I have lost touch with the wind and, in fact, do not like the
wind anymore. It jiggles me up, the wind does, and what I really love
are windless days, when all is peace. There is a great question in my
mind whether a man who is against wind should longer try to sail a
boat. But this is an intellectual response—the old yearning is still in
me, belonging to the past, to youth, and so I am torn between past
and present, a common disease of later life.

When does a man quit the sea? How dizzy, how bumbling must 9
he be? Does he quit while he's ahead, or wait till he makes some
major mistake, like falling overboard or being flattened by an acci-
dental jibe? This past winter I spent hours arguing the question with
myself. Finally, deciding that I had come to the end of the road, I
wrote a note to the boatyard, putting my boat up for sale. I said I was
"coming off the water." But as I typed the sentence, I doubted that
I meant a word of it.

If no buyer turns up, I know what will happen: I will instruct 10
the yard to put her in again—"just till somebody comes along." And
then there will be the old uneasiness, the old uncertainty, as the mild
southeast breeze ruffles the cove, a gentle, steady, morning breeze,
bringing the taint of the distant wet world, the smell that takes a
man back to the very beginning of time, linking him to all that has
gone before. There will lie the sloop, there will blow the wind, once
more I will get under way. And as I reach across to the red nun off
the Torry Islands, dodging the trap buoys and toggles, the shags
gathered on the ledge will note my passage. "There goes the old boy
again," they will say. "One more rounding of his little Horn, one
more conquest of his Roaring Forties." And with the tiller in my
hand, I'll feel again the wind imparting life to a boat, will smell again
the old menace, the one that imparts life to me: the cruel beauty of
the salt world, the barnacle's tiny knives, the sharp spine of the
urchin, the stinger of the sun jelly, the claw of the crab.

Questions on Meaning

1   Why are boats seductive to White? In what way is his attraction to boats
similar to his attraction to the sea? In what way are these two attractions
different?

2   Why did White, as he tells us in paragraph 7, never learn to sail properly?
What connection does this have with the "chill" White always feels
upon casting off?

3   What is the difference between what White in paragraph 8 calls his
"intellectual response" to sailing and what he calls his "old yearning" for
sailing? How does our understanding of this difference help us understand
why sailing, for White, has become " a compulsive activity rather than
a simple source of pleasure"? Explain what White means by calling his
conflict over sailing an example of "a common disease of later life."

4   What does White mean in paragraph 10 when he says that the smell of
the sea "takes a man back to the very beginning of time, linking him to
all that has gone before"? How realistic is his final view of the sea,
especially compared to what at the start of the essay he calls the "unreality" of his habit of dreaming about boats?

Questions on Method

1   What causes lie behind the effect that the sea has on White? Does White make these causes clear, or must the reader interpret them?

2   In the second paragraph White tells us that often he dreams about boats when he is waiting to get a haircut or to board a train or to see a dentist. Why does he describe himself as waiting in these places?

3   Why does White in paragraph 3 compare an "auxiliary cruising boat" to "a home that is stable without being stationary"? How do the details of his description of such a boat help us understand the meaning of this comparison?

4   Discuss the simile that White offers in paragraph 3 comparing a boat to a girl. What do you make of the fact that in paragraph 7 he uses the same image to describe the sea? What other images does White use to good effect in his essay?

5   How does the description in paragraph 5 of White's first encounter with the sea illustrate an important theme of the essay? Is the "case of hate at first sight" typical of a child's first experience at the beach? How much did you enjoy your first visit to the beach?

6   How do White's last two paragraphs illustrate the contrast that he sets up in paragraph 8 between his intellectual and his emotional response to the sea? What are some of the differences between how our intellect works and how our emotions work?

Vocabulary and Diction

1   Why at the end of paragraph 7 does White say that the gulls "jeer" and the empty mainsail "claps"?

2   In what sense is the phrase "manual control" in paragraph 7 a humorous play on words? In what sense is the phrase in paragraph 8, " a man who is against wind," a play on words? In what sense is this phrase ironic? In what sense is it sad?

3   How many times does White use the words "compulsion" and "compulsive" in his essay? Does he use other words as synonyms for these? How does White's stress on such words suggest a main theme of his essay?

4   Define the following words and phrases used by White: a slight press of sail (1), compact and ingenious (3), sprawling panoply (4), liquid delirium (4), stench of the tide flats (5), pelagic (6), bluff (6), wariness (7), coiled halyard (7), jibe (9), sloop (10), trap buoys (10), toggles (10), shags (10).

Writing Topics

1   Describe something you disliked as a child about which your feelings changed as you grew older, such as a place you visited or an activity you engaged in. What caused your feelings to change? What lesson can you draw from your analysis of how and why your feelings changed?

2   Write an essay analyzing how and why one of your dreams has had an important effect on your life.

3   Analyze a compulsion you may have to do something that frightens you. Which of your feelings, your compulsion to act or your fear of acting, seems more reasonable to you? Describe the conflict that is thus set up between your reason and your emotions.

4   White talks about the "cruel beauty" of the sea. Can a person, like the sea, be both cruel and beautiful? Write an essay in which you analyze what effect the cruelty of a person has on the beauty of that person.

5   Recall an experience that caused you to feel a singularly strong emotion. Pick one word that denotes this emotion, then make use of as many synonyms for this word as you can think of in the course of describing the experience and its effect on you. Once the essay is written, replace those synonyms that seem repetitious with whatever metaphors the details of your description suggest might better symbolize the emotion.

ANNE TAYLOR FLEMING is a frequent contributor to *Newsweek* and other periodicals. She currently lives in New York City.

The Fear of Being Alone

Anne Taylor Fleming

At the end of this past summer I had plans to go away for a week, 1 simply a week, without my husband. It was the first time in three years that I was making such a solo pilgrimage, and I was frightened. As I walked down the long corridor to the plane, I looked straight ahead, turning a bottle of tranquilizers over and over in my pocket. I felt like a child lost in a department store; my palms were sweaty and my face was flushed. I tried to remember other solitary departures when I had been similarly discomfited; the walk to the first day of school; the bus ride to Girl Scout camp when I was 9 and my sister, who was also on the bus, was 10 and suddenly wanted nothing to do with me; the first midnight jet to college.

Of what was I so afraid? I was afraid of being by myself, of being 2 wholly quiet, of being with people who did not know my name and did not care. I was afraid of being liked by strangers and of not being liked by strangers. Mostly I was afraid of being alone again, even for so short a time. After four and a half years of marriage I had simply lost the habit.

Marriage is not the culprit, though it is an obvious protective   3
mantle against aloneness. The fear of being alone is not reserved for
the married just as it is not reserved for women. I have heard stories
like mine from young boys and have seen the same childlike fear in
the faces of middle-aged men. Nor is this fear the special property of
Americans. But we seem, in this country, to fan the fear of being
alone. We are raised and in turn raise our children in clumps, in
groups, in auditoriums and car pools and locker rooms and scout dens.
Great emphasis is placed on how sociable we are as children, on how
popular we are with our peers. Great emphasis is also placed on how
well children mix in their own families. Despite the alleged falling
apart of the American family, the dialogue about familial relations is
constant, binding. If only in talk, parents and children do not leave
each other much alone. Great nostalgic emphasis is still placed on
the ritual togetherness of the family meal. A solitary eater, anytime,
anywhere, conjures up one of those sad, empty, too well-lighted
diners of an Edward Hopper painting.

And when for children there is no meal to attend, no group   4
activity, no distraction planned by a weekend father, there is the
constant company of the people on TV. A child need never be alone,
need never know silence except when asleep. Even then, for urban
and suburban children, there are the nonceasing nighttime noises of
cars, of neighbors, of arguing or partying parents. To be away from
the noise, away from the group—parents or peers—becomes a scary
thing and aloneness becomes confused and synonymous with loneliness.

I used to think that the worst thing I could say to my husband   5
when lying next to him was, "I'm lonely." That, I thought, was very
wounding, a reflection on his inability to be company to me. I think
now that it's a reflection on me, on my inability to be gracefully
alone even in the presence of someone I love. We all marry, in part,
to avoid being alone; many of us divorce when we find we can be just
as alone in marriage as before, and sometimes more so. Often, women
in crumbling marriages conceive babies not to try to hold a man, as
the cliche goes, but to guarantee themselves some company—even
that of an infant—when that man is gone. After the divorce, for a
man or woman, comes the frantic search for a replacement, a new
lover, a dog, a singles club, a stronger drink or drug. Waking next to
strangers in strange beds—surely, the loneliest habit—is considered
preferable to being alone.

Of this random bedding there has been much written lately,   6
especially by a handful of philosopher-journalists who blame such
"promiscuity" on what they call the New Narcissism, the inward-
turning, selfish, self-absorption of the American people. Each one of
us, their lament goes, is "into" his or her own jollies—the pursuit of
happiness having become the pursuit of hedonism—our faces reso-
lutely turned away from the world and its problems. But this is the
oddest of narcissisms then, the insecure narcissism of people who do
not like to be alone. The anti-narcissists point to the prodigious
number and variety of soul searchers—est devotees, Aricans, Moon-
ies, meditators and Rolfers—as proof of the neurotic self-celebration
of Americans. But even these soul searchings go on in huge groups;
they are orgies of mass psyche scratching. Hundreds of people writhe
together on auditorium floors in an attempt to soothe their individual
wounds. They jog together and ride bicycles together and walk the
most beautiful country roads together in an effort to slim their individual thighs.

So even if Americans are involved in a manic and somewhat   7
selfish pursuit of psychic and physical fitness, it is a collective not a
private pursuit. Everyone is holding hands; they're one long daisy
chain of self-improvement. This is, at best, a symbiotic narcissism,
the narcissism of people very dependent on one another, of people
afraid or bored to be alone, of people homogenizing into one sex—it
is less scary and less lonely, perhaps, to bed with a body that looks
and feels more like one's own—of people who need to see reflected
in the water not only their own faces but countless other faces as
well.

I do not mean to advertise the advantages of being alone. Many   8
have done that with more conviction than I could. I regard aloneness
not as a pleasure so much as an accident that, if one is to be at all
happy, must be survived. Nor do I mean to put down narcissism. On
the contrary, I find no fault with a certain healthy narcissism. Few
among us would undertake the saving of other souls until we first
have a stab of saving our own.

The point is simply that narcissism is not the point and that in   9
many ways it's a misnomer. A true narcissist is a true loner and most
of us, raised as we are, make lousy loners. We share each other's beds
somewhat freely not out of boldness but out of timidity, out of the
fear of being alone. We hunt for gurus not out of self-love, or
narcissism, but out of self-doubt. If we are to be even mildly happy

and therefore generous of spirit—as the anti-narcissists would have us be—then what we need is more narcissism, more privatism, not less. What we need instead of soul-searching sessions are classes on how to be alone: Aloneness 1A, Intermediary Aloneness, Advanced Aloneness. The great joy of these new classes is that attendance would not only not be required, it would be forbidden.

Questions on Meaning

1   According to Fleming, what causes Americans to fear being alone? What effects does this fear have on them?

2   What is the "New Narcissism" to which Fleming refers in paragraph 6? Why does she think it is incorrect to blame the "promiscuity" of contemporary American life on narcissism?

3   In what way, according to Fleming, might learning to cope better with being alone improve the quality of life in America? Do you agree with her analysis?

Questions on Method

1   List the effects of loneliness Fleming describes in paragraphs 1 and 2. How does her consideration, then rejection, of two alleged causes of loneliness strengthen her analysis when she later reveals the "real" cause?

2   What is the evidence Fleming produces to prove that Americans are trained to regard aloneness as loneliness?

3   How well does Fleming use cause-and-effect analysis to support her thesis? Can you point out other prose patterns that she depends on to make her point?

4   In what sense is Fleming's conclusion paradoxical or ironic? Can you point out other examples of paradox or irony in the essay?

Vocabulary and Diction

1   What is the difference, as Fleming sees it, between "aloneness" and "loneliness"?

2   What does the phrase "one long daisy chain of self-improvement" in paragraph 7 mean? What does Fleming's use of this phrase indicate about her attitude toward the people she calls "soul searchers"?

3 Look up Narcissus in a dictionary of Greek mythology. How accurately does Fleming's definition in paragraph 9 of a "true narcissist" as a "true loner" reflect the moral of the myth of Narcissus?

4 Define the following words used by Fleming: discomfited (1), conjures (3), hedonism (6), prodigious (6), writhe (6), manic (7), psychic (7), symbiotic (7), homogenizing (7), misnomer (9), privatism (9).

Writing Topics

1 Write an essay in which you argue, against Fleming, that Americans are skilled at the art of being alone.

2 Fleming mentions the "alleged" falling apart of the American family. Is family life falling apart in America? Write an essay that analyzes the causes behind either the weakness or the strength of American family life.

3 To what extent do you identify with Fleming's opening description of one of her "solitary departures"? Recall a similar experience you had, either as a child or as an adult. Offer your own analysis of the emotional effect such a solitary departure produced in you.

FRANK TRIPPETT (1926–   ) is a journalist and photographer
who lives in New York City. He worked as senior editor for
Look magazine from 1968 to 1971 and since then has been a
free-lance writer and editor contributing regularly to *Time*
magazine. His books include *The States: United They Fell* (1969)
and *Child Ellen* (1975). The essay that follows is one of
Trippett's frequent analyses of contemporary issues.

The Great American Cooling Machine

FrankTrippett

"The greatest contribution to civilization in this century may well be   1
air conditioning—and America leads the way." So wrote British
Scholar-Politician S. F. Markham 32 years ago when a modern cooling system was still an exotic luxury. In a century that has yielded
such treasures as the electric knife, spray-on deodorant and disposable
diapers, anybody might question whether air conditioning is the
supreme gift. There is not a whiff of doubt, however, that America
is far out front in its use. As a matter of lopsided fact, the U.S. today,
with a mere 5% of the population, consumes as much man-made
coolness as the whole rest of the world put together.

Just as amazing is the speed with which this situation came to   2
be. Air conditioning began to spread in industries as a production aid
during World War II. Yet only a generation ago a chilled sanctuary
during summer's stewing heat was a happy frill that ordinary people
sampled only in movie houses. Today most Americans tend to take
air conditioning for granted in homes, offices, factories, stores, thea-

ters, shops, studios, schools, hotels and restaurants. They travel in chilled buses, trains, planes and private cars. Sporting events once associated with open sky and fresh air are increasingly boxed in and air cooled. Skiing still takes place outdoors, but such attractions as tennis, rodeos, football and, alas, even baseball are now often staged in synthetic climates like those of Houston's Astrodome and New Orleans' Superdome. A great many of the country's farming tractors are now, yup, air-conditioned.

It is thus no exaggeration to say that Americans have taken to 3 mechanical cooling avidly and greedily. Many have become all but addicted, refusing to go places that are not air-conditioned. In Atlanta, shoppers in Lenox Square so resented having to endure natural heat while walking outdoors from chilled store to chilled store that the mall management enclosed and air-conditioned the whole sprawling shebang. The widespread whining about Washington's raising of thermostats to a mandatory 78°F suggests that people no longer think of interior coolness as an amenity but consider it a necessity, almost a birthright, like suffrage. The existence of such a view was proved last month when a number of federal judges, sitting too high and mighty to suffer 78°, defied and denounced the Government's energy-saving order to cut back on cooling. Significantly, there was no popular outrage at this judicial insolence; many citizens probably wished that they could be so highhanded.

Everybody by now is aware that the cost of the American way 4 is enormous, that air conditioning is an energy glutton. It uses some 9% of all electricity produced. Such an extravagance merely to provide comfort is peculiarly American and strikingly at odds with all the recent rhetoric about national sacrifice in a period of menacing energy shortages. Other modern industrial nations such as Japan, Germany and France have managed all along to thrive with mere fractions of the man-made coolness used in the U.S., and precious little of that in private dwellings. Here, so profligate has its use become that the air conditioner is almost as glaring a symptom as the automobile of the national tendency to overindulge in every technical possibility, to use every convenience to such excess that the country looks downright coddled.

But not everybody is aware that high cost and easy comfort are 5 merely two of the effects of the vast cooling of America. In fact, air conditioning has substantially altered the country's character and folkways. With the dog days at hand and the thermostats ostensibly up, it is a good time to begin taking stock of what air conditioning has done besides lower the indoor temperature.

Many of its byproducts are so conspicuous that they are scarcely   6
noticed. To begin with, air conditioning transformed the face of urban America by making possible those glassy, boxy, sealed-in skyscrapers on which the once humane geometries of places like San Francisco, Boston and Manhattan have been impaled. It has been indispensable, no less, to the functioning of sensitive advanced computers, whose high operating temperatures require that they be constantly cooled. Thus, in a very real way, air conditioning has made possible the ascendancy of computerized civilization. Its cooling protection has given rise not only to moon landings, space shuttles and Skylabs but to the depersonalized punch-cardification of society that regularly gets people hot under the collar even in swelterproof environments. It has also reshaped the national economy and redistributed political power simply by encouraging the burgeoning of the sultry southerly swatch of the country, profoundly influencing major migration trends of people and industry. Sunbelt cities like Phoenix, Atlanta, Dallas and Houston (where shivering indoor frigidity became a mark of status) could never have mushroomed so prosperously without air conditioning; some communities—Las Vegas in the Nevada desert and Lake Havasu City on the Arizona-California border—would shrivel and die overnight if it were turned off.

It has, as well, seduced families into retreating into houses with   7
closed doors and shut windows, reducing the commonalty of neighborhood life and all but obsoleting the front-porch society whose open casual folkways were an appealing hallmark of a sweatier America. Is it really surprising that the public's often noted withdrawal into self-pursuit and privatism has coincided with the epic spread of air conditioning? Though science has little studied how habitual air conditioning affects mind or body, some medical experts suggest that, like other technical avoidance of natural swings in climate, air conditioning may take a toll on the human capacity to adapt to stress. If so, air conditioning is only like many other greatly useful technical developments that liberate man from nature by increasing his productivity and power in some ways—while subtly weakening him in others.

Neither scholars nor pop sociologists have really got around to   8
charting and diagnosing all the changes brought about by air conditioning. Professional observers have for years been preoccupied with

307

the social implications of the automobile and television. Mere glancing analysis suggests that the car and TV, in their most decisive influences on American habits, have been powerfully aided and abetted by air conditioning. The car may have created all those shopping centers in the boondocks, but only air conditioning has made them attractive to mass clienteles. Similarly, the artificial cooling of the living room undoubtedly helped turn the typical American into a year-round TV addict. Without air conditioning, how many viewers would endure reruns (or even Johnny Carson) on one of those pestilential summer nights that used to send people out to collapse on the lawn or to sleep on the roof?

Many of the side effects of air conditioning are far from being 9 fully pinned down. It is a reasonable suspicion, though, that controlled climate, by inducing Congress to stay in Washington longer than it used to during the swelter season, thus presumably passing more laws, has contributed to bloated Government. One can only speculate that the advent of the supercooled bedroom may be linked to the carnal adventurism associated with the mid-century sexual revolution. Surely it is a fact—if restaurant complaints about raised thermostats are to be believed—that air conditioning induces at least expense-account diners to eat and drink more; if so, it must be credited with adding to the national fat problem.

Perhaps only a sophist might be tempted to tie the spread of air 10 conditioning to the coincidentally rising divorce rate, but every attentive realist must have noticed that even a little window unit can instigate domestic tension and chronic bickering between couples composed of one who likes it on all the time and another who does not. In fact, perhaps surprisingly, not everybody likes air conditioning. The necessarily sealed rooms or buildings make some feel claustrophobic, cut off from the real world. The rush, whir and clatter of cooling units annoy others. There are even a few eccentrics who object to man-made cool simply because they like hot weather. Still, the overwhelming majority of Americans have taken to air conditioning like hogs to a wet wallow.

It might be tempting, and even fair, to chastise that vast majority 11 for being spoiled rotten in their cool ascendancy. It would be more just, however, to observe that their great cooling machine carries with it a perpetual price tag that is going to provide continued and increasing chastisement during the energy crisis. Ultimately, the air conditioner, and the hermetic buildings it requires, may turn out to be a more pertinent technical symbol of the American personality than the car. While the car has been a fine sign of the American impulse to dart hither and yon about the world, the mechanical cooler more neatly suggests the maturing national compulsion to flee the natural world in favor of a technological cocoon.

Already architectural designers are toiling to find ways out of the technical trap represented by sealed buildings with immovable glass, ways that might let in some of the naturally cool air outside. Some have lately come up with a remarkable discovery: the openable window. Presumably, that represents progress. 12

Questions on Meaning

1 According to Trippett, why did Americans begin to use air conditioning during World War II? At that time, what did most Americans do to escape "summer's stewing heat"? Since then, how pervasive has the use of air conditioning become?

2 What has caused Americans to think of air conditioning as "a necessity, almost a birthright," rather than simply "an amenity"?

3 What are the two most obvious immediate effects that air conditioning has had on America? What in the most general terms has been its long-range effect?

4 How has air conditioning made possible, as Trippett says in paragraph 6, "the ascendancy of computerized civilization"? Why does Trippett think this in turn has caused society to become more "depersonalized"?

5 According to Trippett, what "conspicuous" effects has air conditioning had on the distribution of economic and political power in America and on American habits of shopping and recreation? What "side" effects has air conditioning had on politics and pleasure in America?

Questions on Method

1 What do you consider Trippett's most convincing evidence in support of the effects of air conditioning? What is his least convincing? How could the latter be made more convincing?

2 Although the air conditioner may be a good symbol of certain American character traits, is it responsible for altering "the country's character and folkways," as Trippett claims? How reasonable is Trippett's cause-and-effect analysis?

3 In paragraph 11 Trippett says that the air conditioner may turn out to be "a more pertinent technical symbol of the American personality than the car." What is it about the American personality that Trippett sees symbolized in the air conditioner? How does Trippett feel about what he sees?

4 What is the rationale for Trippett's progression from "obvious" to "scarcely noticed" effects? Do hints that there are yet unknown effects strengthen or weaken his claim to have found some "scarcely noticed" effects? How?

5 At the end of paragraph 10 Trippett says that most Americans have taken to air conditioning "like hogs to a wet wallow." What does this simile convey about Trippett's attitude toward air conditioning? Would you say that this simile is characteristic of the whole tone of the essay? What is that tone?

Vocabulary and Diction

1 In what sense is Trippett's use of the word "treasures" in paragraph 7 facetious, that is, humorously insincere or jesting? Would you say that Trippett's use of the word "progress" in the last paragraph of the essay is similarly facetious? How much is the essay characterized generally by a facetious quality of style and diction?

2 In paragraph 10 Trippett says that perhaps only a "sophist" would link the spread of air conditioning to the rise in divorce rates. What is a "sophist"? How "sophistic" do you find Trippett?

3 Define the following words and phrases used by Trippett: shebang (3), suffrage (3), judicial insolence (3), highhanded (3), rhetoric (4), profligate (4), dog days (5), humane geometries (6), punch-cardification (6), sultry southerly swatch (6), commonalty (7), obsoleting (7), boondocks (8), pestilential (8), carnal adventurism (9), chronic bickering (10), claustrophobic (10), eccentrics (10), chastise (11), hermetic (11), hither and yon (11).

Writing Topics

1 Are Americans as extravagantly self-indulgent, as "spoiled rotten," as Trippett argues they are? Write an essay in which you support your answer to this question with a logical cause-and-effect analysis.

2 Does technological advancement, however useful to people in some ways, in other ways weaken them? Write an essay in which you discuss

both the positive and the negative effects that technological progress has on the human race.

3   Trippett calls the typical American "a year-round TV addict." Do you think that this is a fair characterization? Write an essay analyzing the reasons Americans watch television as much as they do and the effects that this habit has on them.

4   What image would you say best symbolizes the American personality? Write an essay that fully explains your reasons for selecting that image.

KENNETH B. CLARK (1914–   ) received his doctorate in
psychology from Columbia University and taught at the City
College of New York for over thirty years. His work in civil
rights contributed to the 1954 Supreme Court ruling that
school segregation is unconstitutional. He is the founder of
Harlem Youth Opportunities Unlimited and is currently
president of his own consulting firm concerned with race
relations and affirmative action programs. He is a member of
the Board of Regents of the state of New York. In the following
autobiographical essay Clark describes the "guts" one needs to
succeed.

Why I Succeeded

Kenneth B. Clark

I always enjoyed school and admired my good teachers. One of the 1
reasons I ended up teaching is because I so admired them. All the
teachers I respected had in common the ability to take their particular
subject matter and give it a perspective, an order, a meaning. They
made ideas come to life. They also set standards. They would not
accept shoddy work, and I did not respect the teachers who did.

My mother set that standard for me too. She would not accept 2
race or color as alibis, either as excuses for inferior performance or as
insurmountable barriers. It was the one message with which she
bludgeoned me and my sister. She was aware of racial prejudice and
discrimination. She didn't tell us to pretend they didn't exist, but she
wouldn't let them shackle us. She just said, "Look, to hell with it.
Whatever anyone else can do, you can do." That's what I later told
my children and what they tell theirs.

My mother and father were from Jamaica, but with the building 3
of the Panama Canal their families migrated to the Canal Zone for

312

economic reasons. That's where my mother and father met, and they lived there until my mother left my father in 1918, when I was four years old. She came to New York like most immigrants, seeking a better way of life but also escaping my father and the problems he posed. Judging from my correspondence with him, my father—who is now dead—was an arrogant man. I am sure my mother's leaving him was a very positive influence on my life. He would not have been as totally supportive as she was.

He had a good job in Panama as superintendent of cargo with the United Fruit Company. It was quite something for a black man to have a white-collar job, and his father had had the same job before him. But my mother felt, and rightly so, that if we stayed in Panama the most she could look forward to for her son would be to follow in their footsteps. She was and still is a very firm, forthright and ambitious woman, and that didn't satisfy her. She knew what she wanted—particularly for her children. She wanted us to have educational opportunities and the ability to advance.

When we arrived in New York she got a job in a garment factory and worked there until she retired in the 1960s. Single-handedly she saw me and my sister—who was three years younger—through college and into graduate school. She stimulated my sister and me to improve ourselves, and she earned her high school diploma at George Washington High School—the same school I attended—by going nights.

Aside from my mother, my teachers always were my most positive influence. I still have in my mind rather clear, vivid images of significant teachers throughout my school days—from elementary school through college. I can see them smiling—Miss Maguire, Mr. Deegan, Miss Smith, Mr. Mitchell. I especially remember a junior high school speech teacher, Mr. Dixon, who was the first person to indicate to me that I could take ideas and transform them into words in which other people would be interested. He had me give a three-minute speech one day and was very positive in his reaction to it. I didn't understand what was so special about it, but he continued to draw me out. He had me enter an essay contest sponsored by Bond Bread. I don't remember what I wrote about, but I gave it to him and he turned it in, and I won a gold medal. I was very proud when I received it during an assembly period, and Mr. Dixon was proud too. I don't know why it is, but I remember the names of only the teachers I admired. I have been able to block out the others.

There was a guidance counselor in junior high school who tried to direct me to a vocational high school. I do not remember that woman's name. She had the feeling that black students—we were called "colored" then—should be realistic and not go on to academic schools. I suppose she was in the vanguard of counselors who interpreted their roles as protecting us from frustration and unhappiness by shunting us off to meaningless vocational schools, which were of a lower status than academic schools. She was persistent about it, but my mother took care of her. I was in the room the day my mother stormed in and said to her, "I don't care where you send your son, but mine is going to George Washington High School." My mother was not in any way awed by authority, and I think that saved my sister and me.

The only other bad memory I have is of an economics teacher, 8 although he was a good teacher. I was the best student in his class, and he determined who would get the economics prize at the high school graduation. I was shocked and so were my classmates when, even though I deserved it, it went to someone else. Frankly, he wasn't ready at that time to award it to a black student.

My mother's dream was for me to become an Episcopal priest, 9 but I had no illusions about priests and the priesthood, for the simple reason that I had been an altar boy from the time I was six until I was sixteen and went to college. During high school I decided I wanted to become a physician. I guess that came from observing the status and prestige physicians seemed to have. But also I had a crafts teacher at a summer playground who was a medical student at Howard University in Washington, D.C. She was very attractive, and I admired her so much I decided I wanted to go to Howard. That turned out to be the most influential decision to affect my future career.

Throughout my freshman year and part of my sophomore year 10 at Howard, I took all the pre-medical courses I could—biology, chemistry, physics. Then as a luxury I registered for an introductory course in psychology for the second half of my sophomore year. Dr. Francis Cecil Sumner taught it, and as I listened to this man I heard a wisdom, a comprehensive view of man in society, an attempt to deal rationally and systematically with human problems—human dignity. I don't know whether or not it was at any given moment, but as I listened and listened I decided I was not going to go to medical school; that I was going to pursue the study of psychology. Dr. Sumner, without being aware of it, had made it clear to me that that

314

was probably the most important area in which human intelligence should be involved.

Other things happening to me in my sophomore year supported 11 me in that choice. I remember the day in chemistry lab when a senior who was working close-by showed me the letter of admission to medical school he had received that morning. Paradoxically, that incident confirmed my intent not to go to medical school. It put the finishing touch on my decision, because I had seen him cheating on exams. I did not respect him, and it seemed to me that almost anybody could go to medical school. It perhaps was unfair, but I had seen other classmates too doing almost anything to get the grades they needed to gain admission to medical school. But that only confirmed the decision Dr. Sumner's influence had led me to make. He became my intellectual father, my friend, my adviser, my confidant, and from my sophomore year on everything in my choice of courses converged around my primary interest in psychology. No teacher before or since ever had the impact he had. He was totally supportive.

I've been very fortunate in the positive influences the significant 12 people in my life have had on me—including my wife, who was a freshman at Howard when I was a senior. I remember when, as a freshman, she said, "Kenneth, one of these days you're going to be a great psychologist." I took it just as courtship talk, but she always believed it, and that was a great support.

The shift to psychology gave a great deal of meaning to my life. 13 I saw psychology as a systematic rational use of human intelligence, not only to understand social problems but to help in finding answers to them. Although my primary activity throughout my career has been as an academician, my laboratory always was society, the social environment. My involvement in various social issues was never in competition or conflict with my academic role but was quite compatible with it. I never regarded the academic role—particularly in the social sciences—as one which can be fulfilled in isolation.

As I look back on my experiences as an undergraduate at Howard 14 University during the 1930s, I am convinced that my philosophy of the social role of disciplined human intelligence was being skillfully shaped by significant teachers. In addition to Dr. Sumner, such professors as Alvin L. Locke, Ralph Bunche, E. Franklin Frazier, Sterling Brown, and a few others not only taught me subject matter in the classroom but became my counselors and friends. They were my models and they identified with me, encouraged me, and advised me in the early stages of my academic career. If Dr. Sumner was my intellectual father, they were my intellectual godfathers, who made social sensitivity an integral part of all of my work as a social psychologist.

After I graduated from Howard I decided to stay on studying 15 with Dr. Sumner to get my master's degree, which I received at the end of the next year. He then kept me on to teach with him. That was quite an honor, but he soon encouraged me to go for my Ph.D., and I agreed. I applied to just two schools—Cornell and Columbia. Cornell wrote back and said they were sorry but, since Ph.D. candidates worked so closely together, they couldn't admit me because I was black. It was a stupid letter, and I was angry. I don't believe I answered it, but if I did I would have told them I was planning to go there to learn—not to socialize. I wish I had saved that letter, but every time I have gone to Cornell to give a talk I've been mean enough to remind them of it.

Columbia did accept me, and I was glad because Dr. Otto 16 Klineberg was there. I had heard him speak when he lectured at Howard while I was a graduate student, and he and his ideas impressed me. I enjoyed Columbia and speaking with the professors both inside and outside of class. Dr. Sumner had prepared me so well for the Ph.D. work, it was almost leisurely. During my studies at Columbia I also worked with Gunnar Myrdal, the Swedish sociologist and economist. Dr. Klineberg had recommended me to him, and the work consisted of studying and synthesizing the psychological literature on race. Also, my wife and I were doing research on racial awareness of children, but even that, as far as we were concerned, was pure research. It was for her master's thesis at Howard, and we conceived of it as an abstract problem. We had no such intent at the time, but it later became an important component of social policy and social change. I wasn't aware of it, but everything I was doing was preparing me for my involvement in the 1950s with the *Brown* decision by which the U.S. Supreme Court declared school segregation unconstitutional.

After I received my Ph.D. and completed my work with Myrdal, 17 I taught for a while at Hampton Institute, a black college in Virginia. I left there within a year and went into the Office of War Information, where in 1941–42 I was involved in a study of the morale of blacks

316

in America. Then in 1943 I joined the psychology department of the College of the City of New York and stayed there until I retired from teaching in 1975. The whole experience of teaching was a thrilling, stimulating, growing experience. You cannot teach without learning, and I don't recall a single class I had in all the years of teaching in which I didn't learn something. My wife would say to me, "You know, with all these other things you're doing, the real thing you enjoy—the thing you really thrive on—is teaching." She was right, because Dr. Sumner, a person whose life was devoted to teaching, was my model. I could go into a classroom with a headache or a cold, and within ten or fifteen minutes I was feeling wonderful. I remember ten or twelve of my students from all those years as vividly as I remember my teachers. I remember them not because of a surface brilliance or because they could write excellent papers. They went beyond that. They brought to their studies a passionate sensitivity, and a critical probing intelligence.

The action part of my career didn't surface until 1950. The 18 lawyers of the NAACP had gone to Dr. Klineberg for guidance as to how psychologists could help them on school segregation cases. He referred them to me because he knew of the work I had been doing on racial awareness and the effects of prejudice, discrimination, and segregation on personality development in children. From that point on my life was changed because I got involved with those cases on the trial level.

There were five cases—in Delaware, Kansas, South Carolina, 19 Virginia, and the District of Columbia. My involvement was as a social scientist testifying on the effects of discrimination and segregation and helping to write a brief, which was a social science brief, for submission to the Supreme Court. The Supreme Court's decision that segregation in schools was in violation of the Fourteenth Amendment was a highlight of my career. My immediate reaction was one of regret that Dr. Sumner—who had died of a heart attack—was not there to share my pleasure in being involved with that decision.

When it comes right down to it, I guess the principal guideline— 20 one which people important to me throughout my life have helped me to establish and which I have tried to follow—is the sense of the personal worth and substance of every individual. Everything else converges on that. The work my wife does at the Northside Center for Child Development, which we founded, is an acting out of that belief. So was our work with Harlem Youth Opportunities Unlimited and the Metropolitan Applied Research Center. It is what I tried to tell my students. It is what I try to say in my books. It is what I try to communicate to my children and grandchildren—that no human being is expendable and that we have a responsibility to our fellow human beings. Selfish pursuits are easy, but life is not worth much if spent on that.

Questions on Meaning

1   What are the two characteristics in a teacher that Clark says earned his admiration? In what way does Clark's admiration for certain teachers reflect his admiration for his mother?

2   Why did Clark's mother leave Panama? How would Clark have been affected had his mother stayed in Panama? What was the principal effect on him of his mother's decision to leave?

3   Why did Mr. Dixon, the junior high school speech teacher, earn Clark's admiration? What effect did he have on Clark? What was the main difference between Mr. Dixon and the guidance counselor or the economics teacher?

4   Why did Clark decide to become a physician rather than a priest? How did this decision influence Clark's choice about where to attend college? Why does Clark in paragraph 9 call his decision to attend Howard University "the most influential decision to affect my future career"?

5   What caused Clark to change his ambition and become a psychologist?

6   How did the graduate work that Clark and his wife did at Columbia become, as Clark says in paragraph 16, "an important component of social policy and social change"? How did this "action" part of his career, as Clark calls it, change his life?

7   What is Clark's "principal guideline"? In what sense have all the influences on Clark come together to result in this lesson that he draws from his life?

Questions on Method

1   How deeply does Clark probe the complex causes of some of his decisions in life? For example, what effect, only hinted at by Clark, did his father have on him?

2   Although Clark explores numerous cause-and-effect relationships, his essay is organized as a narration. Does Clark's use of narrative techniques help increase our sense of the complexity of the cause-and-effect rela-

tionships he analyzes? In what ways is narration the most subtle technique for exploring cause-and-effect relationships?

3 Clark says in paragraph 11 that seeing a senior's letter of acceptance to medical school paradoxically confirmed his intention not to apply to one. In what ways is there a sense of paradox associated with Clark's other career decisions?

Vocabulary and Diction

1 In paragraph 7 Clark says that the guidance counselor who tried to direct him to vocational school did so because she felt that black students should be "realistic." What did she mean by the word "realistic"? Was Clark's mother more or less realistic than the guidance counselor?

2 In paragraph 13 Clark defines "psychology" as being "a systematic, rational use of human intelligence, not only to understand social problems but to help in finding answers to them." In what sense is this definition overspecialized? In what sense is it too broad?

3 Define the following words used by Clark: shackle (2), vanguard (7), shunting (7), confidant (11), converged (11), academician (13), synthesizing (16), brief (19), expendable (20).

Writing Topics

1 Clark has spent a good deal of his life studying the effects of racial prejudice. What would you say are the most damaging effects of racial prejudice in America? Write an essay in which you use illustrative examples to answer this question.

2 Do some research on the *Brown* decision that declared school segregation unconstitutional. Write an essay in which you analyze the effects this decision has had on Americans. How, for example, has compulsory school busing, one result of the *Brown* decision, affected the country? Has it improved educational opportunities for black children? Has it caused new problems?

3 Clark was strongly influenced by certain teachers. How important an influence can a teacher have on a student? Should a teacher's influence be limited in any way? Do teachers have too much influence on their students? Do they have too little influence? Write an essay that answers these questions.

4 Write an essay in which you narrate how influential others have been in causing you to make a crucial decision in your life. How fully can you explain all the causes that led you to make your decision?

319

PATRICK FENTON (1944–   ) is employed as a cargo handler for an airline company in New York. In "Confessions of a Working Stiff" he writes about himself and his co-workers. His essay reflects his and their experiences after seven years on the job.

Confessions of a Working Stiff

Patrick Fenton

The Big Ben is hammering out its 5:45 alarm in the half-dark of 1 another Tuesday morning. If I'm lucky, my car down in the street will kick over for me. I don't want to think about that now; all I want to do is roll over into the warm covers that hug my wife. I can hear the wind as it whistles up and down the sides of the building. Tuesday is always the worst day—it's the day the drudgery, boredom, and fatigue start all over again. I'm off from work on Sunday and Monday, so Tuesday is my blue Monday.

I make my living humping cargo for Seaboard World Airlines, 2 one of the big international airlines at Kennedy Airport. They handle strictly all cargo. I was once told that one of the Rockefellers is the major stockholder for the airline, but I don't really think about that too much. I don't get paid to think. The big thing is to beat that race with the time clock every morning of your life so the airline will be happy. The worst thing a man could ever do is to make suggestions about building a better airline. They pay people $40,000 a year to come up with better ideas. It doesn't matter that these ideas never work; it's just that they get nervous when a guy from South Brooklyn or Ozone Park acts like he actually has a brain.

I throw a Myadec high-potency vitamin into my mouth to ward 3 off one of the ten colds I get every year from humping mailbags out in the cold rain at Kennedy. A huge DC-8 stretch jet waits impatiently for the 8,000 pounds of mail that I will soon feed its empty belly. I wash the Myadec down with some orange juice and grab a brown bag filled with bologna and cheese. Inside the lunch bag there is sometimes a silly note from my wife that says, "I Love You—Guess Who?" It is all that keeps me going to a job that I hate.

I've been going there for seven years now and my job is still the 4 same. It's weary work that makes a man feel used up and worn out. You push and you pull all day long with your back. You tie down pallets loaded with thousands of pounds of freight. You fill igloo-shaped containers with hundreds of boxes that all look the same. If you're assigned to work the warehouse, it's really your hard luck. This is the job all the men hate most. You stack box upon box until the pallet resembles the exact shape of the inside of the plane. You get the same monotonous feeling an adult gets when he plays with a child's blocks. When you finish one pallet, you find another and start the whole dull process over again.

The airline pays me $192 a week for this. After they take out 5 taxes and $5.81 for the pension, I go home with $142. Once a month they take out $10 for term life insurance, and $5.50 for union dues. The week they take out the life insurance is always the worst: I go home with $132. My job will never change. I will fill up the same igloos with the same boxes for the next 34 years of my life, I will hump the same mailbags into the belly of the plane, and push the same 8,000-pound pallets with my back. I will have to do this until I'm 65 years old. Then I'll be free, if I don't die of a heart attack before that, and the airline will let me retire.

In winter the warehouse is cold and damp. There is no heat. 6 The large steel doors that line the warehouse walls stay open most of the day. In the cold months, wind, rain and snow blow across the floor. In the summer the warehouse becomes an oven. Dust and sand from the runways mix with the toxic fumes of fork lifts, leaving a dry, stale taste in your mouth. The high windows above the doors are covered with a thick, black dirt that kills the sun. The men work in shadows with the constant roar of jet engines blowing dangerously in their ears.

机器的
空想

Working the warehouse is a tedious job that leaves a man's mind 7
empty. If he's smart he will spend his days wool-gathering. He will
think about pretty girls that he once knew, or some other daydream
of warm, dry places where you never had a chill. The worst thing he
can do is to think about his problems. If he starts to think about how
he is going to pay the mortgage on the $30,000 home that he can't
afford, it will bring him down. He will wonder why he comes to the
cargo airline every morning of his life, and even on Christmas Day.
He will start to wonder why he has to listen to the deafening sound
of the jets as they rev up their engines. He will wonder why he crawls
on his hands and knees, breaking his back a little bit more every day.

To keep his kids in that great place in the country in the 8
summer, that great place far away from Brooklyn and the South
Bronx, he must work every hour of overtime that the airline offers
him. If he never turns down an hour, if he works some 600 hours
over, he can make about $15,000. To do this he must turn against
himself, he must pray that the phone rings in the middle of the night,
even though it's snowing out and he doesn't feel like working. He
must hump cargo late into the night, eat meatball heroes for supper,
drink coffee that starts to taste like oil, and then hope that his car
starts when it's time to go home. If he gets sick—well, he better not
think about that.

All over Long Island, Ozone Park, Brooklyn, and as far away as 9
the Bronx, men stir in the early morning hours as a new day begins.
Every morning is the same as the last. Some of the men drink beer
for breakfast instead of coffee. Way out in Bay Shore a cargoman
snaps open a can of Budweiser. It's 6 A.M., and he covers the top of
the can with his thumb in order to keep down the loud hiss as the
beer escapes. He doesn't want to awaken his children as they dream
away the morning in the next room. Soon he will swing his Pinto
wagon up onto the crowded Long Island Expressway and start the
long ride to the job. As he slips the car out of the driveway he tucks
another can of beer between his legs.

All the men have something in common: they hate the work 10
they are doing and they drink a little too much. They come to work
only to punch a timecard that has their last name on it. At the end
of the week they will pick up a paycheck with their last name on it.
They will never receive a bonus for a job well done, or even a party.
At Christmastime a card from the president of the airline will arrive
at each one of their houses. It will say Merry Christmas and have the

president's name printed at the bottom of it. They know that the airline will be there long after they are dead. Nothing stops it. It runs non-stop, without sleep, through Christmas Day, New Year's Eve, Martin Luther King's birthday, even the deaths of Presidents.

It's seven in the morning and the day shift is starting to drift in. Huge tractors are backing up to the big-mouth doors of the warehouse. Cattle trucks bring tons of beef to feed its insatiable appetite for cargo. Smoke-covered trailers with refrigerated units packed deep with green peppers sit with their diesel engines idling. Names like White, Mack, and Kenworth are welded to the front of their radiators, which hiss and moan from the overload. The men walk through the factory-type gates of the parking lot with their heads bowed, oblivious of the shuddering diesels that await them. 11

Once inside the warehouse they gather in groups of threes and fours like prisoners in an exercise yard. They stand in front of the two time clocks that hang below a window in the manager's office. They smoke and cough in the early morning hour as they await their work assignments. The manager, a nervous-looking man with a stomach that is starting to push out at his belt, walks out with the pink work sheets in his hand. 12

Eddie, a young Irishman with a mustache, has just bolted in through the door. The manager has his timecard in his hand, holding it so no one else can hit Eddie in. Eddie is four minutes late by the time clock. His name will now go down in the timekeeper's ledger. The manager hands the card to him with a "you'll be up in the office if you don't straighten out" look. Eddie takes the card, hits it in, and slowly takes his place with the rest of the men. He has been out till four in the morning drinking beer in the bars of Ozone Park; the time clock and the manager could blow up, for all he cares. "Jesus," he says to no one in particular, "I hope to Christ they don't put me in the warehouse this morning." 13

Over in another group, Kelly, a tall man wearing a navy knit hat, talks to the men. "You know, I almost didn't make it in this morning. I passed this green VW on the Belt Parkway. The girl driving it was singing. Jesus, I thought to myself, it must be great going somewhere at 6:30 in the morning that makes you want to sing." Kelly is smiling as he talks. "I often think, why the hell don't you keep on going, Kelly? Don't get off at the cargo exit, stay on. Go anywhere, even if it's only Brooklyn. Christ, if I was a single man I think I would do just that. Some morning I'd pass this damn place 14 by and drive as far away as Riverhead. I don't know what I'd do when I got there—maybe I'd pick up a pound of beefsteak tomatoes from one of those roadside stands or something."

The men laugh at Kelly but they know he is serious. "I feel the same way sometimes," the man next to him says. "I find myself daydreaming a lot lately; this place drives you to that. I get up in the morning and I just don't want to come to work. I get sick when I hit that parking lot. If it wasn't for the kids and the house I'd quit." The men then talk about how hard it is to get work on "the outside." They mention "outside" as if they were in a prison. 15

Each morning there is an Army-type roll call from the leads. The leads are foremen who must keep the men moving; if they don't, it could mean their jobs. At one time they had power over the men but as time went by the company took away their little bit of authority. They also lost the deep interest, even enjoyment, for the hard work they once did. As the cargo airline grew, it beat this out of them, leaving only apathy. The ramp area is located in the backyard of the warehouse. This is where the huge jets park to unload their 70,000-pound payloads. A crew of men fall in behind the ramp lead as he mopes out of the warehouse. His long face shows the hopelessness of another day. 16

A brutal rain has started to beat down on the oil-covered concrete of the ramp as the 306 screeches in off the runway. Its engines scream as they spit off sheets of rain and oil. Two of the men cover their ears as they run to put up a ladder to the front of the plane. The airline will give them ear covers only if they pay for half of them. A lot of the men never buy them. If they want, the airline will give them two little plugs free. The plugs don't work and hurt the inside of the ears. 17

The men will spend the rest of the day in the rain. Some of them will set up conveyor belts and trucks to unload the thousands of pounds of cargo that sit in the deep belly of the plane. Then they will feed the awkward bird until it is full and ready to fly again. They will crawl on their hands and knees in its belly, counting and humping hundreds of mailbags. The rest of the men will work up topside on the plane, pushing 8,000-pound pallets with their backs. Like Egyptians building a pyramid, they will pull and push until the pallet finally gives in and moves like a massive stone sliding through sand. They don't complain too much; they know that when the airline comes up with a better system some of them will go. 18

The old-timers at the airline can't understand why the younger   19
men stay on. They know what the cargo airline can do to a man. It
can work him hard but make him lazy at the same time. The work
comes in spurts. Sometimes a man will be pushed for three hours of
sweat, other times he will just stand around bored. It's not the hard
work that breaks a man at the airline, it's the boredom of doing the
same job over and over again.

At the end of the day the men start to move in off the ramp.   20
The rain is still beating down at their backs but they move slowly.
Their faces are red and raw from the rain-soaked wind that has been
snapping at them for eight hours. The harsh wind moves in from the
direction of the city. From the ramp you can see the Manhattan
skyline, gray- and blue-looking, as it peeks up from the west wall of
the warehouse. There is nothing to block the winter weather as it
rolls in like a storm across a prairie. They head down to the locker
room, heads bowed, like a football team that never wins.

With the workday almost over, the men move between the   21
narrow, gray rows of lockers. Up on the dirty walls that surround the
lockers someone has written a couple of four-letter words. There is
no wit to the words; they just say the usual. As they strip off their
wet gear the men seem to come alive.

"Hey, Arnie! You want to stay four hours? They're asking for   22
overtime down in Export," one of the men yells over the lockers.

Arnie is sitting about four rows over, taking off his heavy winter   23
clothing. He thinks about this for a second and yells back, "What
will we be doing?"

"Working the meat trailer." This means that Arnie will be   24
humping huge sides of beef off rows of hooks for four hours. Blood
will drip down onto his clothes as he struggles to the front of the
trailer. Like most of the men, he needs the extra money, and knows
that he should stay. He has Master Charge, Korvettes, Times Square
Stores, and Abraham & Straus to pay.

"Nah, I'm not staying tonight. Not if it's working the meat   25
trailer. Don wanted to stop for a few beers at The Owl; maybe I'll
stay tomorrow night."

It's four o'clock in the afternoon now—the men have twelve   26
minutes to go before they punch out. The airline has stopped for a
few seconds as the men change shifts. Supervisors move frantically
across the floor pushing the fresh lot of new men who have just
started to come in. They hand out work sheets and yell orders: "Jack,

get your men into their rain gear. Put three men in the bellies to finish off the 300 flight. Get someone on the pepper trailers, they've been here all morning."

The morning shift stands around the time clock with three   27
minutes to go. Someone says that Kevin Delahunty has just been appointed to the Fire Department. Kevin, a young Irishman from Ozone Park, has been working the cargo airline for six years. Like most of the men, he has hated every minute of it. The men are openly proud of him as they reach out to shake his hand. Kevin has found a job on "the outside." "Ah, you'll be leaving soon," he tells Pat. "I never thought I'd get out of here either, but you'll see, you're going to make it."

The manager moves through the crowd handing out timecards   28
and stops when he comes to Kevin. Someone told him Kevin is leaving. "Is that right, Delahunty? Well I guess we won't expect you in tomorrow, will we? Going to become a fireman, eh? That means you'll be jumping out of windows like a crazy man. Don't act like you did around here," he adds as he walks back to his office.

The time clock hits 4:12 and the men pour out of the warehouse.   29
Kevin will never be back, but the rest of them will return in the morning to grind out another eight hours. Some of them will head straight home to the bills, screaming children, and a wife who tries to understand them. They'll have a Schaefer or two, then they'll settle down to a night of television.

Some of them will start to fill up the cargo bars that surround   30
Kennedy Airport. They will head to places like Gaylor's on Rockaway Boulevard or The Dew Drop Inn down near Farmers Boulevard. They will drink deep glasses of whiskey and cold mugs of Budweiser. The Dew Drop has a honky-tonk mood of the Old West to it. The barmaid moves around like a modern-day Katie Elder. Like Brandy, she's a fine girl, but she can out-curse any cargoman. She wears a low-cut blouse that reveals most of her breasts. The jukebox will beat out some Country & Western as she says, "Ah, hell, you played my song." The cargomen will hoot and holler as she substitutes some of her own obscene lyrics.

They will drink late into the night, forgetting time clocks,   31
Master Charge, First National City, Korvettes, mortgages, cars that don't start, and jet engines that hurt their ears. They will forget about damp, cold warehouses, winters that get longer and colder every year, minutes that drift by like hours, supervisors that harass, and the

thought of growing old on a job they hate. At midnight they will fall dangerously into their cars and make their way up onto the Southern State Parkway. As they ride into the dark night of Long Island they will forget it all until 5:45 the next morning—when the Big Ben will start up the whole grind all over again.

Questions on Meaning

1 In paragraph 2 Fenton says, "I don't get paid to think." What does he get paid to do? Why does he say in paragraph 7 that the worst thing a man with his job can do is "to think about his problems"?

2 What does Fenton mean when he says in paragraph 8 that to earn $15,000 a year on his job he must "turn against himself"? Is this the worst effect that his job has on him?

3 In paragraph 10 Fenton tells us that all the men hate their work and drink a little too much. What causes the men to keep going to a job they hate? To what extent does the drinking of someone like Eddie, for example, help make the work any easier to accept? Is it fair to say that working for the airline is what causes the men to drink or, as the man next to Kelly says, to daydream a lot?

4 How does the airline treat the men at Christmas? Is this typical of the way the airline treats them everyday?

5 Why don't the men complain about the way the airline treats them? What is it, ultimately, that breaks a man at the airline?

Questions on Method

1 In paragraph 4 Fenton says that this job gives him "the same monotonous feeling an adult gets when he plays with a child's blocks." What other comparisons does Fenton make to convey the feelings of monotony and hopelessness that his job causes in him? Which parts of his description of the job itself and the way he is treated by his employer are most effective in helping us understand why he feels as he does?

2 Why throughout the essay does Fenton picture the planes and the warehouse as creatures with "insatiable" appetites that must be fed?

3 Why does Fenton conclude the essay by contrasting Kevin, who will never be back, with the rest of the men, who either go home to a night of television or go to places like the Dew Drop Inn?

4 Why doesn't Fenton sound angry about his situation? How does his tone help us understand the character and psychology of the sort of men who work loading cargo for the airline?

Vocabulary and Diction

1 How do such slang expressions as "kick over" (1) and "humping" (2) reflect a particular style of speech? Does Fenton maintain this style consistently throughout the essay?

2 How well does Fenton define such terms associated with his job as stretch jet (3), pallet (4), fork lifts (6), leads (16), payloads (16)?

Writing Topics

1 Who, ultimately, is responsible for the poor working conditions from which the men described by Fenton suffer? Do you blame the airline? If so, what causes the airline to exploit the men the way it does? Might you blame the men for allowing themselves to be exploited? If so, what causes them to do so? Write an essay taking one side or the other.

2 Clark's essay deals with the problem of racial prejudice in America. Is there also a prejudice in America against unskilled blue-collar workers? Does Fenton describe a group of men who are suffering from some kind of discrimination? Write an essay in which you analyze what might cause unskilled blue-collar laborers to feel as though they are victims of discrimination.

3 Write an essay describing the different effects, whether positive or negative, that a certain job you held had on you.

4 Did you ever continue working at a job you hated for a longer time than you expected you would? Write an essay in which you analyze what kept you from quitting.

ARNOLD TOYNBEE (1889–1975) was a historian and writer who
graduated from Oxford University. He is best known for his
twelve-volume work *A Study in History*, which analyzes the
origins, development, and disintegration of world civilization.
His other writings include *Civilization on Trial* (1948) and *The
World and the West* (1953). In the following essay Toynbee
advocates prolonging sexual innocence.

Prolonging Sexual Innocence

Arnold Toynbee

Looking back into the past history of the West—a past which was   1
still present when I was a child—I admire the nineteenth-century
West's success in postponing the age of sexual awakening, of sexual
experience and sexual infatuation far beyond the age of physical
puberty. You may tell me that this was against nature; but to be
human consists precisely in transcending nature—in overcoming the
biological limitations that we have inherited from our pre-human
ancestors.

All human societies overcome death by creating and maintaining   2
institutions that are handed on from one generation to another. Sex
is a still more awkward feature of our biological inheritance than
death, and our nineteenth-century Western society handled sex with
relative success. By postponing the age of sexual awakening, it prolonged the length of the period of education. It is this, together with
the seventeenth-century Western achievement of learning to think

for oneself instead of taking tradition on trust, that accounts for the West's preeminence in the world during the last few centuries.

Nineteenth-century Westerners condemned with justice the Hindu institution of child-marriage, and they deplored, also with justice, the spectacle of an intellectually promising Moslem boy being allowed to commit intellectual suicide by sexual indulgence at the age of puberty. The twentieth-century West is now imitating the non-Western habits that the nineteenth-century West rightly— though perhaps self-righteously—condemned.

Our irrational contemporary Western impatience and our blind adulation of speed for speed's sake are making havoc, today, of the education of our children. We force their growth as if they were chicks in a pullet factory. We drive them into a premature awareness of sex even before physical puberty has overtaken them. In fact, we deprive our children of the human right of having a childhood. This forcing of sex-consciousness started in the United States; it has spread to Britain, and who knows how many other Western countries this perverse system of miseducation is going to invade and demoralize?

Our whole present policy in the upbringing of the young is paradoxical. While we are lowering the age of sexual awareness—and frequently the age of sexual experience, too—to a veritably Hindu degree, we are at the same time prolonging the length of education. We force our boys and girls to become sex-conscious at twelve or thirteen, and then we ask them to prolong their post-graduate studies till they are nearly thirty. How are they to be expected to give their minds to education during those last sixteen or seventeen sex-haunted years?

We are proud of ourselves for providing secondary education, college education, postgraduate education for everybody. But we shall be plowing the sands if we do not simultaneously revert to our grandparents' practice of prolonging the age of sexual innocence. If we persist, in this vital matter, on our present Hindu course, our brand-new would-be institutions for higher education will become, in practice, little more than social clubs for sexual mating.

Questions on Meaning

1 Why does Toynbee admire "the nineteenth-century West's success in postponing the age of sexual awakening" even though he admits that such a postponement was "against nature"?

2 According to paragraph 2, what was the immediate effect of this post-ponement? When this effect was combined with "the seventeenth-century Western achievement of learning to think for oneself," what ultimate effect resulted?

3 Why did nineteenth-century Westerners condemn the Hindu institution of child-marriage?

4 What causes the twentieth-century West to drive its children into "a premature awareness of sex"? What immediate effect does this have on children? What long-term effect does it have on the success of the educational process in the West?

Questions on Method

1 What evidence does Toynbee give that prolonging sexual innocence improves education or that forcing sex-consciousness impairs it?

2 What effects of prolonging sexual innocence has Toynbee overlooked?

3 How could Toynbee make clearer what he means by this cause-and-effect relationship: sex "making havoc, today, of the education of our children"?

Vocabulary and Diction

1 Toynbee says in paragraph 1 that "to be human consists precisely in transcending nature." To what extent do you find this an apt definition of the word "human"?

2 Toynbee says that the nineteenth-century West's condemnation of Hindu marriage practices, although right, was also self-righteous. What does it mean to be self-righteous? Are Toynbee's views self-righteous in any way?

Writing Topics

1 American children today do seem to be more sexually conscious at younger ages than children were in the past. Write an essay in which you explain what you think are the main causes of this. Indicate whether you feel the effects of this early sexual consciousness are as destructive as Toynbee fears.

2 The effectiveness of American education seems to have declined in recent years. Have our educational institutions become "little more than social clubs for sexual mating"? Write an essay discussing what causes

you attribute to the crisis that American education seems to be suffering today and what can be done to improve American education.

3 Toynbee argues that we must prolong "the age of sexual innocence," but he offers no suggestions about how to do so. Write an essay in which you discuss whether there are any practical ways to accomplish such a goal.

4 Write an essay analyzing the positive effects of America's sexual revolution.

Cause and Effect—Writing Topics

1 What would you say is the primary difference between a process analysis and a cause-and-effect analysis? Explain your answer in an essay that illustrates its points by describing both how a certain process works and why it works the way it does.

2 Cause-and-effect analysis is one of the most basic mental processes used to interpret what we read. Read one of the essays in the last chapter of this book, determine the essay's thesis, and write a cause-and-effect analysis that explains what details of the essay led you to your interpretation and why they did so.

3 Compare the author in this chapter whom you find the most hopeful or optimistic to the one whom you find the most pessimistic or bleak. Write an essay that analyzes why the two authors might have such differing outlooks.

4 How hopeful do you feel about your prospects in life? Write an essay in which you analyze what causes you to feel the way you do. How much effect do you think your feelings, whether positive or negative, will have on your ultimate success or failure?

5 Frank Trippett seems to think, and many people would agree, that the most appropriate technological symbol of America is the car. Write an essay that analyzes what causes America to be such a car-oriented society and what effects this orientation has had on the life of Americans.

6 Write a cause-and-effect analysis of a current news event. You might, for example, analyze what the results of a current political crisis might be or what reasons lie behind the current success or failure of a sports team.

7 Write a cause-and-effect analysis of a current sociopolitical issue. You might, for example, analyze the handgun control issue. What causes people to oppose or favor handgun control? What effects would tightening or not tightening control have?

8 Write a cause-and-effect analysis of why students are attending college today and whether it is worth their time to do so.

TEN

Argumentation

Argumentation uses all the resources of the other three types of prose—narration, description, and exposition—but for its own purpose: to persuade the reader to take a specific course of action or point of view. Even when it explains, it aims to persuade. It sets out clearly what is to be done or thought and proceeds to tell why, how, when, and so on, in the most compelling fashion. It engages the heart as well as the head. It aims to sell. It uses lively vocabulary and examples and illustrations that are most vivid for its particular audience. More than narration, description, or exposition per se, argumentation is prose whose effectiveness can be tested because it calls for a more or less definite and immediate reaction from the audience. It asks for commitment, and it requires commitment from the author. If it succeeds, the writer's rewards can be immediate and substantial.

A live debater has two audiences, an opponent to defeat and a public or judges to win to his side. Information and imagination are his best weapons. The writer of argumentation likewise must know both sides of the issues so that he or she can refute the opposition. The place for refutation is early in the essay when a reader is most likely to begin raising mental objections. For example, Louise Montague's side in "Straight Talk about the Living-Together Arrangement" is strengthened by her willingness to give prime space (the first four paragraphs) to the opposition. This organization shows that she has considered both sides, has listened to others, and still believes she is right.

The actual job of refutation is handled in essentially the same way as that of advancing your own position: giving evidence or reasons and drawing logical conclusions. If you think the facts, statistics, precedents, and positions of authorities have only to be known to support your conclusion, then emphasize the evidence and the conclusion will probably take care of itself. This is especially true if you are in a unique position to *know* the evidence. A debater's credentials, those of someone like Cyrus Vance, for example, count for a great deal, and if your credentials are not sufficiently indicated by your title, mention them in your introduction.

If, however, it is a question of deriving the correct (from your point of view) conclusion from already known facts or principles, emphasize the logic of your approach. Here you have two methods of arriving at a conclusion: the inductive, which proceeds by building up facts or particulars, and the deductive, which applies a preexisting generalization or principle to a particular circumstance. For example, if over a period of time you observe that most neighbors with stout fences between them never get into fights and you conclude that good fences are the cause, then you have used induction to reach the conclusion that good fences make good neighbors; when you learn that Jones and Grimaglia are fighting and conclude that a fence would prevent them from doing so, you are using deduction, applying a general principle to a particular case. One problem with this logical approach is that your inductive conclusion may be invalid (good fences may *not* make good neighbors) because of insufficient evidence, for example, or misinterpretation of evidence, and that would mean that any deduction based on it would also be invalid—as would, for example, the deduction that these two families need a fence.

One form of deduction is the "syllogism," which arranges two premises, a major and a minor, to reach a conclusion:

1 Good fences make good neighbors.
2 Jones and Grimaglia have a good fence.
3 Therefore (ergo) Jones and Grimaglia are good neighbors.

Syllogisms are seldom introduced complete and undisguised into argument; they appear more often in a shortened form called an "enthymeme":

1 Smith and Grimaglia would be better neighbors if they had a fence.

or

2 A fence would improve relations between the Smith and Grimaglia families.

The main value of studying the syllogism and the enthymeme is to remember that conclusions drawn from false premises are false and that even valid conclusions need the support of evidence. The next step for the writer on Smith and Grimaglia is to support this conclusion with facts about fences and about these two families.

Writing Argumentation

1 Acknowledge and refute the opposition early on.
2 Support your side with evidence, reasons, statistics, precedents, and the opinion of authorities.
3 Draw valid and significant conclusions from valid premises.
4 Cover the bare bones of your logic with graceful narration, description, and all the modes of exposition that suit your subject.

NORMAN COUSINS (1915–   ) became editor of *Saturday
Review* in 1940 after several years on the staff of the *New York
Post.* An essayist and philosopher, he has spent many years
writing on cultural and educational issues. His most recent
book, *Anatomy of an Illness* (1979), reflects his successful
struggle against a degenerative disease. In the following essay he
analyzes the impact of the news on our everyday lives.

Where Is the News Leading Us?

Norman Cousins

Not long ago I was asked to join in a public symposium on the role   1
of the American press. Two other speakers were included on the
program. The first was a distinguished TV anchorman. The other was
the editor of one of the nation's leading papers, a newsman to the
core—tough, aggressive, and savvy in the ways and means of solid
reporting.

The purpose of the symposium, as I understood it, was to scru-   2
tinize the obligations of the media and to suggest the best ways to
meet those obligations.

During the open-discussion period, a gentleman in the audience   3
addressed a question to my two colleagues. Why, he asked, are the
newspapers and the television news programs so disaster-prone? Why
are newsmen and women so attracted to tragedy, violence, failure?

The anchorman and editor reacted as though they had been   4
blamed for the existence of bad news. Newsmen and newswomen,

they said, are only responsible for reporting the news, not for creating it or modifying it.

It didn't seem to me that the newsmen had answered the ques- 5 tion. The gentleman who had asked it was not blaming them for the distortions in the world. He was just wondering why distortions are most reported. The news media seem to operate on the philosophy that all news is bad news. Why? Could it be that the emphasis on downside news is largely the result of tradition—the way newsmen and newswomen are accustomed to respond to daily events?

Perhaps it would be useful here to examine the way we define 6 the word *news*, for this is where the problem begins. *News* is supposed to deal with happenings of the past 12 hours—24 hours at most. Anything that happens so suddenly, however, is apt to be eruptive. A sniper kills some pedestrians; a terrorist holds 250 people hostage in a plane; OPEC announces a 25 percent increase in petroleum prices; Great Britain devalues by another 10 percent; a truck convey-ing radioactive wastes collides with a mobile cement mixer.

Focusing solely on these details, however, produces a misshapen 7 picture. Civilization is a lot more than the sum total of its catastro-phes. The most important ingredient in any civilization is progress. But progress doesn't happen all at once. It is not eruptive. Generally, it comes in bits and pieces, very little of it clearly visible at any given moment, but all of it involved in the making of historical change for the better.

It is this aspect of living history that most news reporting reflects 8 inadequately. The result is that we are underinformed about positive developments and overinformed about disasters. This, in turn, leads to a public mood of defeatism and despair, which in themselves tend to be inhibitors of progress. An unrelieved diet of eruptive news depletes the essential human energies a free society needs. A mood of hopelessness and cynicism is hardly likely to furnish the energy needed to meet serious challenges.

I am not suggesting that "positive" news be contrived as an 9 antidote to the disasters on page one. Nor do I define *positive news* as in-depth reportage of functions of the local YMCA. What I am trying to get across is the notion that the responsibility of the news media is to search out and report on important events—*whether or not* they come under the heading of conflict, confrontation, or catastrophe. The world is a splendid combination of heaven and hell, and *both* sectors call for attention and scrutiny.

My hope is that the profession of journalism will soon see its 10
responsibility in a wider perspective. The time has come to consider
the existence of a large area of human happenings that legitimately
qualify as news. For example, how many news articles have been
written about nitrogen-fixation—the process by which plants can be
made to "fix" their own nitrogen, thus reducing the need for fertilizer?
Scientists all over the world are now pursuing this prospect in the
hope of combating famine. How much is known about the revolutionary changes being made in increasing the rice harvest in the Far
East? There are literally dozens of similar important developments in
the world that are worthy of inclusion in any roundup of major news
stories.

The anchorman and the editor were right in saying that newsmen 11
and women are not responsible for shaping the world. But they *are*
responsible for affecting our attitudes. We are only what we think we
are; we can achieve only those goals we dare to envision. News people
provide us with the only picture we have of ourselves and of the
world. It had better be a true portrait—and not a caricature—for it
is this picture on which we will base our decisions and around which
we will plan our future.

The journalist, to paraphrase Walter Lippmann, is the public's 12
philosopher. "The acquired culture," Lippmann wrote, "is not transmitted in our genes. The good life in the good society, though
attainable, is never attained and possessed once and for all. What
has been attained will again be lost if the wisdom of the good life in
a good society is not transmitted."

With an accurate report of the good life in the good society, we 13
can begin to use the news as Bernard de Chartres suggested we use
history—boosting ourselves up on our experiences, "like dwarfs seated
on the shoulders of giants," enabled, thus, "to see more things than
the Ancients and things more distant."

Questions on Meaning

1   According to Cousins, what did the man in the audience mean when he
    asked why newspapers and television news programs are so "disaster-
    prone"? What was the effect of this question on the editor and the
    anchorman?

2 Why does Cousins think the news media overemphasize bad news?

3 What effect does such news reporting have on the public mood? Why does it have this effect?

4 What suggestion does Cousins make to help remedy the situation?

Questions on Method

1 Where does Cousins state his thesis most clearly?

2 To what extent does Cousins rely on logic to argue his thesis? To what extent does he rely on emotion?

3 Does Cousins exaggerate at all to make his point? Where? Does the exaggeration affect his credibility? Explain.

4 Does Cousins identify the opposition in this argument? Where? What is the opposition's defense? Does Cousins attempt to refute it? Would the opposition accept the definition of "news" given here? Is the definition Cousins's or the opposition's?

Vocabulary and Diction

1 How well, in your opinion, does Cousins define the words "news" and "progress"?

2 In what sense does the use of the word "distortions" in paragraph 5 reflect the bias Cousins has against the news media?

3 Define the following words used by Cousins: symposium (1), savvy (1), eruptive (6), depletes (8), antidote (9), sectors (9), caricature (11), paraphrase (12).

Writing Topics

1 Do you agree with Cousins that the news media are disaster-prone and that therefore we are "underinformed about positive developments and overinformed about disasters"? Write an essay in which you argue your opinion.

2 How responsible are the news media for making us feel either despairing or hopeful about the future? Are there other important causes for these general attitudes? Write an essay in which you explain how much despair and how much hope you feel about the future and what causes lie behind your feelings.

3 Imagine that you, as the anchorman or the editor at this symposium, are given equal time to rebut Cousins. What would you say? After refuting Cousins, explain what you think the problem is and propose your solutions.

Cyrus Vance (1917–   ) graduated from Yale Law School in
1942 and was admitted to the New York Bar in 1947 and the
U.S. Supreme Court Bar in 1960. He was secretary of the
Army from 1962 to 1963, U.S. negotiator at the Paris Peace
Conference on Vietnam in 1968–69, and served from 1977
until spring 1980 as secretary of state in the Carter
administration. He resigned because of his opposition to the
Carter plan to rescue the American hostages in Iran. In the
following excerpt from his 1980 Harvard commencement
address, Vance outlines his views on foreign policy for the
decade ahead.

Foreign Policy: Defining Our Goals

Cyrus Vance

Yours is the first Harvard class to graduate in the decade of the 1980's.   1
The decisions our nation makes now will shape the future of that
decade. We can either work to shape, in a wise and effective manner,
the changes that now engulf our world or, by acting unwisely, become
shackled by them. It is a time to set and stick to basic goals. Neither
we nor the world can afford an American foreign policy which is
hostage to the emotions of the moment. We must have in our minds
a conception of the world we want a decade hence. The 1990 we
seek must shape our actions in 1980, or the decisions of 1980 could
give us a 1990 we will regret.

Supporting the efforts of third world nations to preserve their   2
independence and to improve the quality of life for their people,
particularly those hovering at the edge of survival; strengthening the
health and well-being of our economic system within a strong international economy—these are the decisions, along with preserving the
military balance while effectively managing our competition with the

343

Soviet Union and fostering strong alliances of free nations—these are the decisions we should make now. These goals are ambitious. It would be naive to think otherwise. But unless our reach is bold, our grasp will fall far short.

Let us keep in mind the world from which we start: a world 3 undergoing rapid change, with growing expectations, better education, quickened communications; a world in which neither the United States nor any other country commands a preponderance of power or a monopoly of wisdom. It is a world of conflicts, among nations and values, among social systems and emerging new interests. It is a world in which competitive superpowers hold in their hands our common survival, yet paradoxically find it beyond their power to order events.

There is a disturbing fear in the land that we are no longer 4 capable of shaping our future. Some believe that we have lost our military muscle; others worry that our political will has been sapped. I do not accept this gloom. It discards the abiding pragmatic philosophy that has characterized America ever since its founding.

I consider mistaken the view that we and we alone are respon- 5 sible for all the confusing changes that we see around us. This is a serious misreading of our condition, a perverted hubris that overestimates our power and our responsibility for ill and underestimates our capacity for good. The international diffusion of power and intellect is a fact. It will not change. It requires fresh and vital forms of action, not regret and pining for supposed "good old days." What is to be regretted is a reluctance to relate our basic purposes to these new conditions. Yesterday's answers will not provide tomorrow's solutions.

It seems to me that much of the current dissatisfaction with the 6 world and our role in it rests on certain fallacies. These illusions must be exploded before our nation can chart a coherent and determined course in foreign policy.

The first fallacy is that a single strategy—a master plan—will 7 yield the answers to each and every foreign policy decision we face. Whatever value that approach may have had in a bipolar world, it now serves us badly. The world has become pluralistic, exposing the inadequacy of the single strategy, the grand design, where facts are forced to fit theory. Given the complexity of the world to which we have fallen heir, the effect of a single strategy is to blur this complexity and to divide nations everywhere into friends and enemies.

344

A second widely accepted fallacy is the fear of negotiation, the 8 worry that somehow we will always come out second best in any bargain. This fallacy assumes we have a realistic alternative of going it alone, of not bothering to recognize the legitimate interests and desires of other peoples. Without the fair bargain, achieved through negotiation and diplomacy, there is only a misguided failed effort to impose one will upon another. Denying others a fair bargain and its benefits will not alter their behavior or reduce their power; it will simply have the effect of denying ourselves the same advantages. If America fears to negotiate with our adversaries, or to bargain fairly with third world nations, we will not have a diplomacy. And we, no less than others, will be the loser.

A third myth that needs to be exploded is that there is an 9 incompatibility between the pursuit of America's values in our foreign policy, such as human rights, and the pursuit of our interests. Certainly the pursuit of human rights must be managed in a practical way. We must constantly weigh how best to encourage progress while maintaining an ability to conduct business with governments—even unpopular ones—in countries where we have important security interests.

But we must ultimately recognize that the demand for individual 10 freedom and economic progress cannot be long repressed without sowing the seeds of violent convulsion. Thus it is in our interest to support constructive change, as we did, for example, in the Dominican Republic, and are seeking to do in Central America, before the alternatives of radicalism or repression force out moderate solutions. We know from our own national experience that the drive for human freedom has tremendous force and vitality. It is universal. It is resilient. And, ultimately, it is irrepressible. In a profound sense, then, our ideals and our interests coincide. For we have a stake in the stability that comes when people can express their hopes and build their futures freely.

Further is the dangerous fallacy of the military solution to non- 11 military problems. It arises in particularly acute form at times of frustration, when the processes of negotiation are seen as slow-moving and tedious. American military power is essential to maintaining the global military balance. Our defense forces must be modernized—and they will be. But increased military power is a basis, not a substitute, for diplomacy. I have heard it argued that our response to a changing world must be a new emphasis on American military power and the will to use it. This is reflected in proposed new budget priorities in the Congress, in which unnecessary defense spending squeezes out domestic programs and foreign assistance. There is near-consensus on the need for defense increases. But it is illusion to believe that they are a substitute for the diplomacy and resources needed to address such problems as internal change and basic need in other nations or a battered international economy.

The use of military force is not, and should not be, a desirable 12
American policy response to the internal politics of other nations. We believe we have the right to shape our future; we must respect that right in others. We must clearly understand the distinction between our readiness to act forcefully when the vital interests of our nation, our allies and our friends are threatened, and our recognition that our military force cannot provide a satisfactory answer to the purely internal problems of other nations.

Finally there is a pervasive fallacy that America could have the 13
power to order the world just the way we want it to be. It assumes, for example, that we could dominate the Soviet Union—that we could prevent it from being a super-power—if we chose to do so. This obsolete idea has more to do with nostalgia than with present-day reality. Spread over the widest territory of any nation on earth, the Soviet Union has its own strategic interests and goals. From a state of underdevelopment and the ravages of war, it has built formidable military and industrial resources. We should not underestimate these resources any more than we should exaggerate them. We must preserve and manage a position of essential equivalence with the Soviet Union. It is naive to believe that the Russians will play by our rules any more than we will accept theirs. It is naive to believe that they—any more than we—would willingly accept a position of second best in military strength.

A dangerous new nostalgia underlies all these fallacies—a long- 14
ing for earlier days when the world seemed, at least in retrospect, to have been a more orderly place in which American power could alone preserve that order. That nostalgia continually erodes confidence in our national leadership for it encourages expectations that bear no relationship to reality. And it makes change in the world's condition seem all threat and no opportunity. It makes an unruly world seem more hostile than it is. The fact is that we are a people who not only have adapted well to change but have thrived on it. The new nostalgia leads us to simplistic solutions and go-it-alone illusions, diverting our

energies from the struggle to shape change in constructive directions. It is self-indulgent nonsense, bound to lead us into error, if not disaster.

Questions on Meaning

1   Why does Vance think it is time for America "to set and stick to basic goals"? What are the four basic goals that he argues America should set?

2   In paragraph 5 Vance says, "Yesterday's answers will not provide tomorrow's solutions." In what ways, according to Vance, has the world changed so that what was successful in the past is now outdated? What feelings and opinions must America abandon to relate its basic purposes to the world's new conditions?

3   Vance argues that America's present dissatisfaction with its role in the world is caused by certain "fallacies," certain logically unsound arguments or ideas. What is the first fallacy he thinks must be rejected "before our nation can chart a coherent and determined course in foreign policy"?

4   What are the effects of the second fallacy Vance wishes to dispel? How closely is this fallacy related to the fourth?

5   Do you agree with Vance when he argues that the third fallacy we must reject is the idea that there is "an incompatibility between the pursuit of America's values in our foreign policy, such as human rights, and the pursuit of our interests"?

6   What is the fifth fallacy Vance discusses? How realistic do you find his view of the Soviet Union?

7   What is the "new nostalgia" that underlies all these fallacies? What effect does this nostalgia have on America's view of itself and the world? How convincingly has Vance argued for an alternative point of view?

Questions on Method

1   Where does Vance acknowledge and attempt to refute the opposition?

2   Where does Vance support his argument with evidence, reasons, or statistics?

3   Vance relies on many devices of logic to create a convincing argument. Where and how effectively does he use deductive logic?

4   What tone of voice characterizes the essay as a whole? To what extent does it help make Vance's argument more convincing?

5 In paragraph 3 Vance says that the world today is one where the superpowers "hold in their hands our common survival, yet paradoxically find
it beyond their power to order events." How thoroughly does this sense
of the paradox of the modern world pervade Vance's argument?

Vocabulary and Diction

1 Vance delivered this speech just after he resigned as secretary of state
over his disagreement with former President Carter's decision to attempt
a rescue of the hostages in Iran. Given this fact, how complex are the
connotations held by the word "hostage" in paragraph 1? Can you locate
other subtle references to the hostage crisis in the speech?

2 What is a "pragmatic philosophy," such as that which Vance in paragraph 4 says always has characterized America? How pragmatic do you
find the philosophy behind Vance's view of foreign policy?

3 Define the following words and phrases used by Vance: third world
nations (2), naive (2), a perverted hubris (5), a bipolar world (7),
pluralistic (7), strategic interests (13), retrospect (14), go-it-alone illusions (14), diverting (14), self-indulgent (14).

Writing Topics

1 Write an essay in which you argue that one of Vance's points is fallacious.
How convincingly can you use examples to invalidate his point? To what
extent does invalidating one point in his argument necessarily invalidate
his overall thesis?

2 Vance argues that Americans have lost confidence in their national
leaders because expectations about America's power to control and order
the world are unrealistic. Do you agree with Vance? Are there other
causes that might lie behind the lack of confidence we feel in our leaders?
Write an essay in which you argue whether or not Americans have lost
confidence in their leaders and why.

3 Vance says that Americans are a people "who not only have adapted
well to change but have thrived on it." Write an essay that analyzes
specific examples of changes Americans have thrived on.

4 In paragraph 10 Vance argues that "the drive for human freedom" is
"universal," "resilient," and ultimately "irrepressible." Write an essay in
which you argue your reasons for agreeing or disagreeing.

LOUISE MONTAGUE (1931–   ) has written on a variety of
subjects that ranges from entertaining to divorce. She also
published a novel, *The Sand Castles*, in 1975. Her thoughts
about couples living together as opposed to being married are
certain to provoke your response.

Straight Talk about the
Living-Together Arrangement

Louise Montague

As the author of two books on divorce, I try to accept as many   1
speaking engagements in high-school and college classes as I can. For
it is my feeling that one answer to the soaring divorce rate is "pre-
ventive thinking"—the time to face many of the problems of divorce
is *before* marriage. Lately, however, I find that at every session someone will stand up and state that marriage is outmoded and that the
answer to the divorce problem is to live with a partner without the
legal commitment of marriage.

Unhappily, "living together" is a modern phenomenon, a na-   2
tional trend today. Between 1960 and 1970, according to the U.S.
Department of the Census, there was an eightfold increase in the
Living-Together Arrangement (LTA). Why are so many people opt-
ing for this arrangement? And how do they get into it?

Certainly it's a very attractive idea sexually. But many young   3
people also say it's a good way to "test" marriage. Others claim it's
a terrific financial boon. And some don't even know how they ended

up together. He started staying over or she began to leave clothes in his closet. These young people feel that by not making their relationship permanent they can maintain the spontaneous atmosphere of new love. By eliminating the legal commitment, they feel they have eliminated the "bad" part of marriage.

But the phenomenon is not limited to young people. Many 4 divorced persons burned in marriage are trying it. Some have religious convictions forbidding a second marriage. Divorced men who are financially strapped feel they can't take on the responsibility of a new wife. Or the divorced woman may be reluctant to give up the alimony which would stop with her remarriage.

With all these "pluses" why do so many people engaged in an 5 LTA write to me about the problems they have encountered? Why *is* the Living-Together Arrangement a detriment to those involved? Let's first consider the college students who decide on or slide into an LTA. You'd be surprised, once the subject comes up for discussion in a classroom, how many youngsters tell unhappy stories about themselves or their best friends.

Take the case of the young couple at Stanford. After they moved 6 in together, the boy lost his scholarship and was not able to meet the high tuition costs from his part-time job. The girl quit school in order to work and let him finish his education. When he graduated, he applied for—and received—a scholarship to do graduate work in England. The girl was extremely hurt and angry; she felt he owed it to her to stay and help her finish *her* education. They argued bitterly for a day, and then the young man packed and left!

This situation is typical of dozens I have heard. The LTA simply 7 can't work when it breeds the mutual dependency of marriage without the mutual responsibility.

Another example is a young couple at Georgetown University 8 who moved into an apartment together. The girl's parents, shocked and hurt, cut off all their daughter's funds. The boy suggested they split up and go back to their dorms, but the girl, having had a terrible row with her family, insisted that it was now his responsibility to take care of her! Both got jobs, and the young man, not a strong student, fell behind and was unable to graduate.

Certainly it's difficult to think in realistic terms when a couple 9 imagine themselves in love. But it is unfair to expect parental values to be dropped at a whim. The censure of family and friends is one of the greatest burdens the LTA carries. Young people who need the support of family are very foolish to chuck their long-term goals for short-term pleasures.

To be sure, intimate relationships are widely accepted today, but any resourceful couple can find ways of being together without moving in together. Moreover, living alone at times and developing individuality should be a prime concern of young people. For few can handle the LTA until they have learned to live with themselves. 10

Some of the most heartbreaking stories I hear about LTA's concern children. Whatever life-style a single male or female chooses is that individual's responsibility. But to bring a child into this atmosphere is to involve an innocent third party in an experiment that can leave all parties damaged. Although the law generally requires a father to support his children, it is often difficult to enforce these laws. Women are frequently left with the burden of support while the air of illegitimacy hangs heavy on the child. 11

A divorced or widowed woman who involves her children in an LTA may also be subjecting them to undue stress. Children experience great pressures to conform. What the mother and her companion view as a marvelous, free life-style, a child could see as a freaky embarrassment. The man in question, not being either father or stepfather, has no social definition as to the role he should play in the child's life. In some states, a divorced mother in an LTA stands a good chance of losing not only support payments but custody of her children. 12

Even a highly motivated working couple should be aware of the consequences of their actions. How you present yourself to the world is how you will be judged. A young petroleum engineer, living with a dental hygienist, applied for a much-wanted overseas job with an oil company. When the company conducted its routine investigation, and found that the young woman with whom he was living was not his wife, he was turned down; the firm felt that his LTA smacked of indecisiveness, instability, and failure on his part to accept responsibility. Who is to say if the oil company made the right decision? But, judging from a great many instances, it happens to be the way things are. What a couple may view as a sophisticated way to live, the business community may see as a career impediment. 13

Heartbreak and setback are also in the cards for a woman who moves in with a man in the hope of getting married. My advice is to avoid this strategy. When you demand nothing of a relationship, that's often exactly what you get. The very impermanence of the 14

LTA suggests that that is what each partner has settled for. If marriage is what you want, marriage is what you should have. So why commit yourself to a shaky arrangement that keeps you out of the mainstream of life where you quite possibly will meet someone who shares your views?

Many divorced women with a great need for a little security, and 15 with little faith in themselves, seek an LTA as a temporary answer to help them get on their feet. All this does is prolong their adjust-ment and reinforce their self-doubts. I'm reminded of one such woman who told me she had been living with a man for four years and wanted out but was afraid to leave. "Why?" I asked. Because, she said, she feared to give up the free rent and all that "security" she had with him. "Wrong," I said. "You have no security of any kind. You stand a good chance of being replaced by a younger version of yourself. And as for free rent, that's no security either. Security is owning the building."

Probably the greatest single hazard of the LTA is that it can 16 actually spoil a good relationship between two people who should eventually marry. Because it is entered into out of weakness rather than strength, doubt rather than conviction, drift rather than deci-sion, it offers unnecessary obstacles. Knowing this, you shouldn't casually toss aside those inherited institutions that have had a history of success.

If I were asked to give one reason only why I am opposed to the 17 LTA, I would state quite simply that I am morally against it. As Barbara Tuchman wrote in *McCall's*: "Standards of taste, as well as morality, need continued reaffirmation to stay alive, as liberty needs eternal vigilance." There are valid standards of judgment which come from confidence in yourself and your values. To accept a living pattern that goes against your better judgment is to chip away at your personal freedom.

And what of love? You cannot hope to find love by experi- 18 menting biologically. You don't build love by creating a living situ-ation designed to test it. You don't create love by setting up a forced proximity. Love *is*. And when you love you commit to it—for better or for worse. When we finally realize that all our experiments in alternate life-styles, communal marriage and open-ended covenants are simply a means of running *from* responsibility and love, *not to* them, we will have reached the beginning of maturity.

Questions on Meaning

1 What are some of the advantages an LTA has for young people? What are some of the advantages such an arrangement has for divorced men and women?

2 Why, in Montague's opinion, did the LTA of the young couple at Stanford fail? Do you think they might have behaved differently had they been married? What reasons does Montague give to support her argument that the young couple at Georgetown University would have been better off had they lived separately in their dormitories?

3 In what ways, according to Montague, can an LTA be unfair to children?

4 Do you think Montague is right in arguing that an LTA might prove a "career impediment"? Do you think she is right in arguing that an LTA is unlikely to benefit either an unmarried woman who hopes it will lead to marriage or a divorced woman who hopes it will provide "a temporary answer" for her insecurity and self-doubt?

5 What does Montague think is the greatest single hazard of the LTA? What is her final reason for opposing the LTA?

Questions on Method

1 Why does Montague begin the essay by telling us she is the author of two books on divorce and a frequent lecturer on the subject? Why does she list some of the advantages of the LTA before she details her objections?

2 What tone does Montague adopt to criticize the LTA? How reasonable does she sound? To what extent does she make effective use of induction, deduction, or cause-and-effect analysis to convince us that her argument is sensible? How sensible is her appeal to ethics in paragraph 17?

3 In paragraph 16 Montague says that the LTA is entered into out of "weakness rather than strength, doubt rather than conviction, drift rather than decision," and she goes on to suggest that therefore marriage is preferable. How valid is her implied contrast in this case between the LTA and marriage? How important is the validity of this contrast to the validity of Montague's overall argument?

Vocabulary and Diction

1 In paragraph 9 Montague says that although it is difficult for a young couple to be realistic when they "imagine" themselves to be in love,

nevertheless it is unfair for such a couple to abandon parents' values in order to live together "at a whim." In what sense is Montague's use of the words "imagine" and "whim" condescending?

2 How adequate do you find the definition of "love" that Montague offers in paragraph 18? How broad or narrow is her understanding of the word's meaning?

Writing Topics

1 In paragraph 10 Montague argues that a prime concern of young people should be "living alone at times and developing individuality." Write an essay that argues whether living alone necessarily leads a person to develop individuality.

2 Montague argues that an LTA is detrimental because people tend to enter into such an arrangement for the wrong reasons. Might you argue that many marriages are detrimental for the same reasons? Write an essay in which you argue when and why people are foolish to marry.

3 Write an essay offering your own views about the LTA. How much do your views coincide or conflict with the views of American society today?

4 Would you ever want to become involved in an LTA? If you were a parent of a college student, how would you feel about your son or daughter becoming involved in such an arrangement? Write an essay in which you compare your feelings about yourself, in this respect, with what your feelings would be about your own son or daughter.

RAMON OLDENBURG and DENNIS BRISSETT hold doctorates in
sociology. Oldenburg teaches at the University of West Florida,
and Brissett at the School of Medicine at the University of
Minnesota. Both are currently writing a book on "third places."
This essay is an example of the importance they attach to
having a place of one's own for relaxation.

The Essential Hangout

Ramon Oldenburg and Dennis Brissett

In 18th-century London, prosperous citizens spent many of their free   1
hours in coffeehouses, chatting, exchanging gossip, sipping coffee or
chocolate—in short, just hanging out. Joseph Addison, founder and
editor of *The Spectator*, mused in print about the attractions of these
social centers.

"When Men are thus knit together, by a Love of Society, not   2
a Spirit of Faction, and don't meet to censure or annoy those that
are absent, but to enjoy one another: When they are thus combined
for their own Improvement, or for the Good of others, or at least to
relax themselves from the Business of the Day, by an innocent and
Chearful Conversation, there may be something very useful in these
little Institutions and Establishments."

Once upon a time, American society seems to have had many   3
equivalents of the coffeehouse, places where ordinary people—men,
at least—could find the conviviality Addison described, the "innocent
and cheerful conversation," the "very useful" something that offered
respite from work. There were, for instance, the long benches that

small midwestern business places used to provide on either side of their entrances for the "sunshine club." There was the local tavern, as well as the small-town express office and the corner drugstore.

Today, the neighborhood tavern survives, but most other places 4 of its type are gone. No doubt our memories of them are somewhat clouded by nostalgia for an America that no longer exists—or that perhaps existed mainly in our imaginations. No matter. The hangout is important for what it symbolizes to us; that is, a kind of pure, freewheeling sociability, uncontaminated by status, special purposes, or goals. If there is a malaise in America, we believe it can be partially attributed to the lack of such places. We believe, too, that it could be otherwise, that the loss is not irretrievable.

In recent decades, the range of arenas for social participation has 5 narrowed to the office and the home, joined by the ordeal of commuting.

The quality of many people's lives has come to depend almost 6 exclusively on the quality of their family life and of their jobs. Not surprisingly, they expect too much from both and are, inevitably, disappointed. That is when they dream that all-American dream of "getting away from it all," or turn to psychotherapy or to commercially packaged diversions that often prove to be more enervating than invigorating.

In our view, much of what people seek from such sources is 7 closer at hand and attainable in forms more genuine and less costly in a "third place"; that is, in some informal spot that is remote from the cares of office and home. At its best, a third place provides democratic friendship; a sense of belonging while yet retaining a distinctive personal identity, an opportunity for spontaneity, surprise, and emotional expression; a chance to stand aside from oneself and gain perspective on private idiosyncrasies. Generally, a third place is open to the public and easily accessible to those who have claimed it as their own. It may have some social cachet, but it is not necessarily a place outsiders find interesting or noteworthy. Its regulars take it for granted.

Frequenting a third place guarantees nothing. A hangout is 8 simply there, providing opportunities for relationships that are rarely available in the larger society. People go there not simply to escape from work and relatives, but primarily to enjoy one another's company. The principal activity is conversation; there are no organized goings-on. In family life, work, commerce, and organized groups—in fact, almost everywhere except in a third place—people find themselves in purposive association. Not so in third places. There, to use the words of the sociologist Georg Simmel, the essence of association is "joy, vivacity, and relief."

As in any human relationship, pure sociability has its own versions of good or proper form. No one is to remain silent—or to dominate the talk; people have come to participate, not to listen to monologues. Speakers turn away from the first person singular that is the hallmark of our self-centered age. Discussion of personal problems is anathema. Instead, conversation stems from and is steeped in local heroes and local tragedies, in gossip and romance. This kind of talk ties people to places and yet removes them from the little schemes and strategies of self-interest.   9

Sociability is not premised on the social qualifications of the people involved. Simmel called it life's most purely democratic experience. Participants surrender their worldly status in return for unqualified acceptance into human fellowship. Third places often provide the only common meeting ground for people of diverse background and experience. Depending on when people stop in at a third place (and they are always both unbidden and most welcome), they may chance to meet the friend of a friend, someone's visiting relative, someone new to the neighborhood—or perhaps just some of the regulars. In a third place, one meets and enjoys a human being who, incidentally and secondarily, repairs appliances or teaches school. In this respect, third places are a stronghold of an important vestige of community: concern and appreciation for people different from oneself.   10

In third places, chatter and banter link those different people by spiritual rather than contractual bonds, giving to individuals a sense of wholeness, belonging, and continuity. To take part in this conversation is to stave off a symbolic poverty, a malnutrition of the soul that psychiatrists might call an impaired sense of identity.   11

Along with this combined sense of individual distinctiveness and of comradeship, third places offer an alternative to structure and schedule; they are a reminder that the most enjoyable and memorable moments of our lives are not really planned. An aura of the unexpected surrounds each visit to a third place. One can never be certain who will be there, never predict what the chemistry of a particular mix of people will create. One can, however, count on a lively atmosphere. The hours slip by unnoticed.   12

Rarely a forum for true drama or high excitement, the third   13
place nevertheless encourages and thrives on emotional expression—
often loud and boisterous expression. Third places give people somewhere to bellow like fundamentalist preachers now and then; yet the
average third-place denizen, given the opportunity to let off steam,
is rarely vulgar, obnoxious, or spiteful in the presence of companions.

By providing an emotional outlet, and, even more important,   14
by supplying a sounding board other than spouses or work mates,
third places make a significant, though underrated, contribution to
mental stability. Americans overemphasize the benefits of diet and
exercise, but they tend to think that mental balance, or perspective,
maintains itself. When a man chats with friends in a third place, he
is subjecting his mental processes to the judgment of others, thereby
keeping in touch with the world around him and with other people's
conception of reality. Yet the pure sociability of the third place is the
antithesis of a group-therapy session; if souls are saved therein, as well
they may be, it is only incidentally.

Whether it saves souls or not, the kind of third place we have   15
been describing is badly needed in American society. Both the home
and the work organization inhibit the emotional expressiveness of
their members, who come to feel that they have too much at stake
to sound off in rage, grief, or even great elation. Protest, for instance,
is generally confined to cryptic sarcasms at the water cooler or snipes
at one's spouse across the dinner table.

As social controls have relaxed and personal freedoms increased,   16
the sense of doing something unique and novel—of being oneself—
has declined. Rather than exercising their new freedom to broaden
their social spheres, too many people have turned almost exclusively
to their families. In the suburbs, especially, they have built secure,
orderly familial lives that, ironically, are very similar to their places
of work. Each runs on a tight schedule and offers a small, highly
predictable world with a constant, homogeneous population. As Richard Sennett, the sociologist, says of the suburbs, "People suffocate
there for lack of the new, the unexpected, the diverse in their lives."

The problem is greatest for the middle class. Traditionally,   17
ghetto dwellers have enjoyed storefront gathering places, while the
upper class has had clubs. In New York City, for instance, the
Metropolitan Club and the Union League Club discourage members

from carrying briefcases into the main dining room and from perusing business documents during meals.

In the cities there are, of course, plenty of places where middle- 18 class people meet, but few qualify as third places. Opening the door to a business club, gym, or singles bar, one finds intense concentration on the business at hand: closing a deal, becoming fit, finding a new sexual partner. On commuter trains, people talk, if at all, about their jobs or their families. In discotheques, the din precludes real conversation.

That leaves the tavern, or the bar, as the dominant third place 19 in our society. Set it on the golf links and call it a clubhouse, put it at the water's edge and call it a yacht club, or organize a fraternal order around it and call it a lodge—the bar is the core of the institution. But a third place does not need liquor. It can be established wherever people can gather and linger without being hassled. Today's urban teenagers may have designated points of assemblage at a lunch counter, on the steps of the local library, or at a bowling alley. In small towns of the Deep South, older men play cards and checkers under the shade trees in the town square, while younger men congregate at fishing camps and bait shops. In the north country— wherever frozen lakes make ice fishing possible—humble one-man fishing shacks have given way to larger models complete with carpeting, refrigerators, and poker tables; there, men spend less time fishing, perhaps, than enjoying third-place pleasures.

There ought to be many more such hangouts, in big cities as 20 well as in small-town America, and there could be, if only people were not reluctant to invest time, energy, and emotions in activities that enhance neither home life nor work opportunities.

In our eyes, participation in third places does not weaken, but 21 supports and complements, involvement in home and work. And it provides something extra: a forum for play in a society impoverished by a stubborn overcommitment to work and purpose. What the Dutch historian and social philosopher Johan Huizinga said of play as a human activity is also true of the third place: "Into the confusion of life it brings a temporary, a limited, perfection."

The proprietor of a bar in New York City's Grand Central 22 Station, through which thousands of commuters pass twice a day, may have the right idea. The bar has a glass facade, so that the convivial group inside is clearly visible, and a sign on the door that reads, "Miss your train."

Questions on Meaning

1   What makes a "hangout," a third place, different from either the home or the job? Why do people go to a hangout?

2   What do the authors mean by saying that, unlike most other places, a third place involves no "purposive association"? What sort of association does a third place foster? What beneficial effects does this sort of association have on people who go to a third place?

3   Why do the authors think the lack of structure and schedule in a third place is valuable?

4   Why do the authors argue that third places are badly needed in American society today? What class of people is most in need of such hangouts? Why do business clubs, gyms, and singles bars fail to qualify as third place hangouts?

Questions on Method

1   How technical and abstract do you find the language used by Oldenburg and Brissett to describe the characteristics that define a third place? Does their language strengthen or weaken their argumentative appeal?

2   The authors conclude in paragraph 21 that "participation in third places does not weaken, but supports and complements, involvement in home and work." Why do they choose to emphasize the positive aspects of third places? What groups or individuals might oppose them? Should the authors have acknowledged possible practical or theoretical drawbacks to third places? Why?

3   How logically do the authors argue their case? Where is their reasoning weakest? Where is it strongest?

Vocabulary and Diction

1   Why might many people think it is a contradiction in terms to refer to a "hangout" as "essential"? Do the authors succeed in convincing you that hangouts are essential in some way?

2   In paragraph 11 the authors argue that the "chatter and banter" of barroom conversation links people by "spiritual rather than contractual bonds." What is the difference between a spiritual and a contractual bond?

3   Define the following words and phrases used by Oldenburg and Brissett: mused (1), conviviality (3), malaise (4), enervating (6), idiosyncrasies

(7), cachet (7), anathema (9), premised (10), fundamentalist preachers (13), denizen (13), cryptic sarcasms (15), snipes (15), homogeneous (16), din (18), precludes (18), facade (22).

Writing Topics

1   Write an essay in which you compare the abstract description of a hangout offered by Oldenburg and Brissett to an actual hangout with which you are familiar. How well does the argument of Oldenburg and Brissett hold up in light of your comparison?

2   Oldenburg and Brissett argue that one reason hangouts are needed in America is that "the home and work organization inhibit the emotional expressiveness of their members." Write an essay in which you explain why you agree or disagree.

3   The authors also argue that hangouts are needed because they provide "a forum for play in a society impoverished by a stubborn overcommitment to work." Does American society suffer from such an overcommitment? Write an essay that argues whether Americans need more opportunities and places to play.

4   Write an essay comparing Oldenburg and Brissett's view of the rewards of sociability to Fleming's view of the rewards of being alone in "The Fear of Being Alone."

SHIRLEY CHISHOLM (1924–   ), a graduate of Brooklyn
College, was a teacher and then an educational consultant. In
1969, a few months after becoming the first black woman
elected to Congress, she stated, "I am an historical person and
I'm very much aware of it." In 1964 she was elected to the
New York State Assembly. A frequent lecturer and essayist,
Chisholm often chooses to focus on minority issues in their
broadest sense, as in the following essay.

I'd Rather Be Black than Female

Shirley Chisholm

Being the first black woman elected to Congress has made me some   1
kind of phenomenon. There are nine other blacks in Congress; there
are ten other women. I was the first to overcome both handicaps at
once. Of the two handicaps, being black is much less of a drawback
than being female.

If I said that being black is a greater handicap than being a   2
woman, probably no one would question me. Why? Because "we all
know" there is prejudice against black people in America. That there
is prejudice against women is an idea that still strikes nearly all men—
and, I am afraid, most women—as bizarre.

Prejudice against blacks was invisible to most white Americans   3
for many years. When blacks finally started to "mention" it, with sit-
ins, boycotts, and freedom rides, Americans were incredulous. "Who,
us?" they asked in injured tones. "We're prejudiced?" It was the start
of a long, painful reeducation for white America. It will take years

for whites—including those who think of themselves as liberals—to discover and eliminate the racist attitudes they all actually have.

How much harder will it be to eliminate the prejudice against women? I am sure it will be a longer struggle. Part of the problem is that women in America are much more brainwashed and content with their roles as second-class citizens than blacks ever were.   4

Let me explain. I have been active in politics for more than twenty years. For all but the last six, I have done the work—all the tedious details that make the difference between victory and defeat on election day—while men reaped the rewards, which is almost invariably the lot of women in politics. → 運氣 命運   5

It is still women—about three million volunteers—who do most of this work in the American political world. The best any of them can hope for is the honor of being district or county vice-chairman, a kind of separate-but-equal position with which a woman is rewarded for years of faithful envelope stuffing and card-party organizing. In such a job, she gets a number of free trips to state and sometimes national meetings and conventions, where her role is supposed to be to vote the way her male chairman votes.   6

When I tried to break out of that role in 1963 and run for the New York State Assembly seat from Brooklyn's Bedford-Stuyvesant, the resistance was bitter. From the start of that campaign, I faced undisguised hostility because of my sex.   7

But it was four years later, when I ran for Congress, that the question of my sex became a major issue. Among members of my own party, closed meetings were held to discuss ways of stopping me.   8

My opponent, the famous civil-rights leader James Farmer, tried to project a black, masculine image; he toured the neighborhood with sound trucks filled with young men wearing Afro haircuts, dashikis, and beards. While the television crews ignored me, they were not aware of a very important statistic, which both I and my campaign manager, Wesley MacD. Holder, knew. In my district there are 2.5 women for every man registered to vote. And those women are organized—in PTAs, church societies, card clubs, and other social and service groups. I went to them and asked their help. Mr. Farmer still doesn't quite know what hit him.   9

When a bright young woman graduate starts looking for a job, why is the first question always: "'Can you type?'" A history of prejudice lies behind that question. Why are women thought of as   10 secretaries, not administrators? Librarians and teachers, but not doctors and lawyers? Because they are thought of as different and inferior. The happy homemaker and the contented darky are both stereotypes produced by prejudice.

Women have not even reached the level of tokenism that blacks are reaching. No women sit on the Supreme Court. Only two have held Cabinet rank, and none do at present. Only two women hold ambassadorial rank. But women predominate in the lower-paying, menial, unrewarding, dead-end jobs, and when they do reach better positions, they are invariably paid less than a man gets for the same job. 11

If that is not prejudice, what would you call it? 12

A few years ago, I was talking with a political leader about a promising young woman as a candidate. "Why invest time and effort to build the girl up?" he asked me. "You know she'll only drop out of the game to have a couple of kids just about the time we're ready to run her for mayor." 13

Plenty of people have said similar things about me. Plenty of others have advised me, every time I tried to take another upward step, that I should go back to teaching, a woman's vocation, and leave politics to the men. I love teaching, and I am ready to go back to it as soon as I am convinced that this country no longer needs a woman's contribution. 14

When there are no children going to bed hungry in this rich nation, I may be ready to go back to teaching. When there is a good school for every child, I may be ready. When we do not spend our wealth on hardware to murder people, when we no longer tolerate prejudice against minorities, and when the laws against unfair housing and unfair employment practices are enforced instead of evaded, then there may be nothing more for me to do in politics. 15

But until that happens—and we all know it will not be this year or next—what we need is more women in politics, because we have a very special contribution to make. I hope that the example of my success will convince other women to get into politics—and not just to stuff envelopes, but to run for office. 16

It is women who can bring empathy, tolerance, insight, patience, and persistence to government—the qualities we naturally have or have had to develop because of our suppression by men. The women of a nation mold its morals, its religion, and its politics by the lives 17

they live. At present, our country needs women's idealism and determination, perhaps more in politics than anywhere else.

Questions on Meaning

1 According to Chisholm, why has it been so difficult to begin eliminating
   prejudice against blacks? Why will it be more difficult to eliminate
   prejudice against women?
2 In paragraph 7 Chisholm refers to the role she played during her first
   fourteen years in politics. What was that role? When she tried to break
   out of it, why was the resistance bitter? How did she succeed four years
   later despite continued resistance?
3 What general reasons does Chisholm suggest account for the prejudice
   that she and other women experience? What evidence, other than that
   of her personal experience, does she offer of the reality of this prejudice?
4 When will Chisholm be ready to abandon politics and return to teaching?
   What contribution does she think women can make in politics? Do you
   agree with her?

Questions on Method

1 How reasonable is Chisholm's argument that "being black is much less
   of a drawback than being female"? What hard evidence does she offer
   to support her argument?
2 Discuss Chisholm's conclusion that women have "a very special contribution" to make because they possess "empathy, tolerance, insight,
   patience, and persistence."
3 How much anger does Chisholm's tone reveal? In which parts of the
   essay do you feel her anger most strongly? Does she rely less on logic
   than on emotion, on stirring up the reader's anger over injustice and
   poor government, to persuade the reader? Why?

Vocabulary and Diction

1 Why in paragraph 3 does Chisholm place the word "mention" in quotation marks?

2   In paragraph 10 Chisholm writes, "The happy homemaker and the contented darky are both stereotypes produced by prejudice." What is a stereotype?

3   What is tokenism? If tokenism is evidence of prejudice, might it also, at times, be evidence that prejudice is being overcome?

Writing Topics

1   Are women, as Chisholm asserts, "second-class citizens" in America? Write an essay in which you argue either with or against Chisholm.

2   Given what Chisholm in paragraph 15 says is wrong with America, would you call her political philosophy liberal or conservative? How much is her view of women a product of her political philosophy? How much might her view of women be shared by those who otherwise disagree with her politically? Consider these questions in an essay that argues just how broad the political appeal of women activists like Chisholm will be in the future.

3   Write an essay in which you argue whether America would have fewer or different problems if there were more women holding high government offices.

Argumentation—Writing Topics

1 How different are the techniques used to write an argument that appeals to reason from the techniques used to write an argument that appeals to emotion or ethics? Write an argumentative essay that appeals strictly to logic and reason. Using a different color ink, make additions to the essay that broaden its argumentative appeal emotionally or ethically.

2 Does an argument have to be true to be convincing? Does a lawyer, for example, necessarily have to be defending an innocent client to argue successfully that his or her client is innocent? Write an essay in which you argue when, if ever, the method may be more important in making an argument convincing—whether or not the argument is true.

3 Cousins warns that a mood of hopelessness and cynicism may be threatening to overtake America. Write an essay in which you analyze how one of the other authors in this chapter offers evidence that Cousins's view is either right or wrong.

4 Beginning with the proposition that all men are created equal, write a deductive argument either in favor of or in opposition to an amendment to the Constitution that would guarantee equal rights to women.

5 Find an editorial in your daily newspaper that you disagree with, then write a letter to the editor that argues your side of the issue.

6 Chisholm argues that she would rather be black than female. Write an essay in which you argue either that you would rather be male than female or that you would rather be female than male.

7 Write an essay that employs as many techniques of argumentation as are necessary to convince a reader that English composition should or should not be a required course for college students.

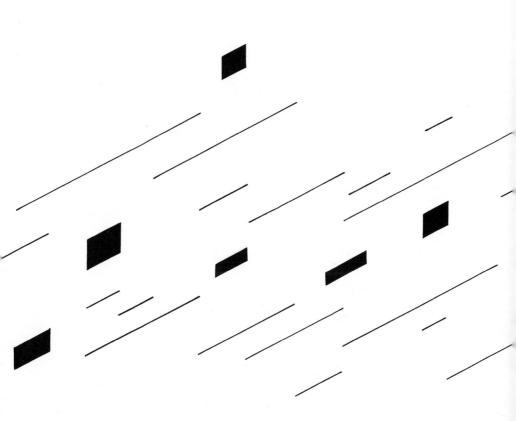

ELEVEN

Further Reading

請簡述大意

A Modest Proposal

Jonathan Swift

It is a melancholy object to those who walk through this great town, 1
or travel in the country, when they see the streets, the roads, and
cabin-doors crowded with beggars of the female sex, followed by
three, four, or six children, *all in rags*, and importuning every passen-
ger for an alms. These mothers, instead of being able to work for
their honest livelihood, are forced to employ all their time in strolling,
to beg sustenance for their helpless infants, who, as they grow up,
either turn thieves for want of work, or leave their dear Native
Country to fight for the Pretender in Spain, or sell themselves to the
Barbadoes.

In think it is agreed by all parties that this prodigious number of 2
children, in the arms, or on the backs, or at the heels of their
mothers, and frequently of their fathers, is in the present deplorable
state of the kingdom a very great additional grievance; and therefore
whoever could find out a fair, cheap, and easy method of making
these children sound useful members of the commonwealth would
deserve so well of the public as to have his statue set up for a preserver
of the nation.

is (...) a very great
additional grievance

But my intention is very far from being confined to provide only 3 for the children of professed beggars; it is of a much greater extent, and shall take in the whole number of infants at a certain age who are born of parents in effect as little able to support them as those who demand our charity in the streets.

As to my own part, having turned my thoughts, for many years, 4 upon this important subject, and maturely weighed the several schemes of other projectors, I have always found them grossly mistaken in their computation. It is true a child, just dropped from its dam, may be supported by her milk for a solar year with little other nourishment, at most not above the value of two shillings, which the mother may certainly get, or the value in scraps, by her lawful occupation of begging, and it is exactly at one year old that I propose to provide for them, in such a manner as, instead of being a charge upon their parents, or the parish, or wanting food and raiment for the rest of their lives, they shall, on the contrary, contribute to the feeding and partly to the clothing of many thousands.

There is likewise another great advantage in my scheme, that it 5 will prevent those voluntary abortions, and that horrid practice of women murdering their bastard children, alas, too frequent among us, sacrificing the poor innocent babes, I doubt, more to avoid the expense than the shame, which would move tears and pity in the most savage and inhuman breast.

The number of souls in this kingdom being usually reckoned one 6 million and a half, of these I calculate there may be about two hundred thousand couple whose wives are breeders, from which number I subtract thirty thousand couples who are able to maintain their own children, although I apprehend there cannot be so many under the present distresses of the kingdom, but this being granted, there will remain an hundred and seventy thousand breeders. I again subtract fifty thousand for those women who miscarry, or whose children die by accident or disease within the year. There only remain an hundred and twenty thousand children of poor parents annually born. The question therefore is, how this number shall be reared, and provided for, which, as I have already said, under the present situation of affairs, is utterly impossible by all the methods hitherto proposed, for we can neither employ them in handicraft, or agriculture; we neither build houses (I mean in the country), nor cultivate land: they can very seldom pick up a livelihood by stealing till they arrive at six

371

years old, except where they are of towardly parts, although I confess they learn the rudiments much earlier, during which time they can however be properly looked upon only as *probationers,* as I have been informed by a principal gentleman in the County of Cavan, who protested to me that he never knew above one or two instances under the age of six, even in a part of the kingdom so renowned for the quickest proficiency in that art.

I am assured by our merchants that a boy or a girl, before twelve 7 years old, is no saleable commodity, and even when they come to this age, they will not yield above three pounds, or three pounds and half-a-crown at most on the Exchange, which cannot turn to account either to the parents or the kingdom, the charge of nutriment and rags having been at least four times that value.

I shall now therefore humbly propose my own thoughts, which 8 I hope will not be liable to the least objection.

I have been assured by a very knowing American of my ac- 9 quaintance in London, that a young healthy child well nursed is at a year old a most delicious, nourishing, and wholesome food, whether stewed, roasted, baked, or boiled, and I make no doubt that it will equally serve in a fricassee, or a ragout.

I do therefore humbly offer it to public consideration, that of 10 the hundred and twenty thousand children already computed, twenty thousand may be reserved for breed, whereof only one fourth part to be males, which is more than we allow to sheep, black-cattle, or swine, and my reason is that these children are seldom the fruits of marriage, a circumstance not much regarded by our savages, therefore one male will be sufficient to serve four females. That the remaining hundred thousand may at a year old be offered in sale to the persons of quality, and fortune, through the kingdom, always advising the mother to let them suck plentifully in the last month, so as to render them plump, and fat for a good table. A child will make two dishes at an entertainment for friends, and when the family dines alone, the fore or hind quarters will make a reasonable dish, and seasoned with a little pepper or salt will be very good boiled on the fourth day, especially in winter.

I have reckoned upon a medium, that a child just born will 11 weigh 12 pounds, and in a solar year if tolerably nursed increaseth to 28 pounds.

I grant this food will be somewhat dear, and therefore very 12 proper for landlords, who, as they have already devoured most of the parents, seem to have the best title to the children.

Infant's flesh will be in season throughout the year, but more 13 plentiful in March, and a little before and after, for we are told by a grave author, an eminent French physician, that fish being a prolific diet, there are more children born in Roman Catholic countries about nine months after Lent than at any other season; therefore reckoning a year after Lent, the markets will be more glutted than usual, because the number of Popish infants is at least three to one in this kingdom, and therefore it will have one other collateral advantage by lessening the number of Papists among us.

I have already computed the charge of nursing a beggar's child 14 (in which list I reckon all cottagers, labourers, and four-fifths of the farmers) to be about two shillings *per annum*, rags included, and I believe no gentleman would repine to give ten shillings for the carcass of a good fat child, which, as I have said, will make four dishes of excellent nutritive meat, when he hath only some particular friend or his own family to dine with him. Thus the Squire will learn to be a good landlord, and grow popular among his tenants, the mother will have eight shillings net profit, and be fit for work till she produces another child.

Those who are more thrifty (as I must confess the times require) 15 may flay the carcass; the skin of which, artificially dressed, will make admirable gloves for ladies, and summer boots for fine gentlemen.

As to our City of Dublin, shambles may be appointed for this 16 purpose, in the most convenient parts of it, and butchers we may be assured will not be wanting, although I rather recommend buying the children alive, and dressing them hot from the knife, as we do roasting pigs.

A very worthy person, a true lover of this country, and whose 17 virtues I highly esteem, was lately pleased, in discoursing on this matter, to offer a refinement upon my scheme. He said that many gentlemen of this kingdom, having of late destroyed their deer, he conceived that the want of venison might be well supplied by the bodies of young lads and maidens, not exceeding fourteen years of age, nor under twelve, so great a number of both sexes in every country being now ready to starve, for want of work and service: and these to be disposed of by their parents if alive, or otherwise by their nearest relations. But with due deference to so excellent a friend, and so deserving a patriot, I cannot be altogether in his sentiments; for as to the males, my American acquaintance assured me from frequent experience that their flesh was generally tough and lean, like that of our schoolboys, by continual exercise, and their taste disagreeable, and to fatten them would not answer the charge. Then as to the females, it would, I think with humble submission, be a loss to the public, because they soon would become breeders themselves: And besides, it is not improbable that some scrupulous people might be apt to censure such a practice (although indeed very unjustly) as a little bordering upon cruelty, which, I confess, hath always been with me the strongest objection against any project, however so well intended.

But in order to justify my friend, he confessed that this expedient 18 was put into his head by the famous Psalmanazer, a native of the island Formosa, who came from thence to London, above twenty years ago, and in conversation told my friend that in his country when any young person happened to be put to death, the executioner sold the carcass to persons of quality, as a prime dainty, and that, in his time, the body of a plump girl of fifteen, who was crucified for an attempt to poison the emperor, was sold to his Imperial Majesty's Prime Minister of State, and other great Mandarins of the Court, in joints from the gibbet, at four hundred crowns. Neither indeed can I deny that if the same use were made of several plump girls in this town, who, without one single groat to their fortunes, cannot stir abroad without a chair, and appear at the playhouse, and assemblies in foreign fineries, which they never will pay for, the kingdom would not be the worse.

Some persons of a desponding spirit are in great concern about 19 that vast number of poor people, who are aged, diseased, or maimed, and I have been desired to employ my thoughts what course may be taken to ease the nation of so grievous an encumbrance. But I am not in the least pain upon that matter, because it is very well known that they are every day dying, and rotting, by cold, and famine, and filth, and vermin, as fast as can be reasonably expected. And as to the younger labourers they are now in almost as hopeful a condition. They cannot get work, and consequently pine away for want of nourishment, to a degree, that if at any time they are accidentally hired to common labour, they have not strength to perform it; and thus the country and themselves are happily delivered from the evils to come.

I have too long digressed, and therefore shall return to my   20
subject. I think the advantages by the proposal which I have made
are obvious and many, as well as of the highest importance.

For first, as I have already observed, it would greatly lessen the   21
number of Papists, with whom we are yearly over-run, being the
principal breeders of the nation, as well as our most dangerous enemies, and who stay at home on purpose with a design to deliver the
kingdom to the Pretender, hoping to take their advantage by the
absence of so many good Protestants, who have chosen rather to
leave their country than stay at home, and pay tithes against their
conscience to an Episcopal curate.

Secondly, The poorer tenants will have something valuable of   22
their own, which by law may be made liable to distress, and help to
pay their landlord's rent, their corn and cattle being already seized
and *money a thing unknown*.

Thirdly, Whereas the maintenance of an hundred thousand chil-   23
dren, from two years old, and upwards, cannot be computed at less
than ten shillings a piece *per annum*, the nation's stock will be thereby
increased fifty thousand pounds *per annum*, besides the profit of a new
dish, introduced to the tables of all gentlemen of fortune in the
kingdom, who have any refinement in taste, and the money will
circulate among ourselves, the goods being entirely of our own growth
and manufacture.

Fourthly, The constant breeders, besides the gain of eight shillings   24
sterling *per annum*, by the sale of their children, will be rid of the
charge of maintaining them after the first year.

Fifthly, This food would likewise bring great custom to taverns,   25
where the vintners will certainly be prudent as to procure the best
receipts for dressing it up to perfection, and consequently have their
houses frequented by all the fine gentlemen, who justly value themselves upon their knowledge in good eating; and a skillful cook, who
understands how to oblige his guests, will contrive to make it as
expensive as they please.

Sixthly, This would be a great inducement to marriage, which   26
all wise nations have either encouraged by rewards, or enforced by
laws and penalties. It would increase the care and tenderness of
mothers toward their children, when they were sure of a settlement
for life, to the poor babes, provided in some sort by the public to
their annual profit instead of expense. We should see an honest
emulation among the married women, which of them could bring the

375

fattest child to the market, men would become as fond of their wives, during the time of their pregnancy, as they are now of their mares in foal, their cows in calf, or sows when they are ready to farrow, nor offer to beat or kick them (as it is too frequent a practice) for fear of miscarriage.

Many other advantages might be enumerated: For instance, the addition of some thousand carcasses in our exportation of barrelled beef; the propagation of swine's flesh, and improvement in the art of making good bacon, so much wanted among us by the great destruction of pigs, too frequent at our tables, which are no way comparable in taste or magnificence to a well-grown, fat yearling child, which roasted whole will make a considerable figure at a Lord Mayor's feast, or any other public entertainment. But this and many others I omit, being studious of brevity.

Supposing that one thousand families in this city would be constant customers for infants' flesh, besides others who might have it at merry-meetings, particularly weddings and christenings, I compute that Dublin would take off annually about twenty thousand carcasses, and the rest of the kingdom (where probably they will be sold somewhat cheaper) the remaining eighty thousand.

I can think of no one objection that will possibly be raised against this proposal, unless it should be urged that the number of people will be thereby much lessened in the kingdom. This I freely own, and it was indeed one principal design in offering it to the world. I desire the reader will observe, that I calculate my remedy for this one individual *Kingdom of Ireland, and for no other that ever was, is, or, I think, ever can be upon earth.* Therefore let no man talk to me of other expedients: *Of taxing our absentees at five shillings a pound: Of using neither clothes, nor household furniture, except what is of our own growth and manufacture: Of utterly rejecting the materials and instruments that promote foreign luxury: Of curing the expensiveness of pride, vanity, idleness, and gaming in our women: Of introducing a vein of parsimony, prudence, and temperance: Of learning to love our Country, wherein we differ even from* LAPLANDERS, *and the inhabitants of* TOPINAMBOO: *Of quitting our animosities and factions, nor act any longer like the Jews, who were murdering one another at the very moment their city was taken: Of being a little cautious not to sell our country and consciences for nothing: Of teaching landlords to have at least one degree of mercy toward their tenants. Lastly, of putting a spirit of honesty, industry, and skill into our shopkeepers, who, if a resolution could now be taken to buy only our* native goods, would immediately unite to cheat and exact upon us in the price, the measure, and the goodness, nor could ever yet be brought to make one fair proposal of just dealing, though often and earnestly invited to it.

Therefore I repeat, let no man talk to me of these and the like expedients, till he hath at least some glimpse of hope that there will ever be some hearty and sincere attempt to put them in practice. 30

But as to myself, having been wearied out for many years with offering vain, idle, visionary thoughts, and at length utterly despairing of success, I fortunately fell upon this proposal, which as it is wholly new, so it hath something solid and real, of no expense and little trouble, full in our own power, and whereby we can incur no danger in *disobliging* ENGLAND. For this kind of commodity will not bear exportation, the flesh being too tender a consistence to admit a long continuance in salt, *although perhaps I could name a country which would be glad to eat up our whole nation without it.* 31

After all I am not so violently bent upon my own opinion as to reject any offer, proposed by wise men, which shall be found equally innocent, cheap, easy, and effectual. But before something of that kind shall be advanced in contradiction to my scheme, and offering a better, I desire the author, or authors, will be pleased maturely to consider two points. First, as things now stand, how they will be able to find food and raiment for an hundred thousand useless mouths and backs. And secondly, there being a round million of creatures in human figure, throughout this kingdom, whose whole subsistence put into a common stock would leave them in debt two millions of pounds sterling; adding those, who are beggars by profession, to the bulk of farmers, cottagers, and labourers with their wives and children, who are beggars in effect; I desire those politicians, who dislike my overture, and may perhaps be so bold as to attempt an answer, that they will first ask the parents of these mortals whether they would not at this day think it a great happiness to have been sold for food at a year old, in the manner I prescribe, and thereby have avoided such a perpetual scene of misfortunes as they have since gone through, by the oppression of landlords, the impossibility of paying rent without money or trade, the want of common sustenance, with neither house nor clothes to cover them from the inclemencies of the weather, and the most inevitable prospect of entailing the like, or greater miseries upon their breed for ever. 32

I profess in the sincerity of my heart that I have not the least 33 personal interest in endeavoring to promote this necessary work, having no other motive than the *public good of my country, by advancing our trade, providing for infants, relieving the poor, and giving some pleasure to the rich.* I have no children by which I can propose to get a single penny; the youngest being nine years old, and my wife past childbearing.

PLATO (427–338 B.C.) was a Greek philosopher and writer who became actively involved in the politics of the Athenian state. He rebelled against the tyranny that had permeated Athenian democracy, and his reaction to the death of his teacher and friend Socrates led him to search for an alternative life-style. He is best known for his philosophical dialogues, and his philosophical and political ideas have had a significant and lasting impact on Western thought.

The Allegory of the Cave

Plato

And now, I said, let me show in a figure how far our nature is 1 enlightened or unenlightened: Behold! human beings living in an underground den, which has a mouth open towards the light and reaching all along the den; here they have been from their childhood, and have their legs and necks chained so that they cannot move, and can only see before them, being prevented by the chains from turning round their heads. Above and behind them a fire is blazing at a distance, and between the fire and the prisoners there is a raised way; and you will see, if you look, a low wall built along the way, like the screen which marionette players have in front of them, over which they show the puppets.

I see. 2

And do you see, I said, men passing along the wall carrying all 3 sorts of vessels, and statues and figures of animals made of wood and stone and various materials, which appear over the wall? Some of them are talking, others silent.

You have shown me a strange image, and they are strange 4 prisoners.

Like ourselves, I replied; and they see only their own shadows, 5
or the shadows of one another, which the fire throws on the opposite
wall of the cave?

True, he said; how could they see anything but the shadows if 6
they were never allowed to move their heads?

And of the objects which are being carried in like manner they 7
would only see the shadows?

Yes, he said. 8

And if they were able to converse with one another, would they 9
not suppose that they were naming what was actually before them?

Very true. 10

And suppose further that the prison had an echo which came 11
from the other side, would they not be sure to fancy when one of the
passers-by spoke that the voice which they heard came from the
passing shadow?

No question, he replied. 12

To them, I said, the truth would be literally nothing but the 13
shadows of the images.

That is certain. 14

And now look again, and see what will naturally follow if the 15
prisoners are released and disabused of their error. At first, when any
of them is liberated and compelled suddenly to stand up and turn his
neck round and walk and look towards the light, he will suffer sharp
pains; the glare will distress him and he will be unable to see the
realities of which in his former state he had seen the shadows; and
then conceive some one saying to him, that what he saw before was
an illusion, but that now, when he is approaching nearer to being
and his eye is turned towards more real existence, he has a clearer
vision—what will be his reply? And you may further imagine that his
instructor is pointing to the objects as they pass and requiring him to
name them—will he not be perplexed? Will he not fancy that the
shadows which he formerly saw are truer than the objects which are
now shown to him?

Far truer. 16

And if he is compelled to look straight at the light, will he not 17
have a pain in his eyes which will make him turn away to take refuge
in the objects of vision which he can see, and which he will conceive
to be in reality clearer than the things which are now being shown
to him?

True, he said. 18

And suppose once more, that he is reluctantly dragged up a steep 19
and rugged ascent, and held fast until he is forced into the presence
of the sun himself, is he not likely to be pained and irritated? When
he approaches the light his eyes will be dazzled and he will not be
able to see anything at all of what are now called realities.

Not all in a moment, he said. 20

He will require to grow accustomed to the sight of the upper 21
world. And first he will see the shadows best, next the reflections of
men and other objects in the water, and then the objects themselves;
then he will gaze upon the light of the moon and the stars and the
spangled heaven; and he will see the sky and the stars by night better
than the sun or the light of the sun by day?

Certainly. 22

Last of all he will be able to see the sun, and not mere reflections 23
of him in the water, but he will see him in his own proper place, and
not in another; and he will contemplate him as he is.

Certainly. 24

He will then proceed to argue that this is he who gives the 25
season and the years, and is the guardian of all that is in the visible
world, and in a certain way the cause of all things which he and his
fellows have been accustomed to behold?

Clearly, he said, he would first see the sun and then reason about 26
him.

And when he remembered his old habitation, and the wisdom 27
of the den and his fellow-prisoners, do you not suppose that he would
felicitate himself on the change, and pity them?

Certainly, he would. 28

And if they were in the habit of conferring honors among them- 29
selves on those who were quickest to observe the passing shadows and
to remark which of them went before, and which followed after, and
which were together; and who were therefore best able to draw
conclusions as to the future, do you think that he would care for such
honors and glories, or envy the possessors of them? Would he not say
with Homer,

Better to be the poor servant of a poor master,

and to endure anything, rather than think as they do and live after
their manner?

Yes, he said, I think that he would rather suffer anything than 30
entertain these false notions and live in this miserable manner.

Imagine once more, I said, such an one coming suddenly out of 31
the sun to be replaced in his old situation; would he not be certain
to have his eyes full of darkness?

To be sure, he said. 32

And if there were a contest, and he had to compete in measuring 33
the shadows with the prisoners who had never moved out of the den,
while his sight was still weak, and before his eyes had become steady
(and the time which would be needed to acquire this new habit of
sight might be very considerable) would he not be ridiculous? Men
would say of him that up he went and down he came without his
eyes; and that it was better not even to think of ascending; and if
any one tried to loose another and lead him up to the light, let them
only catch the offender, and they would put him to death.

No question, he said. 34

This entire allegory, I said, you may now append, dear Glaucon, 35
to the previous argument; the prison-house is the world of sight, the
light of the fire is the sun, and you will not misapprehend me if you
interpret the journey upwards to be the ascent of the soul into the
intellectual world according to my poor belief, which, at your desire,
I have expressed—whether rightly or wrongly God knows. But,
whether true or false, my opinion is that in the world of knowledge
the idea of good appears last of all, and is seen only with an effort;
and, when seen, is also inferred to be the universal author of all
things beautiful and right, parent of light and of the lord of light in
this visible world, and the immediate source of reason and truth in
the intellectual; and that this is the power upon which he who would
act rationally either in public or private life must have his eye fixed.

I agree, he said, as far as I am able to understand you. 36

Moreover, I said, you must not wonder that those who attain to 37
this beatific vision are unwilling to descend to human affairs; for their
souls are ever hastening into the upper world where they desire to
dwell; which desire of theirs is very natural, if our allegory may be
trusted.

Yes, very natural. 38

And is there anything surprising in one who passes from divine 39
contemplations to the evil state of man, misbehaving himself in a
ridiculous manner; if, while his eyes are blinking and before he has
become accustomed to the surrounding darkness, he is compelled to

fight in courts of law, or in other places, about the images or the shadows of images of justice, and is endeavouring to meet the conceptions of those who have never yet seen absolute justice?

Anything but surprising, he replied. 40

Any one who has common sense will remember that the bewil- 41 derments of the eyes are of two kinds, and arise from two causes, either from coming out of the light or from going into the light, which is true of the mind's eye, quite as much as of the bodily eye; and he who remembers this when he sees any one whose vision is perplexed and weak, will not be too ready to laugh; he will first ask whether that soul of man has come out of the brighter life, and is unable to see because unaccustomed to the dark, or having turned from darkness to the day is dazzled by excess of light. And he will count the one happy in his condition and state of being, and he will pity the other; or, if he have a mind to laugh at the soul which comes from below into the light, there will be more reason in this than in the laugh which greets him who returns from above out of the light into the den.

That, he said, is a very just distinction. 42

GEORGE ORWELL (1903–50) was born in India to British parents, and he spent much of his adult life there. For many years he served with the imperial police in Burma, and "Shooting an Elephant" is the record of an incident that occurred during that period. His best-known novels are *Animal Farm* and *1984*, both of which are political satires.

Shooting an Elephant

George Orwell

In Moulmein, in lower Burma, I was hated by large numbers of 1 people—the only time in my life that I have been important enough for this to happen to me. I was sub-divisional police officer of the town, and in an aimless, petty kind of way anti-European feeling was very bitter. No one had the guts to raise a riot, but if a European woman went through the bazaars alone somebody would probably spit betel juice over her dress. As a police officer I was an obvious target and was baited whenever it seemed safe to do so. When a nimble Burman tripped me up on the football field and the referee (another Burman) looked the other way, the crowd yelled with hideous laughter. This happened more than once. In the end the sneering yellow faces of young men that met me everywhere, the insults hooted after me when I was at a safe distance, got badly on my nerves. The young Buddhist priests were the worst of all. There were several thousands of them in the town and none of them seemed to have anything to do except stand on street corners and jeer at Europeans.

All this was perplexing and upsetting. For at that time I had 2
already made up my mind that imperialism was an evil thing and the
sooner I chucked up my job and got out of it the better. Theoretically—and secretly, of course—I was all for the Burmese and all
against their oppressors, the British. As for the job I was doing, I
hated it more bitterly than I can perhaps make clear. In a job like
that you see the dirty work of Empire at close quarters. The wretched
prisoners huddling in the stinking cages of the lock-ups, the grey,
cowed faces of the long-term convicts, the scarred buttocks of the
men who had been flogged with bamboos—all these oppressed me
with an intolerable sense of guilt. But I could get nothing into
perspective. I was young and ill-educated and I had had to think out
my problems in the utter silence that is imposed on every Englishman
in the East. I did not even know that the British Empire is dying,
still less did I know that it is a great deal better than the younger
empires that are going to supplant it. All I knew was that I was stuck
between my hatred of the empire I served and my rage against the
evil-spirited little beasts who tried to make my job impossible. With
one part of my mind I thought of the British Raj as an unbreakable
tyranny, as something clamped down, in *saecula saeculorum,* upon the
will of prostrate peoples; with another part I thought that the greatest
joy in the world would be to drive a bayonet into a Buddhist priest's
guts. Feelings like these are the normal by-products of imperialism;
ask any Anglo-Indian official, if you can catch him off duty.

One day something happened which in a roundabout way was 3
enlightening. It was a tiny incident in itself, but it gave me a better
glimpse than I had had before of the real nature of imperialism—the
real motives for which despotic governments act. Early one morning
the sub-inspector at a police station the other end of the town rang
me up on the phone and said that an elephant was ravaging the
bazaar. Would I please come and do something about it? I did not
know what I could do, but I wanted to see what was happening and
I got on to a pony and started out. I took my rifle, an old .44
Winchester and much too small to kill an elephant, but I thought
the noise might be useful *in terrorem.* Various Burmans stopped me
on the way and told me about the elephant's doings. It was not, of
course, a wild elephant, but a tame one which had gone "must." It
had been chained up, as tame elephants always are when their attack
of "must" is due, but on the previous night it had broken its chain
and escaped. Its mahout, the only person who could manage it when

it was in that state, had set out in pursuit, but had taken the wrong direction and was now twelve hours' journey away, and in the morning the elephant had suddenly reappeared in the town. The Burmese population had no weapons and were quite helpless against it. It had already destroyed somebody's bamboo hut, killed a cow and raided some fruit-stalls and devoured the stock; also it had met the municipal rubbish van and, when the driver jumped out and took to his heels, had turned the van over and inflicted violences upon it.

The Burmese sub-inspector and some Indian constables were waiting for me in the quarter where the elephant had been seen. It was a very poor quarter, a labyrinth of squalid bamboo huts, thatched with palm-leaf, winding all over a steep hillside. I remember that it was a cloudy, stuffy morning at the beginning of the rains. We began questioning the people as to where the elephant had gone and, as usual, failed to get any definite information. That is invariably the case in the East; a story always sounds clear enough at a distance, but the nearer you get to the scene of events the vaguer it becomes. Some of the people said that the elephant had gone in one direction, some said that he had gone in another, some professed not even to have heard of any elephant. I had almost made up my mind that the whole story was a pack of lies, when we heard yells a little distance away. There was a loud, scandalized cry of "Go away, child! Go away this instant!" and an old woman with a switch in her hand came round the corner of a hut, violently shooing away a crowd of naked children. Some more women followed, clicking their tongues and exclaiming; evidently there was something that the children ought not to have seen. I rounded the hut and saw a man's dead body sprawling in the mud. He was an Indian, a black Dravidian coolie, almost naked, and he could not have been dead many minutes. The people said that the elephant had come suddenly upon him round the corner of the hut, caught him with its trunk, put its foot on his back and ground him into the earth. This was the rainy season and the ground was soft, and his face had scored a trench a foot deep and a couple of yards long. He was lying on his belly with arms crucified and head sharply twisted to one side. His face was coated with mud, the eyes wide open, the teeth bared and grinning with an expression of unendurable agony. (Never tell me, by the way, that the dead look peaceful. Most of the corpses I have seen looked devilish.) The friction of the great beast's foot had stripped the skin from his back as neatly as one skins a rabbit. As soon as I saw the dead man I sent an orderly to a friend's house nearby to borrow an elephant rifle. I had already sent back the pony, not wanting it to go mad with fright and throw me if it smelt the elephant.

The orderly came back in a few minutes with a rifle and five 5 cartridges, and meanwhile some Burmans had arrived and told us that the elephant was in the paddy fields below, only a few hundred yards away. As I started forward practically the whole population of the quarter flocked out of the houses and followed me. They had seen the rifle and were all shouting excitedly that I was going to shoot the elephant. They had not shown much interest in the elephant when he was merely ravaging their homes, but it was different now that he was going to be shot. It was a bit of fun to them, as it would be to an English crowd; besides they wanted the meat. It made me vaguely uneasy. I had no intention of shooting the elephant—I had merely sent for the rifle to defend myself if necessary—and it is always unnerving to have a crowd following you. I marched down the hill, looking and feeling a fool, with the rifle over my shoulder and an ever-growing army of people jostling at my heels. At the bottom, when you got away from the huts, there was a metalled road and beyond that a miry waste of paddy fields a thousand yards across, not yet ploughed but soggy from the first rains and dotted with coarse grass. The elephant was standing eight yards from the road, his left side towards us. He took not the slightest notice of the crowd's approach. He was tearing up bunches of grass, beating them against his knees to clean them and stuffing them into his mouth.

I had halted on the road. As soon as I saw the elephant I knew 6 with perfect certainty that I ought not to shoot him. It is a serious matter to shoot a working elephant—it is comparable to destroying a huge and costly piece of machinery—and obviously one ought not to do it if it can possibly be avoided. And at that distance, peacefully eating, the elephant looked no more dangerous than a cow. I thought then and I think now that his attack of "must" was already passing off; in which case he would merely wander harmlessly about until the mahout came back and caught him. Moreover I did not in the least want to shoot him. I decided that I would watch him for a little while to make sure that he did not turn savage again, and then go home.

But at that moment I glanced round at the crowd that had 7 followed me. It was an immense crowd, two thousand at the least and growing every minute. It blocked the road for a long distance on either side. I looked at the sea of yellow faces above the garish clothes—faces all happy and excited over this bit of fun, all certain that the elephant was going to be shot. They were watching me as they would watch a conjurer about to perform a trick. They did not like me, but with the magical rifle in my hands I was momentarily worth watching. And suddenly I realized that I should have to shoot the elephant after all. The people expected it of me and I had got to do it; I could feel their two thousand wills pressing me forward, irresistibly. And it was at this moment, as I stood there with the rifle in my hands, that I first grasped the hollowness, the futility of the white man's dominion in the East. Here was I, the white man with his gun, standing in front of the unarmed native crowd—seemingly the leading actor of the piece; but in reality I was only an absurd puppet pushed to and fro by the will of those yellow faces behind. I perceived in this moment that when the white man turns tyrant it is his own freedom that he destroys. He becomes a sort of hollow, posing dummy, the conventionalized figure of a sahib. For it is the condition of his rule that he shall spend his life in trying to impress the "natives," and so in every crisis he has got to do what the "natives" expect of him. He wears a mask, and his face grows to fit it. I had got to shoot the elephant. I had committed myself to doing it when I sent for the rifle. A sahib has got to act like a sahib; he has got to appear resolute, to know his own mind and do definite things. To come all that way, rifle in hand, with two thousand people marching at my heels, and then to trail feebly away, having done nothing—no, that was impossible. The crowd would laugh at me. And my whole life, every white man's life in the East, was one long struggle not to be laughed at.

But I did not want to shoot the elephant. I watched him beating his bunch of grass against his knees, with that preoccupied grandmotherly air that elephants have. It seemed to me that it would be murder to shoot him. At that age I was not squeamish about killing animals, but I had never shot an elephant and never wanted to. (Somehow it always seems worse to kill a *large* animal.) Besides, there was the beast's owner to be considered. Alive, the elephant was worth at least a hundred pounds; dead, he would only be worth the value of his tusks, five pounds, possibly. But I had got to act quickly. I turned to some experienced-looking Burmans who had been there when we arrived, and asked them how the elephant had been behaving. They all said the same thing; he took no notice of you if you left him alone, but he might charge if you went too close to him.

8

It was perfectly clear to me what I ought to do. I ought to walk 9
up to within, say, twenty-five yards of the elephant and test his
behavior. If he charged, I could shoot; if he took no notice of me,
it would be safe to leave him until the mahout came back. But also
I knew that I was going to do no such thing. I was a poor shot with
a rifle and the ground was soft mud into which one would sink at
every step. If the elephant charged and I missed him, I should have
about as much chance as a toad under a steam-roller. But even then
I was not thinking particularly of my own skin, only of the watchful
yellow faces behind. For at that moment, with the crowd watching
me, I was not afraid in the ordinary sense, as I would have been if I
had been alone. A white man mustn't be frightened in front of
"natives"; and so, in general, he isn't frightened. The sole thought
in my mind was that if anything went wrong those two thousand
Burmans would see me pursued, caught, trampled on and reduced to
a grinning corpse like that Indian up the hill. And if that happened
it was quite probable that some of them would laugh. That would
never do. There was only one alternative. I shoved the cartridges
into the magazine and lay down on the road to get a better aim.

The crowd grew very still, and a deep, low, happy sigh, as of 10
people who see the theatre curtain go up at last, breathed from
innumerable throats. They were going to have their bit of fun after
all. The rifle was a beautiful German thing with cross-hair sights. I
did not then know that in shooting an elephant one would shoot to
cut an imaginary bar running from ear-hole to ear-hole. I ought,
therefore, as the elephant was sideways on, to have aimed straight at
his ear-hole; actually I aimed several inches in front of this, thinking
the brain would be further forward.

When I pulled the trigger I did not hear the bang or feel the 11
kick—one never does when a shot goes home—but I heard the
devilish roar of glee that went up from the crowd. In that instant, in
too short a time, one would have thought, even for the bullet to get
there, a mysterious, terrible change had come over the elephant. He
neither stirred nor fell, but every line of his body had altered. He
looked suddenly stricken, shrunken, immensely old, as though the
frightful impact of the bullet had paralysed him without knocking
him down. At last, after what seemed a long time—it might have
been five seconds, I dare say—he sagged flabbily to his knees. His
mouth slobbered. An enormous senility seemed to have settled upon
him. One could have imagined him thousands of years old. I fired

again into the same spot. At the second shot he did not collapse but climbed with desperate slowness to his feet and stood weakly upright, with legs sagging and head drooping. I fired a third time. That was the shot that did for him. You could see the agony of it jolt his whole body and knock the last remnant of strength from his legs. But in falling he seemed for a moment to rise, for as his hind legs collapsed beneath him he seemed to tower upward like a huge rock toppling, his trunk reaching skywards like a tree. He trumpeted, for the first and only time. And then down he came, his belly towards me, with a crash that seemed to shake the ground even where I lay.

I got up. The Burmans were already racing past me across the   12
mud. It was obvious that the elephant would never rise again, but he was not dead. He was breathing very rhythmically with long rattling gasps, his great mound of a side painfully rising and falling. His mouth was wide open—I could see far down into caverns of pale pink throat. I waited a long time for him to die, but his breathing did not weaken. Finally, I fired my two remaining shots into the spot where I thought his heart must be. The thick blood welled out of him like red velvet, but still he did not die. His body did not even jerk when the shots hit him, the tortured breathing continued without a pause. He was dying, very slowly and in great agony, but in some world remote from me where not even a bullet could damage him further. I felt that I had got to put an end to that dreadful noise. It seemed dreadful to see the great beast lying there, powerless to move and yet powerless to die, and not even to be able to finish him. I sent back for my small rifle and poured shot after shot into his heart and down his throat. They seemed to make no impression. The tortured gasps continued as steadily as the ticking of a clock.

In the end I could not stand it any longer and went away. I   13
heard later that it took him half an hour to die. Burmans were bringing dahs and baskets even before I left, and I was told they had stripped his body almost to the bones by the afternoon.

Afterwards, of course, there were endless discussions about the   14
shooting of the elephant. The owner was furious, but he was only an Indian and could do nothing. Besides, legally I had done the right thing, for a mad elephant has to be killed, like a mad dog, if its owner fails to control it. Among the Europeans opinion was divided. The older men said I was right, the younger men said it was a damn shame to shoot an elephant for killing a coolie, because an elephant

was worth more than any damn Coringhee coolie. And afterwards I was very glad that the coolie had been killed; it put me legally in the right and it gave me a sufficient pretext for shooting the elephant. I often wondered whether any of the others grasped that I had done it solely to avoid looking a fool.

BERTRAND RUSSELL (1872–1970) held unconventional views on
individual freedom throughout his life. In 1918 he spent several
months in jail for his militant pacificism, and during that
period he wrote *Introduction to Mathematical Philosophy*. In the
1950s and 1960s he led pacificist groups and participated in
antinuclear demonstrations. He was also a violent opponent of
the Vietnam War. A voluminous writer, he is best known for
his *Principia Mathematica* (1913). However, he received the
Nobel Prize in 1950 not for science but for literature. The
following essay is from *The ABC of Relativity* (1925).

Space-Time

Bertrand Russell

Everybody who has ever heard of relativity knows the phrase "space-time," and knows that the correct thing is to use this phrase when formerly we should have said "space *and* time." But very few people who are not mathematicians have any clear idea of what is meant by this change of phraseology. Before dealing further with the special theory of relativity, I want to try to convey to the reader what is involved in the new phrase "space-time," because that is, from a philosophical and imaginative point of view, perhaps the most important of all the novelties that Einstein introduced.

Suppose you wish to say where and when some event has occurred—say an explosion on an airship—you will have to mention four quantities, say the latitude and longitude, the height above the ground, and the time. According to the traditional view, the first three of these give the position in space, while the fourth gives the position in time. The three quantities that give the position in space may be assigned in all sorts of ways. You might, for instance, take

"Space-Time," from *The ABC of Relativity* (1925). Reprinted by permission of George
Allen & Unwin Ltd., London.

the plane of the equator, the plane of the meridian of Greenwich, and the plane of the 90th meridian, and say how far the airship was from each of these planes; these three distances would be what are called "Cartesian co-ordinates," after Descartes. You might take any other three planes all at right angles to each other, and you would still have Cartesian co-ordinates. Or you might take the distance from London to a point vertically below the airship, the direction of this distance (north-east, west-south-west, or whatever it might be), and the height of the airship above the ground. There are an infinite number of such ways of fixing the position in space, all equally legitimate; the choice between them is merely one of convenience.

When people said that space had three dimensions, they meant 3 just this: that three quantities were necessary in order to specify the position of a point in space, but that the method of assigning these quantities was wholly arbitrary.

With regard to time, the matter was thought to be quite differ- 4 ent. The only arbitrary elements in the reckoning of time were the unit, and the point of time from which the reckoning started. One could reckon in Greenwich time, or in Paris time, or in New York time; that made a difference as to the point of departure. One could reckon in seconds, minutes, hours, days, or years; that was a difference of unit. Both these were obvious and trivial matters. There was nothing corresponding to the liberty of choice as to the method of fixing position in space. And, in particular, it was thought that the method of fixing position in space and the method of fixing position in time could be made wholly independent of each other. For these reasons people regarded time and space as quite distinct.

The theory of relativity has changed this. There are now a 5 number of different ways of fixing position in time, which do not differ merely as to the unit and the starting-point. Indeed, as we have seen, if one event is simultaneous with another in one reckoning, it will precede it in another and follow it in a third. Moreover, the space and time reckonings are no longer independent of each other. If you alter the way of reckoning position in space, you may also alter the time-interval between two events. If you alter the way of reckoning time, you may also alter the distance in space between two events. Thus space and time are no longer independent, any more than the three dimensions of space are. We still need four quantities to determine the position of an event, but we cannot, as before, divide off one of the four as quite independent of the other three.

It is not quite true to say that there is no longer any distinction 6
between time and space. As we have seen, there are time-like intervals and space-like intervals. But the distinction is of a different sort
from that which was formerly assumed. There is no longer a universal
time which can be applied without ambiguity to any part of the
universe; there are only the various "proper" times of the various
bodies in the universe, which agree approximately for two bodies
which are not in rapid motion, but never agree exactly except for
two bodies which are at rest relatively to each other.

The picture of the world which is required for this new state of 7
affairs is as follows: Suppose an event E occurs to me, and simultaneously a flash of light goes out from me in all directions. Anything
that happens to any body after the light from the flash has reached
it is definitely after the event E in any system of reckoning time. Any
event anywhere which I could have seen before the event E occurred
to me is definitely before the event E in any system of reckoning
time. But any event which happened in the intervening time is not
definitely either before or after the event E. To make the matter
definite: suppose I could observe a person in Sirius, and he could
observe me. Anything which he does, and which I see before the
event E occurs to me, is definitely before E; anything he does after
he has seen the event E is definitely after E. But anything that he
does before he sees the event E, but so that I see it after the event
E has happened, is not definitely before or after E. Since light takes
many years to travel from Sirius to earth, this gives a period of twice
as many years in Sirius which may be called "contemporary" with E,
since these years are not definitely before or after E.

Dr. A. A. Robb, in his *Theory of Time and Space*, suggested a 8
point of view which may or may not be philosophically fundamental,
but is at any rate a help in understanding the state of affairs we have
been describing. He maintained that one event can only be said to
be definitely *before* another if it can influence that other in some way.
Now influences spread from a centre at varying rates. Newspapers
exercise an influence emanating from London at an average rate of
about twenty miles an hour—rather more for long distances. Anything a man does because of what he reads in the newspaper is clearly
subsequent to the printing of the newspaper. Sounds travel much
faster: it would be possible to arrange a series of loud-speakers along
the main roads, and have newspapers shouted from each to the next.
But telegraphing is quicker, and wireless telegraphy travels with the

velocity of light, so that nothing quicker can ever be hoped for. Now what a man does in consequence of receiving a wireless message he does *after* the message was sent; the meaning here is quite independent of conventions as to the measurement of time. But anything that he does while the message is on its way cannot be influenced by the sending of the message, and cannot influence the sender until some little time after he sent the message, that is to say, if two bodies are widely separated, neither can influence the other except after a certain lapse of time; what happens before that time has elapsed cannot affect the distant body. Suppose, for instance, that some notable event happens on the sun: there is a period of sixteen minutes on the earth during which no event on the earth can have influenced or been influenced by the said notable event on the sun. This gives a substantial ground for regarding that period of sixteen minutes on the earth as neither before nor after the event on the sun.

The paradoxes of the special theory of relativity are only para- 9
doxes because we are unaccustomed to the point of view, and in the habit of taking things for granted when we have no right to do so. This is especially true as regards the measurement of lengths. In daily life, our way of measuring lengths is to apply a foot-rule or some other measure. At the moment when the foot-rule is applied, it is at rest relatively to the body which is being measured. Consequently the length that we arrive at by measurement is the "proper" length, that is to say, the length as estimated by an observer who shares the motion of the body. We never, in ordinary life, have to tackle the problem of measuring a body which is in continual motion. And even if we did, the velocities of visible bodies on the earth are so small relatively to the earth that the anomalies dealt with by the theory of relativity would not appear. But in astronomy, or in the investigation of atomic structure, we are faced with problems which cannot be tackled in this way. Not being Joshua, we cannot make the sun stand still while we measure it; if we are to estimate its size we must do so while it is in motion relatively to us. And similarly if you want to estimate the size of an electron, you have to do so while it is in rapid motion, because it never stands still for a moment. This is the sort of problem with which the theory of relativity is concerned. Measurement with a foot-rule, when it is possible, gives always the same result, because it gives the "proper" length of a body. But when this method is not possible, we find that curious things happen, particularly if the body to be measured is moving very fast relatively

to the observer. A figure like the one at the end of the previous chapter will help us to understand the state of affairs.

Let us suppose that the body on which we wish to measure   10
lengths is moving relatively to ourselves, and that in one second it moves the distance OM. Let us draw a circle round O whose radius is the distance that light travels in a second. Through M draw MP perpendicular to OM, meeting the circle in P. Thus OP is the distance that light travels in a second. The ratio of OP to OM is the ratio of the velocity of light to the velocity of the body. The ratio of OP to MP is the ratio in which apparent lengths are altered by the motion. That is to say, if the observer judges that two points in the line of motion on the moving body are at a distance from each other represented by MP, a person moving with the body would judge that they were at a distance represented (on the same scale) by OP. Distances on the moving body at right angles to the line of motion are not affected by the motion. The whole thing is reciprocal; that is to say, if an observer moving with the body were to measure lengths on the previous observer's body, they would be altered in just the same proportion. When two bodies are moving relatively to each other, lengths on either appear shorter to the other than to themselves. This is the Fitzgerald contraction, which was first invented to account for the result of the Michelson-Morley experiment. But it now emerges naturally from the fact that the two observers do not make the same judgment of simultaneity.

The way in which simultaneity comes in is this: We say that two   11
points on a body are a foot apart when we can *simultaneously* apply one end of a foot-rule to the one and the other end to the other. If, now, two people disagree about simultaneity, and the body is in

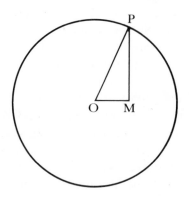

motion, they will obviously get different results from their measurements. Thus the trouble about time is at the bottom of the trouble about distance.

The ratio of OP to MP is the essential thing in all these matters. 12 Times and lengths and masses are all altered in this proportion when the body concerned is in motion relatively to the observer. It will be seen that, if OM is very much smaller than OP, that is to say, if the body is moving very much more slowly than light, MP and OP are very nearly equal, so that the alterations produced by the motion are very small. But if OM is nearly as large as OP, that is to say, if the body is moving nearly as fast as light, MP becomes very small compared to OP, and the effects become very great. The apparent increase of mass in swiftly moving particles had been observed, and the right formula had been found, before Einstein invented his special theory of relativity. In fact, Lorentz had arrived at the formulae called the "Lorentz transformation," which embody the whole mathematical essence of the special theory of relativity. But it was Einstein who showed that the whole thing was what we ought to have expected, and not a set of makeshift devices to account for surprising experimental results. Nevertheless, it must not be forgotten that experimental results were the original motive of the whole theory, and have remained the ground for undertaking the tremendous logical reconstruction involved in Einstein's theories.

We may now recapitulate the reasons which have made it nec- 13 essary to substitute "space-time" for space and time. The old separation of space and time rested upon the belief that there was no ambiguity in saying that two events in distant places happened at the same time; consequently it was thought that we could describe the topography of the universe at a given instant in purely spatial terms. But now that simultaneity has become relative to a particular observer, this is no longer possible. What is, for one observer, a description of the state of the world, at a given instant, is, for another observer, a series of events at various different times, whose relations are not merely spatial but also temporal. For the same reason, we are concerned with *events*, rather than with *bodies*. In the old theory, it was possible to consider a number of bodies all at the same instant, and since the time was the same for all of them it could be ignored. But now we cannot do that if we are to obtain an objective account of physical occurrences. We must mention the date at which a body is to be considered, and thus we arrive at an "event," that is to say, something which happens at a given time. When we know the time and place of an event in one observer's system of reckoning, we can calculate its time and place according to another observer. But we must know the time as well as the place, because we can no longer ask what is its place for the new observer at the "same" time as for the old observer. This is no such thing as the "same" time for different observers, unless they are at rest relatively to each other. We need four measurements to fix a position, and four measurements fix the position of an event in space-time, not merely of a body in space. Three measurements are not enough to fix any position. That is the essence of what is meant by the substitution of space-time for space and time.

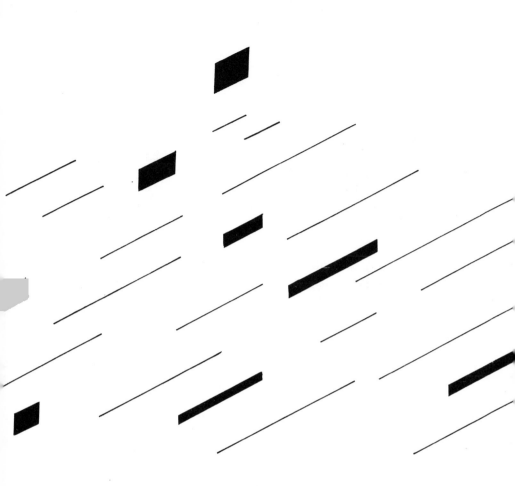

Glossary

ABSTRACT   An abstract word describes a concept or quality that has no physical, tangible existence in itself, a concept such as truth or a quality such as beauty. A "child," for example, is a concrete object that our senses can perceive; but "childishness" is an abstract quality. *See* "Concrete."

ANALOGY   An analogy is a comparison that points out a resemblance between two essentially different things. Sleep and death are analogous, although certainly not identical. Often an analogy is drawn to explain something that is complex or abstract by pointing out one way it resembles something that is simpler or more concrete. For example, to explain how the mind processes and stores information in its memory, an analogy might be drawn to the way a bank processes and stores deposits.

ANTONYM   An antonym is a word of opposite meaning from another word. "Good" is an antonym of "bad". *See* "Synonym."

ARGUMENTATION   *See* Chapter 10.

AUDIENCE   Audience refers to an author's concept of who his or her readers will be, which affects the style and tone. An author may write more technically, for example, if the intended audience is composed of specialists in a certain field and may write less technically if the writing is for the general public.

CAUSE AND EFFECT   *See* Chapter 9.

CLASSIFICATION   *See* Chapter 7.

CLICHÉ   A cliché is an expression that has been so overused it has lost its ability to affect us as a bright and picturesque way of conveying an idea. Clichés, such as "busy as a bee," make writing less clear and precise because we are so used to hearing them, they become little more than vague generalizations to us.

COHERENCE   Coherence refers to a sense of connection and interrelationship among the parts of an essay. In a coherent piece of writing each sentence leads reasonably to the next sentence, and each paragraph follows reasonably from the previous paragraph. A lack of coherence is evident when there are gaps between parts of an essay, when a reader begins to ask, "Why does the writer say this here?" or "How did the writer get to this idea from the previous idea?" *See* "Transition" and "Unity."

COLLOQUIALISM   A colloquialism is a conversational word or phrase that often may be deemed inappropriate in formal writing. It is not wrong to use the colloquialism "booze" for "whiskey" or "loosen up" for "relax," but doing so imparts a less dignified, less studied quality to one's writing. *See* "Slang."

COMPARISON AND CONTRAST   *See* Chapter 6.

CONCLUSION   A conclusion sums up or restates the writer's thesis; it should give a well-rounded sense of completion and finality to a piece of writing. It may be no more than a sentence in a short essay, or it may be many paragraphs in a long report. A short conclusion may restate the writer's thesis in a memorable way, place the specific topic being discussed within or against a broader framework, or suggest answers to questions raised in the essay. A summary of the writer's main points may be effective as the conclusion to a long paper, but in a short essay it will seem unnecessarily repetitious.

CONCRETE   A concrete word describes something specific and tangible as opposed to something general and abstract. "Wealth" is an abstract concept, of which "gold" is a concrete form. The use of concrete details, examples, and illustrations is a key to clear and effective writing. *See* "Abstract."

CONNOTATION   The connotations of a word are its implications and over-tones and the qualities, feelings, and ideas it suggests beyond its literal meaning or dictionary definition. The word "sunshine" literally signifies the lightrays of the sun, but it connotes warmth, cheer, happiness, and even prosperity. *See* "Denotation."

DEDUCTION   Deduction is a mental process in which one first assumes that a broad generalization is valid, then reasons that its validity is applicable to more specific instances. For example, if we assume that cigarette smoking causes cancer, we may deduce that a person who smokes is liable to contract the disease. *See* "Induction" and "Syllogism."

DEFINITION   *See* Chapter 5.

DENOTATION   The denotation of a word is its literal meaning as defined by a dictionary. *See* "Connotation."

DESCRIPTION   *See* Chapter 3.

DICTION   Diction is the writer's choice of words. A writer is said to employ proper diction when the words he or she chooses to express his or her ideas are accurate and appropriate, that is, when what he or she writes says exactly what he or she means. Poor diction stems from choosing words whose denotation does not accurately convey the author's intended meaning or from choosing words regarded as inappropriate because they are nonstandard ("ain't"), colloquial, or obsolete.

EXPOSITION   Exposition is a mode or form of discourse that is designed specifically to convey information, give directions, or explain what is difficult to understand.

FIGURE OF SPEECH   A figure of speech is an imaginative phrase and com-parison that is not meant to be taken literally. "He ran as fast as the wind," for example, is a figure of speech known as a simile. *See* "Analogy," "Hyper-bole," "Metaphor," "Personification," "Simile," and "Understatement."

GENERALIZATION   A generalization is a broad statement, idea or rule that holds a common truth or applicability. For example, it is generally true that a soldier's job is to fight in wars, although there may be many specific exceptions to such a generalization. Writing that relies too much on gen-eralization is likely to be vague and abstract. *See* "Specificity."

HYPERBOLE   Hyperbole is obvious exaggeration, an extravagant statement, intentionally designed to give the reader a memorable image. A fisherman who tells you that the one that got away was "big as a whale" probably is speaking hyperbolically. *See* "Understatement."

ILLUSTRATION AND EXAMPLE   *See* Chapter 4.

IMAGE   In writing, an image is a picture drawn with words, a reproduction of persons, objects, or sensations that are perceived through sight, sound, touch, taste, or smell. Often an image is invoked to visually represent an idea. *See* "Symbol."

IMPRESSIONISTIC   Impressionistic refers to the manner of depicting a scene, emotion, or character so that it evokes subjective or sensory impressions; an impression is an effect produced upon the mind or emotions. The more writing emphasizes the effects of scenes, persons, and ideas on the writer, the more impressionistic, and hence the less purely objective, it will be. *See* "Objectivity" and "Subjectivity."

INDUCTION   Induction is a mental process in which one draws a generalized conclusion from specific, factual evidence. For example, if it is a fact that a high percentage of people who die from cancer each year also smoke cigarettes, one might induce that cigarette smoking is a contributing cause of the disease. *See* "Deduction."

INTRODUCTION   An introduction sets forth the writer's thesis or central themes, establishes the tone (the attitude toward the subject), and, particularly in a long paper, suggests the organizational plan. The introduction or opening of an essay should be designed to capture a reader's attention and interest. Like the conclusion, it may be no more than a sentence in a short essay or many paragraphs in a long paper.

IRONY   Irony is the undercutting or contradicting of someone's expectations. It may be either verbal or dramatic; verbal irony involves a discrepancy, sometimes intentional, sometimes not, between what is said and what is meant; for example, if a dog tries to bite you, you may say, "What a friendly dog!" Dramatic irony involves a discrepancy between what someone expects to happen and what does happen; it would be ironic, for example, if the dog who seemed so unfriendly to you saved your life. *See* "Sarcasm" and "Satire."

JARGON   Jargon is the specialized language of a trade, profession, or other socioeconomic group. Truck drivers, for example, employ a jargon on their CB radios that sounds like jibberish to most people, and writing that employs undefined jargon will sound like jibberish to most readers.

JOURNAL   *See* Chapter 1.

JOURNALISM   Journalism is the profession of writing for newspapers, magazines, wire services, and radio and television. Journalistic writing tends to emphasize objectivity and factual reportage, although the work of editorial writers, columnists, and feature writers often is impressionistic.

LITERAL   Literal refers to the adherence to the ordinary or primary meaning of a word or expression; the literal meaning of a written work is that derived from following the ordinary, straightforward sense of the words. The sentence "Childhood is a time of sunshine" probably should not be read literally as meaning that the sun always shines during childhood, but rather figuratively as meaning that childhood is a happy time.

METAPHOR   A metaphor is a figure of speech in which through an implied comparison one object is identified with another and some qualities of the first object are ascribed to the second. *See* "Simile."

MODE   A mode is a conventional form or usage. In writing there are four customary modes of discourse: descriptive, narrative, expository, and persuasive or argumentative.

NARRATION   *See* Chapter 2.

OBJECTIVITY   Objectivity is freedom from personal bias. A report about a scientific experiment is objective insofar as the facts are explained without reference to the writer's feelings about the experiment. But not even the most factual piece of writing is completely objective, completely uncolored by the writer's attitudes and impressions. Objectivity tends to be a matter of degree, increasing as the writer acts as an observer who distances himself or herself from whatever he or she is writing about. *See* "Subjectivity."

PARADOX   A paradox is a statement that sounds self-contradictory, even absurd, and yet expresses a certain truth. For example, it is paradoxical, though nonetheless true, to say that one person can feel both love and hatred for another person at the same moment.

PARALLEL STRUCTURE   Parallel structure is the association of ideas phrased in parallel or similar ways, thus giving a piece of writing balance and proportion. "He loves wine, women, and singing" lacks parallel structure; "He loves wine, women, and song" is more balanced.

PERSONIFICATION   Personification is a figure of speech in which abstract concepts or inanimate objects are represented as if they had human qualities. To write that "death rides a pale horse," for example, is to personify death.

PERSUASION   Persuasion is the art of convincing someone else to act in a certain way or to believe in a certain idea. Logic and reason are important tools of persuasion. Equally effective may be an appeal either to the emotions or to the ethical sensibilities.

POINT OF VIEW   The point of view is the vantage point from which an author writes. In expository prose an author may adopt a first-person or a third-person point of view. *See* "Style" and "Tone."

PROCESS ANALYSIS   *See* Chapter 8.

SARCASM   Sarcasm is an expression of ridicule, contempt, or derision. Sarcastic remarks are nasty or bitter in tone and tend to be characterized by an irony that is meant to hurt. For example, you might express your displeasure with those who have given you a hard time by sarcastically thanking them for their help. *See* "Irony."

SATIRE   Satire is a form of writing that makes use of irony, sarcasm, ridicule, and humor in order to expose, denounce, and possibly correct the follies and evils of human beings and institutions. The satirist's tone may range from gentle mockery and amused wit to harsh contempt and moral indignation.

SIMILE   A simile is a figure of speech in which a direct, explicit comparison is made between two different things. One thing is expressly *like* or *as* another thing: he ate *like* a pig; her heart felt light *as* a feather. See "Metaphor."

SLANG   Slang refers to colloquialisms and jargon that are deemed inappropriate not only in formal writing but also in the standard speech of educated conversation. Whether a word or phrase is considered colloquial or slang is often a matter of personal taste. A word such as "uptight," which was once considered slang by many cultivated people, is now an acceptable colloquialism.

SPECIFICITY   Specificity is precision, particularity, concreteness. The more detailed a person's writing is, the more specific and hence the less general, vague, and abstract it will be. Specificity, like generalization, is a matter of degree; the word "horse," for example, is more specific than the word "animal" but more general than the word "stallion." See "Generalization."

STYLE   Style is the fingerprint, the identifying mark, of a writer both as an individual personality and as a representative of his or her age and culture. An author's style is a combination of the diction employed, the structure of the sentences and the organization of the material, and the overall form and tone with which the thoughts are expressed. Style may be simple or complex, forthright or subtle, colloquial or formal; it may be modern or classical, romantic or realistic, logical or poetic; it may be anything, in short, that reflects the writer's personality, background, and talent. See "Point of View" and "Tone."

SUBJECTIVITY   Subjectivity in writing is the personal element. The more subjective a piece of writing, the more it will focus on the opinions and feelings of the writer. See "Objectivity."

SYLLOGISM   A syllogism is a highly formalized version of deductive logic. Syllogistic reason argues that if a generalization (major premise) is true and a specific case of the generalization (minor premise) is also true, then whatever conclusion deduction reaches is necessarily true. For example, if the major premise is "smoking causes cancer" and the minor premise is "John Doe smokes," then the conclusion is "John Doe will contract cancer." A syllogism may sound logical yet not be true because one or both of its premises are faulty. See "Deduction."

SYMBOL   A symbol is something that stands for something else. An eagle is a conventional symbol of America. The word "eagle" may bring to mind different images or ideas in different contexts or to different people; it may connote freedom or power or solitude. Any word, image, or description, any name, character, or action, that has a range of meanings and associations beyond its literal denotation may be symbolic, depending on who is interpreting it and the context in which it appears.

SYNONYM   A synonym is one of two or more words having approximately the same meaning. "Happiness" and "joy" for example, are synonyms. *See* "Antonym."

TAUTOLOGY   Tautology is pointless repetition. To write that a person was treated with "cruel inhumanity" would be tautological, as one would assume that inhumanity is always cruel.

THESIS   The thesis of an essay is its main idea or central theme. In expository prose the writer usually will want to state the thesis clearly in the introduction. The thesis statement should establish the point of view, the primary point(s) intended for discussion, and the writer's attitude or tone toward it.

TONE   The tone of voice indicates an author's attitude toward the subject and, at times, the audience. The tone is caught in the "sound" of the writing. The voice of an essay may be angry, resigned, humorous, serious, sentimental, mocking, ironic, sarcastic, satirical, reasonable, emotional, philosophic—anything, in short, that the voice of the author can be. One tone may predominate or many tones may be heard in any single work. *See* "Style."

TOPIC SENTENCE   The topic sentence is the sentence in a paragraph that states clearly the central theme or point of the paragraph.

TRANSITION   A transition is a bridge between one point or topic or idea and another. The transitional movement from sentence to sentence and paragraph to paragraph should be easy to follow if a piece of writing is to achieve coherence. The logic of moving from one point to the next often is emphasized by means of transitional expressions such as "therefore," "hence," "similarly," "however," "but," "furthermore," "also," and "for example." *See* Coherence."

UNDERSTATEMENT   An understatement is an obvious downplaying or underrating of something. It is the opposite of a hyperbole, although similarly designed to create a memorable image or an ironic effect. To say that "after they ate the apple, Adam and Eve found life a bit tougher," is to understate the case. *See* "Hyperbole."

UNITY   Unity refers to the way a basic focus or theme permeates a single piece of writing, lending the piece a sense of wholeness and completeness.

The words and sentences and paragraphs, the images and ideas, the explanations and examples, the characters and actions, the descriptions and arguments—all in some way should be relevant to the overriding purpose or point of the work. *See* "Coherence."

Index of Contributors

To the Student:

We want to hear from you! By now we hope you are an enlightened and satisfied reader of Shaping Prose, one whose own writing has been stimulated by the selections it contains. We believe that your experience with Shaping Prose can help us improve its future editions.

We are seriously interested in improving the textbooks we publish. Please help us with this part of our job by completing the questionnaire below and returning it to College English Developmental Group, Little, Brown and Company, 34 Beacon Street, Boston, MA 02106.

School _____ Course title _____

Instructor's name _____

Other books assigned _____

Please give us your reaction to the selections:

	Liked best				Liked least	Didn't read
Thoreau, from the Journals	5	4	3	2	1	_____
Lindbergh, from War Within and Without	5	4	3	2	1	_____
Nin, from The Diaries of Anaïs Nin	5	4	3	2	1	_____
Frank, from The Diary of a Young Girl	5	4	3	2	1	_____
Scott-Maxwell, from The Measure of My Days	5	4	3	2	1	_____
Camus, from Notebooks 1935–1942	5	4	3	2	1	_____
Theroux, "Soccer in San Salvador"	5	4	3	2	1	_____
Raban, "Qat Chewing"	5	4	3	2	1	_____
Kazantzakis, "Happiness Is a Domestic Bird"	5	4	3	2	1	_____
Arendt, "Denmark and the 'Final Solution'"	5	4	3	2	1	_____
Brown, "The Flight of the Nez Percés"	5	4	3	2	1	_____
Feldman, "The New Student"	5	4	3	2	1	_____
Carson, "The Hidden Pool"	5	4	3	2	1	_____
Kazin, "Brownsville Food"	5	4	3	2	1	_____
Darwin, "Tahiti"	5	4	3	2	1	_____
Eiseley, "How Flowers Changed the World"	5	4	3	2	1	_____
Selzer, "The Discus Thrower"	5	4	3	2	1	_____

	Liked best				Liked least	Didn't read

Allen, "My Speech to the Graduates" 5 4 3 2 1 _____
Morrow, "Back to Reticence!" 5 4 3 2 1 _____
Baker, "The Paradox of the New Leisure" 5 4 3 2 1 _____
Wolfe, "In Our Time" 5 4 3 2 1 _____
Hamill, "Spaldeen Summers" 5 4 3 2 1 _____
Edwards, "Elvira's Story" 5 4 3 2 1 _____

Hellerstein, "Cures That Kill" 5 4 3 2 1 _____
Mead, "New Superstitions for Old" 5 4 3 2 1 _____
Leonard, "Youth" 5 4 3 2 1 _____
Bettelheim, "The Holocaust" 5 4 3 2 1 _____
Yagoda, "The Good, the Bad, and the Cute" 5 4 3 2 1 _____

White, "Education" 5 4 3 2 1 _____
Aristotle, "Youth and Old Age" 5 4 3 2 1 _____
Campa, "Anglo vs. Chicano: Why?" 5 4 3 2 1 _____
Petrunkevitch, "The Spider and the Wasp" 5 4 3 2 1 _____
Baker, "Terminal Education" 5 4 3 2 1 _____

Barber, "Four Types of President" 5 4 3 2 1 _____
Toffler, "The Duration of Human Relationships" 5 4 3 2 1 _____
Cooper, "How Fit Are You?" 5 4 3 2 1 _____
Bacon, "Of Studies" 5 4 3 2 1 _____
Rosen, "Psychobabble" 5 4 3 2 1 _____

Ashe & Graebner, "The Serve" 5 4 3 2 1 _____
Thomas, "On Transcendental Metaworry (TMW)" 5 4 3 2 1 _____
Rosten, "Dear Miss O'Neill" 5 4 3 2 1 _____
Mayleas, "How to Land the Job You Want" 5 4 3 2 1 _____
Miller, "Patients' Rites" 5 4 3 2 1 _____

White, "The Sea and the Wind That Blows" 5 4 3 2 1 _____
Fleming, "The Fear of Being Alone" 5 4 3 2 1 _____
Trippett, "The Great American Cooling Machine" 5 4 3 2 1 _____
Clark, "Why I Succeeded" 5 4 3 2 1 _____
Fenton, "Confessions of a Working Stiff" 5 4 3 2 1 _____
Toynbee, "Prolonging Sexual Innocence" 5 4 3 2 1 _____

Cousins, "Where Is the News Leading Us?" 5 4 3 2 1 _____
Vance, "Foreign Policy: Defining Our Goals" 5 4 3 2 1 _____
Montague, "Straight Talk about the Living-Together Arrangement" 5 4 3 2 1 _____
Oldenburg & Brissett, "The Essential Hangout" 5 4 3 2 1 _____
Chisholm, "I'd Rather Be Black than Female" 5 4 3 2 1 _____

Swift, "A Modest Proposal" 5 4 3 2 1 _____
Plato, "Allegory of the Cave" 5 4 3 2 1 _____
Orwell, "Shooting an Elephant" 5 4 3 2 1 _____
Russell, "Space-Time" 5 4 3 2 1 _____

Glossary 5 4 3 2 1 _____